THE QURAN AND THE BIBLE
IN THE LIGHT OF HISTORY AND
SCIENCE

There is no God apart from me, a righteous God
and a Saviour.
There is none but me!
Turn to me and be saved, all you ends of the earth;
for I am God and there is no other.
By myself I have sworn,
my mouth has uttered In ull integrity
a word that will not be revoked:
Before me every knee will bow;
by me every tongue will swear.
They will say of me,
"In the LORD alone are righteousness and strength."

Isaiah 45:21b-24a

by William F. Campbell M.D.

Middle East Resources
PO Box 96
Upper Darby, PA   19082

TABLE OF CONTENTS

SECTION FOUR
Science and Revelation

SECTION FIVE
Methods of Proof in Revelation

SECTION SIX
Jesus and Muhammad, Two Prophets for a Lost World?

Appendices

PHOTOGRAPHS OF MANUSCRIPTS

PREFACE

WHY A BOOK TO ANSWER A BOOK?

What is this book which still needs to be "revisited" even though it was published ten years ago?

What is this book which would take a doctor away from his medicine for three years in order to write an answer?

It is a *book which one finds in almost every book store in **Tunisia** and **Morocco***.

It is a book which turns up in the **United States** in the hands of a young Egyptian who wishes to use it to influence the girl he is courting.

It is the first book on the book rack, just below the Qur'an and the Hadith, in the Mosque at *Regent's Park in **London***.

It is a book which is considered so valuable by some that as of *1983* it had been translated from the *French original* into *English, Arabic, Indonesian, Persian, Serbo-Croatian, Turkish, Urdu*, and *Goujrati*.

I first heard of this work, written by a French medical doctor, from a young Tunisian. He said, "Have you read the book by Dr. Maurice Bucaille, *The Bible, the Qur'an, and Science*? He has a lot to say about the Bible and the Qur'an. He even says that the Qur'an has no scientific errors."

When I examined the book I found that the author did indeed have much to say about the Bible and the Qur'an, and he does say,

> It was only when I examined the text very closely in Arabic that...I had to acknowledge the evidence in front of me: the **Qur'an did not contain a single statement that was assailable from a modern scientific point of view.**[1]

In contrast, when speaking of the **Bible**, he mentions only "*contradictions, improbabilities and incompatibilities*." He claims that the Biblical specialists usually ignore these, or, if they do mention them, they just "try to camouflage them with dialectical acrobatics."[2]

Muslims are obviously thrilled with Dr. Bucaille's book because, if it is true, it strengthens them in their confidence in the Qur'an. It is a type of second witness.

Equally obvious is the fact that we Christians are sad to see the ease with which strong testimonies to the truth of the Bible have been ignored.

Fulfilled prophecies are not mentioned.

Dr. Bucaille denies that any of the Gospel writings are the work of eye-witnesses.

The earliest copies of the Gospel are dismissed with a few words, leaving the impression that there is no good testimony to the validity of the text which we now have.

---

1. *The Bible, the Qur'an, and Science*, English Edition, American Trust Publications, Indianapolis, 1979, p viii.
2. Ibid., p ix.

In the end, the Gospel is compared to the Song of Roland (Chanson de Roland), "which relates a real event in a fictitious light."[3]

These ideas fit very well, of course, with what most Muslims claim—that we Christians changed the Gospel—that there is no valid witness to Jesus' words and life.

This is a very serious and disturbing charge, but having heard it from almost every Muslim with whom I spoke during long years in North Africa, I thought that I had gotten used to it, that it no longer bothered me. However I was mistaken.

In 1983 while passing through London, I went to the British Museum to see the *Codex Siniaticus*, one of the oldest complete copies of the New Testament — dating from about *350 AD*. I wanted to take the picture which can be seen on page 155. After asking the guard for directions, I went over to the glass-covered case which he indicated, thinking only about how to take a picture through glass without getting a reflection.

Then I saw the book in front of me.

I took one look at that Bible and it was as though all the hundreds of times I had heard "YOU CHANGED YOUR BIBLE" went through my head in one instant. I burst into tears. Even now as I write these words, tears come to my eyes. I wanted to touch it. It would be like touching my brothers who wrote it 1600 years ago. We would be one together even though they had died long ago. It was tangible, touchable proof that the Gospel is as it always has been.

I didn't get to touch it. I asked, but they didn't feel that they could allow it, so I took my picture and left.

This book in your hands, then, is a response to these two evaluations of Dr. Bucaille; but, in fact, it is much more. It is an attempt to examine the real confrontation between Islam and Christianity at the deepest level, both intellectual and emotional.

For example, Muslims claim that Muhammad will intercede for them. This is an emotionally comforting idea, because no one wants to stand alone in the white light of God's final judgment. But is there any evidence for this idea in the Qur'an?

Christians say that God has sent His comfort in Jesus, who died to pay for the sins of the whole world and is now alive to intercede for those who believe in him as Saviour. Is there any evidence for this in the Gospel?

As mentioned above, Muslims claim that the Bible has been changed. Is there any evidence for this in the Qur'an? In the Hadith? In history?

If the two books differ in what they say, how shall we choose between them? How can we know a true prophet?

And who am I that I should try to discuss all these things?

First of all I, too, am a medical doctor. Secondly I, too, have learned Arabic—the Arabic of North Africa. Thirdly I, too, have studied the Qur'an and the Bible.

Even so, some of the areas touched in this book are outside of my

3. Ibid., p 108.

competence. Therefore, I have asked advice from specialists in several fields: astronomy, geology, and even embryology of the human, and have thus tried to avoid errors of fact, in so far as possible. If the rocket-probes sent to investigate Halley's comet make the information about meteors in Chapter I of Section 5 out of date, I ask the reader's patience.

I have asked men whose native language is Arabic to evaluate my word studies in that language. Other friends, including my wife, have given of their time to read and comment on the entire manuscript, and I thank each one. In the final analysis, though, I accept full responsibility for the choice of what is written on these pages.

BASIC ASSUMPTIONS

The first and second chapters speak of basic assumptions and bias on the part of any and every author. My basic assumption and bias is that the Bible is a valid historical document and that the good news of the Gospel is true. In discussing the meaning of the Qur'an and the Gospel, I have tried to understand and stick to the obvious meaning of the text—the meaning that would have been understood by those listening when the verses were given—and avoid the temptation of making a verse say what I want it to say. How successful I have been in curbing my own bias, each reader will decide.

Before closing I would like to explain why I decided to use, almost exclusively, the term "basic assumption." One of my friends suggested that this word was not the best word to express what I wished to say—especially in the chapters on science. He proposed "presupposition," "postulate," "a priori," or "bias." To this could be added "conjecture" and "hypothesis."

It is true that "basic assumption" usually refers to the very important assumptions which serve as a foundation for one's life, or the formation of a hypothesis in science. Therefore, in many places "conjecture" might be a better term, but in the end I have decided to keep basic assumption.

I prefer to keep the term because it follows the idea of a great English philosopher of the 1300's named William of Occam. He said,

> "Essentia non sunt multiplicanda praeter necessitatem," which means, **"Basic assumptions (about the essential nature of things) must not be multiplied beyond necessity."**

This phrase came to be known as Occam's razor. We must cut out, as with a razor or a knife, or at least recognize, all the extra basic assumptions.

Secondly, it keeps before us the idea that each time we make a basic assumption, even a small one, it is a new beginning. We were stuck in our reasoning and we had to think up a NEW possible explanation.

We all make these NEW basic assumptions to try and reconcile problems. In Chapter I of Section 3 we will see that the "higher critics" made a basic assumption that Moses couldn't write.

In Chapter II of Section 1, Dr. Bucaille's basic assumption that the word "smoke" as used in the Qur'an can refer to the primordial gases is compared with the basic assumption of some Christian men of science that the word "water" as used in the Torah can be used in the same way.

In Chapter II of the 4th Section we will see that Dr. Torki makes several basic assumptions in his discussion of the seven heavens.

There is nothing wrong with this activity. It is not a sin. That is what thinking is all about, but we must realize that we do it and try to keep it to a minimum.

Lastly, a few remarks about the usage of Arabic words.

The English names of the Suras are those proposed by Abdullah Yusuf Ali in his English translation of the Qur'an.

International phonetic symbols have been used for the transcription of the Arabic names of Suras and for Arabic words discussed in the text, except for four exceptions such as "th" and "sh" where there are good English equivalents for the sounds.

There are, however, some gray areas. *Personal names of Arab authors writing in French or English have been left as they themselves spell their names in Latin characters.*

Arabic personal names as given in English translations of the Hadith are not uniform. Therefore, I have usually left them as the English author wrote them, since I have not seen them in Arabic.

Most Arabic words which have entered into English in former years and have a "correct" English form, such as Hejira and Shiite, have been left in their English form. However, a few, such as Muslim, Muhammad and Qur'an, have been used in their new modified English form. With these thoughts in mind let us now **revisit and reexamine the Qur'an and the Bible in the light of history and science**.

William F. Campbell M.D.

SECTION ONE

PROLOGUE

CHAPTER I

SOME BASIC ASSUMPTIONS ABOUT WORDS

Every author, every reader, every person who takes part in a discussion brings to the book or to the discussion certain basic ideas which he believes to be true. Sometimes these ideas can be tested by examination or measurement as in science, other times by archaeology, or by reference to historical documents. But often they cannot be tested, and it is especially those ideas which cannot be tested which we refer to as **basic assumptions**.

For example, I believe that matter is real, that the paper on which this book is printed is really here, solidly present in this world. However when I took philosophy at the university, the professor told us about a Greek named Zeno who believed that the world was all an illusion. In my innocence I held up my hand and asked, "But how could he enjoy life if he thought that it was all an illusion?"

Naturally the professor answered, "Why? Can't you enjoy an illusion?"

He was right of course. On a theoretical basis there is no reason why you cannot enjoy an illusion. We spend a lot of time day-dreaming illusions. My problem was that it did not fit my basic assumption that the world is real.

This particular assumption is the same for Muslims, Christians and Jews. All three believe that there is a God who created the existing universe out of nothing—a real universe which can be touched and measured.

When our basic assumptions are not the same, though, we can have all kinds of problems. One time in Morocco, a man came to see me for a medical consultation. When I asked him what his work was, he answered that he was an " 'alim" or religious teacher. We had a little discussion about the Gospel and then he invited me to his home to talk some more. As we talked the word "al-messiyā (المَسِيَّا) of John 1:41 came up in the conversation. I said, "This comes originally from the Hebrew "mashiakh" which corresponds to the Arabic al-masih (المَسِيح)" and equals "the Messiah" in English.

He said, "No, this is another name for Muhammad. Muhammad has many names."

We argued back and forth a bit more and finally I said, "All right, let's look it up in the dictionary. Surely you have a Munjid (Arabic dictionary)."

"Oh no. We can't do that," he answered.

"But why not. I'm sure we'll find it in there."

"No! We can't do that!" he repeated, "You wrote the dictionary!"

"What do you mean 'I wrote the dictionary?' " I asked. "I had nothing to do with writing that dictionary."

"Yes you did. It was written by the Christians."

And that was the end of the conversation. In Morocco 25 years ago the only Arabic dictionary sold had been made by the Catholics in Lebanon and he

3

wouldn't agree that it was valid. If we disagreed about the meaning of a word we couldn't consult a dictionary. We no longer had the same basic assumption about the validity of that dictionary.

THE MEANING OF WORDS

It is obvious from the above example that in order to have any meaningful discussion on scientific or religious matters, we must agree on the meaning of words and how the meaning can be known. This comes up over and over again in Dr. Bucaille's book. He has a whole chapter on the meaning of the Arabic word 'alaqa (العَلَقَة). He has four pages centered around the meanings of the Greek words "laleo," "akouo," and "parakletos."

So how do we know the meaning of words? Who has the power to decide which meaning is correct? How do we make dictionaries?

The answer is that you and I make the dictionaries. We make them by our usage of words over a period of time. Linguists treat oral usage and written usage somewhat differently, but since we are dealing with the Qur'an and the Bible, both written documents, we will illustrate the method used for written language.

Dr. S. I. Hayakawa, Specialist in Linguistics and Professor of English at San Francisco State College,[1] describes the process of making a dictionary as follows:

> Let us see how dictionaries are made and how the editors arrive at definitions…The task of writing a dictionary begins with reading vast amounts of the literature of the period or subject that the dictionary is to cover. As the editors read, they copy on cards every interesting or rare word, every unusual or peculiar occurrence of a common word, a large number of common words in their ordinary uses, and also the sentences in which each of these words appears, thus:

> pail
> The dairy pails bring home increase of milk
> Keats, *Endymion*
> I, 44-45

> That is to say, the context of each word is collected, along with the word itself…When the sorting is completed, there will be for each word anywhere from two or three to several hundred illustrative quotations, each on its card.

> To define a word, then, the dictionary editor places before him the stack of cards illustrating that word. Each of the cards represents

1. *Language in Thought and Action*, New York, Harcourt, Brace and World, Inc. 1964, p 55-56.

an actual use of the word by a writer of some literary or historical importance. He reads the cards carefully, discards some, rereads the rest, and divides up the stack according to what he thinks are the several senses of the word. Finally, he writes his definitions following the hard-and-fast rule that each definition **MUST** be based on what the quotations in front of him reveal about the meaning of the word.

The writing of a dictionary, therefore, is not a task of setting up authoritative statements about the "true meanings" of words, but a task of *recording*, to the best of one's ability, what various words have meant to authors in the distant or immediate past...*The writer of a dictionary is a historian, not a lawgiver.*

MEANING FROM USAGE

As an example of finding the meaning of a word from its usage let us examine the usage of the Arabic noun meaning "burden," (al-wizr الوِزْر), its related noun "burdened one" (al-wāzira الوَازِرَة), and the root verb "to bear" (wazara وَزَرَ) as found in the Qur'an. A Quranic concordance tells us that this word group is used 24 times.[2]

The first passage which we want to examine is in the Sura Ṭā-Hā, 20:87, from the Middle Meccan period, where we read about the Children of Israel after they made the golden calf:

> They said: "We broke not the promise to thee, as far as lay in our power: but we were made to carry the **burdens** of the ornaments of the people..."

If we were to place this on a 3 x 5 card, we would sort it out with other sentences showing that burden means something which you carry. Also it probably represents something heavy or difficult since they were made or forced to carry the burdens.

Next we might look at the Sura Muḥammad, 47:4, from 1 AH,[3] where the Muslims are instructed to fight the blasphemers until subdued:

> ...thereafter either generosity or ransom: until the war lays down its **burdens**...(God lets you fight) in order to test you, some with others. But those who are slain in the way of God, He will never let their deeds be lost.

Here burden takes on a new meaning. It is still difficult, but in the context it now refers to people being wounded and killed in battle and perhaps the sorrow of loss of friends and loved ones.

Finally we come to the following verses. The English nouns and verbs written in boldface represent the Arabic word which we are studying, and we

---

2. The root is also used once for "refuge" and twice for "cabinet minister," meanings which are outside of this study.
3. The dates and English names for the Suras are those suggested by Yusuf Ali in his English translation, The Holy Qur'an, The American International Printing Co. Washington, D.C. 1946.

5

will imagine that we are writing each verse on its own 3 x 5 card.

The Originator of Creation (Fāṭir), Sura 35:16, 18, Early Meccan.

    If He (God) so pleased, He could blot you out and bring in a new creation...Nor can a **burdened one bear** another's **burden**. If one heavily laden should call another to (carry) his load, not the least portion of it can be carried (by the other) even though he be closely related...

The Star (Al-Najm), Sura 53:36-41, Early Meccan.

    Nay, is he not acquainted with what is in the books of Moses and of Abraham, who fulfilled his engagements? Namely, that no **burdened one** can **bear** another's **burdens**; that man can have nothing but what he strives for...then will he be rewarded with a reward complete.

Ṭā-Hā, Sura 20:100-102, Middle Meccan.

    If any do turn away therefrom (from God's message), verily they will carry a **burden** on the Day of Resurrection. They will abide in this (state) and grievous will the load be to them on that day—the day the trumpet will be sounded...

The Cattle (Al-Anʿām), Sura 6:31, Late Meccan.

    Lost indeed are they who treat it as a falsehood that they must meet God, until suddenly the hour is on them, and they say, "Ah! woe unto us that we took no thought of it," for they carry their **burdens** on their backs, and evil indeed (the load) that **they bear**.

Sura 6:164, Late Meccan.

    ...Every soul gathers the result of its acts on none but itself. No **burdened one** can **bear** another's **burdens**. Your goal in the end is towards God. He will tell you the truth of the things wherein you disputed.

The Crowds (Al-Zumar), Sura 39:7, Late Meccan.

    If ye blaspheme, truly God is rich (has no need) toward you, but He does not like blasphemy in His servants. If you are grateful He is pleased with you. No **burdened one** can **bear** another's **burden**. In the end to your Lord is your return when He will tell you the truth of all that ye did, for He knows well all that is in the chests (hearts).

The Bee (Al-Naḥl), Sura 16:25, Late Meccan.

    Let them carry, on the day of resurrection, their total **burdens**, and also some of the **burdens** of those without knowledge, whom they led astray. How grievous (the load) they will **bear**.

The Children of Israel (Banī Isrā'īl), Sura 17:13-15. -1 AH.

> Every man's fate We have fastened on his own neck. On the day of resurrection We shall bring out for him a book which he will find spread open. (He will be told) "Read your book. You are quite able to understand an account against you." Who receives guidance, receives it for his own good. Who goes astray does so to his own loss. And no **burdened one** can **bear** another's **burden**...

It is very clear when we compare these verses with each other that this word is being used for another type of burden. If you deny God's message, you bear this burden. If you blaspheme or deny that there is going to be a day of resurrection, it weighs on you. This burden is a result of the acts of each person, and a record of it is kept in a book which you will read for yourself. It is spoken of as being carried on the back, but also God knows what is in your chest ("heart" in English). From these ideas we easily understand that this burden is **our sins**.

Taking our 3 x 5 cards, our definition of "wizr" as used in Saudi Arabia by the Quraish Tribe in the time of Muhammad might read:

> heavy load, burden — either physical
> or psychological,
> sin, denying God.

When we look up the word "wizr" in Hans Wehr's, *A Dictionary of Modern Written Arabic,*[4] this is what we find:

> heavy load, burden, encumbrance;
> sin, crime;
> responsibleness, responsibility.

We didn't come up with responsibility as one of our meanings, but with "heavy load, burden" and "sin" we were right on the mark.

In a theological dictionary we would expect to find further remarks on these verses, pointing out that no sinner will be able to help another sinner even if he is a close relative. Each person will be punished according to the record book of his own sins. The only exception is that if you lead someone astray you will have added punishment, though the one led astray will have to bear his own sin burden also. Whether a sinless one—someone without any burden of his own—could intercede or take on the burden of another is not dealt with in these verses.

LANGUAGES CONTINUALLY CHANGE

As long ago as his lectures of 1910-1911 Professor Ferdinand de Saussure, the Swiss father of modern linguistics, expressed this fact with the following strong words. He told his students,

> ...language degenerates, or rather evolves, under the influence of all the agents which can reach either the sounds or the meanings. **This evolution is inevitable** ("fatale" in French).

---

4. Otto Harrassowitz, Wiesbaden, 1971.

There is no example of a language which resists it. At the end of a certain time, one can always demonstrate obvious changes.[5]

The French linguistic expert, André Martinet, repeats the same idea in his *Elements of General Linguistics* published in 1964. He writes,

> For the present we shall merely note that languages change constantly, without, of course, ever ceasing to function; and that any language which we approach (in order) to describe its functioning, is in the process of modification (even while we are looking at it). A moment's reflection will serve to convince us that this holds good for all languages at every moment.[6]

Looking under a "hood" 500 years ago would have revealed a monk. Today we find an automobile engine. In addition, a "hood" might be the thief who stole the car.

In his *Semantics and Common Sense*, Louis B. Solomon, Professor of English at Brooklyn College, makes clear that because of this continual change there is only one way to know the meaning of a word.

> The standard meaning of a verbal symbol (word) at any given time is what the users of the symbol do with it at that time.[7]

In summary: as time passes, some words change their meaning while others remain the same. This means that, **TODAY**, you and I are either confirming the previous definition or giving a new definition to each word as we use it, and **usage is the ONLY thing which will affirm the former meaning or indicate a new meaning.**

THE ETYMOLOGICAL FALLACY

Dr. Solomon discusses this common misconception in the following words:

> The *etymological fallacy* (is) the fallacy of holding that the earliest known meaning (perhaps even the meaning of the source word in Latin or Greek or Sanskrit) is the right one and all later meanings are regrettable impurities to be filtered out at the 1st opportunity.[8]

It is a fallacy to look for the meaning of a word in the root meaning—in the original meaning. Rather we must find it in the people who use the word. **The original meaning of a word proves nothing about present usage, and present usage proves nothing about the meaning in former times.** If a word occurs only once in a single document from 500 years ago, or on one clay tablet found in Babylon, then older (or younger) known meanings might help us to guess at a possible meaning, but that is all. It could not prove a meaning. To know what a word meant to the Christians in the first century or among the

---

5. *Cours de Linguistique Gènèrale*, Payot, Paris, 1969, p 111. (translation mine)
6. Max Leclerc et Cie. 1960. Eng. Trans. Univ. of Chicago Press, 1964, p 37.
7. Holt, Rinehart, & Winston, Inc. New York, 1966, p 23.
8. Ibid., p 51.

Muslims in the 7th century, we must examine its usage at that time.

Dr. Bucaille, however, does not agree with these specialists. In his latest book he writes as follows:

> There exists a general rule which I have never found wrong in regard to modern knowledge: the original sense of a word, the oldest sense, is the one which suggests most clearly, the reconciliation which can be made with scientific knowledge, while the derived meanings lead to a false sense or nonsense.[9]

Unfortunately Dr. Bucaille's rule can also lead to nonsense.

As an example let us consider the Arabic word ṭā'ir (الطَّائِر) used in the Sura of the Children of Israel (Banī Isrā'īl) 17:13 from 1 AH, where we read,

> And We (God) have fastened every man's **fate** on his neck...

The root meaning, and one of the current meanings of this word translated **fate**, is *bird*. The Arabs, like the Romans, tried to read the future from the flight of birds, therefore the word came to mean *evil omen* or *evil fate*. To read this Quranic sentence with its root meaning that "God tied every man's bird to his neck" would lead us to absurdity.

As another example let us look at the Hebrew word *rakhamah* found in Deuteronomy 14:17 which comes from the root *rakham* meaning to love. We might expect the word to mean *lover* until we read an article which speaks of a *rakhamah* circling in the sky waiting to eat dead bodies.

The meaning turns out to be **vulture**, but the word was used, according to one dictionary, because these birds keep the same mate for life. In any case it is clear that the root meaning will not lead us to the present meaning, nor can one say that the root meaning is more correct scientifically.

A third example is the word alcohol. The word is derived from the Arabic word al-kuḥl (الكُحْل) which stands for the black antimony powder that Arab women used for eyeliner in the distant past and now. In later Roman times it came to have the meaning of pure. When alcohol was first produced by distillation it was "pure," and therefore "alcohol." This word has now gone back into Arabic as al-kuḥūl (الكُحُول) for alcohol. Both words are from the same root. Both are in use today, and it would be idiotic to ask which meaning is more accurate scientifically.

Finally, to end this section on word meaning, I quote from the introduction to the very excellent translation of the Qur'an into English made by the Egyptian Abdullah Yusuf Ali. He says,

> Every serious writer and thinker has a right to use all the knowledge and experience he possesses in the service of the Qur'an. But he must not mix up his own theories and conclusions, however reasonable, with the interpretation of the Text itself, which is usually perfectly perspicuous, as it claims to be. Our difficulties

---

9. *L'Homme, D'Ou Vient-il*, Seghers, Paris, 1981, p 186. (translation mine)

in interpretation often arise from various causes, of which I will mention just a few:

(1) Arabic words in the Text have acquired other meanings than those which were understood by the Apostle and his Companions. All living languages undergo such transformations. **The early Commentators and Philologists went into these matters with a very comprehensive grasp, and we must accept their conclusions.** Where they are not unanimous, we must use our judgment and historic sense in adopting the interpretation of that authority which appeals to us most. **We must not devise new verbal meanings.**[10]

In other words, we may not lay back on a couch and dream up "new verbal meanings" just because we find ourselves confronted with a difficult passage.

CONTEXT

We have discussed context as the way to understand the meaning of a word from its usage. Now we must discuss the importance of context in establishing the meaning of a word, or a phrase, or a sentence in a document.

As we have already seen in this chapter, a word often has more than one correct current meaning. In our discussion of the Arabic word "wizr" we found that, in addition to burden and sin, it could mean responsibility. Therefore if someone asked the meaning of the phrase "wizr of the Sultan," we would not be able to answer. We could not know from those few words whether it meant the "sin of the Sultan" or the "responsibility of the Sultan." We would have to ask to hear the whole sentence, i.e., **the context**. For it is only by seeing or hearing the context that we would be able to pick out the correct meaning.

De Saussure insists on this when he says,

> ...language is a system in which all the terms are interdependent, and where the one has no value except from the simultaneous presence of the others...[11]

and Solomon expresses it in greater detail when he writes,

> Words are never used in isolation. In organic use the meaning of a word is inevitably affected by its context, which includes at the very least the other words that surround it in a sentence or a paragraph or a lengthy discourse, and actually a great deal more.[12]
>
> To find out what the users of a word in 1787 meant by it we must observe (as far as written records reveal) what the users in 1787 did with it.[13]

---

10. Yusuf Ali, op. cit., p x.
11. de Saussure, op. cit., p 159. (translation mine)
12. Solomon, op. cit., p 49.
13. Ibid., p 51.

In his book *God of Justice*, Dr. Daud Rahbar gives several examples of the importance of context including the following. In the Sura of the Ranks (Al-Ṣāffāt) 37:96 we read,

"وَ اللَّهُ خَلَقَكُمْ وَ مَا تَعْمَلُونَ ,"

This sentence will admit of two alternative translations:

        (a) God has created you and what you do.

        (b) God has created you and what you make.

How shall we choose between them? We will have to look at the sentences, and perhaps the paragraphs, surrounding the phrase in question. By starting at verse 91 we find the following additional information:

> And he (Abraham) went aside unto their gods and said, "Will you not eat? What ails you that you will not speak?" and he attacked them hitting with his right hand.
>
> And they (the people of the city) rushed toward him.
>
> He said, "Do you worship what you (yourselves) carved? When God has created you and what you _____" do? make?

The context of the verse reveals that the words are addressed by Abraham to idol-worshippers telling them that the idols made by them are helpless creatures of God, and that "God has created you and (the idols) **you make**."

By isolating this verse from its context, a great Imam like Al-Ghazali, makes it mean "God has created you and what **you do**," thus contriving to provide Quranic support for the theological idea that God Himself is the creator of each and every deed that men do.[14]

ALL THE CONTEXT

Sometimes, in order to study all the context, we have to include sentences on the same subject from another chapter, or even all the pertinent references in a whole book. An example of this is to be found in an article in *Manār Al-Islām* entitled "The Apostle Was Known Before His Birth," by Professor Hassan 'Abd-al-Fattāḥ Katkat from Jordan.[15] In order to show that the Bible gave prophecies about Muhammad before he was born, the professor quotes Deuteronomy 18:18-19 of the Torah where it reads,

> I (God) will raise up for them a prophet like you (Moses) from among their brothers. I will put my words in his mouth, and he will tell them everything I command him. If anyone does not listen to my words that the prophet speaks in my name, I myself will call him to account.

Secondly he quotes only a part of Deuteronomy 34:10 as follows:

> Since then, no prophet has risen in Israel like Moses...

These two quotations are then summarized as follows:

---

14. Dr. Daud Rahbar, op. cit., E.J. Brill, Leiden, 1960, p 20.
15. Jan-Feb 1981, p 56-57.

a) God promised to raise up another prophet like Moses.

b) But the comment at the end of Deuteronomy itself says that no other prophet has risen in Israel like Moses.

Professor Katkat then concludes that since "no other prophet has risen in Israel like Moses," the words "their brothers" is speaking of the **descendants of Ishmael**, not of Isaac, and this is a prophecy of **Muhammad**.

In order to judge whether this deduction is right we must learn more about the usage of the phrase "their brothers" in the Torah, and how Moses is described. When we examine the context we find that there is more information available. Starting from verse 15, with the newly quoted verses in boldfaced type, Deuteronomy 18:15-19 reads,

> **The LORD your God will raise up for you a prophet like me from among your own brothers. You must listen to him. For this is what you asked of the LORD your God at Horeb (Mt. Sinai) on the day of the assembly when you said, "Let us not hear the voice of the LORD our God (at Mt. Sinai) nor see this great fire anymore, or we will die."**
>
> **The LORD said to me "What they say is good.** I will raise up for them a prophet like you from among their brothers; I will put My words in his mouth, and he will tell them everything I command him." Etc.

When we add these verses we see that Moses was speaking to those of the Children of Israel who had heard the voice of God at Mt. Sinai, and God says that He will do for them what they ask. Therefore "their brothers" can only refer to brothers of those Jews who were present. But if that is still not clear enough the preceding chapter uses the very words "from among your own brothers," and then defines it. Chapter 17:14-15 reads,

> When you enter the land the LORD your God is giving you...and you say, "Let us set a king over us like all the nations around us."..**He must... be from among your own brothers. Do not place a foreigner over you, one who is not a brother Israelite.**

Here the phrase **"from among your own brothers"** is clearly defined as referring to a **"brother Israelite,"** not a descendant of Ishmael.

Furthermore, this is exactly parallel to the Quranic usage in the Late Meccan Sura of the Heights (Al-A'rāf) 7:65,73, where it says.

> And to the 'Aad people (We sent) **their brother**, Hud. He said, ''O my people, worship God''...
>
> And to the Thamud (We sent) **their brother**, Salih...

In his French translation of the Qur'an,[16] Muhammad Hamidullah has a special note here which reads,

> **The Arabic word _akh_ signifies both _brother_ and _member of_**

16. _Le Coran_, Le Club Français du Livre, 1959.

the tribe. (italics his)

The Hebrew word for brother is also "akh," and can also signify both *brother* and *member of the tribe*. In the above passages from Deuteronomy it is being used in exactly the same way—to speak of one who is a member of the same tribe. Clearly God is saying to the Children of Israel, **"I will raise up a prophet from among your brothers, from your own tribe, i.e., from you the Children of Israel."**

When we look at the second passage in Deuteronomy 34:10-12 we find that the context is even more necessary for a proper understanding. It reads,

> Since then, no prophet has risen in Israel like Moses, **whom the LORD knew face to face, who did all those miraculous signs and wonders the LORD sent him to do in Egypt—to Pharaoh and to all his officials and to his whole land.**

This is further explained in the Torah, Numbers 12:6-8 which says,

> And He (God) said, 'Hear My words. If there is a prophet among you, I the Lord make Myself known to him in a vision, I speak with him in a dream. **Not so with My servant Moses... With him I speak mouth to mouth, clearly.'**

What a difference this context makes. It tells us what characteristic of Moses was unique—in what way no other prophet was like him. It describes him as the only prophet **up to that time** whom the Lord knew **"face to face,"** and with whom the LORD spoke **"mouth to mouth."**

Here again we find that the Qur'an confirms the Bible. This very characteristic is mentioned in the Sura of the Women (Al-Nisā') 4:163-164, from 5-6 AH where it says,

> We have inspired you (Muhammad), as We inspired Noah and the prophets after him. We inspired Abraham, and Ishmael, and Isaac, and Jacob and the Tribes, and Jesus, and Job, and Jonah, and Aaron, and Solomon, and to David We gave the Psalms...
> And to Moses, **God spoke directly** (takliman تَكْلِيمًا).

We find Moses listed separately. He is not in the same group with Muhammad and the other prophets, because God spoke to Moses **"directly."**

That Muhammad was a great Warner against polytheism to the people of Mecca is known by all, but the Qur'an never claims that he did miracles like Moses or that God knew him face to face, or spoke to him mouth to mouth.[17]

Therefore, in order to claim that these verses speak about Muhammad, rather than a prophet coming from the tribe of the Children of Israel, Professor Katkat **has ignored the context in both the Torah and the Qur'an.**

---

17. Since Moses there is only one prophet who fulfills these two requirements. Jesus of Nazareth did about fifty individually recorded miracles of healing and prophecy. In addition, Mark 1:32-34, 3:10 and 7:53-56; Luke 10:1,17 and Matthew 15:29-31 say that he healed many or all of those who came to him. As for knowing God "face to face," John 1:1,18, speaking of Jesus as the "Word" of God (الكَلِمَة), says that the "Word" was "in the beginning with God," and after ascending he "is in the bosom of the Father."

CONCLUSION

There is only one way, therefore, to establish a new meaning for a word or a phrase used in a previous age. One must bring examples of the new usage from poetry, or letters, or government documents written during the period in question—the first century AD for New Testament usage—the first century of the Hejira for Quranic usage. This usually happens by discovering new source material from the period under study; such as the Nuzi tablets—clay tablets from the 15th century BC—which have helped us understand the customs of Abraham.

Secondly, if we are going to quote the Bible or the Qur'an or another book or document we must quote all of the context which bears on the subject. As a Christian I must quote the Qur'an with the same honesty that I use in quoting the Bible. A Muslim must quote the Bible with the same honesty he would use in quoting the Qur'an.

To change the meaning of a word or to quote something out of context is obviously a very serious matter when we are dealing with God's word. In reality it is changing God's word and making it into "my" word. At the least this is a form of "alteration of the meaning" (al-taḥrif al-ma'nawī), a type of lying, the very thing which the Jews are accused of doing in the Qur'an; and maybe it is polytheism (al-shirk الشِّرْك), associating myself and my ideas with God. **Therefore we must make every effort to quote things completely and honestly by including the necessary context.**

CHAPTER II

BASIC ASSUMPTIONS PECULIAR TO DR. BUCAILLE'S BOOK

First of all *Dr. Bucaille* claims "*complete objectivity in every respect*"—"une objectivité totale...sans le moindre exclusif." He says,

> It was in a totally objective spirit, and without any preconceived ideas that I first examined the Quranic revelation...I repeated the same test for the Old Testament and the Gospels, always preserving the same objective spirit.[1]

He claims to start from the facts rather than metaphysical concepts, and assumes that one can build inductively from "facts" without injecting any presuppositions into this process.

This, of course, ignores the findings of 20th century social sciences that there is no such thing as a "bare, uninterpreted fact." Kuhn, in his book *The Structure of Scientific Revolutions*, shows that even in science the interpretation of "facts" depends on one's prior metaphysical framework. He says,

> Philosophers of science have repeatedly demonstrated that more than one theoretical construction can always be placed upon a given collection of data.[2]

Earlier scholars have also recognized this. James Orr, writing in 1905, quotes a German theologian, Biedermann (*Christliche Dogmatik*), who put it this way:

> It is "not true, but sand in the eyes," if one asserts that genuinely scientific and historic criticism can and should proceed without dogmatic presuppositions (basic assumptions)... every student brings with him to historical investigations some sort of boundary definitions, be they ever so elastically held, of what is historically possible, and these are for that student dogmatic presuppositions.[3]

Dr. Bucaille's claim of complete objectivity ignores several of his own presuppositions. Therefore, we shall look at four of his **basic assumptions** and bring them out into the light so that every reader can perceive them.

1. Science is the measure of all things

Dr. Bucaille's first assumption is that corroboration between the scriptures and science is the primary measuring scale by which we are to judge the authenticity of a sacred text. There is some truth in this assumption, but a

---

1. *La Bible, Le Coran, et la science*, by Dr. Maurice Bucaille. Edition Seghers, Paris, 1976. Page numbers are from the English translation, *The Bible, the Qur'an, and Science*, American Trust Publications, Indianapolis, 1979. p-viii.
2. Thomas S. Kuhn, 2nd Ed., Univ. of Chicago Press, 1970, p 76.
3. *Old Testament Critics*, Thomas Whitelaw, Kegan, Paul, Trench, Trubner, & Co., Ltd., London, 1903, p 172.

question must be asked: What level of agreement is required? What level of scientific accuracy is necessary?

As everyone knows, scientific "knowledge" has often changed in the past. Dr. Bucaille recognizes this too, so he has proposed the following definition as the basis for his book:

> It must be stressed that when scientific data are discussed here, what is meant is data definitely established. This consideration rules out any explanatory theories, once useful in illuminating a phenomenon and easily dispensed with to make way for further explanations more in keeping with scientific progress. What I intend to consider here are incontrovertible facts and even if science can only provide incomplete data, they will nevertheless be sufficiently well established to be used without fear of error.[4]

Dr. Bucaille's definition of science is a good beginning for our discussion, but it gives the impression that science is limited to water cycles, astrophysics, and embryology.

When we look at the root (as Dr. Bucaille loves to do) of the word science, we find that it comes from the Latin *scientia*, meaning knowledge. Therefore our usage of the word science must include all that we "know." It must include archeological facts and historical facts, as well as how mountains are formed. There are even certain types of religious facts, such as fulfilled prophecy, which must be considered.

Then on page viii he further qualifies his definition by writing,

> This confrontation with science excludes all religious problems strictly speaking.

Again I find myself in disagreement with Dr. Bucaille's attempt to circumscribe the area of discussion and eliminate "religious problems strictly speaking." The only reason for writing and reading either his book or this book is the search for religious truth.

The real questions are, **"Is there a God?"** And if so, **"How can I know Him and be in contact with Him?"**

A biology or chemistry book might have no scientific errors, but it won't tell us about God.

Sometimes scientific knowledge and religious assumptions run into each other. As an example of this type of interaction let us consider pages 156-158 where Dr. Bucaille discusses stars, planets and shooting stars. He quotes the Sura of the Ranks (Al-Ṣāffāt) 37:6, Early Meccan, as follows,

> We (God) have indeed adorned the lowest heaven with the beauty of the planets...

Obviously there is no problem with this, but let us look at the context. When we add verses 7-10 it reads,

> We (God) have indeed adorned the lowest heaven with the

---

4. Bucaille, op. cit., p vii.

beauty of the planets and **for guard against every rebellious evil spirit, (so) they will not hear in the direction of the exalted assembly**, but be cast away from every side, repulsed, for they are under a perpetual penalty, **except such as snatch by stealth and they are pursued by a flaming fire of piercing brightness (a shooting star).**

Here, shooting stars, a scientific fact using Dr. Bucaille's definition, are found in action and reaction with scientifically unverifiable spiritual facts—God and the devils. Everyone with a modern education knows that a shooting star is a meteor. Therefore God, a spiritual being, is throwing material objects at devils which are also spiritual beings.[5]

Dr. Bucaille admits to trouble with this and concludes, "When, however the Qur'an associates material notions intelligible to us, **enlightened as we are today by modern science**, with statements of a purely spiritual nature, their meaning becomes **obscure**." And below, on the same page, "All these observations seem to lie outside the subject of this study."[6]

Whether to call this a scientific difficulty can be questioned, but it is a real difficulty, a "truth" difficulty, a difficulty which cannot be passed over with the statement that "the Qur'an…becomes obscure," or that it "seems to lie outside of the subject of this book." This type of statement where science and religion come together is exactly what one would expect to find discussed in a book called *The Bible, the Qur'an, and Science.*

For these reasons I do not claim that this book deals only with science, or that spiritual matters "lie outside the subject of our study." This book deals with science, but it also deals with the problems which are really basic to any discussion between Muslims and Christians. What does the Qur'an say about the Bible? Has the Bible really been changed? How does the Muslim know that the Qur'an hasn't been changed? What is the place of the Hadith? What does God say about intercession in the Bible and the Qur'an? How can we recognize a **true prophet**?

THE BIBLE AND THE QUR'AN ARE NOT MEASURED WITH THE SAME YARDSTICK

2. The Bible is required to speak in 20th century language

Dr. Bucaille judges the Bible according to 20th century standards, reading it as a scientific document. If a passage appears, according to his understanding, to contain unacceptable scientific data, it is automatically assumed that the passage did not come by revelation. Anything in the Bible that appears to him as "improbable" and/or "unlikely" is proof of error.

Unless the Bible is corroborated/verified by modern scientific knowledge, it is not the Word of God and hardly to be believed even as a human historical document.

---

5. For a complete discussion of all the verses on meteors and meteorites see Chapter II of Section 4.
6. Bucaille, op. cit., p 158.

Any suggestion that his understanding and exegesis of a passage might need to be refined is not admitted. No explanation is allowable, no harmonization. These are merely "cunning dialectical acrobatics orchestrated by apologetic lyricism."[7]

This method of evaluation is called the "conflict" approach. The bias is against the document and great effort is made to find every possible error.

3. The Qur'an may speak in the language of its time

Again it is assumed that modern science is very important and as the ultimate standard—the ultimate knowledge—it is the verifier of the Qur'an. This assumption, as written, seems to be the same as mentioned above for the Bible, but there is a difference.

After quoting Sura 79:27-33 Dr. Bucaille says:

> This list of earthly gifts from God to man, which is **expressed in a language suited to farmers or nomads on the Arabian Peninsula**, is preceded by an invitation to reflect on the creation of the heavens.[8]

Lack of precision is no longer considered error, as he would claim if he were quoting the Bible, but is a concession to people's prescientific state. This allows him to cite various Quranic passages as descriptions of modern science, but in prescientific language.

This type of approach is called "concordist." It is looking for concord or agreement between science and the scriptures.

Standing on this assumption Dr. Bucaille claims that there are no "difficulties" in the Qur'an. Of course, the translation of one single word may be "a very delicate matter,"[9] and we saw above that a reference to shooting stars was "obscure," but there are no "difficulties," "improbabilities" or "unlikelihoods." Perhaps one should say that there are **NO LONGER** any difficulties for Dr. Bucaille admits:

> It is easy to see therefore how for centuries commentators on the Qur'an (including those writing at the height of Islamic culture) have inevitably made errors of interpretation in the case of certain verses whose exact meaning could not possibly have been grasped. It was not until much later, at a period not far from our own, that it was possible to translate and interpret them correctly. **This implies that a thorough linguistic knowledge is not in itself sufficient to understand these verses from the Qur'an.**..As the questions raised are discussed, the variety of scientific knowledge essential to the understanding of certain verses of the Qur'an will become clear.[10]

---

7. Ibid., p 250.
8. Ibid., p 138.
9. Ibid., p 194.
10. Ibid., p 121.

This means that in former times, man could only distinguish an apparent meaning which led him to draw the wrong conclusions on account of the inadequacy of his knowledge at the time in question.[11]

To overcome these "delicate" situations Dr. Bucaille has tried to find (invent?) new meanings for **Arabic words** to bring them into line with modern science.

Many Muslim students—especially those in the sciences—are thrilled with these efforts, but the assumption that the traditional Muslim exegetes, steeped in Arabic grammar and culture, were somehow less able to understand the Qur'an correctly than moderns (especially Europeans) seems rather arrogant—especially since the Qur'an claims that it was written in a "clear Arabic" ('arabīyun mubīnun عَرَ بِيٌ هُبِينٌ) of the Quraish so that they could understand. In addition these efforts of Dr. Bucaille border on making "private interpretations" which the Qur'an prohibits.

THE RESULT

As every reader knows, we often find what we are looking for. If we read the Qur'an or the Bible assuming that it is wrong and that we will find errors, we are using a conflict approach, and we shall surely find errors. If we look at the Qur'an or the Bible with a forgiving spirit and expect God and His science to agree, we are using a concordist approach and we shall find very few errors— perhaps too few, if in our search for agreement, we bend science and/or the interpretation of scripture too far.

Dr. Bucaille has used a "conflict" approach with the Bible and a "concordist" approach with the Qur'an. An example of this is his treatment of the days of creation. Concerning the Bible he writes in Chapter I,

> The idea that successive phases of the Creation…could have been compressed into the space of one week is one that cannot be defended from a scientific point of view. Today we are perfectly aware that the formation of the Universe and the earth took place in stages that lasted for very long periods…Even if, as in the Quranic description, we were permitted to think that they were in fact undefined periods rather than actual days, the description of the Priestly editors would not be any more acceptable.[12]

Thus he admits the possibility in Chapter I that the Biblical "day" could stand for an "**undefined period**" of time, but when he discusses the subject again in Chapter III in relation to the Qur'an he says,

> The way the Bible interprets it, the word "day" means the interval of time between two successive sunrises or sunsets for an inhabitant of the Earth.[13]

11. Ibid., p 122.
12. Ibid., p 27-28.
13. Ibid., p 134.

He has forgotten his admission that the Biblical day could be a period of time—an interpretation which would be scientifically defensible. He now insists that the Biblical account calls for a 24-hour day which cannot be defended scientifically and thus "proves" that there is a "gross error."

On the next page he discusses the Arabic word "yaum" (يَوْم) used for day and quotes two verses from the Qur'an which show that it could mean a period of time.[14] He writes,

> The meaning "period of time" that the word contains is to be found elsewhere in the Qur'an. Hence the following: Sura 32:5,
> …in a period of time (yaum) whereof the measure is a thousand years of your reckoning. (It is to be noted that the creation in six periods is precisely what the verse preceding verse 5 refers to) [Parenthesis Bucaille.] Sura 70:4,
> …in a period of time (yaum) whereof the measure is 50,000 years.

This all sounds very convincing until we look at the verses **in their context**. This Middle Meccan Sura of Adoration (Al-Sajda) 32:4-5 then reads,

> It is God Who has created the heavens and the earth, and all between them in six days (aiyam — plural of yaum), and is firmly established on the throne. Ye have none beside Him to protect or intercede. Will you not then receive admonition? He rules (all) affairs from the heavens to the earth. In the end will (all affairs) go up to Him, in a period of time (yaum) whereof the measure is a thousand years of your reckoning.

and the Early Meccan Sura of the Ways of Ascent (Al-Ma'ārij) 70:4 reads,

> The angels and the Spirit ascend unto Him (God) in a period of time (yaum) whereof the measure is 50,000 years.

When we look at the context we see that these days are special "spiritual days." They both concern the day of judgment, and the second has something to do with the ascension of angels and the Spirit. Neither of them prove how the word "yaum" was understood by the Meccans to whom Muhammad preached before the Hejira. In fact, as special definitions, they may have been needed because the usual understanding was daytime or a day of 24 hours. Again we see the absolute need of context.

However, since these verses do show the Arabic word (yaum) being used for a period of time, let us accept this and admit it as a possibility for reconciling the Qur'an with modern science.

But if Dr. Bucaille wants this meaning accepted for the Quranic word, why did he not quote the following verse from the Bible?

> By the same word the present heavens and earth are reserved for fire, being kept for the day of judgment and destruction of ungodly men. But do not forget this one thing, dear friends.

14. Ibid., p 135.

With the Lord a day is like a thousand years, and a thousand years are like a day...He is patient with you, not wanting anyone to perish, but everyone to come to repentance (II Peter 3:7-9).

It has a "spiritual" meaning. It concerns the day of judgment. In every way it is parallel to the Quranic usage.

In their book *Genesis One and the Origin of the Earth*, Neuman and Eckelmann write,

> An elaborate word study of the Hebrew yom ("day") is not necessary to show that it is used rather like our English word "day." Often it means a period of activity during which the sun is up, roughly twelve hours long, depending on the season (Genesis 1:5; 1:14a). At other times it represents a day-night pair, a 24 hour day (Genesis 1:14b; Numbers 3:13). Less frequently it is used for longer periods of time (Genesis 2:4; Ecclesiastes 12:3).[15]

Why did Dr. Bucaille omit these last mentioned verses? Genesis 2:4 which follows the six days of creative work and the seventh day of rest mentioned in Chapter one reads,

> These are the generations of the heavens and of the earth when they were created. In the **day** that the Lord God made the earth and the heavens.

Here the word **"day"** is used to include the whole seven days of creation. In Ecclesiastes 12:3 the writer says,

> In the **day** when the keepers of the house shall tremble, and the strong men shall bow themselves, and the grinders cease because they are few, and those that look out of the windows be darkened.

This verse is an allegory. In a modern paraphrased translation it reads, "For there will come a **day** when your limbs will tremble with age and your strong legs will become weak, etc." It is using the word "day" for the period of old age.

Dr. Bucaille's idea that the Arabic "yaum" could stand for a period of time is not new. St. Augustine suggested a similar idea for the Hebrew "yom" in the 4th century, saying that the creation days are so great, so majestic, so profound that we cannot consider them as mere sun-divided days, but as God-divided days. They are creative days, not solar days, and so he calls them *natures, growths, "dies ineffabiles."*

The book *Modern Science and Christian Faith*,[16] published in 1948, proposed that the six days of creation were long periods or ages of time, and the idea was called the "day-age theory."

This book and others in English may not have been available to Dr. Bucaille,

---

15. Intervarsity Press, Downers Grove, Illinois 60515, 1977, p 61.
16. Eleven Essays, Van Kampen Press, Wheaton, 1948.

but what of the work of André Neher, *L'essentiel du prophétisme*,[17] published in 1955. In a review of *La Bible, Le Coran, et la science* found in *COMPRENDRE*, the Frère Christian-Marie comments,

> There follows a long study of the Arabic word YAUM…as though the Hebrew word YOM of the Genesis account was not an exact equivalent…It would have been sufficient to consult one of the best exegetes of contemporary Judaism, André Neher:
> "In this (first) chapter of Genesis, the word (YOM) has three different senses. In 1:4 the day is identified as the light, or rather it is the name of the light. YOM has here a cosmic meaning; it is part of the elemental couple of contradictory forces, light-darkness. In verse 1:14, the same word YOM has an astronomical sense; it designates the day—the revolution from one rising of the sun until the next. All through the account, however, appearing at the conclusion of the partial elements of creation, the word YOM has still another sense: **it marks a period**, one time connected to another, which succeeds it and announces the following. It is thus that the Bible later employs the word YOM for the articulations of history. It is of no importance that the seven days of creation will then be abnormal in the sense that they are not equally divided in relation to the sun. They are not astronomical days, but chronometric, if one can say this. They suggest the mobility of time, its advancement, in other words, HISTORY…They are the first days of a succession of days which from now on scan and emphasize the life of the creation…They define history in the larger sense of a DEVELOPMENT (DEVENIR)."[18]

In conclusion we see that in spite of an important amount of evidence to the contrary, Dr. Bucaille has chosen and emphasized an interpretation of the Bible which causes it to be in conflict with science. This, then, is another example of the "conflict" approach.

"WATER" AND "SMOKE"

As a further example of the "conflict" approach vs. the "concordist" approach let us look at a verse in the Qur'an and a verse in the Bible which are applied to the same creational/astronomical event by Bucaille in the one case, and the team of Neuman and Eckelmann in the other.

Dr. Robert C. Neuman has a Ph.D. in astrophysics from Cornell University, and a Master's degree in sacred theology from Biblical School of Theology. Mr. Herman J. Eckelmann, Jr. was a research associate with the Center for Radiophysics and Space Research at Cornell University, and has a Master of

---

17. PUF, 1955, p 135-136.
18. No. 69, 22nd year, 23 Dec. 1977, p 8. (translation mine)

Divinity degree from Faith Theological Seminary. Their book *Genesis One and the Origin of the Earth* is full of modern information and carefully reasoned arguments supporting the idea that Genesis chapter one is in agreement with modern science. Their degrees and experience in astrophysics and the Bible would seem to qualify them to speak both as scientists and theologians. So we shall now look at the following passage from the Torah and compare their "concordist" approach with the "conflict" approach of Dr. Bucaille.

Water: Torah — Genesis 1:1-2.

> In the beginning God created the heavens and the earth. The earth was without form and void, and darkness was upon the face of the deep; and the Spirit of God was moving over the face of the waters."

Conflict approach of Dr. Bucaille

"It is quite possible to admit that before the Creation of the Earth, what was to be come the universe as we know it was covered in darkness. To mention the existence of water at this period is, however, quite simply pure imagination. We shall see in the third part of this book how there is every indication that at the initial stage of the formation of the universe a gaseous mass existed. It is an error to place water in it."[19]

Concordist approach of Dr. Neuman and Mr. Eckelmann

"Likewise the word *mayim* which is nearly always translated 'water' or 'waters' has a broader meaning than one might at first suppose. it is occasionally used for other fluids (or at least mixtures involving more than water (for example; urine, 2 Kings 18:27; semen, Is. 48:1). Also it is used in reference to the solid and vapor states of H_2O (ice – Job 37:10; 38:30; vapor or droplets – 2 Sam. 22:5; Job 26:8; 36:27-28; Jer. 51:16).[20]

"The exact meaning of *mayim* in Gen.1:2 is therefore uncertain, but a large body of ice or water, a mass of ice crystals or droplets, a large cloud of water vapor, or even some other fluid altogether, would be within range of the usage of the word throughout Scripture. All of these would have a surface over which the Spirit of God might 'move' or 'hover.' In agreement with the scientific model proposed, a dark nebula would be expected to contain some water vapor. An alternative possibility is that *mayim* is intended to intimate something of the chemical, rather than the physical, composition of the cloud. Water consists of hydrogen and oxygen, and the cloud consists principally of *hydrogen*, helium, carbon, nitrogen and *oxygen*. *Mayim* is one of the few Hebrew words which could communicate such information."[21]

---

19. Bucaille, op. cit., p 23.
20. For the equivalent Arabic word mā-' pl. miyā-' (مِيَاء مَاء) Wehr's Dict. gives water, liquid, fluid, and juice.
21. Neuman/Eckelmann, op. cit., p 71-72.

Now let us look at the following passage from the Qur'an and compare Dr. Bucaille's "concordist" approach with an imaginary "conflict" approach.

Smoke: Ḥā-Mīm Al-Sajda 41:9b-11, Late Meccan.

...He is the Lord of the worlds. He set on it (the earth) mountains standing firm, high above it, and bestowed blessings on the earth, and measured therein all things to give them nourishment in due proportion, in four days, according to the needs of those who ask.

Then He turned to the heaven when it was smoke and said to it and to the earth: "come willingly or unwillingly!" They said, "We come in willing obedience."

The Concordist approach of Dr. Bucaille

"These four verses of Sura 41 contain several points to which we shall return: The initially gaseous state of celestial matter...[22]

"The statement of the existence of a gaseous mass with fine particles, for this is how the word 'smoke' (dukhān دُخَان) is to be interpreted. Smoke is generally made up of a gaseous substratum, plus, in more or less stable suspension, fine particles that may belong to solid and even liquid states of matter at high or low temperature.[23]

"If we take the sun and its sub product the earth as an example (the only one accessible to us), science informs us that their formation occurred by a process of condensation of the primary nebula and then their separation. This is exactly what the Qur'an expresses very clearly when it refers to the processes that produced a fusion and subsequent separation starting from a celestial 'smoke.' Hence there is complete correspondence between the facts of the Qur'an and the facts of science."[24]

Conflict approach

These verses say that at some point in time the sky or heaven was made out of smoke. Smoke includes organic particles. Therefore this is clearly false because at the time of a primordial gaseous state no organic matter would be found in it. Furthermore, nebulae which might have been supposed to be planetary forerunners are much too dilute to be thought of as "suspending" anything. One has only very dilute gas molecules, a few per ml, and occasional grains of dust.

Also, if it speaks of some early primordial gaseous stage, the earth and sky should have been "smoke" together: but the passage says that there were firm mountains and nourishment on the earth while the heaven was still "smoke." Clearly these verses have serious astronomical errors.

---

22. Bucaille, op. cit., p 136
23. Ibid., p 139.
24. Ibid., p 147.

So what is the result of our little study? Neuman and Eckelmann say that "water" as used in Genesis 1:2 of the Torah refers to the primordial gases. Bucaille says that this is complete error.

Bucaille says that "smoke" as used in Sura 41 of the Qur'an refers to the primordial gases. The conflict author says that this is complete error.

Further knowledge in Hebrew and Arabic word usage and/or further knowledge in astrophysics may allow us to evaluate the validity of the two interpretations and decide whether one is more true than the other; but the real point of this study is to show the effect of bias. If Dr. Bucaille wishes to say that "smoke" stands for the primordial gaseous state, he has no reason to refuse Neuman and Eckelmann the possibility that "water" could be used for such a gaseous state, and vice versa.

It is impossible, of course, to have no bias. I am on the side of myself. I hope that my previous decisions—in this case those which led to my becoming a Christian—are right, and I lean toward anything which confirms them.

Therefore, there is much truth in the little joke which my daughter brought home from the university, "Scientists should always state the opinion on which their facts are based."

We must admit our biases and try to tame them a bit for a discussion such as this. Otherwise, as a raging animal, they make us forget truth. As one friend said,

> When either a Muslim or a Christian starts by postulating that
> he is being scientific and objective, you should see the red light at
> once. That man is dangerous, for he is suffering under a delusion,
> and not even aware of how unscientific and how prejudiced he is.

If I quote only half of a verse in order to make it agree with my ideas, then I have forgotten truth. If I don't bother to mention other verses on the same subject which would contradict my theme, then I am bending the truth.

We must not bow to the level of a second little truism from the university which proposes, "If facts do not conform to theory they must be disposed of."

We must abandon the 100% conflict approach. By that I mean the attitude which can admit to no good thing, to no correct reasoning by the person with whom we disagree. We must admit our bias and then try to look at all the facts and be equal in our judgment.

Surely this attitude is included in Jesus' words when he said, "Do to others as you would have them do to you"; and when he quoted the Torah saying, "Love your brother as yourself."

4. A further assumption concerning the Bible

Dr. Bucaille assumes that the "documentary hypothesis" for the origin and development of the **Torah** is true. This theory, developed in its classical form around 1890, was based on the beliefs that:

A. There is evolution in religion from polytheism to monotheism. As a result, the Old Testament is considered to be more or less the product of the evolving religious consciousness of the Hebrew people. **It had nothing to do with God revealing himself through an angel or the Holy Spirit.**

B. Since the customs mentioned in the life of Abraham are not mentioned outside the Torah (e.g., he married his half-sister, Sarah, and threw out Hagar, his slave-girl wife, when Sarah demanded it), and since people like **the Hittites** are not mentioned outside the Torah, **the accounts of Abraham, Isaac and Jacob, often referred to as the patriarchs, are not historical. They are only myths and stories.**

C. Moses and the Hebrews couldn't write because writing hadn't been invented yet.

D. Therefore the five books of the Torah were not given by Moses in 1400 or 1300 BC, as the Bible (and the Qur'an) repeatedly claim, but were compiled 1000 years later, about 400 BC, by unknown writers and editors who fraudulently used Moses' name. This idea is called the "J,E,D,P theory" or the *"documentary hypothesis."*

E. In addition, whether they stated it or not, the men who first proposed this theory **did not believe in miracles.** They did not believe in the miracles of Moses or Jesus, and they did not believe in the miracle of prophecy — that God reveals himself propositionally in word statements. According to them God never talked to Moses or Jesus and told them words to say. And if they had been studying the Qur'an seriously, they would have said that God never talked to Muhammad either.

We might even say that this **disbelief in miracles and prophecy is the basic assumption behind the whole theory.**

Dr. Bucaille has quoted many Catholic scholars who believe this theory, including[25] J.P. Sandroz, professor at the Dominican Faculties, Saulchoir; R.P. De Vaux, Director of the Ecole Biblique of Jerusalem;[26] Father Kannengiesser of the Catholic Institute of Paris;[27] etc. I do not say that these men deny the possibility of miracles as I have not read their works. Nor does Dr. Bucaille deny the possibility of miracles, as it is clear from his preface, page ii, that he accepts the miracle of Jesus' birth without a human father. What I am saying is that the unbelieving Protestant theologians who developed this theory had the basic assumption that miracles were impossible.

Dr. Bucaille is right to feel angry at church leaders, whether Catholic or Protestant, who quote Moses and Jesus in church before their congregations as though they believe that they spoke from God; and then write scholarly articles showing that they don't believe that at all.

Obviously I disagree completely with this theory. We shall examine some of the evidence and the reasons why it is wrong and invalid in Chapter I of Section 3, but first we must examine what the Qur'an says about the Bible. This

---

25. Bucaille, op. cit., p 9.
26. Ibid., p 11,13.
27. Ibid., p 61.

examination is necessary because it will give a foundation so that the reader may judge for himself and understand that *if the "documentary hypothesis" is true, as Dr. Bucaille claims, then **it falsifies the Qur'an as well as the Bible**.*

THE BIBLE
AS SEEN BY THE QUR'AN
AND THE MUSLIM TRADITIONS

WHAT THE QUR'AN SAYS ABOUT THE BIBLE

Whenever a Christian quotes the Bible to a Muslim in order to establish why he believes something, the Muslim almost always responds by saying, **"BUT YOU CHANGED YOUR BIBLE."** In making this very serious accusation Muslims usually use the word "harrafa" (حَرَّفَ) and quote verses from the Qur'an where this word is used. Therefore in this chapter, we are going to make a detailed study of what the **Qur'an** actually says about the **Torah** of Moses, the **Psalms (Zabūr)** of David and the **Gospel (Injil)** of Jesus.

At this point someone will surely say, "But how can a non-Muslim make any valid study of the Qur'an?" I would be the first to agree that there is some validity to this objection in the sense that to understand a book from "the inside" requires a prior commitment to the "world view" of that book. However, since the Qur'an says of itself that it is a "clear book" written in "a clear Arabic" ('arabiyun mubinun عَرَبِيٌّ مُبِينٌ) so that the unbelieving Quraish could understand, we are going to make a study in the same way that Christians would study such a question in the Bible.

We are going to look at all the verses which have any bearing on the subject and examine them in their context. Sometimes this context is only one verse or even half of a verse. But sometimes it is necessary to examine a whole page in order to show clearly the meaning of a word or phrase.

Muslim writers have also begun to recognize the need for this type of study. In the preface to his book *God of Justice*,[1] Dr. Daud Rahbar writes, "If we are to construct a fair narrative of Muslim Theology and Quranic Exegesis, the first important prerequisite of this study will be a knowledge of what the Qur'an meant to the Prophet and people round him within their historical context."

He goes on to say that commentators of the Qur'an did not coordinate and compare all the verses on a subject before giving their interpretation. As an obvious, but unimportant example, he speaks of Al-Baidawi commenting that in the phrase "earth and heaven," earth is mentioned first "for when you have to climb, you move from bottom upwards." Dr. Rahbar goes on to say, "Thereupon, I looked up Baidawi for several passages of the Qur'an in which the very phrase occurs with 'the heaven' preceding 'the earth,' but here obviously Baidawi failed to remember what he had said previously."[2]

At the end of his preface Dr. Rahbar claims to be the first Muslim to make this type of coordinated study. He says, "After all, an exhaustive collection is the full data. What right have we to quote a couple of passages on a subject when there are another three hundred on the same? Of this pioneer aspect of the work I am absolutely sure. Muslim scholarship is invited to improve upon the analysis or classifications of the exhaustive collections of Quranic contexts made herein,

---

1. Op. cit., E.J. Brill, Leiden, 1960, p xiii. Dr. Daud Rahbar was Specialist-in-charge of the Chair of Urdu and Pakistan Studies at the Ankara University in Turkey from 1956 to 1959.
2. Ibid., p xvii.

but that classified exhaustive collections are made here for the first time none will deny."[3]

For the English translation of the Quranic passages I have used *The Holy Qur'an* as translated by Abdullah Yusuf Ali[4] as a starting point. However, on many occasions where it seemed that Muhammad Pickthall in English[5] or Muhammad Hamidullah's French translation[6] were closer to the original I have used them, and rarely I have used an idea from Masson's French translation.[7]

In addition, there are some verses where the Arabic words were so important to the discussion that I chose to make my own literal translation. This bends the English out of shape, but my purpose was to allow those readers who are not familiar with Arabic to enter into the discussion.

We will start with the Quranic verses referring to the Torah at the time of Jesus and then move forward through history to the verses referring to the Torah and the Gospel during the life of Muhammad. Finally we will look at the verses which specifically refer to tahrīf (change). Now, having set the stage with these explanatory remarks, I here present my exhaustive study of what the Qur'an says about the Bible.

A. VERSES SHOWING THE TORAH TO BE TRUE AT THE TIME OF JESUS

A1. Mary (Maryam) 19:12, Middle Meccan in -7 AH.

God says, " '**Oh Yaḥyā! (John the Baptist) take hold of the Book** with might:' and We gave him wisdom as a child."

A2. The Family of 'Imran (Āli 'Imrān) 3:48, 2-3 AH.

The Angel Gabriel is speaking to Mary about Jesus before Jesus' birth and says: "**And He (God) will teach him the book and wisdom and the Torah and the Gospel.**"

A3. The Forbidding (Al-Taḥrīm) 66:12, 7 AH.

and **Mary** (Jesus' mother)…**believed in the words of her Lord and His Books.**

A4. The Family of 'Imran (Āli 'Imrān) 3:49-50, 2-3 AH.

Jesus says, "I have come to you…attesting to (the truth of) what is between my hands of the Torah, and to make lawful to you a part of that which is forbidden to you."

A5. The Battle Array (Al-Ṣaff) 61:6, from 3 AH.

And remember, **Jesus, the son of Mary, said**: "Oh Children of Israel! **I am the apostle of God to you, confirming that which IS between my hands from the Torah**…"

---

3. Ibid., p xx.
4. Op. cit. in Chapter I.
5. *The Glorious Qur'an*, Muhammad Marmaduke Pickthall, Muslim World League, New York, 1977.
6. *Le Coran*, Muhammad Hamidullah, Le Club Français du Livre, 1959.
7. *Le Coran*, D. Masson, Editions Gallimard, 1967.

A6. The Table (Al-Mā'ida) 5:49, 10 AH.

> And in their footsteps (of Moses and the Jews) We sent **Jesus the son of Mary, attesting to (the truth of) the Torah which was between his hands**; and **We gave him the Gospel**—therein is guidance and light and **attesting to (the truth of) the Torah which was between his hands**: a guidance and an admonition to the righteous.

A7. 5:113.

> Then will God say, "O Jesus son of Mary! Recount my favor to you and to your mother when I strengthened you with the Holy Spirit, so that you spoke to the people in childhood and in maturity. **Behold! I taught you the Book and Wisdom, the Torah and the Gospel...**"

According to these verses, the last of which came in the final revelation of 10 AH, John the Baptist (Yaḥyā) was commanded to take hold of the "Book" [A1]; Mary the mother of Jesus believed in God's "Books" [A3]; God promised before Jesus was born to teach him the Torah [A2]; Jesus said that his Gospel "attested to the truth of the Torah between his hands" [A4,A5]; and God attests, in Muhammad's time, that He taught Jesus the Torah [A6,A7]. **We can only conclude from this that the True Unchanged Torah was present in the first century when Jesus lived.**

Since the Sura of The forbidding (Al-Taḥrīm) from 7 AH quoted above [A3] says that Mary believed in "His (God's) Books" (kutubihi كُتُبِهِ), this must refer to the Books which the other Prophets brought to the Jews, as well as the Torah of Moses.

B. VERSES SHOWING THAT TRUE CHRISTIANS WERE LIVING DURING THE PERIOD BETWEEN JESUS AND MUHAMMAD

B1. The Table (Al-Mā'ida) 5:113-114, 10 AH.

> Then will God say, "O Jesus son of Mary! Recount my favor to you... **Behold! I taught you the Book and Wisdom, the Torah and the Gospel...**"
> And behold! **I inspired the disciples** (al-ḥawārīyūn الْحَوَارِيُّون) to have faith in Me and My apostle (Jesus). **They said (to Jesus), "We have faith and (you must) bear witness that we are Muslims (submitted ones)."**

B2. The Family of 'Imran (Āli 'Imrān) 3:52-53, 2-3 AH.

> When Jesus found unbelief on their part he said, "Who will be my helpers to (the work of) God?" The disciples said, "**We are God's helpers**. We believe in God and (you must) bear witness that we are Muslims (submitted ones). Our Lord, **we believe in what You have revealed and we follow the apostle (Jesus)**."

B3. The Battle Array (Al-Ṣaff) 61:14, 3 AH.

> O ye who believe! Be ye helpers of God: as said Jesus the son of Mary to the disciples, "Who will be my helpers for God?" **The Disciples said, "We are God's helpers!" Then a portion of the Children of Israel believed,** and a portion disbelieved: **but We gave power to those who believed** against their enemies, **and they became the ones that prevailed.**

B4. Iron (Al-Ḥadīd) 57:26-27, from 8 AH.

> And We sent Noah and Abraham, and established in their descendants prophecy and the Book: and some of them are rightly guided, but many are rebellious.
>
> Then We sent after them our apostles and **We sent Jesus the son of Mary, and bestowed on him the Gospel; and We ordained in the hearts of those who followed him compassion and mercy; and monasticism, they invented it**. We did not command it...yet **We bestowed on those among them who believed, their due reward**, but many of them are rebellious. (cp. 5:85)

We learn from this verse that although monasticism is not of God, there were true believers among these followers of Jesus who received their "due reward" (in heaven).

Historically, monasticism started in the 4th century, although certain men, such as Paul of Thebes, lived a separate life as hermits in the third century. St. Anthony of Egypt was the first to organize even a loose group in 305 AD, and in the Sinai, too, monasticism began about the same time.

B5. The Cave (Al-Kahf) 18:10,25, Meccan.

> Behold, the youths betook themselves to the Cave. **They said, "Our Lord! Bestow on us mercy from Yourself, and dispose of our affair for us in the right way"**...
>
> So they stayed in their Cave three hundred years, and (some) add nine (more)...

Yusuf Ali, in several notes to his translation of the Qur'an, refers this to seven young Christian men of Ephesus who, while fleeing from persecution, hid in a cave and did not wake up for 300 years. He discusses various dates which terminate between 440 and 450 AD, and says that the Khalifa Wathiq (842-846 AD) sent an expedition to examine and identify the locality.[8] Hamidullah mentions this possibility, but thinks that the passage refers to a time well before Christianity. However, Toufiq Al-Hakim in his play Ahel Al-Kahf describes them clearly as Christians.

B6. The Zodiacal Signs (Al-Burūj) 85:4-9, Early Meccan.

> Woe to the makers of the pit (of fire), fire supplied with fuel,
> Behold, they sat over against the (fire), and they witnessed (all)

---

8. Yusuf Ali, op. cit., p 730 and 736.

that they were doing **against the believers**. And they ill-treated them for no other reason than that **they believed in God**...

Hamidullah, in the notes to his translation, refers this to a Jewish King of Yemen, Dhou Nuwas, who during the 6th century persecuted the Christians, burning alive those who didn't want to become Jews. The Khalifa Omar built a large Mosque in Yemen to honor these Christians.[9] Yusuf Ali also mentions it as one of three possible explanations.[10]

The first three references clearly refer to **Jesus' followers as being "inspired" by God to follow the Messiah** [B1], choosing to be "God's helpers" [B2,B3], and "becoming the ones who prevailed" [B3]. In addition **some true believers remained** even when monasticism was practiced [B4], starting **in the 4th century in Egypt**.

If references [B5] and [B6] were understood by Muhammad and the people of Mecca in their historical context to refer to Christians, then these are Quranic attestations that there were true Christians, acceptable to God, in Ephesus (Modern Turkey) in 450 AD; and in Yemen in the 6th century when these Christian Martyrs were burned alive.

Admittedly the verses say nothing about the doctrines of these Christians. But true believers in groups as far apart as Turkey and Yemen would surely have left copies of their scriptures and writings—some of which would have come down to us. If their scriptures had been different from the Torah and the Gospel which we know today, then we would certainly have found their traces.

C. VERSES SHOWING THAT THE TORAH AND THE GOSPEL WERE TRUE AND UNCHANGED AT THE TIME OF MUHAMMAD

C1. The City of Saba (Sabā) 34:31, Early Meccan.

> And the unbelievers say, "We will not believe in this Qur'an, **nor in that which IS between his (its) hands (the Torah and the Gospel)**"...

Note: The CAPITAL LETTERS show verbs which are in the present tense for Muhammad and his people. *Italics* have been used for phrases speaking of groups of Jews or Christians at the time of Muhammad spoken of as believers or unbelievers, in order to emphasize that there were always some true believers who would not have changed their own scriptures.

C2. The Originator of Creation (Fāṭir) 35:31, Early Meccan.

> That which We have revealed to you of the Book is the truth, **attesting to (the truth of) that which IS between his (its) hands (the Torah and Gospel)**...

C3. Jonah (Yūnus) 10:37, Late Meccan.

> This Qur'an is not such as can be produced by other than God; but **it is a verification of that (the Torah and Gospel) which IS between his (its) hands**, and the explanation of **the book, wherein there IS no doubt**, from the Lord of the worlds.

---

9. Hamidullah, op. cit., p 593.
10. Yusuf Ali, op. cit., note 6055, p 1714.

C4. Joseph (Yūsuf) 12:111, Late Meccan.

> ...**It (the Qur'an) is** not a fabricated story, but **a verification of that (the Torah and Gospel) which IS between his (its) hands**, a detailed explanation, a guide and a mercy to the people who believe.

C5. The Cattle (Al-An'ām) 6:154-157, Late Meccan.

> Then We gave Moses **the Book complete as to whatever is excellent, and explaining all things in detail, and a guide and a mercy**, that they might believe in the meeting with their Lord. And this (the Qur'an) is a Book which We have revealed, blessed: so follow it and be righteous, that you may receive mercy: lest you should say, **"The Book was sent down to two peoples before us, and for our part, we remained unacquainted with all that they learned by assiduous study"**; or lest you should say: **"If the Book (Torah and Gospel) had only been sent down to us, we should have followed its guidance better than they."**

C6. The Believer (Al-Mū'min) 40:69-70, Late Meccan.

> Do you (Muhammad) not see those who dispute concerning the signs of God? How are they turned away? *Those who **REJECT** the Book*, and **that (book) with which We sent our apostles**, they shall know when the collars shall be around their necks, and the chains, they shall be dragged along.

C7. Winding Sand Tracts (Al-Aḥqāf) 46:12, Late Meccan.

> And before this was the Book of Moses as a guide and a mercy: and **this Book is a verification (of it)** in the Arabic tongue to warn those who transgress and as glad tidings to the righteous.

C8. 46:29-30.

> Behold, We turned towards you a company of Jinns listening to the Qur'an...When the (reading) was finished they returned to their people as warners. They said, "O our people! we have heard a Book revealed after Moses **attesting to (the truth of) that which IS between his (its) hands (the Torah)**—guiding to the truth and to a straight path."

C9. The Heifer (Al-Baqara) 2:91, 2 AH.

> When it is said to them, 'Believe in what God has sent down,' they say, **"We believe in what was sent down to us (the Torah)"**: yet they reject all besides, even if it be truth **attesting to (the truth of) what IS WITH THEM (the Torah)...**

C10. Family of 'Imran (Āli 'Imrān) 3:3, 2-3 AH.

> It is He (God) who sent down to thee the Book in truth, **attesting to (the truth of) what IS between its (his) hands (the Bible), and He sent down the Torah and the Gospel** before this as a guide to mankind.

C11. The Women (Al-Nisā') 4:162-163, 5-6 AH.

But those of them (the Jews) that are grounded in knowledge, and the believers, **BELIEVE in that which has been revealed to you (Muhammad) and in that which has been revealed before you**…We have sent thee inspiration, as We sent it to Noah and the prophets after him, and We sent inspiration to Abraham, Ishmael, Isaac, Jacob and the Tribes, and to Jesus, Job, Jonah, Aaron, and Solomon, and to David We gave the Psalms.

C12. Repentance (Al-Tauba) 9:111, 9 AH.

God has bought from the believers their selves and their wealth, and for them is the garden (of Paradise) if they fight in the ways of God: and whether they kill or are killed, **the promise of God IS true in the Torah and the Gospel and the Qur'an**, and who is more faithful to his promise than God?

C13. The Table (Al-Mā'ida) 5:51, 10 AH.

To you (Muhammad) We revealed the book in truth, **attesting to (the truth of) that which IS between his (its) hands from the scripture (the Torah and Gospel), and guarding it** (wa muhaiminan 'alaihi عَلَيْهِ مُهَيْمِنًا وَ)…

We find in these verses a strong testimony to the Torah and the Gospel as being true and present at the time of Muhammad.

The Qur'an is an Arabic "verification" of the Book of Moses [C7] which is necessary because the Meccans couldn't understand what "the two peoples before" them had learned by "assiduous study"; or they would have followed it better [C5]. Further, **it is an explanation of the Torah and the Gospel "wherein there IS no doubt"** [C3], and a guard over it [C13].

The Meccans say, "We will not believe in the Qur'an, nor in **that which IS between its hands**" of the Torah and the Gospel [C1]. Some of the Jews say that they believe only in what was sent to them **even if the Qur'an attests to (the truth of) "what IS WITH THEM"** [C9]. The warning is given that those who **REJECT (now) the Qur'an and "that (the former books) which We sent our apostles"** will be judged [C6]. "But those of **the Jews who are grounded in knowledge BELIEVE**" in what was revealed to Muhammad and **in (the Torah) which was revealed before him** [C11]; and the Jinns also believe in both the Qur'an and the Torah [C8].

In the Sura of Repentance, one of the last revelations given, it says, **"The promise of God IS true in the Torah, the Gospel, and the Qur'an"** [C12].

Finally it is necessary to mention the phrase "between his hands" (bain yadaihi يَدَيْهِ بَيْنَ) found in many of these verses [C2,C3,C4,C8,C10,C13 and A5,A6 above]. I have chosen to translate it word for word because that gives the sense of the present tense which it has. Sometimes it has the literal meaning "between or in his hands," but usually it is an idiom for "in his presence," or "in his power," or "in his possession," or "at his disposal." Examples are "The words are between your hands," meaning "you have the floor" or "you may speak." "No weapons are between his hands," meaning "he is unarmed." Sura 34:12 speaks of Solomon and "the Jinns who worked between his hands." In the text Yusuf Ali translates this passage as "worked in front of him," but in a note he explains, the Jinns "worked under his eyes."

The sense of these verses, therefore is that the Qur'an has come to confirm, attest to and verify the Torah and the Gospel which are now "in its presence" or "before its eyes." With the other verses discussed above from this section they show that Muhammad acknowledged the existence of a valid Torah and Gospel "under his eyes."

D. VERSES WHERE MUHAMMAD ACTUALLY QUOTES OR APPEALS TO THE TORAH AND/OR THE GOSPEL

D1. The Star (Najm) 53:33-38, Early Meccan.

> Do you (Muhammad) see the one who turns back? Gives a little, then hardens (his heart)? What has he knowledge of the unseen so that he can see? Nay, **IS he not acquainted with what IS in the books of Moses and of Abraham** who fulfilled his engagements?—namely that no bearer of burdens can bear the burden of another.

D2. The Poets (Al-Shu'arā') 26:192-197, Middle Meccan.

> Verily this is a revelation from the Lord of the worlds. The Spirit of faith came down upon your heart with it that you might be one of the warners in the plain Arabic tongue. **And truly it IS in the Scriptures (Zubur) of the former people. IS it not a sign to them that the learned of the Children of Israel RECOGNIZE it?**

D3. Ṭā-Hā 20:133, Middle Meccan from -7 AH.

> They (the Meccans) say, "Why does he not bring us a sign from his Lord?" What! Has not a **clear sign come to them in what IS in the former pages** (al-ṣuḥūf al-aūllā الصُّحُوف الأَثُولَى)?

According to Baidawi's commentary on this verse—The "former pages" refers to "the Torah and the Gospel and all the divine books."

D4. The Prophets (Al-Anbiyā') 21:7, Middle Meccan.

> And before thee (Muhammad), We sent no one, except men, to whom We granted revelation. **ASK (plural) the people of the Scripture message, if you don't know.**

D5. The Prophets (Al-Anbiyā') 21:105, Middle Meccan.

> Before this We wrote in the Psalms, after the Message (given to Moses): **"My servants, the righteous, shall inherit the earth."**

This is a direct quotation from Psalm 37:29 which reads, "The righteous shall inherit the earth and dwell therein forever." When considered with the preceding quotation from the same sura (21:7), **it is clear that, according to the Qur'an,**

God is quoting from the Psalms as still present and true at the time of Muhammad.

D6. Gold Adornments (Al-Zukhruf) 43:44-45, Late Meccan.

> The (Qur'an) is indeed a message for you (Muhammad) and your people, (all of) you shall be brought to account, and **ASK those of Our apostles whom We sent before thee**, "Did We appoint any deities other than the Most Merciful whom they should worship?"

According to Baidawi, Jelaleddin, and Yusuf Ali, "ask those of Our apostles whom We sent before thee" means enquire of their people—those learned in their writings and doctrines. Therefore those writings and doctrines were clearly available in Muhammad's time.

D7. Jonah (Yūnus) 10:94, Late Meccan.

> **If you (Muhammad) are in doubt** regarding that which We have revealed to thee, **ASK those who READ the book from before you**…

D8. The Bee (Al-Naḥl) 16:43-44, Late Meccan.

> And We have not sent before you (Muhammad) other than men to whom We granted revelation. And (all of you) **ASK the people of the (Scripture) Message if you don't know**.

D9. The Children of Israel (Banī Isrā'īl) 17:101, Late Meccan from -1 AH.

> To Moses We gave nine clear signs. **ASK (O Muhammad) the Children of Israel**…

D10. 17:107-108.

> Ṣay, "Whether you believe in it (the Qur'an) or not (O Meccans), it is true that *those to whom knowledge came before it, when they hear it recited unto them, fall down upon their faces worshiping*…and it increases their humility."

D11. Thunder (Al-Ra'd) 13:43, Late Meccan.

> And those who disbelieve say, "You (Muhammad) are not sent." Say, "God is sufficient as a witness between me and you, and also **he who HAS the knowledge of the book**."

D12. The Heights (Al-A'rāf) 7:156-157, Late Meccan.

> And I will write down (my mercy) for those who are righteous and give alms and who believe in our signs; who follow the apostle, the unlettered prophet, **whom they find written in the Torah and the Gospel that IS WITH THEM.**

D13. The Heights (Al-A'rāf) 7:159, Late Meccan.

> Of the people of Moses *there is a group* (umma أُمَّة) *who guide with truth and judge by it.*

D14. 7:168-170, Late Meccan.

> He broke them (the Jews) up into sections on this earth. *Some of them are righteous*, and *some of them are not*. We have tried them with blessings and with adversities in order that they might return to Us…What! has there not been taken from them the covenant of the Book, that they should not say of God other than the truth, **and they diligently STUDY that which is therein**…As to those (Jews) *who HOLD FAST by the Book* and observe prayer; verily We shall not detract from the reward of the righteous.

D15. The Heifer (Al-Baqara) 2:113, 2 AH.

> The Jews say, "The Christians are not (founded) upon anything." And the Christians say, "The Jews are not (founded) upon anything." And yet **they READ the Book.**

D16. The Family of 'Imran (Āli 'Imrān) 3:23, 2-3 AH.

> Do you not see those to whom a portion of the Book came. **They were called to the Book of God (Torah) that it might judge between them.** Then *a party of them* turned aside and declined.

The commentators refer this verse to various incidents, but they agree that a dispute was submitted by the Jews to Muhammad for arbitration. He proposed to these Jews to determine the question by actual reference to their Scriptures, but they refused and went away.

D17. 3:79.

> It is not for a man to whom is given the Book and wisdom and prophecy that he should then say to people, "Be worshipers of me in place of God." But rather, **"Be true teachers**** (rabbāniyīn رَبَّانِيِّين), **since you teach the Book and you STUDY it earnestly."**
>
> (**Every translator is different here. I followed Masson.)

D18. 3:93-94.

> All food was lawful to the Children of Israel except what Israel made unlawful for itself before the Torah was revealed. Say, **"BRING the Torah and READ it, if you are men of truth."** If any, after this, invent a lie and attribute it to God, they are indeed transgressors.

D19. The Women (Al-Nisā') 4:60, 5-6 AH.

> Have you (Muhammad) not seen those who fancy that they believe in that which hath been revealed unto thee, and **in that which has been revealed before thee?** They desire to go for a mutual decision unto the Taghut (an idol); yet verily **they have been commanded (in the Torah) to disbelieve therein,** and Satan desires to deceive them into a wide deception.

D20. The Victory (Al-Fatḥ) 48:29, 6 AH.

On their faces (of the Muslim believers) are their marks, the traces of their bowing (in worship). **This IS their likeness in the Torah**; and **their likeness in the Gospel IS like a seed which sends forth its blade, then makes it strong. It then becomes thick, and it stands on its own stem, and delights the sower.**

This seems to be a definite allusion to Jesus' words as recorded in Mark 4:26-28 which reads:

And he said, "This is what the kingdom of God is like. A man scatters seed on the ground…all by itself the soil produces grain— first the blade, then the head, and then the full kernel in the head. As soon as the grain is ripe he puts the sickle to it because the harvest has come."

D21. The Table (Al-Mā'ida) 5:46, 10 AH.

But why do they (the Jews) come to thee for decision, **when they HAVE the Torah in which IS the command of God**.

D22. 5:48, 10 AH.

We ordained therein for them (the Jews): "Life for life, eye for eye, nose for nose, ear for ear, tooth for tooth, and wounds equal for equal." **But if any one REMITS the retaliation** by way of charity, **it IS an act of atonement** for himself. **And if any fail to JUDGE by what God has revealed, they are wrong-doers.**

Here the Qur'an quotes God as repeating the law which He gave to Moses in the Torah Exodus 21:23-25 where He ordered,

…You are to take life for life, eye for eye, tooth for tooth, hand for hand, foot for foot, burn for burn, wound for wound, bruise for bruise.

Then the Jews of Medina are warned, "If any fail to JUDGE by (the Torah)…they are wrong-doers."

D23. 5:50, 10 AH.

And let the People of the Gospel JUDGE by what God has revealed in it. If any fail to judge by what God has revealed, they are licentious.

D24. 5:68-71, 10 AH.

If only the People of the Book had believed and been righteous, we should have blotted out their sins and admitted them to gardens of bliss.

If only they had performed the Torah and the Gospel and all that was revealed to them from their Lord, they would have eaten from above and from under their feet. *Among them is a People* (umma أُمَّة) *on the right course*, but evil is that which many of them do…

Say, **"O People of the Book! You are not (founded) on anything until you PERFORM the Torah and the Gospel, and what was revealed to you from your Lord."**

In the above verses there is a continuing testimony to the presence during Muhammad's lifetime, of a true Torah and Gospel, recognized by the Muslims and non-Muslims alike.

In Mecca an unbeliever who turns away IS acquainted with **what IS in the books of Moses and Abraham** [D1]. A clear sign has come to them in "what IS in the former pages" [D3], and Muhammad appeals to **"he who HAS the knowledge of the Book"** [D11].

It is stated that the coming of the **Qur'an "IS in the Scripture of the former people"** and **"the learned of the Children of Israel RECOGNIZE it"** [D2]. **Those to whom knowledge came before BELIEVE in it** [D10]. *Some Jews are righteous and "hold fast by the Book"* [D14], but there are others who do not accept Muhammad even though **"they diligently STUDY"** their Book [D14].

Both the Jews and Christians **"READ the book"** [D15], and **"STUDY it earnestly"** [D17].

There are *some* **righteous Jews** [D14] who GUIDE **with truth and JUDGE by it** [D13], and among the Jews and Christians is *a people on the right course* [D24].

Meccans are told, **"ASK the People of the Scripture message if you don't know"** [D4,D8], and **"ASK those of Our apostles whom We sent"**—that is ask their people who are learned in their writings and doctrines [D6].

Muhammad is told, **"ASK those who READ the Book from before you, if you are in doubt"** [D7], and **"ASK the Children of Israel"** about the nine clear signs given to Moses [D9].

According to other passages **God repeats commands from the Torah, warning the Jews to JUDGE by them** [D22], **and quotes from the Psalms of David** [D5]. **He appeals to** worshiping as the likeness of Muslim believers which is to be found in **the Torah, and alludes to growing seed in the Gospel of Jesus** as the likeness of believers from the Gospel [D20].

Muhammad tells the Jews to bring the Torah **that "it might JUDGE between them"** [D16]. On another occasion he tells them, **"BRING the Torah and READ it, if you are men of truth"** [D18].

God asks Muhammad why the Jews come to him for judgment when **"they HAVE the Torah in which IS the command of God"** [D21]; and the Christians are told to **"JUDGE by what God has revealed in it (the Gospel)"** [D23].

God speaks of **"the Torah and the Gospel that IS WITH THEM"** [D12]. And in the last sura which came to Muhammad—the Sura of the Table (Al-Mā'ida) from 10 AH—both Jews and Christians are told **"You are not (founded) on anything until you PERFORM the Torah and the Gospel**, and what was revealed to you from your Lord" [D24].

One of the commentators, Ibn Ishaq, relates the following **hadith** concerning this passage [D24]. He says:

> Rafi son of Haritha and Salam Ibn Mashkum and two others, came to Muhammad and said to him, **"O Muhammad!** do you not claim to be a follower of the religion of Abraham and of his faith,

and **do you not believe in that which we have of the Torah and do you not testify that it is truly from God?"**

He replied, "Yes, in truth, but you have invented new doctrines, and you deny that which is therein regarding which a covenant was taken from you; and you conceal what you have been commanded to show to mankind. Therefore, I separate myself from your new ideas."

They said, "And as for us, we hold by that which is in our hands, and we follow the truth and guidance; and we do not believe in you and we will not follow you."

Then the great and glorious God revealed, "Say, O People of the Book! You are not (founded) on anything until you perform the Torah and the Gospel and what was revealed to you from your Lord."[11]

If this **hadith** is true then, by itself, it proves that Muhammad believed in the Torah available to the Jews in Medina in 10 AH. And, even if it is not a strong **hadith**, it is an important testimony to the fact that Muslims of the first and second century of the Hejira knew about a valid Torah and Gospel with them in Arabia.

With or without the above hadith, the 24 passages which we have looked at in this section and the 13 from the previous section make a total of 37 quotations which testify to a true Torah and Gospel being available to the people of Mecca and Medina while Muhammad was alive.

Muslims may claim that the true Torah and true Gospel, which were present in Arabia, are different from those presently available. But where are they?!? Surely some Muslim would have preserved such important books in one of the many Muslim libraries found throughout the Islamic world, even if only to help the Jews and Christians obey the Quranic instruction to "perform the Torah and the Gospel." Moreover, we would then be able to compare them with the copies which have been preserved by the Jews and Christians.

In fact, this is not the case. No such ancient copies have been preserved by the Muslims. Over the whole world there is only one Torah, which IS WITH both Jews and Christians, and one book called the Gospel, which IS WITH the Christians.

E. VERSES WHICH SAY THE TORAH AND/OR THE GOSPEL ARE GOOD, BUT THE TIME ABOUT WHICH THEY SPEAK IS NOT CLEAR

In the introduction to this chapter I said that a true study of a subject must include all the verses—all the data relevant to the subject. Some 55 other Quranic passages also speak of the Torah and the Gospel, but since they neither deny or affirm the presence of these books at the time of Muhammad, only their verse references are listed.

---

11. *The Coran*, Sir W. Muir, S.P.C.K., E. & J.B. YOUNG & Co. 1896, p 209. Also reported by Tabari.

As an example of this type of passage let us look at the following verse from the Sura of the Women (Al-Nisā') 4:136, 5-6 AH. It reads:

O ye who believe! Believe in God and His apostle, and the book which He has sent to His apostle **and the book (Torah) which He sent down from before.**

When taken by itself, we cannot tell whether Muhammad is commanding the Muslims to believe in a Torah which is present with them while Muhammad is speaking, or only to believe that God gave Moses a true Torah which was "sent down from before" and could have been changed at a later date.

Here are the references, listed from the earliest to the latest.

74:31, 87:18, 25:35, 35:25, 34:23-24, 54:43, 37:114-117, 19:28-29, 21:48, 29:27, 29:46-47, 32:23, 40:53-55, 41:45, 42:15, 45:16-17, 45:28-29, 46:10, 11:16-17, 28:43, 28:48-49, 28:52-53, 23:49, 13:36, 17:2, 17:4-7, 17:55, 6:20, 6:114, 6:124, 98:1, 2:1-5, 2:53, 2:87, 2:121, 2:136, 2:144-145, 2:176, 2:213, 2:285, 3:65, 3:81, 3:84, 3:99, 3:119, 3:183-184, 3:187, 62:5, 4:51, 4:54, 4:131, 4:136, 4:150-153, 4:171, 57:25, 5:62, 5:85-86,

Every reader is free to look them up and bring one or all of them to the discussion, if he feels that they will change the conclusions.

F. VERSES STATING THAT THE CHRISTIANS DIFFERED AND FOUGHT EACH OTHER

F1. The Consultation (Al-Shūrā) 42:13-14, Late Meccan.

He has ordained to you the religion which He commanded to Noah, and which We have revealed to you, and which We commanded to Abraham, Moses, and Jesus—saying, "Maintain the true religion and be not divided (la tatafarraqū لَا تَتَفَرَّقُوا) in it" **...And they became divided only after knowledge reached them, through selfish envy among them.** Had it not been for a word from your Lord to an appointed term, the matter would have been settled between them. **But truly those who inherited the Book after them are in a perplexing doubt concerning it.**

F2. The Clear Evidence (Al-Baiyīna) 98:4, Early Medina.

Nor did **the People of the Book become divided** (tafarraqa تَفَرَّقَ) until after there came to them clear evidence.

F3. The Heifer (Al-Baqara) 2:253, 2 AH.

To Jesus the son of Mary We gave clear (signs) and strengthened him with the Holy Spirit. If God had so willed succeeding generations would not have **fought each other**, after clear (signs) had come to them. **Yet they fell to variance** (akhtalafū اخْتَلَفُوا) and *some believed and some rejected.*

F4. The Family of 'Imran (Āli 'Imrān) 3:19, 2-3 AH.

And those to whom the Book came did not **fall to variance** (akhtalafa اخْتَلَفَ) until after the knowledge (of divine truth) came to them—**envying each other**.

F5. The Table (Al-Mā'ida) 5:15-16, 10 AH.

And of those who say, "We are Christians," We have taken their covenant and **they have forgotten a part** of that whereby they were admonished. So We have placed **enmity and hatred between them**, until the day of judgment. And soon will God show them what it is they have done.

O People of the Book! There has come to you Our Apostle, revealing to you **much that you used to hide in the Book**, and passing over much (that is now unnecessary).

We see from these verses that the Christians became divided [F1,F2] through selfish envy [F2,F4]. They fell to variance [F3,F4]; so God placed enmity and hatred between them [F5]; and they fought each other [F3].

Concerning their Book and their covenant, they forgot a part [F5]; they used to hide much [F5]; and they are in perplexing doubt [F1].

But as we saw in Section B, and as we read here in [F3], **"some believed."**

That the Christians fell to variance and killed each other is confirmed by secular and church history. The Egyptian Coptic Church was declared heretical by the Roman and Byzantine Churches, but they all had exactly the same Bible; just as the Shiites have fought the Sunni Muslims, but they all have the same Qur'an.

In none of these verses does it say that even unbelieving Christians changed their Bible, and certainly the believing Christians wouldn't change it.

G. VERSES STATING THAT THE JEWS REFUSED THE QUR'AN AND TRIED TO CHANGE IT, OR CONCEALED VERSES IN THEIR OWN TORAH AND THREW ITS MEANING BEHIND THEM

G1. The Cattle (Al-An'ām) 6:89-92, Late Meccan.

These were the men (the prophets from Noah to Jesus listed in verses 84-86) to whom We gave **the Book**, and authority, and prophethood: if these reject the same, We shall entrust their charge to a new people who do not reject it...and they do not estimate God with a just estimation, when they say, "God has not revealed anything to man." Say, "Who sent down the book, which Moses brought, a light and a direction to mankind? **You make it upon sheets of paper which you show and conceal much: and you are taught that which you knew not, neither your fathers"**...And this book We have revealed, blessed, **attesting to (the truth of) that which IS between his (its) hands (the Torah),** and that you might admonish the mother of cities and all around her.

45

G2. The Prophet Hud (Hūd) 11:110, Late Meccan.

And verily We gave Moses the book, and **they (the Jews) fell to variance regarding it**. And had not the word gone forth from thy Lord, surely the matter had been decided between them; **and verily they are in perplexing doubt concerning the same.** (Same idea in 10:93)

G3. The Heifer (Al-Baqara) 2:40-44, 2 AH.

O children of Israel!...believe in what I (God) reveal, **attesting to (the truth of) that which IS WITH YOU (the Torah)**, and be not the first to **reject faith in it**, nor **sell my signs for a small price**...and **do not clothe truth with falsehood, nor conceal the truth while you know it**...Do you command righteousness for people and forget yourselves, and yet **you STUDY the book**.

G4. 2:85. 2 AH.

What! Do you believe in part of the book and **reject part**? Whosoever among you does this, his reward shall be none other than disgrace in the present life and in the Day of Judgment they shall be cast into a more awful torment.

G5. 2:89-90.

And when there comes to them a Book from God, **attesting to (the truth of) that which IS WITH THEM (the Torah)**...they refuse to believe in it...miserable is the price for which they have sold their souls.

G6. 2:97,101.

He (Gabriel) brings it (revelation) upon thy heart, **attesting to (the truth of) that which is between his (its) hands (the Torah)**...and when there came to them an apostle from God, **attesting to (the truth of) that which IS WITH THEM (the Torah)**, *a faction* (fariq فَريق) *of those to whom the Book came* threw away the Book of God behind their back as though they didn't know (what was in it).

G7. 2:140, 2 AH.

Or do you say that Abraham, Ishmael, Isaac, Jacob and the Tribes were Jews or Christians? Say, "Do you know better than God?" Ah, who is more unjust than those **who conceal the witness which they HAVE from God?**

G8. 2:146.

The people of the Book know this as they know their own sons; but *some of them* **conceal the truth which they themselves know.**

G9. 2:159.

> *Those* (of the Jews) **who conceal the clear (signs) and the guidance** after we made it clear to the people of the Book, on them shall be God's curse.

G10. 2:174.

> Those **who conceal what God revealed in the Book and purchase with it a small profit,** they shall eat naught but fire in their bellies...

G11. The Family of 'Imran (Āli 'Imrān) 3:69-71, 2-3 AH.

> *A section* (Ṭā'ifa طَائِفَة) *of the People of the Book* desire to lead you astray. But they shall not lead astray any but themselves and they do not perceive. "Ye People of the Book! **Why do you reject the signs of God, and you yourselves are witnesses.** Ye People of the Book! **Why do you clothe truth with falsehood, and conceal truth, and you yourselves HAVE knowledge.**"

G12. 3:75.

> Among the People of the Book are *some* who, if entrusted with a hoard of gold, will (readily) pay it back; *others*, who if entrusted with a single silver coin, will not repay it unless you constantly stand demanding.

G13. 3:199.

> And *there are, certainly, among the People of the Book those who believe in God*, and in that which has been revealed to you (plural), and **in that which has been revealed to them**, bowing in humility to God. **They will not sell the signs of God for a miserable gain.** For them is a reward with their Lord, and God is swift in account.

In these verses many charges are made against the Jews. They "fell to variance" regarding the Torah, and are in perplexing doubt" about it [G2]. They write their books on separate sheets of paper which they "show and conceal much," according to what they want to let the Muslims see [G1].

The main charges, though, are what the Jews do in relation to the Qur'an. They reject faith in the Qur'an [G3,G4] and reject the signs of God [G11]. They sell God's signs and their own souls for a miserable price [G3,G10,G13]. They conceal the truth—the testimony to the Qur'an—in their own Scriptures [G3,G7,G8,G9,G10,G11], and they clothe truth about the Qur'an with falsehood [G3,G11]. They believe in the part of the Qur'an that pleases them and reject part [G4], or they throw it away behind their back [G6].

But at the same time the Qur'an testifies that **they have the Torah "WITH THEM"** [G3,G5,G6]; and **attests to the truth of the Torah "which is between its hands" (in its presence)** [G1,G6]. The Jews **"HAVE a witness from God"** [G7]; they **"are witnesses"** [G11]; they **"HAVE knowledge"** [G8,G11]; and they **"STUDY the Book"** [G3].

This can best be summarized by looking again at quotation G3 from the Sura of the Heifer (Al-Baqara) 2:40-44, from 2 AH.

> O children of Israel!...believe in what I (God) reveal, **attesting to (the truth of) that which IS WITH YOU (the Torah)**, and be not the first to **reject faith in it**, nor **sell my signs for a small price**...and **do not clothe truth with falsehood, nor conceal the truth while you know it**...Do you command righteousness for people and forget yourselves, and yet **you STUDY the book**.

The Qur'an comes attesting and certifying to the truth of **the Torah which is WITH the Jews and which they STUDY**. The unbelieving Jews command righteousness for others, but forget it for themselves because they lie when they reject the Qur'an and conceal the truth about it in their own Scriptures.

The Qur'an also testifies that there are among the people of the Book those who are completely honest [G12], and who believe in God, and some of them also believe in the Qur'an as well as the Torah.

But in all of these verses there is no statement from God that even unbelieving Jews changed the written words of their Torah, and Jews like Abdullah Ibn Salam and Mukhairiq who had accepted the Prophet's message and become Muslims certainly wouldn't have changed it.

H. VERSES SPEAKING SPECIFICALLY OF "TAḤRĪF"

There are four verses in the Qur'an where the Jews are accused of changing or altering (ḥarrafa حَرَّفَ) words, and one verse where they are accused of twisting their tongues when they read. We will now examine these verses in their complete context. However, we must remember that the preceding 50 to 60 quotations also represent a wider context for these verses—the context provided by the **entire Qur'an**.

H1. The Family of 'Imran (Āli 'Imrān) 3:78, 2-3 AH.

> There is among them (the People of the Book) "a party" (farīq فَرِيق) who (in reading) twist their tongues with the Book (يَلْؤُنَ الْسِنَتَهُم) so that you will count it from the Book and it is not from the Book. And they say it is from God and it is not from God. And they say a lie against God and they know (it).

In this verse the People of the Book are accused of twisting the words or the pronunciation while they read. They do this so that the hearers will think that this different meaning is from the Book (the Torah) and from God. But, the verse goes on to say, "it is not from the Book" and "it is not from God."

H2. The Table (Al-Māʾida) 5:12-14, 10 AH.

> God formerly took a covenant from the Children of Israel, and We appointed twelve captains among them... And because of their (the Jews') breach of their covenant, We cursed them, and made their hearts grow hard. **They change the words from their (right)**

places (يُحَرِّفُونَ الكَلِمَ عَنْ مَوَاضِعِهِ) and they forgot a part of that whereby they were admonished. You will not cease to find deceit in them, *excepting a few of them,* but pardon them, and forgive, for God loves those who are kind.

The unbelieving Jews, whose hearts have been made hard because they broke the covenant, "change the words from their (right) places" and "forget (on purpose) a part of" their own law.

Taken by itself, this verse might mean that the Jews were cutting up their Torah with a knife in order to change some verses around and omit other verses completely. But in Sections D and E above, and [H6] below, the Qur'an appeals to the Torah as being present WITH the Jews; as BEING READ by them; as HAVING the command of God in it.

Therefore the passage must mean that the Jews were covering some verses and reading others **out of context**, as in the famous example of the verse of stoning. In Arabic this is called "al-taḥrīf al-maʿnawī" (التَّحْرِيف المَعْنَوِي) or "changing the meaning."[12]

It is also necessary to emphasize the little phrase **"except a few."** There were a few who were serious, who believed, even as the Qur'an attests in the following quotation. They would never have altered either the meaning or the words of their Torah.

H3. The Family of 'Imran (Āli 'Imrān) 3:113-114, 2-3 AH.

> Not all of them are alike. *Some of the People of the Book are an upright people* (أُمَّة قَاءِمَة). They recite the signs (or verses) of God in the night season and they bow down worshiping. They believe in God and the last day. They command what is just, and forbid what is wrong and they hasten in good works, and they are of the righteous.

In the next three quotations I believe that the Qur'an is accusing some of the Jews, not of changing their own Torah, but of altering and distorting what Muhammad said when he was reciting and explaining the Qur'an.

H4. The Heifer (Al-Baqara) 2:75-79, 2 AH.

> Can you (O men of faith) still earnestly desire that they (the Jews) will believe in you? and verily *a party* (fariq فَرِيق) *among them* hear the Word of God; then **they pervert it** (يُحَرِّفُونَهُ) knowingly after they have understood it. And when they meet the believers they say, "We believe"; but when they meet each other in private they say, "Why do you tell them what God has revealed to you (in the Torah), that they may engage you in argument about it before their Lord? What, do you not understand?" Do they not know that God knows what they conceal and what they make public? And there are among them illiterates, who know not the Book except their desires. They follow nothing but what they think.

---

12. Changing the actual words is "al-taḥrīf al-lafẓī" (التَّحْرِيف اللَّفْظِي).

And woe to those who write the book with their own hands and then say, "This is from God," that they may sell it for a small price. Woe unto them for what their hands have written, and woe unto them for that which they gain.

"A party" of the Jews (not all) hear the **Qur'an** and say to the Muslims, "We believe." Then they "pervert" Muhammad's explanations knowingly and respond in the manner described in detail in the following passage from The Women. But in private one rebukes the other saying, "Why do you tell them what the Torah says? The next time they will use it against you."

H5. The Women (Al-Nisā') 4:44-47, 5-6 AH.

Hast thou not turned your vision to those who were given a portion of the Book? They buy and sell error...*Of the Jews there are those who change the words from their (right) places,* (يُحَرِّفُونَ الكَلِمَ عَنْ مَواضِعِهِ) and say: "We hear and we disobey"; and "Hear what is not heard," and "Ra'ina" with a twist of their tongues and a slander to faith. If only they had said: "We hear and we obey"; and "Do hear"; and "Do look at us"; it would have been better for them and more upright; but God has cursed them for their unbelief; and they will not believe *except a few*. O you to whom the Book came, believe in what We sent down (the Qur'an), **attesting to (the truth of) what IS WITH YOU (the Torah)**, before We deface your countenances...

As in the preceding passage, the charge is made against *"those" (some) of the Jews* "who change the words"; but here several examples are given—examples where Muhammad's words are being altered. Yusuf Ali explains this exceedingly well in his notes to this passage. He says,

A trick of the Jews was to twist words and expressions, so as to ridicule the most solemn teaching of Faith. Where they should have said, "We hear and we obey," they said aloud, "We hear," and whispered, "We disobey." Where they should have said respectfully, "We hear," they added in a whisper, "What is not heard," by way of ridicule. Where they claimed the attention of the Teacher, they used an ambiguous word apparently harmless, but in their intention disrespectful. "Ra'ina," if used respectfully in the Arabic way, would have meant "Please attend to us" (or "Do look at us"). With a twist of their tongue, they suggested an insulting meaning, such as "O thou that takest us to pasture!" or in Hebrew, "Our bad one!"[13]

H6. The Table (Al-Mā'ida) 5:41-48, 10 AH.

O Apostle! Let not *those grieve thee*, who race each other into unbelief (whether) among those who say, "We believe" with their mouths but whose hearts have no faith; or *among the Jews* who listen to any lie—who listen to other people that never even come to

13. Yusuf Ali, op. cit., notes 565 and 566, p 194.

thee. **They change the words from their (right) places** (يُحَرِّفُونَ الكَلِمَ مِنْ بَعْدِ مَوَاضِعِهِ).

They say, "If ye are given this, take it, but if not, beware!"…If they do come to you, either judge between them or decline to interfere. If you decline, they cannot hurt you in the least. If you judge, judge between them in equity, for God loves the just. **But why do they (the Jews) come to you (Muhammad) for decision, when they HAVE the Torah in which IS the command of God?** Yet even after that they turn away for they are not believers. **Truly We revealed the Torah in which IS guidance and light.** The prophets that submitted themselves to God judged thereby those that were Jews; and the rabbis and doctors (did the same), for to them was entrusted the protection of God's Book and they were witnesses to it. Therefore (O Jews) fear not men, but fear Me, and sell not My signs for a miserable price. And those who do not judge by what God revealed, they are unbelievers.

We ordained therein for them, "life for life, eye for eye, nose for nose, ear for ear, tooth for tooth, and wounds equal for equal." But if anyone REMITS the retaliation by way of charity, it IS an atonement for him. And those who fail to JUDGE by what God revealed, they are sinners.

And in their footsteps We sent Jesus the son of Mary, **attesting to (the truth of) what was between his hands of the Torah**, and We gave him the **Gospel, in which IS guidance and light, and attesting to the truth of) what was between his hands of the Torah, and guidance and exhortation to the righteous.**

Let the people of the Gospel JUDGE by what God revealed in it. And those who do not judge by what God revealed, they are licentious.

To you (Muhammad) We revealed the Book in truth, **attesting to (the truth of) what is between its hands (in its presence) of the Book, and guarding it.** So judge between them by what God revealed, and do not follow their vain desires —diverging from the truth that has come to you. To each among you We have given a law and a way. If God had so willed, He would have made you a single people, but (His plan is) to test you in what He has given you: so strive as in a race in all virtues. The goal of you all is to God.

In this last passage the situation is the same. *Some "among the Jews"* who will listen to any lie—even to quotations of Muhammad's words from people who never heard him—"change the words from their (right) places." They say, "If Muhammad gives you such and such a statement, accept it. If not, beware." The explanations of Muhammad are being altered and rejected by them, not their own Torah.

However, even if I am mistaken in this interpretation, and these last three passages also speak about "al-taḥrīf al-ma'nawī" where the Jews change the meaning of their own Scriptures, the context of these verses clearly states the following facts.

1. Some? Many? Perhaps even most? of the Jews did not believe. **But SOME DID believe in God and wanted to do His will.**

2. The Qur'an attests to **the truth of the Torah which is WITH THEM.**

3. God is quoted as saying that **the Jews "HAVE the Torah in which is the command of God."**

4. **"Life for life, eye for eye" is quoted from the Torah (Exodus) as valid law by which Jews are to JUDGE** unless they wish to REMIT the penalty.

5. The People of the Gospel are told to **"JUDGE by what God revealed in it."**

We can only conclude from these passages—the very passages which speak about "taḥrīf"—that in the time of Muhammad there were upright Jews and Christians who owned, read, and obeyed the true Torah and the true Gospel.

CONCLUSION

As we have examined what the Qur'an says about the Torah, the Gospel, and the People of the Book, the various groups of verses have led us to the following conclusions:

Group A. The true Torah was available to John the Baptist (Yaḥyā), Mary, Jesus and his disciples in the 1st century.

Group B. The Qur'an attests to the presence of true Christian believers at least to the beginning of monasticism in 300-350 AD. It seems correct to assume that these true believers did not change their own Gospel or the Qur'an would have called them false believers.

Group C. The Qur'an attests to the truth of the former books between its hands, i.e., "in its presence" or "under its eyes." These books are WITH the Meccans, but the Arabic Qur'an was necessary because the Meccans couldn't understand the former books.

Group D. According to the Qur'an, God, or Muhammad under God's orders, appealed to the Torah and Gospel more than 20 times. The Psalms of David and the Torah are quoted. Muhammad asks the Jews to bring the Torah to settle a dispute. People READ the Torah and the Gospel which are WITH THEM.

Group F. The Christians differed and fought each other and forgot part of the Book, but there are no verses which say they ever changed, altered or corrupted the text.

Groups G. and H. Some of the Jews are guilty of "al-taḥrīf al-ma'nawī" because they conceal things written in their own books and throw the references they don't like behind their backs. They reject the Qur'an, clothe it with falsehood, sell the signs of God for a miserable price, and are doubly guilty of "taḥrīf" because they also change Muhammad's explanations. But in all of this, there is not one verse claiming that even these unbelieving Jews changed their own written text of the Torah, and certainly the believing Jews would not change it, nor let the others change it.

The Qur'an says in the Sura of the Cattle (Al-An'ām) 6:34, **"There is no changing to the Words of God"**; and again in Jonah (Yūnus) 10:64, **"There is no change to the Words of God."**

The only possible conclusion from our study of the Qur'an is that copies of THE TRUE TORAH AND THE TRUE GOSPEL were present in Mecca and Medina at the time of Muhammad. Furthermore, since no Muslim has brought forth from one of the great Islamic libraries an ancient manuscript of a different Torah or a different Gospel, and since no archaeological discoveries have shown any carved quotations which differ from the Torah and Gospel present WITH US now; **I am firmly convinced that the books which were available in Mecca during the lifetime of Muhammad were identical to**

THE TORAH AND THE GOSPEL WHICH WE READ TODAY.

CHAPTER II

THE HADITH AND THE SUNNA

In the last chapter we examined the testimony of the Qur'an concerning the integrity of the Torah-Old Testament and the Gospel-New Testament. This does not terminate our investigation, however, because Muslims have another source of information and doctrine called the **Hadith**.

The word "hadith" could be translated as "a speech" or "a saying" or even "small talk," but in Islamic theology the term refers to a narrative concerning a deed or utterance of the Prophet Muhammad reported by his companions. These are broken down into various classes, such as the **Hadith Qudsi** in which God Himself speaks, and the **Hadith Nabawi** in which the words and the custom or practice (Sunna) of Muhammad are recorded.

At one time the words "sunna" and "hadith" were almost synonymous. The word "sunna" means the sayings and practices of Muhammad, and it became a second source of law. The first source of law is the Qur'an. The following story will help us understand the importance of the Sunna/Hadith.[1]

After having lived in Tunisia for some time, I met a Mu'addib. A Mu'addib is a person who helps the families of the dead in their mourning by reciting the Qur'an over the graves of the dead relatives. This man, though poorly dressed, was very well informed. Not only did he know his own religion, but he was knowledgeable about many subjects—quoting Abraham Lincoln and other men of history.

As we talked, the conversation turned to religion, and when he spoke about Islam he made the following statement:

"Our religion is based on the **Qur'an** and the **Hadith**, 50-50."

To give another example of the importance of the Hadith (also called "traditions" in English) it has recently been reported that 200,000 volumes of the Qur'an and the Hadith of Al-Bukhari have now been printed in the Uygur language in China. We would expect that after many years of persecution under atheism and the Red Guard, the Muslims would want to reprint the Qur'an just as the Chinese Christians want to reprint the Bible. But we see that in addition they wished to print a collection of the hadith. (Al-Bukhari, along with Muslim, is one of the most respected of those who collected the traditions of Muhammad.)

When in conversation, Muslims quote the Hadith almost as often as the Qur'an to prove a doctrine under discussion. One friend explained it this way: "The Qur'an gives the basic doctrine. The Hadith shows the things which are not clear in the Qur'an and makes plain the decrees of the Qur'an."

---

1. Any of the several recognized collections of individual hadith (traditions about Muhammad) are commonly referred to as "the Hadith." Thus used, the word is a collective noun.

54

The editor of the book *Quarante Hadiths de Imam Nawawi*[2] says in his preface, "The Qur'an, the word of God revealed to Muhammad; and the Hadith, the teachings of the Prophet, are the two sources of Islam. The knowledge of this religion would be impossible apart from these two texts."

Poetically, it is of course very beautiful to speak of the Hadith as a text, and there is every reason for a believer to do that. However to speak of the Hadith as a text also gives the impression that it has set boundaries and that everyone agrees as to the contents. Unfortunately this is not the case; and it is at this point that there is a very important and difficult problem with the Hadith. **It is the problem of knowing which hadiths are authentic, and which ones are not.**

Over the years many stories were told about Muhammad. Then people began to realize that not all of the hadiths were authentic so they made special studies and searched out the oldest collections. E. K. Ahamed Kutty of the University of Calicut, India, in speaking of the collection made by Bukhari, says,

> He took into consideration 600,000 traditions out of which he accepted only 7,397, or according to some authorities, 7,295. The same tradition is often repeated more than once under different chapters. Disregarding these repetitions, the number of distinct hadith is reduced to 2,762.[3]

From this we understand that only 3000 or 4000 hadiths were judged to be authentic or "strong." The others were thrown out as "weak," or to use a Christian word, "apocryphal."

Why would a false hadith be written? I suppose to glorify Islam and Muhammad, or support a favorite doctrine. Fazlur Rahman in his book *Islam* gives the following example,

> With the growing inner rupture between Sufi practices on the one hand and the emerging orthodox system on the other, a new body of hadith also came into existence. The Sufis, in order to justify their stand, formulated (i.e., verbally invented) statements, sometimes quite fanciful and **historically completely fictitious**, which they attributed to the Prophet.[4]

But it was not only the Sufis, for on page 65, after quoting the so-called hadith according to which the Prophet said,

> Whatever of good speech there be, you can take it to have been said by me.

Rahman goes on to say,

> On no other hypothesis than this can we explain the fact that **palpably post-prophetic developments**—the theological posi-

2. *Quarante Hadiths de Imam Nawawi*, Sud Editions, Tunis, 1980.
3. "The Six Authentic Books of Hadith," *The Muslim World League Journal*, April-May 1983, p 20.
4. University of Chicago Press, Chicago, 2nd Ed., 1979, p 133-34.

tions with regard to human freedom, Divine Attributes, etc.—
were verbally attributed to the Prophet himself.

Therefore, the nagging question still remains, "Which hadiths are true?"
When asked how he knew which hadiths were true, one man answered,
"Whichever one seems to make sense to me." That requires a basic assumption
for each hadith. Another man, a school teacher, responded, "For ten years I have
been asking myself this question and I still don't know." Other Muslims solve
the puzzle by refusing to accept the Hadith as revelation.

Part of the problem may be that religious leaders and speakers continue to
use the doubtful hadiths when it suits their purpose. Imam An-Nawawi chose his
Forty Hadiths in the 7th century AH, or the 14th century AD, and in his
introduction he gives this long explanation concerning the value of choosing and
memorizing 40 hadiths. He says,

> We have been told according to 'Ali ibn Abi Taleb, 'Abdallah
> ibn Mas'ud, Ma'ad ibn Jabal, Abu al-Darda', Ibn 'Umar, Ibn
> 'Abbas, Anas Ibn Malik, Abu Huraira and Abu Sa'id al Khudri
> (may God be pleased with them) through several chains of
> authority[5] and in different versions that the Messenger of God (God
> bless him and grant him salvation) said,
>> Whoever memorizes 40 hadiths concerning the points of
>> his religion for the benefit of my community, God will raise
>> him on the day of resurrection in the rank with the religious
>> teachers and the theologians.
> And in another version it says, "God will raise him on the day of
> resurrection as a completely knowledgeable teacher." And in the
> version of Abu al-Darda' it says, "At the day of resurrection, I will
> be for him an intercessor and a witness." The version of Ibn Mas'ud
> says, "It will be said to him, 'Enter heaven by any gate that you
> wish.'" Finally, according to Ibn 'Umar, "It is written (that he will
> be) in the rank of the theologians and he will be assembled with the
> martyrs."

How great is our surprise then, after all these proof texts, to find that he
continues with the following words,

> However, the theologian specialists in hadiths are agreed that
> this hadith has a weak coefficient of authenticity in spite of the
> numerous paths of transmission. [sic][6] (translations mine)

Continuing, he goes on to say that although "The theologians have agreed
that one can refer to **weak (doubtful) hadiths** when it is a matter of good
works," he decided to refer only to **strong (authentic) hadiths**: especially those

---

5. Whenever a hadith is memorized, the Isnad, the supporting chain of people who passed on the information, is
memorized and often quoted with the text. In the above quotation the author has given only the original witnesses
and omitted the chains.
6. An-Nawawi, op. cit., p 8-10.

from the collections of Al-Bukhari and Muslim.[7]

When we read that the specialists have decided that the above tradition concerning hadiths is **weak** (doubtful), in spite of all those paths of transmission, we can only conclude that it must be very difficult for a person of only average religious education to make a judgment in relation to the validity of any given hadith.

Secondly, when we see the type of discussion which the experts themselves can have on the subject, it must be even more discouraging for the ordinary believer. In an article called "The Antichrist—between Truth and Fantasy" by Dr. Ahmad 'ud An-Nashash,[8] the author quotes three other writers concerning the subject of the Antichrist who is mentioned in certain hadiths. In two of the quotations the authors' criteria for judging a hadith as valid are also mentioned.

'Abd-ar-razzaq Naufal, after stating that there is no mention of the Antichrist in the Qur'an and some other discussion as to why he thinks that the hadiths in question are not valid, goes on to ask, "How then can we hold on to **these hadiths which have no Quranic support**?"

Later in the same article Mustapha Mahmud is quoted in the following words, "The Muslims receive their religious beliefs from two sources: the Book (Qur'an) and the Sunna, without making any distinction between them because the strong, or authentic sunna is revelation." (Then he gives the following Quranic quotation from the Sura of the Star (Al-Najm) 53:3-4 to prove it.)

> He (Muhammad) does not speak on the basis of desire. It** is no less than revelation revealed.[9]

Therefore whenever we find a **strong (authentic) hadith we must accept it, whether it has corresponding proof from the Qur'an or not.** But, if a **strong hadith contradicts the text of the Qur'an**, that is another matter…and would require exegesis of the hadith and discussion of the antecedence of one over the other…"

And so we see that one expert, Naufal, says that a hadith must have some support from the Qur'an. The second one, Mahmud, says that this is not necessary; that everything that the Prophet said is by revelation, whether Qur'an or hadith. In addition the possibility is raised that a strong (well-attested) hadith could contradict the Qur'an and then a study would have to be made.

That some **hadith are strong** is no doubt true. There is at least one which even has Biblical confirmation as we shall see later in this chapter. Hamidullah is convinced that Al-Bukhari's collection is valid. He says, in the introduction to his translation of the Qur'an,

> Suppose that Al-Bukhari says, "I heard from Ahmad ibn Hanbal, who received it from 'Abdar-Razzaq, who received it from Ma'mar, who received it from Hammam, who heard it from Abu Huraira, that the Prophet said such and such." Since the end

---

7. Ibid., p 11-14.
8. See the magazine *Manār Al-Islām*, Jan-Feb, 1981, p 109-112.
9. To me it seems that the word "it" marked with a "**" refers to the Qur'an. The context (verse 10) speaks of a being who "revealed unto his slave that which he revealed." That the Hadith is intended seems doubtful.

of the 2nd World War, Manuscripts of Hammam, Ma'mar, and 'Abdar-Razzaq have been found. (However he does not give the dates of these copies.) The work of Ahmad has been known for a long time. Thus, in searching in the sources from before Al-Bukhari, we find that he neither lied, nor gathered the simple folklore of his time, but he based his work on authentic written sources.[10]

But in spite of Hamidullah's defense of the Hadith, the uncertainty remains for each Muslim. In addition it spills over into Christianity.

THE GOSPEL AS HADITHS

When Muslims read the Gospel of Jesus Christ according to Matthew, Mark, Luke and John, they sometimes complain and say, "These accounts are only hadith. This is not like the Qur'an." I understand by this that for them the Qur'an is revealed law telling them how to live, while most of the hadiths are narrative accounts of events in the life of Muhammad—especially events which explain why certain verses were revealed. They believe that the Bible ought to be like the Qur'an, and when they find large sections of narrative material they say, **"These are just hadiths,"** implying that it is not the true Word of God, or that it is on some lower second-class level.

As an example let us look at a few verses from the Gospel according to Luke 8:19-21 where it reads,

> Now Jesus' mother and brothers came to see him, but they were not able to get near him because of the crowd. Someone told him, "Your mother and brothers are standing outside, waiting to see you."
>
> He replied, **"My mother and brothers are those who hear God's word and put it into practice."**

As I understand it, Muslims would expect the true Gospel to include only the words in boldfaced type which would be considered the words of God through Jesus. Then in another book there would be a hadith saying,

> *According to James the half-brother of Jesus (may God be pleased with him) the occasion for the revelation of Luke 8:21 was as follows:*
>
> Now *my* mother and brothers and *myself* came to see *Jesus*, but *we* were not able to get near him because of the crowd. Someone told him, "Your mother and brothers are standing outside, wanting to see you."
>
> And then the verse was revealed, **"My mother and brothers are those who hear God's word and put it into practice."**
>
> *This hadith was transmitted by Luke and Mark in their books,*

---

10. Hamidullah, op.cit., p xiii.

which (along with those of Matthew and John) are the most valuable among the collections of hadiths.) (Material in Italics arranged or added by me)

As a second example we might take Jesus' teaching on food as found in Mark 7:15 where he said,

Nothing outside a man can make him "unclean" by going into him. Rather it is what comes out of a man that makes him "unclean."

This would be considered Quranic type material and then in some other book we would find the following hadith.

According to Peter, one of the twelve closest disciples (may God be pleased with him and with them), Jesus' teaching about food as found in Mark 7:15 and 20-23 was revealed in the following manner:

The Pharisees and some of the teachers of the law who had come from Jerusalem...saw some of *us* eating food with "unclean"—that is ceremonially unwashed—hands...

So the Pharisees and teachers...asked Jesus, "Why don't your disciples live according to the tradition of the elders instead of eating their food with 'unclean' hands?"...

Again Jesus called the crowd to him and said, "Listen to me, everyone, and understand this. **Nothing outside a man can make him 'unclean' by going into him. Rather, it is what comes out of a man that makes him 'unclean.'**"

After he had left the crowd, *we* entered the house, *and we* asked him about this parable.

"Are you so dull?" he asked. "Don't you see that nothing that enters a man from the outside can make him 'unclean?' For it doesn't go into his heart but into his stomach, and then out of his body"...

Then he went on *and the whole saying was revealed*: **"What comes out of a man is what makes him 'unclean.' For from within, out of men's hearts, come evil thoughts, sexual immorality, theft, murder, adultery, greed, malice, deceit, lewdness, envy, slander, arrogance and folly. All these evils come from inside and make a man 'unclean.'"**

This hadith was transmitted by Mark who wrote it down from Peter. Matthew also transmitted it.

Again the material in Italics has been added by me, but everything else is included in the Gospel account as given in Mark 7:1-2,5,14-23.

Therefore, it is clear to all who have read it that the Gospel does not correspond to Muslim expectations. As these examples show, Jesus' words from God and the historical explanatory material are woven together.

This situation puzzled me for a long time and I didn't really know how to answer when someone said, "These accounts are only hadith." For the majority of Muslims, any single hadith is not in the same class as the Qur'an. It can be accepted or rejected according to the understanding of the individual. Other Muslims, because of the difficulties mentioned above, refuse to accept the Hadith as revelation. Since neither of these views represent Christian belief about the Bible, I could not agree and say that the Gospel is just hadith.

Another thing which puzzled me was that the Qur'an also contains much "hadith" or "narrative material." Extensive accounts are given about the Devil's fall, Adam and Eve, Noah, Mary the mother of Jesus, and especially Abraham and Moses. The history of Abraham being told the good news of his son Isaac is described in detail in three different passages—the Early Meccan Sura 51:24-37, the Late Meccan Sura 11:69-83, and the Late Meccan Sura 15:51-77. Moreover, the 28th sura is even named "The Story" (Al-Qaṣaṣ). Why, then, should anyone complain because the Gospel has narrative material when the Qur'an also has a considerable amount?

THE KEY TO THE PUZZLE

As I said above, this was all very puzzling. On the one hand the Hadith seemed extremely important; and on the other hand it seemed arbitrary and not important at all. Then I read Fazlur Rahman's book entitled *Islam*, in which he makes the following statement:

> "For, if the **Hadith** *as a whole* is cast away, the basis for the
> **historicity of the Qur'an** is removed at one stroke."[11] (Italics
> his, boldfacing mine)

Some readers may disagree with this statement, but if they consider it carefully, I think that they will have to agree that it is true. For although the Qur'an contains narrative material, it has very little narrative material about Muhammad's life, the battles he fought, etc.

Therefore it is true, if the **Hadith as a whole** were removed, we would know almost nothing about how Muhammad used to go out to fast and meditate in a cave, or how the first revelation came, or the flight to Medina. Though the Battle of Badr is very important to Islamic history, it is mentioned by name exactly one time in the Qur'an, in the Sura of the Family of 'Imran (Īli 'Imrān) 3:123 from 2-3 AH. To understand what happened and why it was so important one must turn to the Hadith, and in Section Three, Chapter III of this book, almost all the material on the origin of the Qur'an is from the Hadith.

The logical conclusion is that the Qur'an, believed by every Muslim to be pure revelation, can only be proved and justified as pure revelation by using the human,[12] less certain material from the Hadith. Therefore every Muslim, even one who belittles the Hadith, must decide whether the testimony

---

11. Rahman, op. cit., p 66.
12. "Human" in the sense that a human decision is involved as to whether it is a "weak" or a "strong" hadith.

of Abu Bakr, 'Umar Ibn Khattab, 'Uthman, and the others quoted in the Hadith is true enough and has been transmitted with enough accuracy so that their reports of Muhammad bringing the Qur'an can be believed.

This understanding of the absolute necessity of the Hadith shows that a Muslim has no basis for complaining about narrative material in the Torah and the Gospel. **If the great truth of the coming of the Qur'an is validated by human hadiths which are outside of the revelation**—hadiths which often have disagreements in their details and sometimes severe scientific errors—**on what basis will a Muslim say that the great truth of Jesus' death for our sins cannot be validated by "hadith type material" included in the Gospel revelation?**

EXPLANATORY MATERIAL IN THE GOSPEL REVELATION

Christians believe that the men who recorded the Gospel were guided by the Holy Spirit in their choice of "hadith explanatory material" just as they were guided in recording Jesus' words.

The historical narrative truths of
> Gabriel speaking to Mary;
> Jesus' birth from a virgin;
> the signs and miracles which he did to prove himself apostle,
> > Messiah, and the "Word of God";
> his death for our sins;
> his resurrection from the dead;
> and his ascension;

were included by the guidance of the Holy Spirit; just as Jesus' words of law in the Sermon on the Mount and his parables teaching how God wants us to live were given by the Holy Spirit. Or, to put it another way, we believe that the words **"God said"** (qāla Allāh قَالَ اللهُ) are understood to be present at the beginning of every chapter.

WHY CONSIDER THE HADITHS IN THIS BOOK?

The reader may be asking himself by this time why the Hadith should be brought up in a book concerned with *The Bible, the Qur'an, and Science*? It is because, as we have just seen, the Qur'an is only half of the basis of faith for many Muslims. Any book on the subject should probably be called *The Bible, the Qur'an-Hadiths, and Science*.

Therefore, it is not enough to study only what the Qur'an says about the Torah and the Gospel. We must also examine what the hadiths say about them. Specifically, we want to see whether they give any support to the charge that Jews and Christians changed the Bible.

Moreover, a number of hadith have something to say about science. Dr. Bucaille recognizes this and discusses the subject in a short chapter starting on page 242 of his book. He finds that even some **strong hadiths** have severe scientific errors in them. This raises theological difficulties, as well as scientific ones, and we will examine one example in detail later on when we discuss scientific problems.

The Integrity of the Bible according to the Hadith[13]

In Chapter I of Section Two we saw that the Qur'an contains more than one hundred references to the Torah and the Gospel. Therefore it is no surprise to find that they are also mentioned in a number of hadiths. Thus, according to *Mishkat al-Masabih*,[14] Book I, ch. VI:

> Abu Huraira reported God's messenger as saying, "In the last days there will be lying *dajjals* who will bring you traditions of which neither you nor your fathers have heard, so beware of them. They will neither lead you astray nor seduce you." Muslim transmitted it.
>
> He also said that the people of the Book used to read the Torah in Hebrew and expound it in Arabic to the Muslims, so God's messenger said, "Neither believe nor disbelieve the people of the Book, but say,
>
> Say (O Muslims): "We believe in Allah and that which is revealed unto Abraham, and Ishmael, and Isaac, and Jacob, and the tribes, and that which Moses and Jesus received, and that which the Prophets received from their Lord. We make no distinction between any of them, and unto Him we have surrendered." (Qur'an 2:136) Bukhari transmitted it.

Muhammad neither affirms nor denies the interpretation of the People of the Book. Nor does he comment on the actual text of the Torah. In his commentary of Bukhari, Ayni explains that the Muslims were unable to know whether or not the interpretations given by the People of the Book really accorded with the Torah, adding that confirming a lie or denying the truth provokes the wrath of God.

Somewhat similar are the traditions found in *Mishkat al-Masabih*, Book VIII, ch. I, p. 454; Book I, ch. VI, p. 49; Book XX, ch. I, p. 892:

> Abu Huraira told that when God's messenger once asked Ubai b. Ka'b how he recited in the course of the prayer and he recited **Umm al-Qur'an**, he said, "By Him in whose hand my soul is, nothing like it has been sent down in the Torah, the Injīl, the Testament Zabūr, or the Qur'an and it is seven of the oft-repeated verses and mighty Qur'an which I have been given." Tirmidhi transmitted it...

---

13. Most of this section is taken from *The Integrity of the Bible according to the Qur'an and the Hadith*, by Ghiyathuddin Adelphi and Ernest Hahn, Henry Martyn Institute, Hyderabad, 1977, p 29-38, and is used by permission of the authors.
14. *Mishkat al-Masabih*, tr. by James Robson, Ashraf, Lahore, 1963, p. 42.

Jabir told how 'Umar b. al-Khattab brought God's messenger a copy of the Torah saying, "Messenger of God, this is a copy of the Torah." When he received no reply he began to read to the obvious displeasure of God's messenger, so Abu Bakr said, "Confound you, do you not see how God's messenger is looking?" So 'Umar looked at God's messenger's face and said, "I seek refuge in God from the anger of God and His messenger. We are satisfied with God as Lord, with Islam as religion, and with Muhammad as Prophet." Then God's messenger said, "By Him in whose hand Muhammad's soul is, were Moses to appear to you and you were to follow him and abandon me, you would err from the right way. Were he alive and came in touch with my prophetic mission he would follow me." Darimi transmitted it.[15]

Salman said he read in the Torah that the blessing of food consists in ablution after it, and when he mentioned that to the Prophet he said, "The blessing of food consists in ablution before it and ablution after it." Tirmidhi and Abu Dawud transmitted it.

Here also Muhammad neither forbids the reading of the Torah nor denies its existence. His silence really confirms its existence. Likewise, according to *Mishkat al-Masabih*, Book XXVI, ch. XXXIX, pp. 1371, 1372:

Khaithama b. Abu Sabra said: I came to Medina and asked God to grant me a good companion to sit with and He granted me Abu Huraira. I sat with him and told him I had asked God to grant me a good companion to sit with and that he suited me. He asked where I came from and I replied that I belonged to al-Kufa and had come desiring and seeking good. He then said, "Do you not have among you Sa'd b. Malik whose prayers are answered, Ibn Mas'ud who looked after God's messenger's water for ablution and his sandals, Hudhaifa who was God's messenger's confident, 'Ammar to whom God gave protection from the devil at the tongue of His Prophet, and Salman who was a believer in the two Books? meaning the Injil and the Qur'an. Tirmidhi transmitted it.

It is beside the point that this tradition identifies the two books (kitabain) as the Injil and the Qur'an rather than the Torah-Old Testament and the Gospel-New Testament. To the point is the fact that this tradition also assumes the existence of a valid Injil.

The following tradition is also found in *Mishkat al-Masabih*, Book II, ch I, pp. 62,63:

Ziyad b. Labid said: The Prophet mentioned a matter, saying, "that will be at the time when knowledge departs." I asked, "How

---

15. This hadith seems incredible to Christians. Why was Muhammad angry when 'Umar brought the Torah? Why would he not want to rejoice in the Word of God given to Moses? Jesus was always appealing to the Torah-Old Testament and rebuked the Jewish leaders for not looking in it to see where it spoke of him. (John 5:39-40,45-47).

can knowledge depart when we recite the Qur'an and teach it to our children and they will teach it to their children up till the Day of Resurrection?" He replied, "I am astonished at you, Ziyad. I thought you were the most learned man in Medina. Do not these Jews and Christians read the Torah and the Injīl without knowing a thing about their contents?" Ahmad and Ibn Majah transmitted it, Tirmidhi transmitted something similar from him, as did Darimi from Abu Umama.

As the Qur'an, so the Hadith criticizes Jews and Christians for their ignorance. Yet Muhammad clearly shows that they read the Torah and the Injīl, not a corrupted or abrogated Torah or Injīl. Perhaps he was referring to Arab Jews and Christians who could not understand the languages of the Torah and Injīl. Here we must ask how many people read any sacred Scriptures with understanding?

But what of Waraqa bin Naufal? There is no question about whether he could read. In the chapter "How Revelation First Began" Bukhari describes how Muhammad received his first revelation, the initial verses of Sura 96, and how he first returned to Khadijah. Then, to quote the part of the Hadith which is relevant here.

> Khadijah took him to her cousin Waraqa ben Naufal. He had accepted Christianity during the Age of Ignorance and he used to write the Hebrew Scripture and the Injīl from Hebrew as God granted him strength. Waraqa had become very aged and was bereft of his sight.[16]

This tradition indicates that "**the Scripture**" (al-kitāb), probably the Torah-Old Testament and the Gospel-New Testament, were available and were even known in isolated areas of Arabia.

The following tradition is also found in *Mishkat al-Masabih*, Book VI, ch. XLIII, p. 285:

> Abu Huraira said: I went out to at-Tur and met Ka'b al-Ahbar with whom I sat, he telling me about the Torah and I telling him about God's messenger. One of the things I told him was that God's messenger had said, "The best day on which the sun has risen is Friday; on it his repentance was accepted, on it he died, on it the last hour will come, on Friday every beast is on the outlook from dawn to sunrise from fear of the last hour, but not jinn and men, and it contains a time at which no Muslim will pray and ask anything from God without His giving him it." Ka'b said that was one day every year, but when I insisted that it was on every Friday Ka'b read the Torah and said that God's messenger had spoken the truth. Abu Huraira said, "I met 'Abdallah b. Salam and told him of my meeting with Ka'b al-Ahbar and of what I had told him about

16. Translation of the authors, Adelphi and Hahn.

Friday, telling him that Ka'b had said that was one day every year. 'Abdallah b. Salam said that Ka'b had lied, but when I told him that Ka'b afterwards read the Torah and said that it was every Friday he said that Ka'b had spoken the truth."

Malik, Abu Dawud, Tirmidhi and Nisa'i transmitted it, and Ahmad transmitted it up to the statement that Ka'b had spoken the truth.

Initially Ka'b misrepresents the Torah, i.e., he is guilty of al-taḥrif al-ma'nawī. Ka'b then refers to the Torah, not a corrupted Torah, and admits his error.

Mishkat al-Masabih cites several traditions (Book XXVI, ch. XVIII, pp. 1232, 1233 and ch. XIX, p. 1244) which indicate that the Torah prophesies the coming of Muhammad.

'Ata b. Yasar told that he met 'Abdallah b. 'Amr b. al-'As and asked him to inform him of the description of God's messenger given in the Torah. He agreed, swearing by God that he was certainly described in the Torah by part of the description of him given in the Qur'an when it says, "O prophet, We have sent you as a witness, a bearer of good tidings, and a warner, and a guard for the common people" (from Al-Aḥzāb 33:45). (The following is from the Torah-Old Testament, Isaiah 42:1-3,6-7)[17] "You are My servant and My messenger; I have called you the one who trusts, not harsh or rough, nor loud-voiced in the streets. He will not repulse evil with evil, but will pardon and forgive, and God will not take him till He uses him to straighten the crooked creed so that people may say there is no god but God, and he opens thereby blind eyes, deaf ears and hardened hearts."

Bukhari transmitted it, and Darimi also gives something to the same effect on the authority of 'Ata who gave as his authority Ibn Salam.

Anas told that when a young Jew who was a servant of the Prophet became ill, he went to visit him and found his father sitting by his head reciting the Torah. God's messenger said to him, "I adjure you, Jew, by God who sent down the Torah to Moses, do you find in the Torah any description of me, or anything about my coming forth?" On his replying that he did not, the young man said, "Certainly, messenger of God, I swear by God that we do find in the Torah an account and description of you and a statement about your coming forth, and I testify that there is no god but God and that you are God's messenger." The Prophet then said to his companions. "Remove this man from beside his head and look after your brother."

Baihaqi transmitted it in *Dala'il al-Nubuwa*.

---

17. Material in parentheses mine.

Other traditions making the same claim are recorded in *Mishkat al-Masabih* (pp. 1237, 1249). Again all these traditions presume the existence of the genuine Torah. The father and the young man who is ill disagree about what the Torah says, but none of these traditions claims that the Jews have corrupted the text of the Torah.

Editor's comments: The quotation from the Torah-Old Testament repeated in the first of the above two passages was accepted as valid by 'Ata b. Yasar; and it can be found now, today, in the prophecy of Isaiah written more than 700 years before the Messiah came and more than 1300 years before Muhammad came. It reads,

> Here is My servant, whom I uphold,
>> My chosen one in whom I delight;
> I will put My Spirit on him
>> and he will bring justice to the nations.
> He will not shout or cry out,
>> or raise his voice in the streets.
> A bruised reed He will not break,
>> and a smoldering wick he will not snuff out...
> I, the LORD, have called you in righteousness...
>> I will keep you and will make you to be a covenant
>> for the people...
> to open eyes that are blind,
>> to free captives from prison, and
>> to release from the dungeon those who sit in
>> darkness.   Isaiah 42:1-3a, 6-7

Thus we have two witnesses—**the text of Isaiah in the Torah-Old Testament** and **the hadith**. Since they show some agreement, it indicates that Isaiah hasn't been changed and allows us to suppose that the rest of the hadith is probably a fairly reliable record of the conversation.

It is another question, of course, as to whether 'Abdallah b. Amr is right in referring the prophecy to Muhammad. The Injil refers it to Jesus in Matthew 12:18-21, and both the Qur'an and the Injil say that it was Jesus who opened the eyes of the blind. That is strong evidence, not to be easily dismissed!

According to the *Mishkat al-Masabih*, Book XVI, ch. I, p. 758:

> 'Abdallah b. Umar told that the Jews came to God's messenger and mentioned to him that a man and a woman of their number had committed fornication. He asked them what they found in the Torah about stoning and they replied that they should disgrace them and that they should be beaten. 'Abdallah b. Salam then said, "You lie; it contains instruction that they should be stoned to death, so bring the Torah." They spread it out, and one of them put his hand over the verse of stoning and read what preceded it and what followed it. 'Abdallah b. Salam told him to lift his hand and when he did so the verse of stoning was seen to

be in it. They then said, "He has spoken the truth, Muhammad; the verse of stoning is in it." The Prophet then gave command regarding them and they were stoned to death. In another version it says that he told him to lift his hand and that when he did so, the verse of stoning was clearly in it. The man then said, "It contains the verse of stoning, Muhammad, but we have been concealing it from one another." He then gave command regarding them and they were stoned to death (Bukhari and Muslim).

Here Muhammad openly accepts the command of the Torah and gives no indication that it has been abrogated or corrupted. This is one instance to which the Qur'an refers when it accuses the Jews of concealing and changing the Torah, verbally but not textually.

Furthermore in the *Mishkat al-Masabih*, Book XIII, ch. III, p. 667:

'Umar b. al-Khattab and Anas b. Malik reported God's messenger as saying that it is written in the Torah, "If anyone does not give his daughter in marriage when she reaches twelve and she commits sin, the guilt of that rests on him." Baihaqi transmitted both traditions in *Shu'ab al-iman*.

According to this passage Muhammad has knowledge of the Torah and even quotes it. Moreover he indicates what **is** written in the Torah, not what was written in the Torah and is now corrupted or abrogated.

Two traditions from the time when Omar was Khalifa (13-23 AH) also relate to our discussion. According to the *Mishkat al-Masabih*, Book XVII, ch. III, p. 795:

Sa'id b. al-Musayyib told that a Muslim and a Jew brought a dispute before 'Umar, and as he considered the Jew was in the right he pronounced judgment in his favor, but when the Jew said, "I swear by God that you have pronounced just judgment" he struck him with the whip and asked him what caused him to know that.

The Jew replied, "I swear by God that we find in the Torah that no *qadi* judges rightly without having an angel at his right hand and an angel at his left who direct him and dispose him to what is right as long as he adheres to the right; but when he abandons the right, they ascend and leave him." Malik transmitted it.

The second one is reported by Darimi in Sunan, Muqaddima 56. Abbad ben Abbad Abu Ataba quotes a letter of Omar ben Al-Khattab as saying:

If the doctors and the monks had not feared the disappearance of their ranks and the destruction of their prestige by the observance of the Scripture and expounding it (correctly), they would not have falsified (ḥarrafū حَرَّفُوا) or hidden (katamū كَتَمُوا) it. But as they went against the Scripture by their acts, they tried to fool the people about what they had done. Fearing the destruction of their prestige and that their corruption would be revealed to men, they falsified (ḥarrafū حَرَّفُوا) the Scripture by their interpretation, and what they could not falsify they hid (katamū كَتَمُوا). They were silent about their acts in order to keep their prestige and they were silent about the acts of their people acting in complicity. And truly God made a covenant with those to whom the Scripture came that they should make it known to the people and not hide it, but they deceived with it and were accommodating to themselves with it.

In the first of these hadiths there is no suggestion that Omar refused the right of the Jew to appeal to the Torah. In the second, he accuses the Jews and Christians of "**falsifying the Scripture by their interpretation,** and what they could not falsify **they hid**." As does the Qur'an, this last tradition accuses the people of the book of interpreting the Scriptures falsely (al-taḥrif al-ma'nawī), but it does not speak of corrupting the actual text of the Scriptures (al-taḥrif al-lafẓī).

When these two hadiths are considered along with the previously quoted hadith which tells of Omar bringing a copy of the Torah to read in Muhammad's presence, we can only conclude that Omar also considered that the Torah was available in an uncorrupted condition.

One exception has come to our attention, a tradition from Bukhari which supports the frequent claim of Muslims that the People of the Book corrupt the actual text of their Scriptures. It is attributed to Abdallah Ibn Abbas who was 14 when Muhammad died and later was appointed Governor of Al-Basrah by Ali. According to Obaidullah ben Abdallah ben Otba, Abdallah Ibn Abbas said:

> O Congregation of Muslims, how can you ask questions of the People of the Book, when your book which God revealed to His prophet brings the best tidings about God: Ye read it unfalsified and God has told you that the People of the Book have altered (baddalū بَدَّلُوا) what God wrote, and have falsified (ghaiyarū غَيَّرُوا) the book with their hands, and said, "This is from God," in order to get some paltry reward for it. Has He not forbidden you to ask those people about what you have received in the way of knowledge? By God, we have never seen any one of them asking you about what has been revealed to you.[18]

If this were the sole reference to the previous Scriptures in the Hadith, it would certainly fortify the Muslim claim that the People of the Book corrupt their Scriptures. Yet, to the best of our present knowledge, it must be considered as a single negative reference among the many other references within the Hadith which confirm the presence of a valid Torah and Gospel in the early Muslim community.

It is true that our evidence from the Hadith on this issue may be meaningless to those Muslims who have little trust in them. Yet, regardless of anyone's

---

18. Bukhari, *Sahih, Kitab al-Shahada*, No 29, as noted in J.W. Sweetman. *Islam and Christian Theology*, Part One, Vol. II, Lutterworth Press, London, 1947, p 139.

opinion about the importance of the Hadith, it must be noted that the *Mishkat al-Masabih* does not include a single reference to corruption of the previous Scriptures. Moreover, assuming we have not missed any pertinent references, it is clear that all the hadith, with one exception, are devoid of any reference to the corruption of previous Scriptures.

It is possible, of course, that individual Jews foolishly corrupted individual texts of their books, or in other words, that there were isolated instances of actual textual corruption. This would allow us to reconcile this single tradition with the remaining traditions which accept the genuineness of these previous Scriptures.

In summary, according to the hadiths which we have examined, Waraqa writes or translates the "Hebrew Scriptures," not *corrupted* Scriptures; Muhammad says that the "Jews and Christians read the Torah and the Injil, not a *corrupted* Torah or Injil. With a copy of the Torah at hand, Muhammad judges according to it, and on another occasion he quotes the Torah and says nothing about it being a corrupted Torah.

Thus **the Hadith** leads us to the same conclusion as our Quranic study in the last chapter. **THERE WAS AN UNCORRUPTED TORAH AND AN UNCORRUPTED GOSPEL WITH MUHAMMAD in Mecca and Medina during the first century of the Hejira.**

THE BIBLE AND THE QUR'AN:

TWO BOOKS
WITH MANY SIMILARITIES
IN THEIR COLLECTION

THE DOCUMENTARY HYPOTHESIS —
ITS EFFECT ON THE TORAH AND THE QUR'AN

In Chapter II of Section One we discussed assumptions. The last assumption mentioned was that Dr. Bucaille believes that the "documentary hypothesis" for the origin and development of the Torah is true. This hypothesis, sometimes called the "higher critical theory," or the "Graf-Wellhausen theory" after two of the men who proposed it, was developed in its classical form around 1880 AD, and was built **on the following basic assumptions**:

1. There is evolution in religion from polytheism to monotheism. As a result, the Old Testament is considered to be more or less the product of the evolving religious consciousness of the Hebrew people. **It had nothing to do with God revealing himself through an angel or the Holy Spirit.**

2. Since the customs mentioned in the life of Abraham are not mentioned outside the Torah (e.g., he married his half-sister, Sarah, and threw out Hagar his slave-girl wife when Sarah demanded it), and since people like **the Hittites** are not mentioned outside the Torah, **the accounts of Abraham, Isaac and Jacob, often referred to as the patriarchs, are not historical. They are only myths and stories.**

3. Moses and the Hebrews couldn't write because writing hadn't been invented yet.

4. The five books of the Torah were not, therefore, given by Moses in 1400 or 1300 BC, as the Bible (and the Qur'an) repeatedly claim, but were compiled hundreds of years later by unknown writers and editors.

According to the theory the first of these men, writing in about 900 BC, spoke of God as Yahweh or **J**ehovah, meaning the Eternal One. He is supposed to have composed Genesis chapters 2 and 3 among other passages.

A second writer, living a hundred years later is said to have used the Hebrew name **E**lohim for God. He was responsible for other large sections of the Torah. These two documents were then woven together sometime about 650 BC; and the theory holds that one can distinguish between these two authors according to whether the name Jehovah or Elohim is used for God. The divine names being insufficient in themselves, however, the "critics" took into consideration language, style, and theological concepts as criteria which they believed would allow them to identify the different documents.

The fifth book of the Torah called **D**euteronomy was written (as a complete fabrication—a lie) in 621 BC.

Finally some of the Jewish priests, called **P**riestly Editors added a fourth document which begins with the great creation epic of Genesis 1. They then assembled the Torah in its present form sometime about 400 BC—**fully 1000 years after Moses was alive**. Following the boldfaced letters shown above this idea is called the "**J,E,D,P** theory" or the **"documentary hypothesis."**

From this very brief summary we see that the "documentary hypothesis" calls into question the credibility of the entire Old Testament. **One would have to conclude, if these assertions are correct, that the Old Testament is a gigantic literary fraud.**

5. In addition, whether they stated it or not, **the men who first proposed this theory did not believe in miracles.** They did not believe in the miracles of Moses or Jesus, and they did not believe in the miracle of prophecy—that God reveals himself propositionally in word statements. God never talked to Moses or the prophets, or spoke through them. And if these men had been studying the Qur'an seriously they would have said that God never talked to Muhammad.

We might even say that this **disbelief in miracles and prophecy is the basic assumption behind the whole theory.**

Dr. Bucaille spent many pages of his book giving a detailed analysis of this theory and came out with the conclusion that the Bible is full of contradictions, improbabilities, etc. Muslims have been saying for centuries that we Christians changed our Scriptures. So when Dr. Bucaille, coming from a Christian background and upbringing, says the same thing, Muslims conclude that it must surely be true and are only too glad to accept it.

When I did my premedical studies at the College of Wooster, I was taught this theory as truth. The college was related to the Presbyterian church and my professor was a Ph.D. in religion. One day, the student sitting next to me said to the professor,

> "But if what you say is true, then the Bible is not true."
> He answered, as though talking to a six-year-old, "Well, you can believe the Bible if you want to."

Not having any facts with which to test the professor's statement that the Torah was not written by Moses, even though Jesus said it was, I accepted the professor's words—words which I now believe to be false. This destroyed my confidence that the Bible was a true revelation from God, so I gave up the Christian faith and became an agnostic. I was not against God, but I no longer knew what to believe about Him.

Praise be to God, "who wants all men to be saved and to come to the knowledge of the truth,"[1] He did not leave me in ignorance! He led me to men and women who could show me other facts—facts which confirm the Torah and the prophets—facts which we will look at in this chapter.

THE EFFECT ON THE QUR'AN

In Chapter I, A of Section Two, we saw that the Qur'an says there was a true unchanged Torah with Mary, Yaḥyā (John the Baptist), and Jesus in 34 AD. Though all readers may not agree with me that it was the same as our present Torah, there are some facts in those Quranic verses about which we can all agree.

The Qur'an says clearly that Abraham was a real person, to whom God spoke.

---

1. I Timothy 2:4.

It says clearly that Moses performed many miracles and was given tablets from God inscribed with the Torah.

As an example, let us look at the Late Meccan Sura of the Heights (Al-A'rāf) 7:144-145:

> God said, "O Moses, I have chosen thee above other men"...and We (God) ordained laws for him in the **tablets** in all matters, both commanding and explaining all things.

Any person familiar with the Qur'an will say, "Of course our Book teaches these things. Even the most uninstructed Muslim knows these two facts. Why mention them?"

Because if the stories of Abraham, Ishmael, Isaac and Jacob are myths in the Torah, then they are myths in the Qur'an. If writing was unknown at the time of Moses in 1400 BC, then neither Moses or anyone else could read written tablets, and the Qur'an which says that God gave them to Moses is in complete error along with the Torah.

For this reason it is necessary to look very carefully at this **"documentary hypothesis,"** and we shall start our investigation by looking at what these "higher critics" say about miracles.

MIRACLES AND PROPHECY ARE IMPOSSIBLE

In one of his works (*De Profeten en de Profetie onder Israel*, Vol. I, pp.5,585) A. Kuenen states his anti-supernaturalist position:

> So long as we attribute a part of Israel's religious life directly to God and allow **supernatural or immediate revelation (prophecy) to intervene even in one instance**, just so long does our view of the whole remain **inexact**, and we see ourselves obliged to do violence here or there to the well-assured content of the historical accounts. It is only the assumption of a **natural development** that takes account of all the phenomena.

In *De Godsdienst van Israel* (Vol. I, p.111) Kuenen confesses that,

> The familiar intercourse of the divinity with the patriarchs constitutes for me one of the determining considerations **against the historical character of the narratives**.

In the first quotation Kuenen says that even one supernatural event makes our view inexact.

In the second he says that because God speaks to Abraham, Hagar, Isaac, and Jacob (the patriarchs), that is **proof** that the Books of Moses are not historical.

Julius Wellhausen, one of the originators of the Graf-Wellhausen theory, **ridicules the account of the miracles that occurred at Sinai when God gave Moses the law (on the tablets)** with the scornful exclamation, **"Who can seriously believe all that?"**[2]

---

2. *Israelitische und Juedische Geschichte*, p. 12.

Many modern teachers continue to hold and teach these same ideas because of their continued unbelief in miracles. Langdon B. Gilkey, from the University of Chicago, writing in 1962, describes the Biblical account of the entire Exodus-Sinai experience as

> the acts (which the) Hebrews believed God might have done and the words he might have said, had he done and said them— **but of course we recognize he did not.**

Referring to the Hebrews' crossing of the Red Sea, Gilkey goes on,

> **We deny the miraculous character of the event** and say its cause was merely an East wind, and then we point to the unusual response of Hebrew faith.[3]

In these few quotations we see that miracles are considered impossible: the very miracles which we mentioned are all denied.

> It is impossible that God would have spoken to Abraham.
> It is impossible that Moses could have received the Law from God.
> No miracle was done, when by the power of God the Red Sea was divided and then closed again, drowning Pharaoh and his army.

The logical result of such a theory was not lost on Yusuf Ali. On page 283 of his translation of the Qur'an he warns,

> The view of the school of Higher Criticism is radically destructive. According to Renan it is doubtful whether Moses was not a myth.
> ...**we reject the premise which we believe to be false, *viz.*, that God does not send inspired Books through inspired Prophets.**

Again it must be stressed, if there is no such thing as prophecy, or if Moses never existed, the Qur'an falls along with the Bible.

UNBELIEF AND DATING

The unbelief of these men in miracles has a profound affect on their dating of the **Old Testament** documents. As an example, let us consider the prophet Daniel. By revelation, Daniel was told to record his conversations with the Babylonian king Nebuchadnezzar. Both Biblical history and secular history give a date of about 600 BC for the life of this king, so we would expect that the book of Daniel was written at that time.

Not so for the higher critics! Why? Because in addition to various miracles which are recorded, chapter 8:20-21 gives a detailed prophecy of the political future for the next 300 years. It reads,

> The two-horned ram that you saw represents the kings of Media and Persia. The shaggy goat is the king of Greece, and the large horn between his eyes is the first king.

---

3. *Cosmology, Ontology, & the Travail of Biblical Language*, Concordia Theological Monthly. Mar. 1962, Vol. 33, p 148-150.

This prophecy was given when Belshazzar, the grandson of Nebuchadnezzar, was still ruler of the Babylonian kingdom. It predicts that the Medes and Persians will overthrow Babylon. They in turn will be conquered by the Greeks, which happened under Alexander the Great around 330 BC, or almost 300 years after Daniel gave his prophecy.

But the "higher critics" don't believe in the miracle of prophecy, so what do they do with a wonderful prophecy like this?

They say that since the book of Daniel prophesies things that happened in 330 BC, the book *had to have been written* after **330 BC** when the events took place, by a writer who just used the name of Daniel so that people would believe what he said. In other words, **since miracles are impossible, Daniel cannot have prophesied the future, and the book called by his name is a forgery.**

Bucaille quotes one of these "higher critics" as saying that the book of Daniel is "a 'disconcerting' apocalypse from an historical point of view." [4] But the reason that it is disconcerting is because it is so accurate in foretelling hundreds of years of history.

Another reason that it is disconcerting is that it foretells things which did not happen until Jesus Christ came and ascended into heaven. In chapter 9:25-26, **Daniel**, who is prophesying in the sixth century BC about 30 years after Jerusalem and the first Temple had been destroyed, **foretells** that (1) **Jerusalem and the Temple will be rebuilt,** that (2) **the Messiah will come,** that (3) **"the Messiah will be cut off, but not for himself,"** and (4) **"the people of the ruler who will come will destroy the city and the sanctuary"**—which the troops of the Roman General Titus did in 70 AD.

The higher critics and Dr. Bucaille have no answer for these fulfilled prophecies, especially the last one which happened more than 200 years after Bucaille himself says that Daniel was written,[5] so they just ignore them. We shall not ignore them, however. In a later chapter we shall examine fulfilled prophecy in detail as a proof of the validity of the Bible.

1. EVOLUTION IN RELIGION

Just as Darwin applied the evolutionary concept to biology and Hegel applied the evolutionary concept to history, so the higher critics proposed and believed that religious development went through an evolutionary process which commenced with a belief in spirits in the days of primitive man, to finally arrive at true monotheism. Wellhausen even tried, by means of Hegelian analogy with pre-Islamic and Islamic Arabia, to build a system for the development of Israel's religion.

G. E. Wright explains the view of Wellhausen and many other radical critics as follows:

---

4. Bucaille, op. cit., p 18.
5. Bucaille, op. cit., p 18. He writes, "It is probably a work from the Maccabean period, second century BC." Fragments of Daniel found among the Dead Sea Scrolls now prove this impossible. The previous manuscript from which the copy in our possession was made could not have been later than the 4th century BC, or at least 200 years before the Maccabees.

The Graf-Wellhausen reconstruction of the history of Israel's religion was, in effect, an assertion that within the pages of the Old Testament we have a perfect example of the evolution of religion from animism in patriarchal times…to monotheism. The last was first achieved in pure form during the sixth and fifth centuries BC. **The patriarchs (Abraham and his sons in 1800 BC) worshiped the spirits in trees, stones, springs, mountains, etc.** The God of pre-prophetic Israel (1000 BC) was a tribal deity, limited in his power to the land of Palestine…It was the prophets who were the true innovators (inventors of monotheism)…[6]

Thus, according to their theory, there was animism first, then a limited tribal deity, and finally explicit and universal monotheism in the history of Israel.

The higher critics went on from this to conclude that a piece of literature can be dated by its stage of religious teaching. They believed that the high conception of God which the Torah attributes to Abraham and the other patriarchs, was *impossible* for them. The idea of the unity of God was too elevated and spiritual for their minds. Wellhausen, speaking on the creation of the world by One God, says that **"in a youthful people such a theological abstraction is unheard of."**[7]

The reasoning now goes like this: Having already **assumed** that there was evolution in religion, the history of Abraham as written in the Torah does not fit. Genesis 22:18 says,

> In your seed all the nations of the earth shall be blessed, because you have obeyed Me.

But this can't be true of Abraham. According to the theory he wasn't developed enough to know that there was One God over "all the nations of the earth." **THEREFORE, that sentence from the Torah had to have been written 1000 years later.**

But if this reasoning is true, what about the Qur'an? In the Late Meccan Sura of the Cattle (Al-An'ām) 6:79 Abraham says,

> For me, I have set my face, firmly and truly towards Him who created the heavens and the earth, and never shall I give partners to God.

The higher critical theory says that Abraham could not have said those words because he was worshiping the spirits in trees and stones. Therefore, if the documentary hypothesis, taken up by Dr. Bucaille, is true, then the Qur'an is also false along with the Torah.

Furthermore, recent investigations of primitive cultures have shown that this idea of "evolution in religion" is completely false. In a book called *Eternity in*

---

6. *The Study of the Bible Today and Tomorrow.* Edited by Harold R. Willoughby. U. of Chicago Press, Chicago, 1947, p 89-90.
7. *Prolegomena to the History of Israel*, Julius Wellhausen, Adam and Charles Black, Edinburgh, 1885, p 305.

Their Hearts,[8] the author, Don Richardson, demonstrates conclusively that in addition to their animism or polytheism, almost all primitive tribes and cultures believe in "a supreme creator god" who made the heavens and the earth. In addition, these tribes often have a story giving some sort of explanation as to why contact was lost with the great supreme god.

Was this not, in fact, the situation among the Quraish in Mecca at the time of Muhammad? Muhammad's father was named Abd-allah, and the Qur'an makes it clear that the Meccans believed that Allah was the chief. The others were secondary gods, employed to intercede with Allah on behalf of the Quraish.

Anthropological evidence, therefore, is against any theory of evolution in religion. It supports the **Biblical** teaching that men knew of the Supreme Creator God from the beginning, but then separated themselves away by sin.

2a. THE CULTURE AND SOCIAL CUSTOMS OF ABRAHAM

As for the criticism in point 2 above that the social customs of Abraham are just myth and fiction, the Nuzi tablets from 1500 BC mention these very customs.

A.   There are several accounts of a barren wife who asked her husband to produce a child for her by her maidservant, just as Sarah did using Hagar. "In a marriage contract from Nuzi, the bride Kelim-ninu promises in written form to procure for her husband Shennima a slave girl as a second wife, if she fails to bear him children. She also promises that she will not drive out the offspring of such a union"[9] as Sarah did when she threw out Hagar and Ishmael.

B.   The victory of Abraham over Chedolaomer and the Mesopotamian kings, described in the Torah, Genesis 14, has been described by the higher critics as "fictitious" and the five Cities of the Plain (Sodom, Gomorrah, Admah, Zeboiim and Zoar) as legendary. Yet the Ebla archives (described in the next section) seem to refer to all five Cities of the Plain, and on one tablet the Cities are listed in the exact same sequence as in Genesis 14.[10]

In addition, the language of Genesis 14 contains some unique or very rare words and phrases which were not commonly used in later Hebrew writing. "One such word, 'hanikh' in verse 14, meaning 'an armed retainer,' appears but this once in the Bible, where it is used to describe men born and trained in Abraham's household. But it is found in the Egyptian execration texts of the nineteenth-eighteenth centuries BC when Abraham was alive, and in a fifteenth century cuneiform inscription from Taanach" in Palestine.[11]

C.   Genesis 29 tells how Jacob, the grandson of Abraham, was followed by his father-in-law Laban, because Laban thought that Jacob had stolen the family images or "teraphim." "Commentators have long wondered why he

8. Regal Books, Ventura, California 93006, 1981.
9. *More Evidence That Demands a Verdict*, Josh McDowell, Campus Crusade for Christ, San Bernardino, CA 92414, 1975, p 74.
10. *Evidence That Demands a Verdict*, Josh McDowell, Here's Life Publishers Inc., San Bernardino, p 68. (henceforth called "*Evidence*")
11. *Understanding Genesis*, Naham Sarna, McGraw-Hill, New York, 1966, p 111.

would go to such pains to recover images which he could have replaced by buying others in the local shops. The Nuzi tablets tell of a son-in-law who, because he possessed the family images, had the legal right to claim his father-in-law's property." This new finding explains Laban's anxiety. He was afraid that Jacob would come back and use the idols to take the inheritance away from Laban's own sons.[12]

Cyrus Gordon, who abandoned the **"documentary hypothesis"** after his study of the ancient history and archaeology of the Middle East, writes,

> The cuneiform contracts from Nuzu have demonstrated that the social institutions of the patriarchs (Abraham, Isaac, Jacob, etc.) are genuine and pre-Mosaic. They cannot have been invented by any post-Mosaic **J,E,D, or P.**[13]

2b. THE LONG-LOST HITTITES

This negative argument that "since the Hittites are not mentioned outside of the Bible, then the Bible must be wrong," was still being taught to me at Wooster College in 1946, even though Hugo Winckler had discovered the Hittite capital of Boghaz-koi in central Turkey in 1906. In an archive of clay tablets, Winckler found a military treaty between the Hittites and the Egyptians written nearly 1300 years before Christ.

In addition, an Egyptian tablet has been found which records a fierce battle between Ramses II and the Hittites at Kadesh on the Orontes river in 1287 BC.[14]

3. WRITING HAD NOT YET BEEN INVENTED

We saw above that the critics who proposed this hypothesis said that Moses couldn't write. Julius Wellhausen wrote in 1885 that Israel certainly had its laws,

> **only they were not fixed in writing.**[15]

and Hermann Schultz, in 1898 said,

> Of the legendary character of the pre-Mosaic **narrators** (not writers), the time of which they treat is sufficient proof. **It was a time prior to all knowledge of writing.**[16]

Then in 1902, a French archaeological expedition under the direction of M. Jacques de Morgan found the law code of Hammurabi at the site of ancient Susa, to the east of Mesopotamia. The code, engraved in stone sometime between 1700 and 2000 BC, contained 282 sections or paragraphs, and was found to contain many laws similar to the Mosaic law.

---

12. "Archeology and the Bible," J. P. Free, *His Magazine*, May 1949, Vol. 9, p 20.
13. "The Patriarchal Age," *Journal of Bible and Religion*, October 1955, Vol. 21, No. 4, p 241.
14. McDowell, *More Evidence*, p 309-311.
15. Wellhausen, op. cit., 1885, p 393.
16. *Old Testament Theology*, Edinburgh, T. & T. Clark, 1898, p 25.

Since then, archaeological discoveries have been made which prove that writing existed in Moses day and long before him. Here is a partial list, including the fact that inscriptions have even been found at Mt. Sinai.

1. In 1917 Alan Gardiner, noted British Egyptologist, made the first decipherment of the Proto-Semitic inscriptions found at Mt. Sinai... These inscriptions, written in a pictorial script by Canaanites before the middle of the second millennium (1500) BC, prove that alphabetic writing existed before the time of Moses.[17]

2. Starting in 1925, more than 4000 tablets, dating from 1500-1400 BC, have been found in the town of Nuzi, near ancient Ninevah in Iraq.

3. In 1929 tablets were found at Ugarit and Ras Shamra on the Syrian north coast. These tablets are from the 14th and 13th centuries BC, the very age of Moses. The language corresponds closely to the Hebrew poetic language from the **Torah-Old Testament**, such as the Song of Miriam from Exodus 15:21, and the song of Deborah found in Judges 5 (12th century BC).

4. In 1933 excavations were started at Mari on the Middle Euphrates in Syria. Three years later thousands of cuneiform tablets were found which dated from 1700 BC.

5. In 1964 the ruins of Ebla were discovered in northern Syria. By 1974, more than 17,000 clay tablets written in 2200 BC had been found.

6. Finally, I myself sat at the base of an Egyptian obelisk at the Place de la Concorde while in Paris in 1961, the sides of which are covered with hieroglyphics from the time of Ramses II.

As early as 1938, without the later finds, W. F. Albright, discussing the various writing systems that existed in the ancient Orient during pre-Mosaic patriarchal times, could write,

> In this connection it may be said that writing was well known **in Palestine** and Syria throughout the Patriarchal Age (Middle Bronze, 2100-1500 BC). **No fewer than five scripts are known to have been in use:** (1) Egyptian hieroglyphs, used for personal and place names by the Canaanites; (2) Accadian Cuneiform; (3) the hieroglyphiform syllabary of Phoenicia; (4) the linear alphabet of Sinai; and (5) the cuneiform alphabet of Ugarit which was discovered in 1929.[18]

---

17. "Recent Illumination of the Old Testament," S. H. Horn, *Christianity Today*, June 21, 1968, Vol. 12, pp 925-929.
18. "Archaeology Confronts Biblical Criticism," W. F. Albright, *The American Scholar*, April 1938, Vol. 7, p 186.

More evidence that demands a verdict [**]

One can go on and on like this.

The higher critics said that the laws found in Exodus, Leviticus, and Deuteronomy of the Torah were too advanced and complicated for Moses' knowledge. Then the Code of Hammurabi was found, which was just as complicated, but written between 300 and 500 years before Moses. [**p 63]

The statement was made that extensive travel such as would be necessary for Abraham to come from Ur of the Chaldees (Iraq) to Palestine (Torah, Genesis 11 and 12) was unknown in those days. But Babylonian excavators (at Mari) have uncovered a tablet with a wagon contract dating from the time of Abraham. The owner of the wagon leased it to a man for a year on condition that it wouldn't be driven to Kittim on the Mediterranean coast north of Palestine. [**p 75]

Another tablet found in Babylon records that a man named "Abarama" paid his rent, showing that this form of the name "Abram" (Abraham's original name) was in use when Abraham lived in that area. [**p 75]

The complicated tent, called a tabernacle, which God ordered Moses to build for the place of worship (Torah, Exodus 36) was considered pure imagination. It was thought to be much too elaborate for the time of Moses. But in 2600 BC, 1200 years before Moses, the Egyptians had a portable bed canopy, used for their queen, made of vertical rods and corner posts with beams across the top, overlaid with gold, and fitted together with tenons in sockets for rapid erection and dismantling, just like the Hebrew tabernacle. [**p 110]

Wellhausen says that the bronze mirrors donated by the Jewish woman for the construction of a ceremonial basin (Torah, Exodus 38:8) were unknown until much later. Now, specific archaeological evidence proves their existence in Egypt during the Empire Period of 1500-1400 BC. [19]

In view of all this modern evidence, it is sad to find Dr. Bucaille repeating the following quotation from E. Jacobs who says,

It is probable that what the Old Testament narrates about Moses and the patriarchs only roughly corresponds to the succession of historic facts... (boldfacing mine)[20]

What a contrast there is between this statement and the following quotation from Nelson Glueck, former president of the Jewish Theological Seminary in the Hebrew Union College in Cincinnati, Ohio, and one of the three greatest archaeologists of our time.

...In all of my archaeological investigation I have never found

---

[**] Summarized from *More Evidence That Demands a Verdict*, Josh McDowell, Campus Crusade for Christ, San Bernardino, CA. 1975. This book and his first volume, *Evidence That Demands a Verdict*, are full of quotations indicating the beliefs of the critics, followed by archaeological evidence proving that the critics and their **"documentary hypothesis"** are wrong, and that the Torah and Gospel are trustworthy and reliable. They have very complete bibliographies and should be read by anyone interested in this problem.

19. McDowell, *Evidence*, p 70.
20. Bucaille, BQ&S, p 4.

one artifact of antiquity that contradicts any statement of the Word of God (the **Torah-Old Testament**).[21]

4. THE TORAH IS MADE UP OF MULTIPLE DOCUMENTS WRITTEN LONG AFTER MOSES

In the outline at the beginning of this chapter we saw that Graf and Wellhausen proposed that there were at least four documents which were woven together to make the present Torah. Some later men have pretended to find evidence for many more—ten, twelve, fifteen. They attempt to make these divisions on the basis of word usage.

The most outstanding example of this is the division according to the use of the divine names: Elohim which is used in the Torah, Genesis 1; and Jehovah which is used in Genesis 2 and 3.

A second assumption is that when the Elohim writer, called **"E,"** and the Jehovah (Yahweh) writer, called **"J,"** or one of the other writers, would tell the same story in a slightly different form, a later editor would use all of the accounts as different episodes in one story. An example of this is to be found in the naming of Isaac which means Laughter.

In Genesis 17 we read how God through His angel told Abraham that he would have a son in his old age, and verses 15-19 say,

> God also said to Abraham, "As for Sarai your wife...her name will be Sarah. I will bless her and will surely give you a son by her. I will bless her so that she will be the mother of nations; kings of peoples will come from her."
>
> **Abraham fell face down; he laughed** and said to himself, "Will a son be born to a man a hundred years old? Will Sarah bear a child at the age of ninety?"...
>
> Then God said, "Yes, but your wife Sarah will bear you a son, and you will call him Isaac." (Isaac means *he laughs* in Hebrew)

Sometime later God speaks to Abraham again and repeats this promise in the hearing of Sarah as recorded in Genesis 18:10-15.

> Then the LORD said, "I will surely return to you about this time next year, and Sarah your wife will have a son."
>
> Now Sarah was listening at the entrance to the tent... Abraham and Sarah were already old and well advanced in years, and Sarah was past the age of childbearing. **So Sarah laughed to herself** as she thought, "After I am worn out and my master is old, will I now have this pleasure?"
>
> Then the LORD said to Abraham, "Why did Sarah laugh...Is anything too hard for the LORD?..."
>
> Sarah was afraid, so she lied and said, "I did not laugh."
>
> But He said, "Yes, you did laugh."

---

21. McDowell, *Evidence*, p 22.

Finally there is a third passage concerning laughter at the time of the birth. Genesis 21:1-6 reads,

> Now the LORD was gracious to Sarah as He had said...Sarah became pregnant and bore a son to Abraham in his old age, at the very time God had promised him. Abraham gave the name Isaac to the son Sarah bore him. When his son Isaac was eight days old, Abraham circumcised him, as God commanded him. Abraham was a hundred years old...
>
> Sarah said, **"God has brought me laughter, and everyone who hears about this will laugh with me."**

What do the critics do with these seemingly straightforward passages? They theorize that three different documents had differing accounts of one event, the naming of Isaac. The three were then woven into one in Genesis. They propose that the first account in Genesis 17 is from the *Priestly Editors*, the second one is from the **"J"** document, and the third one is from the **"E"** document. But is it really unreasonable to assume that both Abraham and Sarah laughed with disbelief when they were individually told that Isaac would be born, and that she later laughed with joy at the birth?

Henri Blocher summarizes the whole process very nicely in his book *Révélation des Origines—Le Début de la Genèse*. He writes:

> The critics, when they judge the internal phenomena (of the Bible) project into it their customs as modern western readers, and neglect all that we know today of the writing customs used in Biblical times. The taste for repetition, the structure of a global statement—repeated with development, the replacement of a word by its synonyms, especially the change of a divine name in a text (i.e., the names of Osiris on the stele of Ikhernofret), are well attested characteristics of ancient Middle Eastern texts...The Biblical text, *as it is*, agrees with the literary canons of its time.[22]

IF "HIGHER CRITICISM" WERE APPLIED TO THE QUR'AN?

In Arabic the name for God **"Allāh"** (الله) parallels the Hebrew **Elohim** and the name **"Rabb"** (الرَّبّ) corresponds to the Hebrew Adonai (Lord) which the Jews used later to refer to **Jehovah**. When we examine the Qur'an we find that the name **Rabb** is never used in 11 suras: 24, 48, 49, 58, 61, 62, 77, 88, 95, 104, and 112; and the name **Allah** is absent in 18 suras: 54-56, 68, 75, 78, 83, 89, 92-94, 99, 100, 105, 106, 108, 113, and 114. In addition there are 10 very short Early Meccan suras in which, like the Book of Esther in the **Torah-Old Testament**, the name of God is not mentioned at all.

---

22. Op. cit., Presses Bibliques Universitaires, rue de l'Ale 29, 1003 Lausanne, Switzerland, 1979, p 234. (translation mine)

Below is an analysis of the use of **Allah** and **Rabb** in Suras 48 to 64. I have chosen these 17 suras because 8 of them are in the above lists.

Sura Number Verse	Date of Sura	Times Allah used	Number of Verses	Times per Verse	Times Rabb Used	Times per
48	6 AH	19	29	.65	0	0.
49	9 AH	27	18	1.50	0	0.
50	Early Meccan	1	45	.02	2	.04
51	Early Meccan	3	60	.05	5	.08
52	Early Meccan	3	49	.06	6	.12
53	Early Meccan	6	62	.10	7	.11
54	Early Meccan	0	55	0.	1	.02
55	Early Meccan	0	78	0.	36	.46
56	Early Meccan	0	96	0.	3	.03
57	8 AH	32	29	1.10	3	.10
58	5-7 AH	40	22	1.81	0	0.
59	4 AH	29	24	1.21	1	.04
60	8 AH	21	13	1.61	4	.31
61	3 AH	17	14	1.21	0	0.
62	2-5 AH	12	11	1.09	0	0.
63	4-5 AH	14	11	1.27	1	.09
64	1 AH	20	18	1.11	1	.06

When we look at this information we see that in Sura 55 the word Rabb was used 36 times — 31 of them along with the word "favors" (al-ālā' الآلَاء). This word ālā' is a rare word in the Qur'an, being found only three other times—once in the Early Meccan Sura 53 and twice in the Late Meccan Sura 7. Furthermore, when we examine Sura 53:19-20, we find that it is the only sura which mentions the three Goddesses Al-Llāt, and Al-'Uzzā, and Manāt.

A higher critic who believes in the "documentary hypothesis" would now say, "We see here that Allah is used much less often during the Meccan period, never more than once in every 10 verses. While in the Medina period this name is used at least once a verse except for Sura 48.

In addition, the word ālā' and the three idol goddesses are found only in these Meccan suras. Therefore there must have been an early Meccan writer called "**R**" because he used "Rabb" as the name for God, but who was still interested in idols. Later there was a second writer called "**A**" who used "Allah and wrote when pure monotheism had developed. It is true, of course, that in Sura 53, Manāt, Al-Llāt and Al-'Uzzā are mentioned with disapproval, so these disapproving words must have been added at a later date by "**Q**" which stands for editing done by the "Qurrā" (قُرَّاء).[23]

23. The "qurrā," singular "qāri," are those responsible for the correct reading of the Qur'an.

Next we find that there are four accounts in the Qur'an telling how the honored guests came to inform Abraham that he would have a son in his old age. The Early Meccan Sura 51:24-30 mentions how Abraham's wife didn't believe and said "a barren old woman." This was obviously done by "R." The Late Meccan Sura 15:51-56 tells how Abraham didn't believe the news and said, "Do you give me glad tidings that old age has seized me?" Since this is Late Meccan the "A" writer was starting to have an influence.

In the Late Meccan Sura 11:69-74 the two stories have been worked together by one of the "Q" editors and the fact is added that Abraham's wife laughed.

Finally there is the early Mid-Meccan account in Sura 37:99-103 which is really concerned with Abraham's sacrifice of his son. Since sacrifices are mentioned, this represents another document which we will call the "D" document for (al-dabīha الذَّبِيحة) sacrifice.

As the reader can see, we easily made up a new four-document theory for the origin of the Qur'an. We could call it the **R, A, Q, D** theory. Though this **R, A, Q, D theory is completely fictitious, it demonstrates the type of arbitrary reasoning used by the authors of the "documentary hypothesis"** and shows what would have happened if they had applied the same type of analysis to the Qur'an.

CONCLUSION

In the light of all this evidence it seems incredible that men would continue to accept and teach this outmoded idea unless it is because of hard-hearted unbelief. Perhaps there is some excuse for Graf and Wellhausen, who developed their theory before the archaeological finds of the 20th century. But why modern scholars and Dr. Bucaille continue to present this hypothesis is difficult to understand. Henri Blocher thinks it is because they have the same **basic assumption**. "They share, in general, Wellhausen's hostility toward any intrusion of the supernatural in the narratives."[24]

There is no objective evidence for the existence of the **J, E,** or any of the other documents that are alleged to have been used to construct the Torah. And there is no history, no isnād (الإسْنَاد)[25] of anyone claiming to have ever seen them.

K.A. Kitchen, Lecturer in Archaeology at Liverpool University, says,

> The conventional forms of literary criticism ("**J, E, P, D**," etc., oral tradition) were evolved in a vacuum and their criteria can be proven to be non-significant and just plain wrong when compared with the ways in which people *really* wrote in the Biblical world. The evolutionary scheme of concepts…is wholly illusory when measured against the entire Biblical world of the Near East…When the Old Testament writings and the theoretical reevaluations of

---

24. Op. cit., p 236. (translation mine)

25. The Arabic word for the chain of people through whom a tradition about the prophet Muhammad or/and the Qur'an passed.

86

them are finally measured against the visible, tangible...Old Testament world—**then it is the extant documents (of the Old Testament) that match with their Near Eastern context**, and not the reconstructions based on false premises and false criteria.[26]

The same conclusion was reached by the late Jewish scholar Umberto Cassuto. In his book *The Documentary Hypothesis*, he devotes six chapters to the five most significant arguments which the higher critics use to support the theory that Moses did not write the Torah. He compares the five reasons to pillars which hold up a house. About these supports or "pillars" of the **"documentary hypothesis,"** Cassuto says in his concluding chapter,

> I did not prove that the pillars were weak or that each one failed to give decisive support, but **I established that they were not pillars at all, that they did not exist, that they were purely imaginary.**[27]

In our little study we have only considered four points or pillars, but I think that we have come to the same conclusion as Cassuto. **"They are not pillars, they do not exist, they are purely imaginary."**

Finally, we must realize that this theory assumes something about the Jews that few of us are prepared to say. **It assumes that ALL of the Jews from Moses' time down to the time of Christ were dishonest—that there were no God-fearing men who would defend and preserve copies of the true Torah.** Yet even the Qur'an does not make such an accusation against the Jews of Mecca and Medina. As we saw in Chapter I of Section Two, it admits that some of them were honest and sincere in their religion. The Late Meccan Sura of the Heights (Al-A'rāf) 7:159 says,

> Of the people of Moses there is a group who guide with truth and judge by it.

The **"documentary hypothesis"** stating that Moses did not write the Torah is clearly false, and men have followed it because they have made false assumptions in their analysis of the Scriptures. When we analyze the Bible or the Qur'an we should follow in the footsteps of the literary genius and critic Coleridge. Long ago he established this basic rule for the analysis of literature.

> When we meet an apparent error in a good author, we are to presume ourselves *ignorant of his understanding*, until we are certain that we *understand his ignorance.*

As Aristotle said in [*de Arte Poetica*, 14606-14616], **"The benefit of the doubt is to be given to the document itself, not arrogated [arrogantly taken] by the critic to himself."**

---

26. "The Old Testament in Its Context," K.A. Kitchen, Lecturer in the School of Archaeology and Oriental Studies, Liverpool University; from the *Theological Student Fellowship Bulletin*, 39 Bedford Square, London WC1B 3EY, 1972, p 15.

27. Cassuto, op. cit., Magnes Press, Jerusalem, 1941, 1st Eng. Edition 1961, p 100.

NEW TESTAMENT FORM CRITICISM — ITS EFFECT ON THE GOSPEL AND THE QUR'AN

"**Form criticism,**" which also originated in Germany, is an attempt to analyze the Gospel on the basis of literary forms much as the "**documentary hypothesis**" did with the Torah of Moses.

The form critics assume that the **Gospels** are composed of small independent units or episodes which were circulated orally. During the 30 years between Jesus ascension and the writing of the first Gospel, the critics believe, these small units which they named "**pericopes**" gradually changed and took on the forms of folk literature, such as **legends, tales, myths and parables**.

The formation of these units and their preservation was not under the control of God but was determined by the needs of the Christian community. In other words, when the community had a problem, they either used one of the circulating sayings of Jesus or they **created a new saying**. That is, they lied about what Jesus said in order to answer that particular problem.

Dr. Bucaille gives a fairly comprehensive summary of this method of study (p. 71-76), but again he does not seem to have realized that those who proposed this method (one could rightfully call it a "theory" because of the large number of basic assumptions) did not believe anything which seemed to be supernatural or miraculous. They did not believe that God spoke to the prophets by means of angels or the Holy Spirit. They did not believe that Jesus brought a special revelation in the Gospel.

Rudolph Bultmann, one of the three most-well-known proponents of "**form criticism,**" wrote,

> **A historical fact which involves a resurrection from the dead is utterly inconceivable.**[1]

W. J. Sparrow-Simpson, speaking of another form critic, David Strauss, says,

> Nothing can be more genuine than Strauss' acknowledgement that he was controlled by *a priori* considerations, to which **the fact of a resurrection was inadmissible.**[2]

In summary, according to the form critics the four accounts of the Gospel of Jesus the Messiah are not historic witnesses to the life and words of Jesus, but rather what the church believed and eventually put together from older sources.

The conclusion of Martin Dibelius, another of the three most-well-known form critics, is:

> ...there never was a "purely" historical witness to Jesus.[3]

---

1. *Kerygma and Myth*, Rudolph Bultmann, English Trans. Harper and Row, New York, 1961, p 39.

2. "Resurrection and Christ," *A Dictionary of Christ and the Gospels,* Vol. 2, T.&T. Clark, Edinburgh, 1908, p 511.

3. *From Tradition to Gospel*, Martin Dibelius, Charles Scribner's Sons, New York, 1949, p 295.

And Eduard Ellwein summarizes Bultmann's ideas as follows:

> Who is this man Jesus? He is a man like ourselves, not a mythical figure (which means, for Bultmann, that he never did those miracles); he is **without messianic radiance**...(a man) who renewed and radicalized the protest of the great Old Testament prophets against legalism and cultic worship of God, and who was delivered up by the Jews to the Romans and was crucified. **Everything else is uncertain and legendary.**[4]

SOURCES

In contrast to this skepticism of the form critics, serious Christians everywhere, including many scholars, believe that we have and know accurate history about the Messiah, Jesus, the son of Mary. This does not mean that Christians deny the use of oral and written source material from eyewitnesses by some or all of the Gospel writers. Luke acknowledges the fact in his preface with the following words:

> Many have undertaken to draw up an account of the things that have been fulfilled among us, just as they were handed down to us by those who from the first were **eyewitnesses and servants of the word**.
>
> Therefore, since **I myself have carefully investigated everything from the beginning**, it seemed good also to me to write an orderly account for you, most excellent Theophilus, so that you may know the certainty of the things you have been taught. (Luke 1:1-4).

Muhammad must have also used sources when he told the story of the Christians who slept 300 years, as recorded in the Middle Meccan Sura of the Cave (Al-Kahf) 18:9-26. If someone answers and says, "Ah, but Muhammad was ordered to include that by revelation," that is exactly what we Christians mean when we say that Luke was guided by the Holy Spirit in the things which he recorded.

When the form critics quoted by Bucaille on page 76, propose that there was a proto-Luke and proto-Mark, based on document this and document that, and when they say that everything is "uncertain and legendary," they ignore three things:

1. They ignore (or disbelieve) the fact that Jesus' disciples were around to verify what was being taught.

2. They ignore all the witnesses to Jesus' miracles. Dozens were present, if not hundreds, when he raised Lazarus from the dead. 5000 people ate the meal he provided by multiplying five loaves and two fish.

---

4. "Rudolf Bultmann's Interpretation of the Kerygma," *Kerygma and History*, Abingdon Press, New York, 1962, p 34.

3. They ignore the enemies of the early Christians. These people would quickly discredit any false stories.[5]

DISBELIEF IN THE ACCURACY OF ORAL TRADITION

It is clear from the above statements that the early form critics did not believe that oral tradition can be accurately remembered and transmitted. They did not believe that the original Christians could memorize Jesus' words and remember his miracles accurately for 30 or 35 years until the first Gospel account was completed sometime between 62 and 64 AD.

That these **European "form critics"** would deny the possibility of accurate memorization and transmission of facts may be understandable, but what of Dr. Bucaille? He has undoubtedly met Muslims who have memorized the whole Qur'an; and for him to quote these false ideas and agree with them is difficult to accept.

ROOTS—A SECULAR EXAMPLE

This ability of men to memorize and preserve history accurately has been popularized recently in the historical novel *Roots* by Alex Haley. In 1767, his great-great-great-great grandfather, a Gambian named Kunta Kinte, went out to the forest to find just the right tree for a drum. He was caught by slave traders, brought to the United States and sold as a slave. Always proud of his African heritage, he insisted that his family remember that his real name was Kunta Kinte; and he taught his daughter that in his African language a river was "Kamby Bolongo" (the Gambia river) and a guitar was called a "ko."

Starting with this information, Haley finally arrived at the village of Juffure in Gambia where there was a "griot" familiar with the history of the Kinte clan. Griots are men who have memorized the history of their tribe. They are walking archives of oral history and, according to Haley, "there were certain legendary griots who could narrate facets of African history for as long as three days without ever repeating themselves."[6]

When Haley got to Juffure, the griot began to recite the history of the Kinte clan from the time that their ancestors came from Mali, giving all the sons and daughters, the marriages, and certain historical events to fix things in time. After almost two hours, the griot said, **"About the time the King's soldiers came, the oldest of these four sons, Kunta, went away from his village to chop wood...and he was never seen again."**[7] Haley burst into tears and calls this the epic event in his life.

Going to London, later, Haley found the record of the "King's soldiers" being sent to Gambia, and he writes of the griot in Africa, "He had been so correct that I felt embarrassed that...I had been checking behind him." As Haley

---

5. For a complete and well-documented analysis of "form criticism" see *More Evidence That Demands a Verdict*, Josh McDowell, Campus Crusade, San Bernardino, CA 92414, 1975, p 183-299.
6. Haley, op.cit., p 715. Well written and worth reading.
7. Ibid., p 719.

continued searching he found the London record of the ship which had taken his ancestor to the U.S., and the U.S. record of the ship's arrival in "Naplis" (his grandmother's pronunciation of Annapolis).

After 200 years, the essential facts had been preserved solely by oral transmission on both sides of the Atlantic—by a chain of trained griots in Africa, and by a family of untrained men and women in America.

If men and women are able to memorize secular history and keep it correct for hundreds of years, and Muslims believe that their forefathers were able to memorize the entire Qur'an and transmit it correctly for 40 years before Othman made his recension, on what basis shall anyone say that Christians were not able to transmit the words and essential facts of Jesus' life for 20 to 60 years until they were written down between 50 and 90 AD?

If Muslims can memorize the 111 verses of the Sura of Joseph (Yūsuf), Sura 12, and transmit it correctly, on what basis shall anyone say that Christians were unable to memorize and transmit the 111 verses of the Sermon on the Mount as recorded in Matthew chapters 5-7?

If Muslims were able to memorize and transmit the hadiths about the battles of Badr and Uhud correctly, on what basis will anyone say that Christians were not able to transmit what the eyewitnesses said about Jesus' resurrection from the dead?

Who can imagine that Talha Ibn 'Ubaidu'llah ever forgot saving Muhammad's life at the battle of Uhud? It is inconceivable!

It is just as inconceivable that Jesus' disciples would ever forget seeing the nail marks in his hands, or how he ate fish with them when they saw him alive again after having witnessed his death on the cross.[8]

THE EFFECT OF FORM CRITICISM ON THE QURAN

Again I invite my Muslim readers to think carefully before they accept the theories of **"form criticism"** as proposed by Dr. Bucaille. Having made the assumption that Christians couldn't remember what Jesus said for thirty years, the form critics would certainly assume that the Muslims couldn't remember what Muhammad brought to them during the forty years from the first Meccan suras until Othman made the official copies of the Qur'an in about 26 AH. By then the suras would have become tales and myths—uncertain and legendary.

If the Christians went around inventing **"pericopes"** according to the needs of the Christian community, the form critics would surely say that the Muslims must have gone around inventing suras according to the needs of the Muslim nation.

If a "resurrection from the dead is utterly inconceivable" and giving sight to the blind is impossible, then the Qur'an is wrong when it says in the Sura of the Table (Al-Mā'ida) 5:113, from 10 AH,

> And you (Jesus) **heal those born blind**, and the lepers by My leave, and behold! **you bring forth the dead** by My leave.

---

8. These events are all found in Luke 24:36-49.

If the Virgin Birth is impossible, then the Qur'an is wrong when it tells, in the Middle Meccan Sura of Mary (Maryam) 19:19-21, how Gabriel promised Mary that she would have a "holy son" even though no man had touched her, and claims again that she was a virgin in the Sura of the Forbidding (Al-Taḥrim) 66:12, from 7 AH, saying,

> And Mary, the daughter of Imran, **who guarded her maidenhood**, and We breathed into it our Spirit; and she believed the words of her Lord, and His books, and **was of the devout**.

If God does not guide His prophets by the Holy Spirit then the Qur'an is wrong when it says twice in the Sura of the Heifer (Al-Baqara) 2:87 and 2:253, from 2 AH,

> ...We (God) gave Jesus the son of Mary clear signs and strengthened him with the **Holy Spirit**.

RELIGIOUS SKEPTICS?!?

The obvious question is how can people who call themselves Christians say such things? But it should be no surprise to Muslim readers that among those who call themselves "Christians" there could be men who do not believe in the supernatural. Have there not been similar writers among those who call themselves "Muslims"?

In his very evenly balanced book, *Islam—A Christian Perspective*, Michael Nazir-Ali of Pakistan writes as follows concerning the Muslim reformer Sir Syed Ahmad Khan,

> Theologically Sir Syed was of deistic inclinations and held that God was indeed the Ground of the Universe and it was he who had created nature and her laws...God does not, however, interfere in the course of nature, and occasional divine intervention in the affairs of man is ruled out altogether...
>
> **Sir Syed denies the Quranic doctrine of the Virgin Birth of Jesus Christ**, holding that such a birth would be an interference in the course of nature and was, therefore, impossible. In order to reconcile this *a priori* attitude with the testimony of the Qur'an, he offers the somewhat feeble explanation that when the Qur'an speaks of Mary's virginity it really means that she had intercourse only with her husband! An examination of the Quranic texts shows us the absurdity of such a position, and it is indeed true that no competent commentator of the Qur'an has attempted a denial of the fact that the Qur'an teaches her virginity.
>
> ...Sir Syed repeatedly affirms his belief in the inerrancy of the Qur'an and pleads only for a correct interpretation of it. In some cases it is quite clear, however, that his deism will not be reconciled to the supernaturalism of the Qur'an.[9]

9. The Paternoster Press, Exeter, 1983, p 109-110.

Conservative Muslims like the Wahhabis violently oppose these ideas of Sir Syed. Similarly a large number of conservative Christians, who **do believe in miracles** and **do believe the Gospel is true**, strongly oppose the anti-supernatural **basic assumptions** of both **"form criticism"** and the **"documentary hypothesis"** and consider them as lies of the Devil.

By now it should be clear that this theory is as harmful to the Qur'an as it is to the Gospel. If a fact found in both books, such as Jesus raising men from the dead, is false in the Gospel, then that same fact is false in the Qur'an; and the Qur'an is found to have been changed, altered, and corrupted—a conclusion which is clearly unacceptable to Muslims.

In the next chapter we shall examine the development of both the Qur'an and the Gospel, and hopefully it will become clear to everyone that there is absolutely no documentary or historical evidence for **"form criticism"** as it was conceived of by the above-mentioned German theologians; but first I should like to present a modern **pericope**.

THE SHORT CHAPTER WITHOUT A NUMBER
JUST A PERICOPE —
FOR THE NEEDS OF THE COMMUNITY

Recently Dr. Bucaille has written another book entitled *L'Homme D'Ou Vient-il?*[10] In this book he evaluates the evidence for evolution and finds it sadly wanting.

He quotes the well-known evolutionist J. Monod who acknowledges in his book *Le Hasard et la nécessité* his complete inability to explain the origin of new gene material with these words:

> The major problem is the origin of the genetic code and the mechanism of its translation. In fact, it is not just a "problem" of which one must speak, but rather a genuine riddle. p 82.

Over many pages Dr. Bucaille demonstrates in a very able manner that chance mutations cannot be the cause of a complicated organ like the eye, nor the complicated instinctive activity of birds or monkeys; nor will they explain the development and order of the complicated proteins used for the storage of the genetic code in the genes. On page 51 he says,

> This notion of the production of new structures, more and more complicated, unquestionably eliminates the effect of chance. Fortuitous and unforeseen variations, even though corrected by natural selection, would never have been able to assure such a progression in perfect order.

Or, in other words, **CHANCE WAS NOT THE CAUSE!** — a conclusion with which I am in complete agreement. He then goes on to ask the following question:

WHY THIS SLAVISH ACCEPTANCE OF EVOLUTION AS A FACT?

Dr. Bucaille analyses the cause of this almost total acceptance of an unproved theory in the following words:

> We live, unfortunately, at a time when sensational but erroneous information often captures the interest of the public, much more quickly than does a carefully weighed judgment, expressing some reservations and admitting those things which are unknown. p 11.
>
> This (information) has even more impact on the public, the greater the authority of the one who presents it, and the more that its expression receives image reinforcement like that offered by prime-time television. p 118.

Then in a third passage he makes the following analysis:

> "But if we lose sight of the real (of the genuine), even the

---

10. Seghers, Paris, 1982, page numbers are in the text. (translations mine)

wisest logic can only lead to falsehoods; which is precisely what happens with certain theories, such as neo-darwinism... p 48.

Dr. Bucaille wrote these words about evolution. They are equally true of the **"documentary hypothesis"** and **"form criticism."** The men who originated these theories **lost sight of the real**, and in spite of all the logic which they invested **the result was and is only falsehood**.

The "hackers," the modern-day computer specialists, say the same thing about their computers, but in less refined language. They have proposed the following "pericope" for the needs of the community:

Garbage (false information) in,
Garbage (false conclusions) out.

CHAPTER III

HISTORICAL DEVELOPMENT OF THE QUR'AN AND THE GOSPEL COMPARED

In Section Two we examined what the Qur'an and the Hadith say about this question of "taḥrif," of purposely changing the Gospel, and we found that neither of them support the charge. They both confirm the fact that **there was a valid Torah and Gospel present WITH Muhammad in Mecca and Medina during the 1st century of the Hejira.**

In the six parts of this chapter we want to approach the problem from another angle. We are going to compare the textual development of the Qur'an with the textual development of the Bible in order to see whether it is really possible that such lying changes could have been made; and if so, when and where this changing might have been done.

A. THE BEGINNING DEVELOPMENT OF THE QUR'AN AND THE GOSPEL

We shall start this discussion by "putting the shoe on the other foot," as we say in English. I shall pretend to claim that since the Qur'an doesn't say what I think a Qur'an ought to say, it must be that you—my Muslim readers—or your ancestors, changed the Qur'an. You purposely altered the Qur'an to make it say what pleases you.

What would you say? How would you try to answer this accusation?

First, you would say that the Qur'an was given by God. Then, when I asked how you know this, you would have to start telling me how it came into existence historically.

FIRST STAGES OF THE QUR'AN

According to those with whom I have discussed this question, the first verses of the Qur'an came to Muhammad thirteen or fourteen years before the Hejira, or sometime in the year 609 AD. During the next 13 years until the Hejira, almost exactly **two thirds of the Qur'an** was given. It was written down on the shoulder-blades of cattle, on leather, on white stones, on anything at hand, and it was memorized.

When I have asked how many believers fled with Muhammad from Mecca to Medina at the time of the Hejira, some have answered 75, others 150. The Qur'an does not give any definite number, but in the Sura of the Spoils of War (Al-Anfāl) 8:26, from 2 AH, it describes these believers using the following words:

> Call to mind when you were a small (band), despised through the
> land and afraid that men might despoil and kidnap you.

J. M. Rodwell in his English translation of the Qur'an agrees, saying, "The numbers who emigrated with Muhammad at first, were about 150 persons." [1] In addition, of course, there were already some believers at Medina who had invited Muhammad to join them, and probably others—especially slaves—who couldn't leave Mecca with Muhammad. However, for our discussion let us use this figure of **150 strong believers** who were willing to leave their homes because of their faith.

With this information in our minds we must now ask the following question. **How do you know that the Qur'an was accurately transmitted when there were only 150 strong believers?** Maybe some pieces of leather parchment were lost. Maybe a shoulder blade with two suras written on it fell off a camel. Do not think that I am laughing or making a joke! This is serious. **HOW DO YOU KNOW THAT THERE WEREN'T ANY CHANGES?**

You will no doubt say to me, "But they memorized the Qur'an; and some of those 150 believers were present when Muhammad first repeated the suras; and anyway, Muhammad was still with them to correct them."

I do not say "No" to this, but I want you to realize something. You can't prove this. You don't have even one original sura written on a shoulder blade. You **BELIEVE** it. This is **A BASIC ASSUMPTION**.

FROM THE HEJIRA TO MUHAMMAD'S DEATH

In the second or third year of the Hejira when the Muslims were victorious at the Battle of Badr, there were about 300 soldiers who defeated a much larger force from Mecca. Yusuf Ali in his translation of the Qur'an[2] says, "The Muslim force consisted of only about 313 men, mostly unarmed…The Meccan army, well-armed and well-equipped, numbered over a thousand." If we assume that each of these fighters had a wife and a couple of children at home, it would seem logical to suppose that there were 1500 Muslims at that time. It may have been more, but that is not important for our discussion.

In the year 6 AH Muhammad started toward Mecca to perform the pilgrimage. He was met by the Quraish at Hudaibiya and a truce was made. On that trip there were 1400 men with him, and so again we might suppose that altogether there were 6000 to 8000 Muslims.

After taking Mecca in 8 AH, and continuing to increase in numbers over the next two years, there were tens of thousands of believers when Muhammad died in 10 AH. Hamidullah says that at the last pilgrimage, Muhammad spoke to 140,000 Muslims.[3]

In those first ten years of the Hejira the last third of the Qur'an was given. So now again we must ask our questions. **How do you know that it was kept accurate in those ten years?** Maybe they never got to Mecca? Maybe there was no Battle of Badr? Maybe some of it got lost? **HOW DO YOU KNOW THAT IT WASN'T CHANGED?**

---

1. Koran, trans. by J. M. Rodwell, Everyman's Library, 1978. p 338, Note 1.
2. Yusuf Ali, op. cit., p 125, note 352 on Sura 3:13.
3. Hamidullah, op. cit., Introduction, p xiii.

Again you will answer, "But they memorized the Qur'an and Muhammad was still alive. And even after he died, many of those who fought at Badr—maybe as many as 200 or 250—were still alive. They were witnesses of that battle and of the words of Muhammad." And again I won't say "No," but I will point out the same truth to you.

You don't have a copy of the Qur'an from the year 10 AH. YOU BELIEVE that the Qur'an which is now in your hand is the same as the suras which the Muslims were memorizing in those first years. **YOU BELIEVE** the hadiths which tell about the origin of the Qur'an, and the Battle of Badr, and the treaty of Hudaibiya.

THE FIRST COLLECTION OF THE QUR'AN

We must now consider the manner in which the scattered suras and verses of the Qur'an were brought together into one book. Al Bukhari informs us that about a year after Muhammad's death, the Qur'an was first put together into one collection by Zaid ibn Thabit at the command of the Khalifa Abu Bakr. Zaid's own account, quoted by Al Bukhari, is this:

At the time of the slaughter of the people of Al Yamamah, Abu Bakr sent for me, and lo! Omar ibn al Khattab was with him. Abu Bakr said: "Verily Omar has come to me and has said, 'Truly the slaughter on the day of Al Yamamah was severe among the Reciters of the Qur'an and indeed I fear that there has been severe slaughter in the battlefields among the Reciters, therefore much of the Book is going away (being lost), and I consider that you should give orders for the collecting of the Qur'an.'

(Abu Bakr continued) "I said to Omar, 'How will you do a thing which the Apostle of God did not do?'

"Then Omar said, 'By God this is good,' and Omar did not stop from repeatedly urging me, until God expanded my breast to the idea and I have formed the same opinion as Omar has."

(Then) Abu Bakr said (to me), "Verily you are an intelligent young man. We do not distrust you, and you used to write out the revelation for the Apostle of God. Therefore search out the [various chapters and verses of] the Qur'an and gather it together."

And by God, if he had enjoined upon me the removal of one of the mountains, it would not have been heavier upon me than what he commanded me regarding the collecting of the Qur'an. I said, "How will you do a thing which the Apostle of God did not do?"

He said, "By God, it is good." Accordingly Abu Bakr did not desist from repeatedly urging me, until God expanded my breast to that which Abu Bakr's breast and that of Omar had explained to him.

Accordingly I sought out the Qur'an. I gathered it together from leafless palm branches, and thin white stones, and men's breasts, until I found the end of Surat Al-Tauba (9:128-129) with Abu Khuzaimah the Ansari. I didn't find it with anyone except him. "There came unto you an Apostle from among yourselves" to the conclusion of Bara'ah. And the sheets were with Abu Bakr until God caused him to die, then with Omar during his life, then with Hafsa, Omar's daughter.[4]

Hamidullah, in the introduction to his translation of the Qur'an, gives other interesting information from the hadiths about this collecting process, including a statement by Zaid that if the end of Surat Al-Tauba would have been three verses instead of two, he would have made it a separate Sura. Hamidullah also says that the sources are unanimous in saying that Abu Bakr ordered Zaid to not rely only on memory, but to find for each verse at least two written copies with two different people.[5]

As far as is known, this was the only copy of the Qur'an which might be termed an official copy, until Othman became khalifa. There were men such as Ubai b. Ka'b in Medina and Ibn Mas'ud in Kufa in Iraq who had made their own fairly complete copies, but most men and women were depending on what was memorized. **We may say then that for 40 years**, from 13 years before the Hejira when the first revelation was given until about 27 AH, when Othman made his official recension, **the transmission of the Qur'an was almost completely oral.**

So now the question must again be asked: **How do you know that the Qur'an was kept unchanged during those years when the transmission was almost entirely oral?** Maybe someone forgot something! Maybe a few verses were eaten by an animal! **HOW DO YOU KNOW THAT IT WASN'T CHANGED?**

There are hadiths which speak of these problems. On the authority of Omar himself, Muslim, the great collector of hadiths, quotes him as saying,

> Verily God sent Muhammad with the truth, and He sent down upon him the Book. Accordingly the Verse of Stoning was part of what God Most High sent down. The Apostle of God stoned, and we stoned after him, and in the Book of God stoning is the Adulterer's due. Mishkat, Kitab al Ḥudūd, p. 301.

Elsewhere Ibn Majah informs us that Aisha said:

> The verse of stoning and of sucking (See Section Four, Chapter II, 8a, Genetics and Milk-mothers.) came down...and its sheet was under my bed: when therefore the Apostle of God died, and we were occupied about his death, a tame animal came in and ate it.

And Hamidullah quotes Omar as saying,

---

4. Mishkat al Masabih, p 185. Also Al Suyuti, *Tārīkh al Khulafā',* Muhammadi Press, Lahore, 1304 AH, p 53.
5. Hamidullah, op. cit., p xxix and xxx.

If I hadn't feared the accusation of adding just anything to the Qur'an, I would have written the verse on the stoning of the adulterers.[6]

Again you will answer me and say, "I don't know about the validity of these hadiths, especially the one about Aisha; but even if they are true, no important change could possibly be made as late as 27 years after the Hejira. If one Muslim forgot something, the others would remember it. Besides, many of the Ansar and Companions were still alive to correct any errors."

THE SPREAD OF ISLAM OUTSIDE OF ARABIA

Moreover you would tell me that during these 27 years after the Hejira, Islam spread into many other countries. In 13 AH, Damascus and Syria were taken. The next year Muslim armies had reached Persia. In 19 AH or 641 AD Egypt was occupied, and by 25 AH the "futūḥāt" or wars of conquest had reached Armenia in northern Turkey.

Many of the soldiers and administrators who went into these countries had memorized parts of the Qur'an and knew the historical events concerning its origin. Some would have memorized all the suras of which they had knowledge.

Then you would conclude your answer and say to me, "**It is impossible** that as late as 27 AH anyone could have changed any important part of the Qur'an, the knowledge of which extended from Egypt to Persia and from Turkey to Arabia.

And again I won't say "No." But I will point out to you that **YOU BELIEVE IT.** You do not have this copy of the Qur'an gathered by Zaid Ibn Thabit from 12 AH "between your hands" (بَيْنَ يَدَيْكُمْ).

There is nothing wrong or illogical about believing these things, but when we turn now and examine the development of the Gospel, we are going to find that the reasoning and beliefs are almost exactly the same.

FIRST STAGES IN THE HISTORICAL DEVELOPMENT OF THE GOSPEL (INJĪL)

In this second part we shall see what Christians know and believe about how the Gospel came. But before we look at that, it is necessary to state clearly what is meant by the word "gospel." This English word is used to translate the Greek word EUANGELION which means **GOOD NEWS**. And though it is not commonly known, the Arabic word "Injīl" (الإنْجِيل) is a loan word derived from this same Greek word. The Greek EUANGELION entered into the popular languages used by the Christians in the Near East and Arabia during the first centuries of the Christian era, and finally came to be pronounced "Injīl" in the colloquial Arabic of the Quraish, the language in which the Qur'an was given.

What is this news that God named **GOOD NEWS**? It is the good news that

---

6. Hamidullah, op. cit., p xxx. (translation mine)

Jesus the Messiah died on the cross to bring forgiveness of sin; forgiveness to every one who believes him to be the suffering Saviour. We use such terms as "He shed his blood for us." "He was our sacrifice." "He redeemed or ransomed us." "He was the Lamb who took away the sins of the world."

Jesus, himself, taught this while celebrating the Jewish Passover with his disciples. Matthew tells us that "He took the cup, gave thanks and offered it to them, saying, 'Drink from it, all of you. This is my blood of the covenant, which is poured out for many for the forgiveness of sins' " (Matthew 26:27). We shall call this **"Doctrine A."**

We also believe that he could only do this because the **ONE CREATOR GOD**—Father, Son, and Holy Spirit—willed with one will that the Son—the Eternal Word or Kalima (الكَلِمَة), Jesus the Messiah—should come and do this task of redeeming men. We believe this because Jesus taught it. When he was brought to trial just before his death "the High Priest asked him,

'Are you the Christ, the Son of the Blessed One?'
'**I am**,' said Jesus" (Mark 14:61-62).

Thus, in his own words he claimed to be the Son of God, and we shall call this second belief **"Doctrine B."**

It is necessary to state clearly here that we do not believe that God had relations with a wife, a "ṣāḥiba" (الصَّاحِبَة), or with Mary. We agree completely with the Qur'an when it says in the Late Meccan Sura of the Cattle (Al-An'ām) 6:101,

How can He (God) have a son when He has no consort (ṣāḥiba)? He created all things, and He has full knowledge of all things."

Such a thought would be blasphemy. We understand and believe that the "Word" or "kalima" was in a spiritual unity with God the Father from eternity. The only new thing which was formed at his earthly appearance was a body in the womb of Mary.

Together "Doctrine A" and "Doctrine B" make up what I shall call the **Doctrinal Gospel**. As we consider the historical development of the Gospel, we shall be following the oral transmission of this **Doctrinal meaning** as well as the development of the written text.

A second meaning of the word "gospel" has grown out of the first one. It has come to be used for the **written** accounts of Jesus' life, death, and resurrection. From these written accounts, it is clear that Jesus knew how to read and write. In Luke 4:16 it says:

…on the Sabbath day he (Jesus) went into the synagogue, as was his custom. **And he stood up to read**.

But Jesus did not write down the Gospel himself.

Four different men were guided by the Holy Spirit of God as they told of Jesus' life here on earth. Originally people spoke of these accounts as "the Gospel of Jesus Christ according to Matthew" or "the Gospel of Jesus Christ according to Luke." However as time went on, Christians began to speak of them as the four **Gospels**. This may sound as though each man brought his own Gospel, but this is not what is meant. **We believe that Jesus the Messiah brought one true "good news" of salvation from sin—the one true Gospel.**

Lastly, there is another name which must be mentioned—the New Testament. This term refers to the book which contains the four Gospel accounts of Jesus' life and teaching, plus the letters of counsel and doctrine written by Jesus' disciples to different groups of Christians.

The Quranic word "Injil" clearly speaks of something written, but whether it includes these writings of Jesus' disciples and stands for the whole New Testament, or whether it refers only to the Gospel accounts of Jesus' life and work, is not clear.

Now back to the question of how the written Gospel came into existence. We too would say that it was given by God—that serious "men of God were led by the Holy Spirit" as they wrote. When asked how we know this, we too would have to start telling about the historical development.

THE BEGINNINGS OF THE GOSPEL

Christians understand that Jesus began to preach the Gospel when he was thirty years old. We know this from the third chapter of the Gospel of Jesus Christ according to Luke where we read,

> Now Jesus himself was about thirty years old when he began his ministry (Luke 3:23).

The problem with these early dates is rather similar to the problem which Muslims have with dating events in Muhammad's life before the Hejira. Christians were a disliked and often persecuted group for the first three hundred years after Christ ascended, so obviously the Roman authorities were not keeping records about them. However, there are two facts in the Gospels which help us to approximate the date of Jesus' birth.

The first one is that Herod the Great was king when Jesus was born (Matthew 2:1), and the second is that Pontius Pilate was already governor when Jesus started to preach (Luke 3:1,23).

According to secular history, Herod died in 4 BC, and Pilate became governor in 26 AD. If Jesus was born in 4 BC just before Herod died, and he started preaching at the age of 30 in 26 AD just after Pilate came to Jerusalem, then all the facts would fit, so we shall use this date of 26 AD for the beginning of Jesus' ministry.[7]

As Jesus went around Palestine preaching the Gospel, many people heard him. He challenged these hearers to follow him and some did. After some months he chose twelve for special training.[8] These men are called the twelve disciples, or twelve apostles (sent ones), because after Jesus ascended into heaven, they

---

7. Our calendar which was supposed to count from the birth of Christ was only adopted in about 550 AD. We now know that the calculations were in error by four years.

8. Luke 6:13.

were "sent" by Jesus to preach the "good news." The Qur'an refers to them as "al-ḥawāriyūn" (الْحَوَارِيُونَ) and, as we saw in Chapter I B of Section Two, it speaks highly of them, saying that they were "inspired" to believe in God and Jesus, and that they wanted to be God's helpers.

These men left everything to follow Jesus. Some gave up their fishing. Matthew left his job as a tax collector. For about three and a half years these men went everywhere that Jesus went. They heard his preaching. They saw his miracles. They were witnesses of all that he said and did.

According to Papias (a man who collected Christian hadiths and wrote them down sometime between 120 and 130 AD), "Matthew compiled the sayings (of Jesus) in the Hebrew language."[9] I believe that Matthew started collecting these "logia" or sayings during Jesus' lifetime, although he, or someone else, could have rearranged them and compiled them in a final form later, just as Zaid did with the Qur'an.

These men were also present when Jesus ascended into heaven. In Acts 1:9 we read,

> After he (Jesus) said this, he was taken up before their very eyes, and a cloud hid him from their sight.

Then the brothers of Jesus, his mother, and others who had been witnesses of Jesus' teaching and miracles also gathered with the apostles. The account continues:

> Then they returned to Jerusalem…Those present were Peter, John, James and Andrew; Philip and Thomas, Bartholomew and Matthew; James the son of Alphaeus and Simon the Zealot, and Judas son of James.[10] They all joined together constantly in prayer, along with the women and Mary the mother of Jesus, and his brothers. In those days Peter stood up among the believers **(a group numbering about a hundred and twenty)** and said… (Acts 1:12-16a).

From this information we can conclude that when Jesus ascended after three and a half years of preaching, **there were at least 120 strong believers who had left their homes for their faith**.

---

9. Papias was born between 50 and 60 AD when many people who had heard and seen Jesus were still alive. He became a bishop in what is now Turkey, and wrote "Interpretations of the Sayings of the Lord" sometime between 120 and 130 AD. Quotations from this work were given in 180 AD by Ireneus who wrote that Papias was a "hearer of John the Apostle and a companion of Polycarp" who was martyred as a Christian in 155 AD. This tradition or Christian Hadith with the above mentioned "isnad" is given by Eusebius in his *Church History*, V. 33, 4.1

10. Only 11 are named here. Judas Iscariot had hanged himself in remorse for his betrayal of Jesus.

OTHER WITNESSES

In addition to the twelve disciples there were hundreds of others who had heard Jesus' commands and had seen his miracles. Once, after preaching all day to a crowd of 5000 people and healing the ill and demon possessed among them, he fed them all by multiplying five loaves of bread and two fish, and there were twelve basketsful left over.[11]

At least three times Jesus raised people from the dead. The first time he raised the only son of a poor widow. The second time it was the daughter of an important Jewish leader. The third time it was Lazarus, an important man of Bethany.

The Qur'an also testifies to this healing power in the Sura of the Table (Al-M'ida) 5:113, from 10 AH, where it reads:

> And you (Jesus) heal those born blind, and the lepers, by My
> leave, and behold! you bring forth the dead by My leave.

Based on the information in the written Gospel, Jesus did at least 900 to 1000 miracles which were seen by as many as 15,000 people. In addition another 86,000 friends and family would have known the sick people and could testify that they had been ill or dead and were now healed.[12]

It is important to know about this vast number of people who were witnesses of Jesus' power in order to understand what happened next. Ten days after Jesus ascended into heaven, on the Jewish feast of Pentecost, Jesus' disciples began to preach this **Doctrinal Gospel** and the result was that **3000 people believed in one day**. In the book of Acts we read,

> When the day of Pentecost came, they (the apostles) were all
> together in one place....Then Peter stood up with the Eleven, raised
> his voice and addressed the crowd: "Men of Israel, listen to this:
> Jesus of Nazareth was a man accredited by God to you by **miracles,
> wonders and signs, which God did AMONG YOU** through him,
> **AS YOU YOURSELVES KNOW.** This man was handed over to
> YOU by God's set purpose and foreknowledge; and **YOU, with the
> help of wicked men, put him to death** by nailing him to the cross.
>
> "But God raised him from the dead, freeing him from the agony
> of death, because it was impossible for death to keep its hold on
> him" (Acts 2:1,14a,22-24).

It is clear from this quotation and the whole chapter that Peter was sure that his audience knew about Jesus' life and miracles, and that the listeners did not deny it. For when he ended his speech there was a tremendous response and they asked what they should do. Peter answered,

> "Repent and be baptized, every one of you in the name of Jesus
> Christ for the forgiveness of your sins. And you will receive the gift
> of the Holy Spirit."

---

11. John 6:1-40.

12. See Appendix A for a complete list of these miracles including estimates of the number of people present. This represented one out of every 20 people in the country at that time.

...Those who accepted his message were baptized, **and about three thousand were added to their number that day** (Acts 2:38 and 41).

This is the first public preaching of the **Doctrinal Gospel**. It took place ten days after Jesus ascended to heaven in about 30 AD and about 3000 people accepted Christ as their Saviour in one day.

Why am I discussing all this? Because it may be that this is the period of time when Muslims believe that we changed the Gospel. Therefore we will pose the questions concerning the Gospel in the very same words which we used concerning the Qur'an. **How do we Christians know that the Gospel was accurately transmitted when there were only 120 strong believers?** Maybe some pieces of papyrus paper were lost from Matthew's collection as they were traveling around Palestine with Jesus. Or, perhaps an animal ate a page while they stayed overnight in some home. **HOW DO WE CHRISTIANS KNOW THAT THERE WEREN'T ANY CHANGES?**

We also will answer that Jesus' followers memorized his words. While it is true that he did not give a direct command to memorize the Gospel, we have two reasons for saying this. First of all, the Jews had a strong tradition (and still do) of memorizing their Scriptures. It was customary in the Jewish religion for a student to memorize a rabbi's teaching. The Mishna says, "A good pupil is like a plastered cistern that loses not a drop" (Aboth ii, 8).

Secondly, it is certainly implied in the following words of Jesus:

> Why do you call me, "Lord, Lord," and do not do what I say? **I will show you what he is like who comes to me and hears my words and puts then into practice.** He is like a man building a house, who dug down deep and laid the foundation on rock. When a flood came, the torrent struck that house but could not shake it, because it was well built.
>
> **But the one who hears my words and does not put them into practice** is like a man who built a house on the ground without a foundation. The moment the torrent struck that house, it collapsed and its destruction was complete (Luke 6:46-49).

If you were a disciple and heard these words you would obviously try to memorize Jesus' sayings so that you could put them into practice and avoid "destruction."

And finally, we too would answer that his disciples were present when Jesus gave his teachings; and anyway, Jesus was with them and could correct them through this whole four years until he ascended just ten days before Peter spoke. But we can't prove this. That is, we do not have the original manuscript of Matthew's "oracles," or a tape recording of Peter's first preaching. We **BELIEVE** it. It is **A BASIC ASSUMPTION**.

FROM THE ASCENSION OF JESUS TO THE FIRST WRITTEN MANUSCRIPT

Over the next months the number of believers continued to increase. Following a miracle done in Jesus' name by Peter and John, Luke writes that "many who heard the message believed, and the number of men grew to about **five thousand**" (Acts 4:4).

The apostles were arrested and threatened by the Jewish leaders, but "day after day, in the temple courts and from house to house, they never stopped teaching and proclaiming the good news that Jesus is the Christ" (Acts 5:42). The result was that "the number of disciples in Jerusalem **increased rapidly**, and a large number of priests became obedient to the faith" (Acts 6:7).

THE SPREAD OF CHRISTIANITY OUTSIDE OF PALESTINE

When Peter preached the **Doctrinal Gospel** on that first Pentecost, there were Jews present from many nations. Luke described them as follows,

> Now there were staying in Jerusalem God-fearing Jews from every nation under heaven...Parthians, Medes, and Elamites (all in present-day Iran); residents of Mesopotamia (Iraq), Judea, and Cappadocia, Pontus and Asia, Phrygia, and Pamphylia (all in present-day Turkey), Egypt and the parts of Libya near Cyrene; visitors from Rome—both Jews and converts to Judaism; Cretans and Arabs... (Acts 2:5,9-11).

Many of these believed when they heard Peter's preaching and the testimony of the other disciples. They returned home to **Iran, Iraq, Rome, and Arabia**, and gave the Gospel message in their own lands to their own people.

Then persecution arose in Palestine against the Christians. Some were killed. Others scattered **into Judea and north into Samaria**, and "those who were scattered preached the word wherever they went." Philip preached to an **Ethiopian** who took the Gospel back to Ethiopia (Acts 8).

When Saul, who later became Paul the Apostle, was persecuting the Christians he traveled to **Damascus in Syria** because there were already believers there (Acts 9). Others, scattered by the persecutions mentioned above, traveled as far as **Phoenicia (Tyre and Sidon) and Cyprus**, and men from **Cyprus and Cyrene (Libya)** went to **Antioch in northern Syria (now southern Turkey)** (See Acts 11:l9-20).

In this same 11th chapter of Acts it mentions a famine that took place while Claudius was Emperor. He took office in 41 AD, so we can assume that the Gospel had spread to all these countries during the first 12 to 15 year of preaching.

In the next few years, this **Doctrinal Good News** was preached through **Turkey and Greece**, and by the year 49 AD we have extra-Biblical testimony that there were already Christians in **Rome**. In that year Claudius the Emperor began a persecution of the Jews and Christians which is mentioned by the Roman historian Suetonius. Writing in 120 AD, he recorded that,

As the Jews were making constant disturbances at the instigation of Chrestus (another spelling of Christ), he (Claudius) expelled them from Rome.[13]

Luke gives the same information in Acts 18:1-2 where we read,

> After this, Paul left Athens and went to Corinth. There he met a Jew named Aquila, a native of Pontus, who had recently come from Italy with his wife Priscilla, because Claudius had ordered all the Jews to leave Rome.

It is clear from these two witnesses that many Jews in Rome had become Christians, and that their witness had angered the unbelieving Jews so that they caused disturbances.

Thus, by 49 AD, or 23 years after Christ started preaching, Christians were to be found all over the Eastern Mediterranean and toward the West—at least as far as Rome. By now there were tens of thousands of believers, and probably hundreds of thousands.

A second event in this same chapter of Acts can be dated with great accuracy. The text says,

> So Paul stayed for a year and a half (in Corinth), teaching them the word of God. **While Gallio was proconsul of Achaia**, the Jews made a united attack on Paul and brought him into court (Acts 18:11-12).

At the beginning of this century, many scholars attacked Luke's truthfulness as a historian because of this statement. They said that there was no mention of Gallio having ever been in Corinth; and in addition they claimed that the Roman title "proconsul" had been used only in Gaul.

Since the writing of those attacks, a mutilated stone fragment has been found at Delphi, Greece, which states in part: "As Lucius Junius Gallio, my friend, and the Proconsul of Achaia..." The date of this inscription is 52 AD. From other sources we now know that he took office on July 1st and that his proconsulship lasted only one year. Thus it is clear that there was such a person as Gallio, that the title of proconsul was used outside of Gaul, that Paul's stay in Corinth included 52 AD, and that Luke's history is absolutely correct.

Sometime about the year **55 AD** while in Ephesus, Paul wrote a letter back to the church at Corinth—a letter which Christians refer to as I Corinthians. All Biblical scholars agree on the date of this letter, and we shall examine two passages in some detail. They are as follows:

> Paul, called to be an apostle of Christ Jesus by the will of God...to the church of God in Corinth...**Grace and peace to you from God our Father and the Lord Jesus Christ...God, who has called you into fellowship with his Son Jesus Christ our Lord**, is faithful (I Corinthians 1:1,2a,3,9).

---

13. *Life of Claudius* 25,4.

Now, brothers, I want to remind you of the **Gospel I preached to you**, which you received and on which you have taken your stand. **By this Gospel you are saved**...

For what I received I passed on to you as of first importance: that **Christ died for our sins** according to the Scriptures, that **he was buried**, that **he was raised on the third day** according to the Scriptures,

> and that **he appeared to Peter**,
> and **then to the Twelve**.
> After that, **he appeared to more than five hundred** of the brothers at the same time, most of whom are still living, though some have fallen asleep.
> Then **he appeared to James**, then **to all the apostles**, and last of all **he appeared to me** also, as to one abnormally born.

(I Corinthians 15:1-8)

You will notice that some phrases are in boldfaced type. When we look at these phrases, we find that:

> Paul believes Doctrine A that Jesus died for our sins and rose from the dead the third day.
> He believes Doctrine B that Jesus is the Son of God.

He preached this **Doctrinal Gospel** to them orally when he was with them in 52 AD so that they might be saved. Now he is repeating the same thing to the Corinthians in his letter written in 55 AD.

Though Matthew probably wrote his "oracles" while Jesus was on earth, and Luke says that, "Many (undertook) to draw up an account of the things that have been fulfilled among us,"[14] this letter to the Corinthians is the first portion of the **New Testament** which can be precisely dated. Therefore, although some other portions may have been earlier,[15] we can say with assurance that when Paul wrote the above two passages, the **Doctrinal Gospel**, which for 25 years until 55 AD had been transmitted largely by oral proclamation, **now became the Written Gospel**, which has been transmitted unchanged from that point in history until the present.

In photograph No 1 you can see part of I Corinthians 14 and 15 from the papyrus manuscript p46, preserved at the Chester Beatty Library in Dublin, Ireland. The text of this copy, which dates from around 200 AD, is used as the basis of our modern translations.

So now the questions must again be asked. **How do we know that the Gospel was kept unchanged during these years when the transmission was almost entirely oral?** Maybe someone forgot something. Maybe Jesus didn't raise Lazarus from the dead and claim, "I am the resurrection and the life." Maybe Jesus never ascended into heaven. **HOW DO WE KNOW THAT IT WASN'T CHANGED?**

---

14. Luke 1:1.
15. Many scholars believe that Mark's **Gospel** and James' letter date from the 50's, but there's no sure proof.

Photograph 1 —
Papyrus p 46 from 200 AD (145 years after the original).
Two sides of the same page showing I Corinthians 14:34b-15:15a
which lists five appearances of Jesus to one or more of his disciples.
By Permission of the Chester Beatty Library.

And we too will answer, **"No important change could possibly have been made during this 25 years since Jesus ascended**. They memorized Jesus' words. If one Christian forgot something the others would remember it. Moreover, John, Peter, James, Paul and others of the twelve special disciples were still alive to verify the things which Jesus said, and thousands were still alive who had seen Jesus' miracles. It is impossible that anyone could have changed any important part of the **Gospel**, the knowledge of which extended in 55 AD from Rome eastward to Syria and Iraq, and from Turkey south to Libya."

WE BELIEVE Paul's letter to the Corinthians to be valid even though we don't have the original copy "between our hands." **WE BELIEVE** the history recorded by Luke in the book of Acts to be reliable history because he was guided by the Holy Spirit of God while writing. In addition, his word is supported by Roman historians, and by documents and archaeological inscriptions which we, ourselves, can see today.

B. THE FINAL COLLECTION OF THE
QUR'AN AND THE GOSPEL

THE QUR'AN BY ZAID IBN THABIT AND HIS COMMITTEE

In the preceding section we followed the development of the Qur'an through to the completion of the first official copy when Abu Bakr was still Khalifa. There were, however, other men who made their own collections of suras, either as they heard them from Muhammad or by copying them from those who had.

One of the most well known is that of Abdullah Ibn Mas'ud who was the personal servant of Muhammad and was present at both Badr and Uhud. He claimed to have learned some seventy suras directly from the mouth of Muhammad, and tradition says that he was one of the first to teach Qur'an reading. It is also well-known that his collection differed in its order of the suras, and that it did not include Suras 1, 113, and 114.

Another of Muhammad's companions who made his own collection of suras was Ubai b. Ka'b. One of the Ansar, he served as Muhammad's secretary after Muhammad came to Medina. Ubai's codex was known to contain two suras not found in the Othmanic text—Surat al-Khal' and Surat al-Ḥafd, as well as a verse on men's greed following Sura 10:24. Before the appearance of Othman's text, Ubai's text was much used in Syria; and Ubai may have even helped Zaid prepare the official text for Othman.

In addition to these two men, Islamic history and hadiths mention primary collections made by Ali Ibn Abi Talib, the Prophet's son-in-law, whose codex was arranged in chronological order starting with Sura 96; by Ibn Abbas, whose codex is mentioned by al-Suyuti (Itqan, 154) as including the two extra suras of Ubai; and by Abu Musa, whose codex was used by the people of Basra. It also contained the two extra suras of Ubai (Itqan, 154) as well as the verse on the greed of men (Muslim, Sahih, 1, 285, 286).[1]

As we shall see in the following hadith, differences between collections were so great that Muslim soldiers from Iraq who followed Ibn Mas'ud's collection and the soldiers of Syria who followed Ubai's collection, accused each other of lying.

The problem became so severe that while Othman was engaged in the conquest of Armenia and Azerbaijan (in the year 25 or 30 AH), he was warned of what might happen by Hudhaifah ibn al Yaman as is explained in the following hadith:

> Hudhaifah therefore said to Othman: "Oh Commander of the Faithful, be careful of the people."
> He answered, "What is the problem?"
> Hudhaifah said, "I took part in the expedition against Armenia

---

1. Much of the information in this section is from *Materials for the History of the Text of the Qur'an*, Arthur Jeffery, E.J. Brill, Leiden, 1937.

where there were Iraqis as well as Syrians. But the Syrians follow the reading of the Qur'an according to Ubai ibn Ka'b, and they say some things which the Iraqis have not heard, so the latter accuse them of unbelief. In the same way the Iraqis, who follow the reading of Ibn Mas'ud, read some things which the Syrians have not heard, and the Syrians accuse them of unbelief. Restrain this people before they differ in the book, as do the Jews and the Christians."

Accordingly Othman sent to Hafsa, saying, "Send us the sheets that we may copy them into the volumes. Then we shall return them to you." Hafsa therefore sent them to Othman. Then he commanded Zaid ibn Thabit and Abdullah ibn al Zubair and Said ibn al As and Abdullah ibn Harith ibn Hisham, and they copied them into the volumes. And Othman said to the company of the three Quraishites, "When you differ, you and Zaid ibn Thabit, in any portion of the Qur'an write it in the dialect of the Quraish, for verily it came down in their dialect." And they did so until, when they had copied the sheets into the volumes, Othman restored the sheets to Hafsa. **And he** sent to every region a volume from what they had copied, and **commanded regarding everything of the Qur'an besides it**, in every sheet and volume, **that it should be burned.**[2]

Further evidence demonstrating the great effort made by Zaid and his committee in compiling their collection is found in the following hadith:

Ibn Shahab said that Kharijah ibn Zaid ibn Thabit told me that he heard Zaid ibn Thabit say, "When we copied the volume, there was missing from Sura al Aḥzāb a verse (33:23) which I used to hear the Apostle of God recite. Therefore we sought for it. And we found it with Khuzaimah ibn Thabit the Ansari from among the believers... Therefore we inserted it in its sura in the volume."[3]

Now that we have seen how Zaid Ibn Thabit went about his task of collecting and assembling the suras of the Qur'an, let us consider what is known about the composition of the Gospel accounts with special emphasis on Luke because we have the most information about his methods.

THE RECORDING OF THE GOSPEL ACCOUNTS

During the first 25 years after the ascension of Jesus all preaching of the Gospel was based on **(a) the prophecies about Jesus** found in the Torah of Moses, the Zabūr or Psalms of David, and the other Old Testament prophets; plus **(b) the eyewitness accounts of the apostles that the prophecies had been fulfilled**.

---

2. Tabari's Commentary, I, 20.
3. Mishkat, p 185. Bukhari derived this from Anas ibn Malik.

As time went on the Holy Spirit led the four evangelists to write down the life of Christ and his teachings. However, like the suras in the Qur'an, there is no date of composition in the text, so we don't know exactly when they were written. Papias, already mentioned above as a collector of Christian traditions, says that Matthew wrote the "oracles" (or sayings) of Jesus first; that Mark wrote what the Apostle Peter told him; that Luke was the companion of the Apostle Paul; and that John wrote the fourth Gospel in his old age at Ephesus.

Nevertheless, extra-Biblical history helps in approximating a date. Thus Tacitus, a Roman historian, mentions the Christians in his account of the burning of Rome in 64 AD while Nero was Emperor. He writes:

> But not all the relief that could come from man, not all the bounties that the prince could bestow, nor all the atonements which could be presented to the gods, availed to relieve Nero from the infamy of being believed to have ordered the conflagration, the fire of Rome. Hence to suppress the rumor, he falsely charged with guilt, and punished with the most exquisite tortures, the persons commonly called Christians, who were hated for their enormities. **Christus, the founder of the name, was put to death by Pontius Pilate, procurator of Judea in the reign of Tiberius**: but the pernicious superstition, repressed for a time broke out again, not only through Judea, where the mischief originated, but through the city of Rome also.[4] (boldfacing mine)

It is clear from the words in boldfaced type that Tacitus and the Romans believed that Jesus had been crucified under Pontius Pilate just as the Gospel accounts say. In addition, Tacitus confirms Nero's severe persecution of the Christians.

According to tradition, both Peter and Paul died in this persecution. Since Luke **does not** mentioned either the persecution or their death at the end of the book of Acts, evangelical Christian scholars think that Acts must have been written before this persecution, during the two years that Luke was with Paul in Rome. If this is true, then Acts would have been written in 62-63 AD, and Luke would have written his Gospel around 60 AD while waiting for Paul to be tried in Palestine.

LUKE'S QUALIFICATIONS AS A COLLECTOR

In Colossians 4:14 the Apostle Paul says of him that, "Luke, the physician…sends greetings." This, plus the quality of his Greek writing, shows him to have been an educated person.

He accompanied Paul personally on at least two occasions, once for a short time from Troas in Turkey to Philippi in Greece (Acts 16:10 to 16:40), and again for several years when he traveled with Paul from Philippi to Jerusalem, waited with Paul through more than two years of imprisonment in Palestine, and

---

4. Tacitus' Annals XV.44. Tacitus was born in 52-54 AD, and in ll2 AD was Governor of Asia (western Turkey).

then waited with him another two years during Paul's imprisonment in Rome (Acts 20:6 to Acts 28:31).

While in Jerusalem and Palestine, Luke had the opportunity to talk with many people who knew Jesus, including **James the half-brother of Jesus**. Luke describes his meeting with James in these words,

> The next day Paul and the rest of **US** went to see James, and all the elders (Acts 21:18 capitals mine).

James, as a full son of Mary and Joseph would have known about Jesus' miraculous birth and how he worked with Joseph in the carpenter shop. Luke is the only writer to tell of Jesus' conversation with the teachers in the Temple at the age of 12 (Luke 2:41-50), a fact which he could have easily learned from James.

It is recorded in I Corinthians 15:7 that after Jesus rose from the dead he appeared to James. Obviously when Luke saw James, he would have asked James about this appearance and what Jesus said to him.

In addition to asking James, if **Mary** was still alive Luke would have been able to ask her personally about the miraculous birth of the Messiah. For Luke is the only writer who tells how the Angel Gabriel spoke to Mary and said,

> The Holy Spirit will come upon you, and the power of the Most High will overshadow you, and the child to be born will be called, "holy, the son of God." (See Luke 1:26-38.)

During the more than two years that Paul was in prison in Palestine, Luke would have been able to contact literally **hundreds of people** who had seen Jesus' miracles and heard his words; and he would have been able to interview **many of the "more than five hundred"** who saw Jesus at one time after he rose from the dead (I Corinthians 15:6).

Lastly, we know that Luke knew **Mark** because they were with Paul at the same time. At the end of his letter to the Colossians, Paul writes,

> My fellow prisoner Aristarchus sends you his greetings, as does Mark, the cousin of Barnabas...Our dear friend Luke, the doctor, and Demas send greetings (Colossians 4:10,14).

According to a hadith of Papias, Mark wrote his record of Jesus' life and sayings from the mouth of Peter. Comparison of the two Gospel accounts suggest that Luke almost certainly knew about Mark's work and used it as one of his sources. He may have even gotten his copy of Mark's Gospel directly from the author right there in Paul's prison. All this information indicates clearly that Luke had excellent opportunities to verify the facts of the Gospel, just as Zaid Ibn Thabit and his committee verified the collection of the Qur'an.

LUKE'S COLLECTION METHOD

As with the Qur'an, so with the Gospel, various men made collections of Jesus' words and acts. Luke mentions this in the preface of his Gospel where he describes his own collecting activities in these words:

> **Many have undertaken to draw up an account of the things that have been fulfilled among us**, just as they were handed down to us by those who from the first were eyewitnesses and servants of the word. Therefore, **since I myself have carefully investigated everything from the beginning**, it seemed good also to me to write an orderly account for you, most excellent Theophilus, so that you may know the certainty of the things you have been taught (Luke 1:1-4).

Luke first tells us that many people made collections of Jesus' sayings, including descriptions of his miracles, which they heard from those who were "eyewitnesses and servants of the word." "Word" here means Jesus, who is called the "Word of God" (Kalimatu Allāh أللهِ كَلِمَةُ) first in the Gospel and then in the Qur'an. Then Luke says, "I, myself, have carefully investigated everything" (e.g., he searched for at least two witnesses), and finally he wrote it up in an orderly account for a man named Theophilus.

Neither Luke, nor any traditions, say "two witnesses." I assume this from Deuteronomy 19:15 which says,

> One witness is not enough to convict a man accused of any crime or offense he may have committed. A matter must be established by the testimony of two or three witnesses.

If two witnesses are necessary to verify human crimes and offenses, how much greater the necessity for two witnesses in matters of God's holy word. Now let us look quickly at what is known about the other **Gospels**.

MARK

Mark was originally from Jerusalem and could have known Peter and the other apostles in his youth. We know that later in his life he was with Peter in Rome because in his second general letter to the Christians Peter writes,

> She (the church) who is in Babylon (Rome), chosen together with you, sends you her greetings, and **so does my son, Mark** (I Peter 5:13).

Therefore, the statement of Papias that Mark wrote down what Peter told him is quite possible. Whether Peter told the Gospel in Aramaic and Mark was translator as well as scribe, we do not know, but those who are familiar with both Aramaic and Greek say,

> There is no lack of evidence in (Mark's) Gospel that much of the material originally existed in Aramaic; his Greek in places preserves the Aramaic idiom quite unmistakably.[5]

---

5. *The New Testament Documents: Are They Reliable*, F.F. Bruce, Intervarsity Press, Downers Grove, Ill. 5th Ed., 1960, p 37.

According to tradition, Peter was executed during the persecution of the Christians by Nero which began in 64 AD. Mark could have written things down from memory after Peter's death as Dr. Bucaille suggests when he gives a date of 70 AD; but since Luke, who probably wrote his Gospel account in 60 AD, knew of Mark's Gospel and used it as one of his sources, most conservative scholars, along with early church fathers like Origen, Jerome and Clement of Alexandria, place it in the 50's.

As we shall see later, Dr. Bucaille's choice of the year 70 AD has nothing to do with either internal or external evidence. It follows from the "**basic assumption**" underlying "form criticism," the assumption that miracles of prophecy are impossible.

MATTHEW

Concerning Matthew's account, again the date is not known. As we shall see later, Matthew is quoted in the earliest Christian letters and writings which we have, and Papias says that Matthew was the first to write down the "sayings" of Jesus.

From the Gospel accounts we know that Matthew was a tax-collector before he responded to Jesus' call to follow him. As a tax collector he would have needed to know Latin and Aramaic to keep records of the debts people owed the Romans, and he would probably have known Greek, the trade language of the epoch. Thus there is good reason to believe that he possessed the skills necessary to record Jesus' words, and Papias says in another hadith that Matthew wrote the "logia" or sayings of Jesus in the Hebrew dialect (Aramaic).

As Matthew followed Jesus around from village to village and listened to his preaching, he wrote down the lessons which Jesus taught. These notes were probably not dated, just as the suras of the Qur'an are not dated, and it obviously makes no difference on what day or in which village Jesus said, "Be perfect as your Father in heaven is perfect" (Matthew 5:48).

Later another person, who like Luke made his own collection of Jesus' acts and sayings, took the material Mark had gotten from Peter, translated Matthew's collection of Jesus' sayings into Greek, and added them to Mark in the form of five teaching lessons—the most famous of which is the "Sermon on the Mount" (Matthew 5-7).

In this sermon Jesus speaks of prayer, fasting, divorce, adultery in the heart and other attitudes of the inner spiritual life, including one of the most difficult commands ever given by God. Jesus said,

> But I tell you: **Love your enemies and pray for those who persecute you**, that you may be sons of your Father in heaven (Matthew 5:44-45a).

Jesus kept this commandment and fulfilled it when he prayed for those who were crucifying him, saying, "Father (God), forgive them, for they do not know what they are doing" (Luke 23:34).

Also it is very clear from this commandment that **"sons of your Father in heaven" speaks of a spiritual relationship.** There is absolutely NOTHING physical about it.

Other materials found only in the Gospel of Matthew include the account of the wise men who came from the East to bow down to Jesus as the newborn king of the Jewish nation. Whether this account came from Matthew's collection or not we just don't know, for no copy of Matthew's collection of "sayings" has come down to us, just as there is no longer any copy of Ibn Mas'ud's collection of the Qur'an.

Finally, in the same way that the suras of the Qur'an received names from some word found in them, so this collection was named "according to Matthew" because of the material which came from him.

JOHN

The date of John's Gospel has usually been given as 90-95 AD in the Apostle's old age, but there are no statements in the Gospel which will allow us to date it. In recent years, scholars have begun to propose an earlier date.

William Foxwell Albright, who was one of the world's foremost Biblical archaeologists, said: "We can already say emphatically that there is no longer any solid basis for dating any book of the new Testament after about 80 AD."[6]

DR. BUCAILLE'S DATES AND WHY

Dr. Bucaille quotes several New Testament scholars in the field, and settles on the following dates for the composition of the four Gospel accounts: Matthew in 80 AD, Mark 70 AD, Luke 70-90 AD, and John in the 90's. Notice that all of these dates are after 70 AD!! Why? Because Jerusalem was destroyed in 70 AD, and Matthew, Mark, and Luke all record Jesus' prophecy that Jerusalem and the temple would be destroyed. Mark records the prophecy with these words:

> As he (Jesus) was leaving the temple, one of his disciples said to him, "Look, Teacher! What massive stones! What magnificent buildings!"
>
> "Do you see all these great buildings?" replied Jesus. **"Not one stone here will be left on another; every one will be thrown down"** (Mark 13:1-2).

The men whom Dr. Bucaille has chosen to quote are those who accept the **"documentary hypothesis"** and **"form criticism"** which we discussed in Chapters II and III of this section. You will remember that the men who first proposed these theories had as one of their **BASIC ASSUMPTIONS** that miracles, including prophecy, are impossible.

Therefore, because of this "basic assumption," **they HAVE to place the date of writing of these words** after the destruction of Jerusalem—i.e., **after the event which was prophesied took place.**

---

6. Albright, *Recent Discoveries in Bible Lands,* Funk and Wagnalls, New York, 1955, p 136.

As was stated above, there is not one fact in any of the four Gospel accounts which indicates the date when they were written. They could have been written in the first decade immediately after Jesus' death. A recent author, John A. T. Robinson, in his book entitled *Redating the New Testament,* published in 1976, concludes that the whole New Testament was written before the Fall of Jerusalem in 70 AD.[7]

Dr. Bucaille included a diagram of the collection of the Gospel accounts in his book on page 76 and presented it as proof that the Bible has been manhandled, altered, and changed. Diagram 1 demonstrates the collection of the Gospel material as it has been described in these pages.

Diagram 1 — THE COLLECTION OF THE GOSPEL

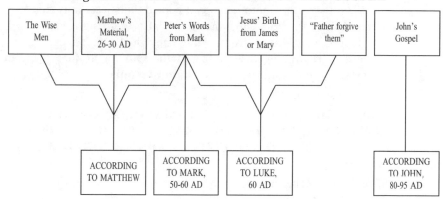

It is obvious from this diagram that I do not agree at all with Dr. Bucaille's dating. But even if we accept his dates instead of mine, all scholars are agreed that many of the New Testament books were written between 52 and 70 AD; that all of them were written by 95 AD; and that all of the New Testament authors believed firmly in the Doctrinal Gospel.

I stress these dates of 52 to 70 AD because they represent a time period of 26 to 44 years after Jesus first started preaching. When we remember that Othman's official copies of the Qur'an were sent out, at the earliest, around 26 AH or **40 years after Muhammad started preaching**, we see that the time frames for the distribution of the written Gospel and the distribution of the written Qur'an are very similar.

And again you may ask the question, **"BUT HOW DO YOU KNOW?"**

We will answer:

WE BELIEVE the disciples were upright men who wanted to know and obey God's truth, and the Qur'an agrees with this statement when it says that they were "inspired" and wanted to be God's helpers.

WE BELIEVE that there were many other eyewitnesses to Jesus' life and miracles who could control the truth.

7. Robinson, *Redating the New Testament,* London: SCM Press, 1976.

WE BELIEVE that the accounts were written early, and of even more importance **WE BELIEVE** that the Holy Spirit guided in the writing.

But we don't have absolute proof in the sense of having the original copy of the book of Acts, or of Luke's Gospel.

OTHMAN'S "VERY SPECIAL AND UNIQUE PRECAUTIONS" WITH THE TEXT OF THE QUR'AN

At the beginning of this section several hadiths were quoted telling about the final collection of the Qur'an by the committee of Zaid ibn Thabit. I am repeating here the last few lines of one of these hadiths because we must now talk about the last sentence. It reads as follows,

> ...When they (the committee) had copied the sheets into the volumes, Othman restored the sheets to Hafsa. **And he** sent to every region a volume from what they had copied, and **commanded, regarding everything of the Qur'an besides it, in every sheet and volume, that it should be burned.**[8]

We must note carefully that last sentence.

...AND HE (OTHMAN)...COMMANDED, REGARDING EVERYTHING OF THE QURAN BESIDES IT, IN EVERY SHEET AND VOLUME, THAT IT SHOULD BE BURNED.

Othman decided to make sure that there were no variations in the Qur'an. To do this he burned all the copies, except the one made by ibn Thabit's committee.

He burned the copy of Ali, the prophet's son-in-law.

He burned the copy of Ubai b. Ka'b. Ibn Abi Dawud records that when some Iraqis asked the son of Ubai to see his father's collection of suras, the son answered that Othman "had seized it" (qabaḍahu قَبَضَهُ).[9]

He ordered Ibn Mas'ud far away in Iraq to destroy his private copy. Ibn Mas'ud refused while alive, but it also was eventually destroyed.

If Othman had not ordered all the other copies of the Qur'an to be burned, there would be four (or more) separate testimonies to its validity. **He burned Qur'ans which were the primary collections, made by eyewitnesses and earwitnesses of what Muhammad said.**

We saw above that the Torah says that there must be at least two witnesses, but Othman destroyed the plurality of witnesses and turned them into one. At least one hadith says, "He found the Qur'ans many and left one; he tore up the Book."[10]

In all seriousness I now ask my Muslim readers: On what basis can you prove to yourselves, let alone to non-Muslims, that there was **no "changing of the text"** (al-taḥrīf al-lafẓī اَلتَّحْرِيفُ اَللَّفْظِي)؟

---

8. Tabari's *Commentary*, I, 20.

9. Ibn Abi Dawud, (Died 316 AH/928 AD) *Kitab al-Maṣaḥif*, hand copied by Arthur Jeffery from a hand-written copy in the Zahiriya Library at Damascus (Hadith, No. 407), p 25, reproduced in *Materials for the History of the text of the Qur'an*, Arthur Jeffery, E. J. Brill, Leiden, 1937.

10. Tabari, I, 2952, 10; II, 516, 5.

118

And what does Dr. Bucaille say about this action of Othman?! He has a tiny paragraph with one carefully constructed sentence!! He writes:

> We know that after the death of Muhammad, Islam spread with great rapidity, and far from its region of origin, among people, of whom a large number did not know Arabic. **They took SOME SPECIAL AND UNIQUE PRECAUTIONS (des précautions toutes particulières) so that the Quranic text did not suffer from this expansion.**[11] <sic> (capitals and translation mine)

Let us repeat that last sentence.

> **They took SOME SPECIAL AND UNIQUE PRECAUTIONS so that the Quranic text did not suffer from this expansion.**!! <sic><sic><sic>

Imagine what Dr. Maurice Bucaille would have said if Christians wrote one tiny line like this? We would have been accused of dialectical acrobatics, hiding the truth, deceiving the faithful, etc. We will now have a new sign in our book. Our new sign is made like this (-@-@-@). It represents three somersaults of dialectical acrobatics.

Dr. Bucaille condemns the Christians in strong language, saying that **"Perhaps** a hundred gospels were suppressed"[12] (though he gives no reference for this information), and that certain texts were "brutally thrust aside." This may have been true in some local area, but since church leaders had no political power until a number of years after Constantine I became Emperor in 324 AD, it was impossible for them to have taken such an action.

That books were burned in those early years is true, but it was done on the orders of a non-Christian. **In 303 AD, the pagan Emperor Diocletian ordered the destruction of all of the sacred books of the Christians—both Canonical and apocryphal.** This, no doubt, resulted in the destruction of many books, **but it was not done by the church.**

Not until **393 AD** at the Synod of Hippo in North Africa did any church council make a list of the books officially accepted as having been written under the direction of the apostles. But when we realize that the Codex Vaticanus and the Codex Sinaiticus were both written 40-50 years before this Synod met, and both contain all 27 books of the present **Gospel-New Testament**, it is clear that those 27 books were accepted by the believers during three centuries of open discussion, during a time when the church had no political power to enforce its rules.

That Dr. Bucaille should bring this up at all when he has said nothing about Othman's actions is incredible. Moreover, he dares to go on with these words:

> One may join Father Boismard in regretting the disappearance of a vast quantity of literature declared apocryphal by the

---

11. L'Homme, p 163.
12. Bucaille, BQ&S, p 78.

Church although it was of historical interest.[13] <sic>

Dr. Maurice Bucaille "regrets" with Father Boismard "the disappearance of a vast quantity of literature declared apocryphal, etc," yet he has so little regret over Othman's action of burning the original copies of the Qur'an that he doesn't even consider it worth mentioning. He slides right over it with the polite little phrase **"SPECIAL AND UNIQUE PRECAUTIONS"** (-@-@-@).

Jesus said,

> Why do you look at the speck of sawdust in your brother's eye
> and pay no attention to the plank in your own eye? (Matthew 7:3).

Thrusting some texts aside, even if done "brutally" (to use Dr. Bucaille's word), is surely a "speck of sawdust" compared to the "plank" of burning original collections of the Qur'an—collections made by some of the most trusted companions of Muhammad.

Furthermore, it should be noted that the rejected Gospels and letters which Dr. Bucaille does mention by name, some of which we shall consider in Part D of this chapter, all contain the **Doctrinal Gospel** with one exception.[14]

THE FATE OF THE UNIQUE FIRST COPY OF THE QUR'AN

Finally, we must mention the destruction of the unique first copy of the Qur'an collected at the order of Abu Bakr, which, because of his oath, Othman had returned to Hafsa. After Othman's death, Marwan the Governor of Medina sent to Hafsa and demanded it. She refused to give it up, so it stayed with her until she died. But Marwan was so concerned to have it that as soon as he returned from her funeral, he immediately sent to get it. The story is recorded by Ibn Abi Dawud (died 316 AH) in his *Kitab Al-Maṣaḥif*. He gives the isnad down to Salem ben Abdullah who said,

> When Hafsa died and we returned from her funeral, Marwan
> sent with firm intention to Abdullah ben Omar (Hafsa's brother)
> that he must send him those pages, and Abdullah ben Omar sent
> them to him, and Marwan ordered it and they were torn up. And
> he said, "I did this because whatever was in it was surely written
> and preserved in the (official) volume and I was afraid that after a
> time people will be suspicious of this copy or they will say there is
> something in it that wasn't written."[15] (translation mine)

With that destruction and the eventual destruction of Ibn Mas'ud's copy in Kufa, the primary sources were all destroyed with no copies having been made of them. However, for the first two or three centuries after the Hejira, called the

---

13. Ibid., p 78.

14. The exception is the Gospel of Barnabas. This gospel contradicts the Qur'an 20 times, calls Muhammad the Messiah seven times, has severe scientific errors, and over 30 errors of history, geography, social customs, religious customs and religious language which no first century Jew would make. It was probably written between 1500 and 1600 AD as an intentional forgery. For details see *The Gospel of Barnabas – Its True Value*, William F. Campbell M.D., Christian Study Center, Rawalpindi, 1989.

15. Ibn Abi Dawud, p 24-25, reproduced in Jeffery, op. cit.

period of original thinking (ijtihād), Quranic teachers would speak of preferring the reading of one or another of the companions of the prophet. But finally this became so intolerable for orthodoxy that even such an eminent Quranic authority as the great Baghdad scholar Ibn Shanabudh (245-328 AH) was forced to make public recantation of his use of readings from the old codices.[16]

Dr. Bucaille has repeated many times in his book that Christians altered, changed, and manhandled the Gospel. If that is true, what is to be said about Othman and his committee, and Marwan? Did they not manhandle, alter, and do as they pleased with the Qur'an?

A few pages back, the origin of the four **Gospels** was presented in the form of a diagram. The same thing can be done for the Qur'an. Diagram 2 portrays the origin and transmission of the Qur'an as it was recounted for us in the above hadiths.

Diagram 2 — THE COLLECTION OF THE QURAN

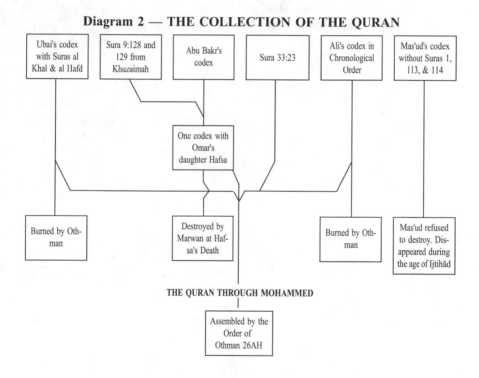

The diagram could be made much more complicated by adding other codices such as that of Abu Musa Al-Ash'ari which was used at Basra, but the essential information is clear and shows the many parallels in the recording of the Gospel and the Qur'an.

---

16. Jeffery, op. cit., p 9.

We shall now ask the question again. **HOW DO YOU KNOW that the Qur'an which you have WITH YOU is exactly the same as that given by Muhammad?**

CONCLUSION

If, in spite of this "manhandling" and suppression of evidence by Othman, Muslims **BELIEVE** that there has been no change of any importance in the essential doctrines of the Qur'an, on what basis shall anyone say that the Gospel does not contain the essential doctrines of Jesus?

If the Qur'an, which came 600 years later, does not agree with the Gospel-New Testament, Muslims will have to find some other explanation than "Taḥrif." To charge lightly and easily that "the Christians changed the Gospel" is a **basic assumption** for which no proof has been provided.

Christians agree wholeheartedly with the idea expressed in the Late Meccan Sura of Jonah (Yūnus) 10:64 when it declares,

"There is no change in the Words of God."

VARIANTS IN THE QUR'AN

In spite of this great effort to prevent the occurrence of variant readings in the text of the Qur'an, quite a number may still be found. Al Baidawi mentions some in his commentary on Suras 3:100; 6:91; 19:35; 28:48, 33:6, etc. This last one from the Sura of the Confederates (Al-Aḥzāb) 33:6, from 5-7 AH, is also mentioned by Yusuf Ali. The Othmanic text reads,

> The prophet is closer to the believers than their own selves, and his wives are their mothers.

but there are reports stating that Ubai b. Ka'b's text read,

> The prophet is closer to the believers than their own selves, **and he is a father to them**, and his wives are their mothers.[1]

Muhammad Hamidullah has quite a detailed discussion of these variations in the preface to his French translation of the Qur'an.[2] He divides them into four classes.

1. Variations caused by a scribe who makes an error while copying. Naturally these are easy to find by comparing with other copies.

2. Variations caused by someone writing notes of explanation in the margin. Hamidullah writes:

> The style of the Qur'an was such that sometimes even the companions of the Prophet had to ask him for explanations. Sometimes they noted these explanations in the margin of their personal copies in order to not forget them. It is completely understandable that sometimes the scribe mixed the text and the commentary while trying to faithfully make a new copy from an old one. We know of the famous order of Omar, which formally forbids the adding of commentary to copies of the Qur'an.
>
> **There are hundreds of variant readings of this type.** But the fact that "the Qur'an of such and such a teacher" has a certain addition which the others don't have, leaves no doubt as to the origin of that addition. Also, the information concerning this type of variant given by the classical authors is sometimes contradictory— some saying that the Qur'an of so-and-so had a certain addition— others denying it.

3. Variations caused by the permission originally given by Muhammad to recite the Qur'an in other dialects than that used by the people of Mecca.

> Muhammad tried to make religion easy for even the most

---

1. Yusuf Ali, op. cit., Note 3674, p 1104.
2. Hamidullah, op. cit., p xxxiii, (translation mine of all his notes).

humble. Therefore, he tolerated some dialectical variations even for the text of the Qur'an because the essential thing was not the word but the sense; not the recitation, but the application and the assimilation. He said willingly, "Gabriel permitted me to have up to seven different readings." While guarding for himself and his fellow citizens a certain reading, he permitted the members of different tribes to replace certain words by their equivalents—better known in their tribe. (Later Othman stopped this also.) But from copies made in outer areas and kept by their descendants, the teachers from previous centuries were able to gather a certain number of such words, which are exact equivalents of those used in the official version.

4. Variations coming from the fact that for the first 150 to 200 years after the Hejira, the handwritten copies of the Qur'an were written without vowel marks, and without dots to distinguish between different letters written in the same way.

What does it mean to write without vowel marks? It is hard to give an example that would be clear to English readers, but perhaps the following will help. The sentence "he painted the barn" would be "h pntd th brn" if written without vowels as in Arabic. After one tries this for a while, one gets used to it, and the above sentence couldn't be anything else. However, if we consider the sentence "h gv hm a bd," it might mean "he gave him a bed" if he was in a furniture store, or "he gave him a bud" in a florist's shop, or "he gave him a bid" if he was a contractor. In most cases the context would make this type of situation clear, but not always.

Secondly, to compound the problem, there are certain letters in Arabic which are written in exactly the same way except that they have dots over them or under them to show the difference. One of these letters is made somewhat like an English "i," but in Arabic one dot above ن = n, 2 dots above ت = t, three dots above ث = th, one dot below ب = b, and two dots below ي = y as in the words "you" or "yours."

There are seven other pairs of letters in which the two members of the pair are told apart by the number of dots, and one group of three. Or, to put the problem simply, there are only 15 letter forms to represent 28 different letters.

I have spoken to many Muslims who do not know that the first copies of the Qur'an were written without vowel marks and without dots; and perhaps some among my readers are among them. Photograph 3 shows verses 34-36 of Sura 24, the Sura of the Light (Al-Nūr), as found in an old Qur'an preserved at the British Museum in London. According to the experts it is from the end of the eighth century AD, or about 150 AH.[3]

---

3. This is the oldest copy of the Qur'an that I have been able to verify personally (have "between my hands").

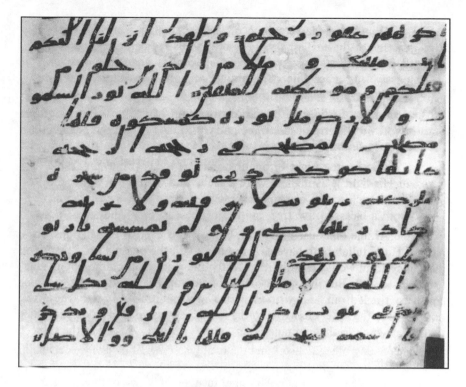

Photograph 2 —

A Qur'an from 150 AH without vowels and without dots
to differentiate the letters, showing Sura 24:34-36.
By Permission of the British Library.

In order that non-Arabic-speaking readers may appreciate the problem
clearly, I have reproduced the seventh line from the top of the picture:

As in the
Qur'an above. (149a)

With dots to
distinguish between
the consonants. (149b)

With the vowel
marks added. (149c)

Hamidullah discusses this lack of vowels and dots in another passage from
the same page. He writes,

125

Finally, a (last) source of variants comes from the Arab writing of the earliest times, before the use of diacritical marks. It is sometimes possible to read a word as an active verb or passive, as masculine or feminine, and the context sometimes admits several possibilities.

An example of this type of variant is found in the above photograph. Starting toward the end of line three and continuing to the end of line seven, the text reads:

God is the Light of the heavens and the earth. The parable of His light is as if there were a niche and within it a lamp: the lamp enclosed in glass: the **glass** as it were a brilliant **star**: **lit** from a blessed olive tree, neither of the east nor of the west...

In the Arabic texts used for their English and French translations Yusuf Ali and Hamidullah both have يُوقَدُ (yūqadu) for the passive verb "lit." This masculine form would usually refer to the preceding masculine noun "star" (kaukab كَوْكَب). But in line six of the photograph we find one letter which has been singled out and written with vowel points. It is توقد. These two points above the letter change it to the feminine passive تُوقَدُ (tūqadu) which then refers back to the feminine noun "glass" (zujāja زُجَاجَة) as the subject.

This Qur'an was copied when it was still possible for a scholar to say, "I prefer the reading of so-and-so," and the man who ordered the copy, or made it, believed that the feminine passive form was correct.

Since a translator like Yusuf Ali might mention only two or three variants in his whole translation, the impression is given that there are very few. Hamidullah is one of the few Muslim authors who has been willing to admit, as we saw above, that "there are hundreds of variant readings." In fact, there are thousands. In Arthur Jeffery's work where he has listed all the variants which he has found reported in any document, there are more than 1700 attributed to Ibn Mas'ud alone.

Most of them, 99.9%, are like the above example and have very little importance, but a few represent real problems such as the following example from the Sura of the Table (Al-Mā'ida) 5:63, from 10 AH. The verse reads:

Shall I tell you of an evil worse than that, for retribution with God? He who **God cursed** him, and **was angry with** him, and **made some** of them into monkeys and pigs, **and worshiped (the idol) al-ṭāghūt**.

قُلْ هَلْ أُنَبِّئُكُمْ بِشَرٍّ مِنْ ذَلِكَ مَثُوبَةً عِنْدَ اللهِ
مَنْ لَعَنَهُ اللهُ وَ غَضِبَ عَلَيْهِ وَ جَعَلَ مِنْهُمُ الْقِرَدَةَ
وَالْخَنَازِيرَ وَ عَبَدَ الطَّاغُوتَ

The translation is mine, and it represents what the Arabic says, because according to the vowel marks "God" is the subject of the verb "worshiped"! But it is impossible to have a sentence in the Qur'an which says that God worshiped (the idol) al-ṭāghūt"! No translator has translated it this way, and I, myself, know this is impossible, so something has to be wrong.

It could be my faulty knowledge of Arabic, and that would be the first thing to suspect if I were the only one with a problem. However, when we look at Arthur Jeffery's *Materials for the History of the Text of the Qur'an* we find that this is not the case. Jeffery has found a record of 19 alternate readings; seven attributed to Ibn Mas'ud, four to Ubai b. Ka'b, six to Ibn Abbas, and one each to 'Ubaid b. 'Umair and Anas b. Malik.[4] Obviously each man could have had only one alternate reading. But the multiplication of possibilities shows that the scholars recognized the problem.

Here are the readings attributed to Ibn Mas'ud.

** wa man 'abadu al-ṭāghūta — وَ مَنْ عَبَدُوا الطَّاغُوتَ

wa 'abadata al-ṭāghūti — وَ عَبَدَةَ الطَّاغُوتِ

wa 'ubada al-ṭāghūtu — وَ عُبَدَ الطَّاغُوتُ

wa 'abuda al-ṭāghūtu — وَ عَبُدَ الطَّاغُوتُ

wa 'ubuda al-ṭāghūti — وَ عُبُدَ الطَّاغُوتِ

wa 'ubidati al-ṭāghūtu — وَ عُبِدَتِ الطَّاغُوتُ

'ubbada al-ṭāghūta — عُبِّدَ الطَّاغُوتَ

For those who don't know Arabic, these alternate readings can be divided into three classes: the verb is made plural so that the monkeys and swine are "those who worship (the idol) al-ṭāghut," or the verb is put in the passive tense so that "al-ṭāghut is worshiped" by the monkeys and swine, or the word 'abada is changed to a noun form making the monkeys and swine "slaves" or "worshipers of al-ṭāghut."

Moreover, in 14 out of the 19 changes all that was done was to change the vowel combinations. In the other 5 cases one or two consonants were also added.

I have chosen to reproduce the readings attributed to Ibn Mas'ud because his first reading above (marked **) is the one which has been chosen by all the translators. The verse then reads,

> ...(God) made some of them into monkeys and pigs, **and who served (the idol) al-ṭāghut**...

The fact that this difficult reading has been maintained in spite of the ease with which it could have been eliminated by altering two or three vowel marks, certainly **proves the care with which copies were made after the vowels were added**.

However, to paraphrase Dr. Bucaille's comment concerning the Christian apocryphal writings,

> One can only regret the disappearance of a number of primary collections of the Qur'an declared unnecessary by Othman, although they might have allowed present-day Muslims to know the correct text in difficult passages like the one concerning "al-ṭāghut."

---

4. Jeffery, op. cit., pages 39, 129, 198, 216, and 237.

127

THE CONCLUSION

Now that we have gone over this material, it is time to again ask our questions. **How do you know that there have been no changes in the Qur'an in the 163 years between the giving of the first verse of the Qur'an and the oldest known copy? What about these variants? How do you know that it is just the way it came from Muhammad?**

And again you are going to answer me that these variants are just little changes. You are going to tell me that the members of Zaid ibn Thabit's committee were serious men and they never would have made any changes on purpose. And you will tell me that even if the Qur'an was first written without the vowels and without the dots to distinguish the letters, this was controlled by the custom of memorizing the whole Qur'an.

And finally you might point out that in 150 AH there were men still alive who had heard about Muhammad's life and teachings and learned the Qur'an directly from their fathers and from other men who had known Muhammad or some of the companions personally. Therefore it is not possible that there could be important errors which would change the doctrines of the Qur'an.

And this is exactly the conclusion made by Hamidullah when he writes:

> Furthermore, in gathering all the variations and studying them carefully, we are sure that not one of them changes the sense of the common text so carefully codified and so carefully transmitted.[5]

The modern Christian translator, D. Masson, comes to the same conclusion. In the introduction to her French translation of the Qur'an she says,

> Finally, in spite of these points of debate, we can say that the text presently in our possession contains the criteria of a substantial fidelity.[6]

Having arrived at this conclusion we must now look at what is known about variant readings in the Gospel.

VARIANT READINGS IN THE GOSPEL-NEW TESTAMENT

With the **New Testament** as with the Qur'an, there are variant readings in different copies. In his book *The Text of the New Testament*,[7] Dr. Bruce M. Metzger, who is Professor of New Testament Language and Literature at Princeton Theological Seminary, devotes a whole chapter to a detailed discussion of the way in which these variant readings came about. In the following paragraphs we shall look at some examples.

---

5. Hamidullah, op. cit., p. xxxiii.
6. *Le Coran*, trad. de D. Masson, Editions Gallimard, 1967, p xl.
7. Oxford University Press, New York, Second Edition, 6th printing, 1968.

1. Variations Caused by Scribal Errors.

A. Through faulty eyesight.

In the Greek language, in which the Gospel-New Testament was originally written, the letters sigma, epsilon, theta, and omicron were sometimes confused with each other. If a scribe copied the wrong letter this would lead to a variant reading. The same thing can be seen in Arabic where the letter "r" or rā' can easily be confused with "d" or dāl.

In certain manuscripts a whole line has been omitted, because two lines ended with the same word or words. The eye of the scribe jumped down to the second use of the word and the intermediate line was left out. I am sure that each reader has had the same experience at some time during his schooling when he had to copy a quotation or some poetry.

B. Arising from faulty hearing.

When scribes made copies from dictation, confusion would sometimes arise over words having the same pronunciation, but differing in spelling (as the English words "there" and "their" or "grate" and "great." An example of this is found in Revelation 1:5. The translators in 1611 followed a text which read, "Unto him that loved us, and *washed* us from our sins by his blood," whereas older Greek texts used by modern translators read correctly "Unto him that loved us and *freed* us from our sins by his blood." This difference, which arose because of confusion between the pronunciation of *ou* and *u*, obviously makes no difference in the spiritual meaning.

C. Variants caused by holding a phrase in the mind while copying.

Sometimes this caused a change in the sequence of the words. Other times, the scribe would write the phrase as found in a parallel passage. As Hamidullah stated in relation to the Qur'an, almost all of these scribal errors are easily detected by comparison with other manuscripts.

2. Variants caused by including marginal notes or comparing manuscripts.

Words and notes standing in the margin of the older copy were occasionally incorporated into the text of the new manuscript. Synonyms of hard words or notes of explanation could pose a problem which a scribe sometimes solved by putting both the original word and the synonym or explanation into the text.

A similar type of variation happened in later years when a scribe might have more than one copy of the **Gospels** in front of him. What would a conscientious scribe do when he found that the same passage was given differently in two or more manuscripts? Rather than make a choice between them and copy only one of the two variant readings, the scribe might incorporate both readings in the new copy. For example, in some early manuscripts the Gospel of Luke closes with the statement that the disciples "were continually in the temple *blessing* God," while others read "were continually in the temple *praising* God." Rather than choose between the two, later scribes put the two together and wrote that the disciples "were continually in the temple *praising* and *blessing* God."

3. Variants caused by addition.

A scribe supposed that something was lacking in Jesus' statement in Matthew 9:13, "For I came not to call the righteous, but sinners," and added the words *"unto repentance"* to make it agree with Luke 5:32.

At Romans 13:9 Paul's reference to four of the Ten Commandments was expanded in one family of manuscripts when a scribe inadvertently added a fifth one—*"You shall not bear false witness"*—from memory.

4. Variations caused by attempts to solve difficulties.

The most obvious example of this is Mark 16 where the end of the Gospel is missing. After telling how the women who came to embalm Jesus' body were told by a man (angel) dressed in white, "He (Jesus) has risen! He is not here," the oldest texts of Codex Sinaiticus and Codex Vaticanus end with the words:

> Trembling and bewildered, the women went out and fled from the tomb. They said nothing to anyone. They were afraid for - - -

The Greek word translated "for" is the conjunction "gar" and Metzger says that in all of Greek literature "no instance has been found where "gar" stands at the end of a book" as it does in this case.[8]

Metzger suggests that Mark was interrupted while writing and prevented (perhaps by death) from finishing, or that the last leaf was lost before other copies were made. All that is known is that toward the end of the second century some Christian added a summary of Jesus' resurrection appearances which he made from the other Gospel accounts. Eventually this got included in the text, as discussed above concerning other marginal notes in the Qur'an and the Gospel.

ACCURACY OF THE SCRIBES

However, just as we saw with the Qur'an, the very fact that difficult passages were left intact until today shows that the scribes were usually very careful in their work. If they had not been careful and afraid to change God's word, they would have removed everything that they considered a problem.

Even in incidental details one observes their faithfulness. For example, in the Codex Vaticanus from 350 AD, there are section numbers which run in a series throughout the body of Paul's letters. They were placed there when the book of Hebrews was between Galatians and Ephesians. The scribe carefully copied these section numbers just as they had been, even though they were no longer correct because the order of the books had been changed.[9]

Interestingly enough, this is the very copy of the **Gospel-New Testament** which is singled out by Dr. Bucaille to be challenged. He writes:

> **The authenticity of a text, and of even the most venerable manuscript, is always open to debate**. *The Codex Vaticanus* is a good example of this. (See Photograph No. 3) The facsimile

---

8. For his complete discussion see Metzger, op. cit., p 226-229. Also Bucaille, BQ&S, p 65.
9. Metzger, op. cit., footnote 1, p 48.

reproductions edited by the Vatican City, 1965, contain an accompanying note from its editors informing us that "several centuries after it was copied a scribe inked over all the letters except those he thought were a mistake." There are passages in the text where the original letters in light brown still show through, contrasting visibly with the rest of the text which is in dark brown. **There is no indication that it was a faithful restoration.**[10] (boldfacing mine)

Metzger, a specialist in New Testament Greek, who has spent his whole academic life studying the source documents and has written the textbook called *The Text of the New Testament*, from which much of this chapter is adapted, also includes the information about the later scribe re-inking the text. He doesn't hide it. But his conclusion is:

> The text which it (Codex Vaticanus) contains has been regarded by many scholars as an excellent representative of the Alexandrian type text of the New Testament.[11]

And his own evaluation is summarized in the following statement:

> One of the most valuable of all the manuscripts of the Greek Bible is Codex Vaticanus.[12]

Dr. Bucaille passes the whole thing off by saying "The authenticity of a text is always open to debate" and **"There is no indication that it was a faithful restoration."**

Yet, Dr. Bucaille has not mentioned one single example of a word which was wrongly restored, or given us a percentage of words wrongly restored if there were any. **He has ASSUMED that it WAS NOT a faithful restoration**, and that others must prove to him that it was. Included, of course, is the further implication that possibly? probably? the validity of the **Doctrinal Gospel** is therefore in question.

When we examine Photograph No. 3 we can see, even in the photographic reproduction, the traces of the original letters as well as the newly restored ones. Thus we have both the original and the restoration, and if the reader wishes to spend the time learning Greek he will be able to verify for himself that the restoration is faithful.

---

10. Bucaille, BQ&S, p 79.
11. Metzger, op. cit., p 48.
12. Ibid., p 47.

Photograph 3 —

Codex Vaticanus from 350 AD. John 8:46 to 9:14,
including the healing of a man born blind.
By permission of the Vatican Library.

The problem is that this type of doubting, attacking statement, so easily written on a piece of paper by Dr. Bucaille, can be made about any document, including the Qur'an pictured in Photograph No. 2. "The authenticity of a text, and of even the most venerable manuscript, is always open to debate." Prove to us, therefore, that this first complete copy of the Qur'an is a valid copy!

I am a Christian and each reader will have to evaluate my success at controlling my own biases in this book, but until Dr. Bucaille comes up with some hard facts to support his slander against the Codex Vaticanus, I am going to continue to align myself with the specialist Dr. Metzger and the scribe who slavishly copied numbers which were no longer of any value when he copied them. For Christians, the Codex Vaticanus pictured in Photograph No. 3 is a valid and excellent fourth century witness to the text of the original Gospel—just as valid as the codex of the Qur'an pictured in Photograph No. 2.

FURTHER PROOF FOR THE ACCURACY OF THE SCRIBES FROM THE TRANSMISSION OF UNFAMILIAR NAMES AND WORDS

In the Old Testament, proper names of kings, both Hebrew and foreign, were transmitted with great fidelity—even though they had been dead and gone for hundreds, some for more than a thousand years. Dr. Bucaille himself mentions this when he discusses the name of the Egyptian Pharaoh *Rameses*. He says, "The name of Rameses was almost lost except in the Bible and a few Greek and Latin books where it was more or less deformed…The Bible, though, preserved the name very exactly. It is mentioned four times in the Torah."[13]

Another example is found in the **Torah-Old Testament** book of I Samuel where chapter 13:21 was originally translated,

Yet they had a **file** for the mattocks…

The Hebrew word, translated as "file," is "pim." It's meaning was unknown and the translation was strictly a guess from the context. Then, in one of the archaeological excavations, they found a previously unknown type of coin. When they cleaned it off and were able to decipher the name written on it, they found that it was a "Pim." So the verse is now understood to give the price for sharpening the mattocks and is translated,

"and the price was two-thirds of a shekel (pim) for sharpening plowshares and mattocks…"

The word "pim" is unimportant. It has no bearing on any doctrine, but it was copied correctly by the scribes for 2000 years from 1000 BC to 1000 AD even though, for most of that time, nobody knew what it meant.

The reader has probably realized by this time, that the types of variant readings which we have discussed in relation to the Torah and the Gospel, like those we examined from the Qur'an, have no effect at all on the validity of the message. Whether the verse mentioned in Luke 24 says *"praising* God" or *"blessing* God," or *"praising and blessing* God," changes nothing. Whether it says Jesus *"washed* us from our sins" or *"freed* us from our sins," the **DOCTRINAL GOSPEL** is the same.

There are now more than 5,300 old copies or portions of the Gospel in Greek alone. It is not surprising therefore to know that there are thousands of minor differences in these handmade copies. *LOOK* magazine once printed a headline reading *50,000 Errors in the Bible*. But for all practical purposes that headline was a lie, just as a statement saying that there are 5000 errors in the Qur'an would be a lie. The author used the word "error" for "variant reading," and the reader is not told that most of them are easily checked out against the other manuscripts; or that thousands are in later manuscripts which are controlled by the earlier ones.

---

13. Bucaille, BQ&S, p 232.

Dr. Bucaille has made the same type of misleading statement on page 3 where he writes,

> It is not difficult to understand why from version to version, and translation to translation, with all the corrections inevitably resulting, it was possible for the original text to have been transformed **during the course of more than two thousand years**.[14]

But we are not dealing with two thousand years. Our present **Bibles** are translated from copies of the Gospel made in the second, third, and fourth centuries. A scribal error made in 900 AD can have no effect on our present copies of the **Gospel-New Testament**, which are translated from the Codex Vaticanus and the Codex Sinaiticus of 350 AD, and papyri from 200 AD.

In their edition of the Greek New Testament, Westcott and Hort,[15] who spent 28 years from 1853 to 1881 comparing in great detail all the Greek manuscripts available to them, marked "about **sixty passages** (only seven of which are from the four **Gospels**) which they (or one of them) suspected involved a 'primitive error.'" By "primitive error" they meant an error older than the existing manuscript witnesses. What a fantastic difference to change from speaking about 50,000 errors to talking about having a question on 60 places in the New Testament.

Since those lines were written in 1881, many earlier Greek manuscripts and papyrus copies have been found. In every case, these new finds continue to demonstrate that the confidence of Westcott and Hort in the present texts of the Gospel was well founded.

The editors of the Revised Standard Version of the English Bible published in 1946 say,

> It will be obvious to the careful reader that still in 1946, as in 1881 and 1901, no doctrine of the Christian faith has been affected by the revision, for the simple reason that, out of the thousands of variant readings in the manuscripts, none has turned up thus far that requires a revision of Christian doctrine.

Professor Metzger, writing in 1968, summarizes the present situation with the following remarks.

> It is widely agreed that the Alexandrian text (passed on by Christians from Alexandria in Egypt) was prepared by skillful editors trained in the scholarly traditions of Alexandria...Until recently the two chief witnesses to this form of text were Codex Vaticanus and Codex Sinaiticus, dating from about the middle of the fourth century.
>
> With the discovery, however, of papyrus p66 (Photograph 9 in Chapter IV of Section Six) and papyrus p75 (Photograph 5 in III E

---

14. Bucaille, BQ&S, p 3.
15. Westcott and Hort, *The New Testament in the Original Greek,* Cambridge, 1881. Cited by Metzger, including the 60 references, op. cit., p 184.

of this Section),[16] both dating from about the end of the second or the beginning of the third century, **proof is now available that (this text) goes back to an older copy from early in the second century.**[17]

The end of the second century or the beginning of the third century speaks of 200 AD. That is 170 years after Jesus' ascension and only 110-120 years after John wrote his Gospel. At that date men were still alive who had heard the **Doctrinal Gospel** from their fathers and from other men who had known the apostles personally.

On good evidence then, we BELIEVE that the text which we have is essentially the text which the apostles of Jesus originally gave us.

CONCLUSION

Abundant evidence from the Hadith and from Muslim commentaries prove that there were variant readings in the copies of the Qur'an made by the companions of the Prophet. This contradicts the frequent Muslim claim that the present text is a "photographic copy" of the original. Nevertheless, these variant readings are not important enough to undermine Muslim confidence that they have the essential message of the Qur'an as it was proclaimed by Muhammad.

Likewise for the **Gospel-New Testament**. It is impossible to support a "Christian" contention that the present text of the **Gospel-New Testament** is a perfect reproduction of the original autographs. Nevertheless, the variant readings are not important enough to alter Christian confidence that we have the **essential message of the Gospel** as it was proclaimed by Jesus.

---

16. See III E for a more detailed description of these papyrus manuscripts.
17. Metzger, op. cit., p 215-216.

D. STRUGGLE AND CONFLICT IN EARLY CHRISTIANITY COMPARED WITH STRUGGLE AND CONFLICT IN EARLY ISLAM

In his short second chapter Dr. Bucaille focuses upon internal struggle in the young Christian community, with the implication that this could effect the validity of the **Gospel message**. His presentation can be summarized as follows:

1. This struggle involved one group of Christians who followed the doctrines of Paul and opposed another group, called the Judeo-Christians, led by the Apostles Peter and John along with James the brother of Jesus.
2. Many of the Gospel-New Testament books were a result of this struggle.
3. The Judeo-Christian group eventually lost out and their books were called apocryphal and hidden or suppressed by the Church.

Dr. Bucaille elaborates on these three points with these words:

> **1.** From the time Jesus left earth (30 AD) until the second half of the second century (150 AD), **there was a struggle between two factions**. One was what one might call Pauline Christianity and the other Judeo-Christianity. It was only very slowly that... **Pauline Christianity triumphed over Judeo-Christianity.**[1]

Next he claims,

> **"Until 70 AD, Judeo-Christianity represents the majority of the Church"** and "Paul remains an isolated case." **The head of the community at that time was James, a relation of Jesus. With him were Peter (at the beginning) and John. "James may be considered to represent the Judeo-Christian camp**, which deliberately clung to Judaism as opposed to Pauline Christianity."[2]

And again on the following page,

> Paul is the most controversial figure in Christianity. **He was considered to be a traitor to Jesus' thought by the latter's family** and by the apostles who had stayed in Jerusalem in the circle around James. Paul **created** Christianity at the expense of those whom Jesus had gathered around him to spread his teachings.[3]

Thus Paul is considered a traitor to Jesus' thought and from this presentation a reader not well instructed in the Bible and the facts of the situation, is again given the impression that the Christians have changed, altered, suppressed and hidden the true Gospel.

Dr. Bucaille's second point that many of the New Testament books were the result of this struggle, is set forth in the following words:

> **2.** As far as the Gospels are concerned however, it is almost

1. BQ&S, p 50.
2. Ibid., p 51. Words in single quotation marks are from Daniélou, the others from Bucaille.
3. Ibid., p 52.

certain that if this atmosphere of struggle between communities had not existed, we would not have had the writings we possess today. They appeared at a time of fierce struggle between the two communities. These "combat writings," as Father Kannengiesser calls them, emerged from the multitude of writings on Jesus...

This then leads to his third point that,

> **3.** These texts constituted the "Canon" which condemned and excluded as unorthodox any other documents that were not suited to the line adopted by the Church.[4]

It is certainly true that some of the Gospel-New Testament books bear the imprint of struggle, but two questions must be asked.

Is Dr. Bucaille correct in saying that this struggle was between Paul and the other disciples of Jesus?

Does the existence of a struggle prove that the Gospel-New Testament was not written by revelation?

WERE PETER, JOHN AND JAMES IN MAJOR DISAGREEMENT WITH PAUL?

The following passages from the Gospel-New Testament prove that these men were friends and in complete doctrinal agreement.

A. Paul says in his letter to the Galatians 2:1-2,9-10:

> Fourteen years later I went up again to Jerusalem, this time with Barnabas...I went in response to a revelation and set before them the Gospel that I preach among the Gentiles (uncircumcised pagans)... for fear that I was running or had run my race in vain.
>
> **James (the brother of Jesus), Peter and John**, those reputed to be pillars, **gave me and Barnabas the right hand of fellowship** when they recognized the grace given to me...All they asked was that we should continue to remember the poor...

B. In Acts 21:17-20, perhaps five years before his death, we read of Paul's last voyage to Jerusalem. It says,

> When we arrived at Jerusalem, **the brothers received us warmly**. The next day **Paul** and the rest of us went to see **James (the brother of Jesus), and all the elders were present**. Paul greeted them and reported in detail what God had done among the Gentiles through his ministry. **When they heard this they praised God**...

C. Finally, in the second of the two letters which Peter himself wrote we read these words:

> Bear in mind that our Lord's patience means salvation, **just as our dear brother Paul also wrote you** with the wisdom that God gave him...His letters contain some things that are hard to understand, which

---

4. Ibid., p 53.

137

ignorant and unstable people distort, **as they do the other Scriptures**, to their own destruction (II Peter 3:15-16).

These verses show Paul traveling to Jerusalem to check whether his preaching agrees with the preaching of Peter, John and James.

They show him having good relations with James at the end of his life.

They show that Peter calls Paul's letters "Scripture."

Galatians 2:11-16 does report a confrontation where Paul rebukes Peter, but the last quotation above proves that they were later reconciled.

Why does Dr. Bucaille ignore these verses? If I omitted important verses like these when quoting the Qur'an, would it not be **changing the context** by suppression of evidence? It is as though I were to say that there was great disagreement between Abu Bakr, Omar, and Othman, in spite of evidence in the Hadith to the contrary.

There was a struggle. That is true. But the struggle was between **Paul, Peter, John and James on one side** and **a party of Jewish Christians on the other**.

THE EFFECT OF THE STRUGGLE ON THE GOSPEL-NEW TESTAMENT

The Book of Acts and Paul's letters show three levels of struggle.

First of all there was struggle between Paul and the pagan idol-worshipers. According to Acts 19, when people accepted Christ as Saviour because of Paul's preaching, they turned **"from dead idols to serve the living God"** and stopped buying silver images. This made the silversmiths in Ephesus so angry they went on a riot and forced Paul to leave.

Secondly there was struggle between the apostles and those Jews who did not accept the Gospel. In Acts 12 it tells of King Herold killing James the brother of John and putting Peter in Jail, and in Acts 14:19 we read,

> Then some Jews came from Antioch and Iconium and won the crowd over. **They stoned Paul** and dragged him outside the city, thinking he was dead.

Thirdly there was struggle between Peter, John and Paul on one side and some Jewish Christians on the other. It is this third type of conflict about which Dr. Bucaille is concerned.

The reader may be asking himself by this time what is meant by the term "Jewish Christian"? Were not Peter, James, John and all of Jesus' disciples Jews who became Christians? What is the difference between them and the other group called "Jewish Christians"?

WHAT DID THE JEWISH CHRISTIANS BELIEVE?

Contrary to all we might have imagined, we are astonished to find that they believed the **Doctrinal Gospel**.

Dr. Bucaille speaks of Cardinal Daniélou's studies of the Judeo-Christian writings several times in his book. On page 19 he writes,

> Christianity, which was initially Judeo-Christianity, has been

carefully studied…by modern authors, such as Cardinal Daniélou. Before it was transformed under Paul's influence, Christianity accepted the heritage of the Old Testament (Torah) without difficulty.

In another quotation on page 50 Bucaille writes,

> He (Cardinal Daniélou) reviews past works, retraces Judeo-Christian history and enables us to place the appearance of the Gospels in quite a different context from the one that emerges on reading accounts intended for mass publication.

These quotations give the impression that Daniélou has demonstrated a different Gospel in the Jewish Christian community, but when we turn to Cardinal Daniélou's own works we discover that his conclusions are exactly the opposite.

At the end of his epic work, *Théologie du Judéo-Christianisme*,[5] in which the Cardinal deals with every document which had been discovered up to its publication in 1964, he says,

> The task which we set ourselves at the beginning of this volume was to examine the documents which have come down to us from the Jewish Christian period of the Early Church in order to draw…a picture of the theology of Jewish Christianity… p 405.

> Its concern is with cosmic history, from the Beginning of things…to the last infinite Heaven of God. **The axis pinning together this immeasurable sphere of things and events is the Incarnation, the tabernacling in human flesh and season of the concealed glory of the Son (Jesus).** p 405.

> **For them redemption was a cosmic matter**; the action of the Word (Jesus) extended through every region of the spiritual universe, from Sheol (hell) to the seventh heaven, and touched every creature. **The cross, the instrument of redemption, is…the double axis of the universe**, transcending space by **stretching out its arms to unite all nations** of men and by **reaching up its head to join heaven and earth**… p 407.

> **Here, so early** as in some instances even to go behind the New Testament (he means, be earlier than the **written Gospel**),

> **we find still the divine preexistent Christ**—Name, Son and Word…

> **we find the divine Person of the Holy Spirit**…

> **we find the *virginitas in partu* (virgin birth)**…

> and the elaborate doctrine of the Church (the Christian Nation of believers)…

> These, and other instances…leave little room to doubt that **IN ALL MAJOR FEATURES THE CHRISTIAN FAITH IN ITS MOST ARCHAIC EXPRESSION WAS EVEN THEN WHAT IT ALWAYS HAS BEEN.** p 408. (capitals mine)

---

5. English translation, *The Theology of Jewish Christianity*, The Westminster Press, Philadelphia, 1978.

Not only does Cardinal Daniélou show that the Jewish Christians had the same beliefs about God and Jesus as Paul, but there are at least ten places in his book where he **quotes from Paul to illustrate the Jewish Christian beliefs**.

THE DISAGREEMENT BETWEEN THE APOSTLES AND THE JEWISH CHRISTIANS

If this struggle was not because of disagreement concerning belief in Jesus as Saviour, what could be the cause of so much division? According to the Gospel-New Testament the struggle started when some of the pagan idol-worshipers became Christians.

Then the question was raised as to whether, in addition to accepting Christ as Saviour, they had to be circumcised and keep the religious ceremonies of the Torah? Or stated differently, do you have to also become a Jew and be circumcised in order to be a complete Christian? From this stems the term JEWISH-Christians.

Paul said, "Jesus has paid for every one of our sins as a free gift—by grace. Period!"

The Judeo-Christians said, "It is true that Jesus paid for our sins, but one must also obey the law." Their teaching is described in Acts 15:1 as follows:

> Some men came down from Judea to Antioch and were teaching the (Christian) brothers: **"Unless you are circumcised, according to the custom taught by Moses, you cannot be saved** (even though you have accepted Jesus, the Messiah, as Saviour)."

Because of this disagreement, Paul and Barnabas traveled to Jerusalem to discuss the question with the other apostles.

In the discussion which followed, **Peter** answered the Jewish-Christians with these words:

> Why do you try to test God by putting on the necks of the disciples a yoke (the Torah) that neither we nor our fathers have been able to bear (to keep completely)? No! We believe **it is through the grace of our Lord Jesus that we (Jews) are saved**, just as they (the pagans) are (Acts 15:10,11).

We might paraphrase this as Peter saying, "No, we Jews were not saved by being Jews. We were saved by accepting Christ and becoming Christians. Therefore it is unnecessary for pagans who turn to Christ to become Jews." And that was the final decision of the meeting. Christians who believed from pagan religions did not have to be circumcised.

The complete discussion is found in the Gospel-New Testament in Paul's letter to the Galatians and the Book of Acts, chapters 10-15 and shows that **James, the brother of Jesus, and Peter were there and agreed with Paul.** The JEWISH-Christians refused to accept this decision, and considering Paul responsible for it, they persecuted him as the main leader.

ISLAM AND THE PREVIOUS REVELATIONS

This question of the relation between Islam and the previous revelations does not seem to have come up among the early Muslims, and I am not sure why it didn't. Theoretically one could say that unless the Qur'an abrogated a command found in the Torah or the Gospel, that command or teaching should still be binding on the Muslims.

For example, why don't Muslims circumcise their sons on the 8th day as God commanded Abraham in Genesis 17:9-12, which reads,

> **Then God said to Abraham...,"This is My covenant** with you and your descendants after you, the covenant you are to keep: **Every male among you shall be circumcised**. You are to undergo circumcision, and it will be the sign of the covenant between Me and you. **For the generations to come every male among you who is eight days old must be circumcised**, including those born in your household or bought with money."

The Qur'an emphasizes that it is going back to the true religion of Abraham. Yet Muslims usually circumcise their sons when older, between three and six years of age, which seems to be disobeying God's straight, clear command ordering Abraham to do it on the 8th day.

Anyway, if we imagine two groups of Muslims arguing with each other— one saying, "We must circumcise on the 8th day as God told Abraham," and the other saying, "No, that is no longer necessary"— that is an imperfect example of the struggle in the early church. It is imperfect because the disagreement in the early church was much more basic.

Are we saved by our efforts in keeping the Law found in the Torah (or in the Qur'an)?

Or are we saved uniquely and solely by the grace and mercy of God who paid for all our sins in Christ?

APOCRYPHAL BOOKS

Finally, we must consider Dr. Bucaille's third point concerning the rejected documents which are usually referred to as "apocryphal." This word comes from the Greek "apokryphos" which means "hidden." Dr. Bucaille claims that these documents were called "apocrypha" because the church hid them. In a note on page 51 he says,

> One could note here that all these writings were later to be classed as apocrypha, i.e., they had to be **concealed** by the victorious church...

Dr. Bucaille is right that the original Greek root meaning of the word "apocryphal" is "hidden," but once again he has refused to limit himself to those meanings of a word which can be established by usage, feeling free to make up his own meaning based on its root.

In the 1st and 2nd century AD, the word "apokryphos" (secret) was used by a group of men called Gnostics for their own works. For example, one of their books is called the *Apocryphon of John* or the Secret of John. The Gnostics claimed to have "apocryphal" or secret knowledge which others did not have, and salvation was to be found in the form of knowledge coming from the gnostic revealer—usually Jesus—though other revealers were also named.

In contrast to both Christianity and Islam, Gnostic works ridicule the "creator god" as blind and unaware of another higher, purely spiritual deity. In the *Apocryphon of John*, for example, the creator God is said to be weak and "impious in his madness...for he said, 'I am God and there is no other God beside me' (reference to Isaiah 46:9), for he is ignorant of his strength, the place from which he had come."[6]

Later in the fourth century the word was used to refer to books not publicly read in churches. It meant apocryphal in the modern sense (i.e., fictitious) only by implication, as when the church historian Eusebius speaks of some of "the so-called secret (apocryphal) books" as forgeries composed by heretics.[7]

There is not the least bit of evidence for Dr. Bucaille's statement that these books were called "apocryphal" because the church hid them.

EXAMPLES OF JEWISH CHRISTIAN APOCRYPHAL WORKS

At this point it may be helpful to point out that **because a book was declared apocryphal by the church does not mean that it agreed with the doctrines of Islam.** This is simply not the case.

A **Jewish-Christian "Gospel of Peter"** which claimed clearly that Jesus is the Divine Word of God who died on the cross for our sins was rejected by the church because, first of all, it was not written by Peter, and secondly **it denied Jesus' true humanity**, saying that when he was on the cross he felt no pain.[8] Daniélou says of this *false* gospel that "its purpose is to throw into bold relief the divine character of the person of Christ."[9] Certainly Islam would not be sympathetic to this!

There was an **"Acts of Paul"** which agrees completely with the Christian doctrine of Jesus' death for our sins, but it also says that "you shall have no part in the resurrection unless you remain chaste and defile not the flesh," **which to them meant no sexual intercourse even for married people**. The church rejected it because this is against Christian teaching (as it is also against Quranic teaching), and its author, who admitted that his work was a forgery, was removed as a church leader for this lie.[10] This prohibition of sexual relations even in marriage is also found in the **Judeo-Christian books—The Gospel of Thomas** and **The Gospel of the Egyptians.**[11]

Finally, I will mention the **Judeo-Christian Epistle of Barnabas** which was

---

6. *Apocryphon of John* of Nag Hammadi Codex II, page 11, lines 18-22, quoted from a review of *The Gnostic Gospels* by Elaine Pagels, Random House.
7. Adapted from *Encyclopedia Britannica*, 15th Ed, 1982, vol 2, p 973.
8. *International Standard Bible Encyclopedia* (ISBE), Eerdmans, Grand Rapids, 1955, p. 197.
9. Daniélou, op. cit., p 21.
10. ISBE, op. cit., p 188-190.
11. Daniélou, op. cit., p 24.

written about 120 AD. This work was very highly respected by many second and third century Christians and the teaching which it contains about Christ is orthodox, but it was declared apocryphal. Why? First, there was no proof that it was written by Barnabas, and secondly **it attributes the Law of Moses to the wiles of a demon,**[12] a statement which contradicts Jesus' words and **which contradicts the Qur'an too**.

Every one of these Jewish-Christian works is mentioned by Bucaille and quoted by Daniélou. It is clear from these examples that although most of these apocryphal books had considerable orthodox doctrine about Christ, they were excluded from being read in churches because they taught false doctrine and were not written on the authority of the apostles of Jesus.

WEAK HADITHS

Have you Muslims not had the same problem with your Hadith? We learned in Chapter II of Section Two that Bukhari started with 600,000 and judged that only 2,762 were "strong," or authentic. When a hadith is declared weak, are you not saying, "We don't really believe that this was said by Muhammad or one of the original companions"? **The doctrine in it might be correct, but you doubt that it is authentic. This is exactly what we Christians mean when we use the words "apocryphal" or "uncanonical."**

CONCLUSION

Examination of Dr. Bucaille's three points has shown them to be invalid. **There is no evidence that the struggles of the 1st century AD limited the ability of God's Holy Spirit to guide His prophets and apostles in any way.** After all, He is God Almighty, Maker of heaven and earth. What man can alter His will or His Word?

Furthermore, Dr. Bucaille's thesis contradicts the Qur'an. We saw in Section Two, Chapter I that the Qur'an says in the Sura of the Battle Array (Al-Ṣaff) 61:14, from 3AH, that,

> ...a portion of the Children of Israel believed (in Jesus), and a portion disbelieved: **but We gave power to those who believed, against their enemies, and they became the ones that prevailed.**

Moreover, we saw in the Sura of Iron (Al-Ḥadīd) 57:27, from 8 AH, that there were true Christian believers present when monasticism started in 300 AD, long after Jewish Christianity had disappeared, **Therefore, according to the Qur'an, the Christianity which prevailed could not have been changed by any type of struggle in the 1st century as Dr. Bucaille has suggested.**

---

12. *Early Christian Writings*, Penguin Books, Baltimore, 1972, p 190 & 205.

STRUGGLE DURING THE GIVING OF THE QUR'AN

If we are to take seriously the idea that struggle and conflict can falsify revelation, what about the Qur'an? When the Qur'an was given, was there not struggle between the Muslims and the Meccans? Was there not struggle between the Muslims and the Jews? Was there not struggle between Muhammad and others who claimed to be Muslims and even prophets? The answer to all three of these questions is "yes"!

Is this struggle with the Meccans not mentioned in the Qur'an? What of the Sura of the Family of 'Imran (Āli 'Imrān) 3:123, which refers to the battle fought with the Meccans at Badr?

> God had helped you at Badr, when you were a contemptible
> little force. Then fear God; thus may you show gratitude.

And in the same Sura 3:140-180, the Prophet rebukes and encourages the believers in relation to what happened at the battle of Uhud. And what of Muhammad's struggle with the Jews? In Chapter I of Section Two we looked at nearly 40 passages given because of the struggle between the Muslims and the Jews. One example from the Late Meccan Sura of the Cattle (Al-An'ām) 6:124, is enough. There we read about the Jew's request for a sign in these words:

> When there comes to them a sign they say, "We shall not
> believe until we receive one like those received by God's
> Apostles."

The third type of struggle, between Muhammad and others who also claimed to be Muslims, is even somewhat parallel to the struggle in the early church with the Jewish Christians. As an example we shall consider Musailama who headed an embassy sent by his tribe to see Muhammad in 9 AH and professed Islam. The next year he claimed also to be a prophet of the One True God and began to publish written revelations in imitation of the Qur'an. Abu 'l-Faraj has preserved this example:

> Now has God been gracious unto her that was with child, and
> has brought forth from her the soul which runs between the
> peritoneum and the bowels.

He even wrote to Muhammad, starting the letter with the words, "From Musailama, the Apostle of God, to Muhammad, the Apostle of God." Muhammad answered calling him "Musailama, the Liar."

Even so, Musailama continued to increase in importance and was only stopped when he was killed during the defeat of his army by General Khalid in 11 AH, one year after Muhammad's death.[13]

Does that mean that the Qur'an was changed because of this struggle, or that revelation was broken and crooked because of it? No Muslim would admit to that. In fact the Qur'an says just the opposite! It says that there was conflict and struggle every time a prophet was sent to a people, whether it was Moses with Bani Israel or Salih with the Thamud.

---

13. Adapted from Hughes, op. cit., p 422.

STRUGGLE IN ISLAM AFTER MUHAMMAD'S DEATH

Musailama was not the only person to claim prophethood. During the period immediately after Muhammad's death, three false prophets and a prophetess gathered increasing numbers around their standards. In the north, east and south of the Peninsula, tribe after tribe apostasized from the newly-adopted creed, and Medina itself was attacked.[14] This is the very period during which Abu Bakr ordered Zaid ibn Thabit to make the first collection of the Qur'an.

If Dr. Bucaille's theories are correct concerning the Gospel, then we must assume that all these false prophets, wars, and rebellions must have in some way affected the collection of the Qur'an. Furthermore, we ought to regret the disappearance of the words of Musailama and the other prophets, words which were declared apocryphal by the Muslim Nation, "although (they were) of historical interest."

In the succeeding years there were other struggles. The second Khalifa, Omar, was assassinated by a Persian slave, Firoz, in 23 AH., and less than 25 years after Muhammad's death, in 35 AH, unhappy Muslims entered the headquarters of Othman, the 3rd Khalifa, and mortally wounded him.

Ali, the Prophet's son-in-law, was named successor, but there was much opposition to this action. Aisha, the widow of the Prophet, along with two men named Talha and Zubair, eventually gathered forces in an attempt to overthrow him. In October 656 AD/35 AH, Ali marched out of Medina leading, for the first time, a Muslim army to put down a civil insurrection raised by brother Muslims. Some months later he defeated the triumvirate at the "Battle of the Camel." Talha and Zubair were killed and Aisha was sent back to Mecca.

Some of the emotional weight of this struggle can, perhaps, be realized when we understand who these people were in relation to Muhammad.

Ali was a cousin of Muhammad who adopted him as his son. He was one of the first believers and married Fatima, Muhammad's daughter.

Zubair was also a cousin of Muhammad, one of the first to believe, and one of the ten, called al-'Ashara al-Mubashshara, to whom the Prophet promised sure entry into Paradise.

Talha, a grand-nephew of Abu Bakr the first Khalifa, was a distinguished Companion (term for those who saw Muhammad with their own eyes, embraced Islam, and accompanied him). He saved the life of Muhammad at the battle of Uhud and was also included in the list of al-'Ashara al-Mubashshara, who were promised paradise.[15]

Ali himself was then murdered in 661 AD/40 AH by one of the Kharijites, a group of Muslims who had revolted against him.

---

14. Ibid., p 651.
15. Above information adapted from Hughes, op. cit, pages 716, 626, & 13.

This bit of history demonstrates the struggles and conflicts in the early Islamic political situation. But, Shiite claims aside, **is any Muslim willing to say that these struggles caused a change in the Qur'an?**[16] Certainly not! Such a conclusion would be considered ridiculous.

On what basis, then, shall Dr. Bucaille or anyone else say that the Holy Spirit could not guide Paul, or Peter, or James, even while they were in the midst of struggle and controversy?

SUMMARY AND CONCLUSION CONCERNING THE DEVELOPMENT OF THE QUR'AN

We have now made a fairly complete study of the historical development of the Qur'an. We started with the first preaching of Muhammad 13 years before the Hejira and followed through to one of the oldest copies of the Qur'an from about 150 AH. To see this progression in the development of the Qur'an easily, look at the summarization in Diagram 3.

Diagram 3 — THE HISTORICAL DEVELOPMENT OF THE QURAN

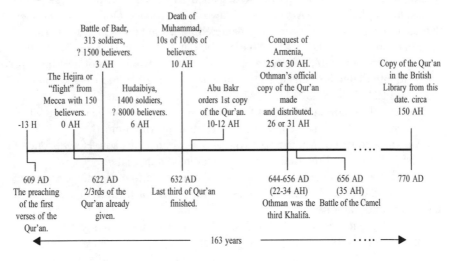

Having considered all this information, it seems correct to summarize Muslim beliefs about the collection and transmission of the Qur'an in the following statements.

Even though you do not have the original copy of the Qur'an in your hands, you **BELIEVE** that Zaid and Omar gathered the Qur'an as it was given.

You **BELIEVE** that if something was missed when Othman burned the original copies, or even if Omar and 'Ubai were right about the verse of stoning and the two extra suras, it doesn't make a difference to any basic Islamic doctrine.

---

16. The Shiites charge that certain Quranic verses which said that Ali should have been the first Khalifa, were suppressed. However, there is no documentary proof; and Ali never claimed this when he was the Khalifa and had the power to put them back.

You **BELIEVE** that those who copied the Qur'an did it carefully; and that when errors were made because the scribes were human, they could be controlled by comparison with other copies.

You **BELIEVE** that the hadith gathered by Muslim and Bukhari describing the life of Muhammad and the collection of the Qur'an are essentially true and to be relied upon.

You **BELIEVE** that those original Muslims would not have given of their money and their time and even been ready to die for something that they knew to be a lie.

In summary, **YOU BELIEVE** that the evidence in favor of the reliable transmission of the Qur'an is so great that you **ARE SURE** you can use it with complete confidence.

E. THE SECOND HUNDRED YEARS OF THE GOSPEL

In following the historical development of the Gospel-New Testament from the time Jesus started preaching until John wrote the last Gospel account between 80 and 95 AD, we have found no evidence for alteration or falsification of the Bible.

Photograph 1 of Part A in this chapter and Photograph 5 in this part show papyrus manuscripts dating from 200 AD. These two documents alone represent almost 40% of our present Gospel-New Testament, and where applicable, the English, French and Arabic New Testaments which we use every day are translated from these Greek papyri.

That leaves the time from **90 AD to 200 AD** as a period when theoretically some change might have taken place in the Gospel-New Testament, so we shall now turn our attention to this period.

POST-APOSTOLIC WITNESSES

Clement of Rome — 96 AD

In Part A of this chapter we saw that I Corinthians was written in 55 AD. Forty years later in about 96 AD, a man named Clement, a bishop in Rome, wrote a letter to the church at Corinth just as Paul had done. In that letter he writes:

> Read your letter from the blessed Apostle Paul again.[1]

What letter is Clement referring to? He is referring to I Corinthians, the very letter in which the **Doctrinal Gospel** was written down for the first time, and he quotes from I Corinthians 15:20 saying,

> He (God) has made Jesus Christ the firstfruits by raising him from the dead.[2]

In addition to other quotations from I Corinthians, he paraphrases or quotes from the so-called "Judeo-Christian" Gospel of Matthew, and five other New Testament books: I Peter, James, Hebrews, and Paul's letters to the Romans and the Ephesians.

It is natural that he would know about the letter to the Romans since it had been written to Clement's own church in Rome. But the other letters had been written to churches in Greece and what is now Turkey. This shows that they were quickly circulated among the early Christians, just as the new verses and suras of the Qur'an were quickly circulated among the early Muslims.

Moreover, we can see from the above tiny quotation that there was no change in the **Doctrinal Gospel** between the time when Paul wrote it down in 55 AD and the moment when Clement quoted it 40 years later.

---

1. Epistle of Clement to Corinth, *Early Christian Writings*, op. cit., p 48, section 47.
2. Ibid., p 36, section 24.

Polycarp's letter to Philippi—107 AD

Polycarp was born in 69 or 70 AD in Asia (now Turkey). **He heard the Gospel from the Apostle John** who lived in Turkey in his old age, and according to Irenaeus, Polycarp "had had familiar intercourse with many who had seen Christ."[3] In his later years he became Bishop of the church in Smyrna, about 40 miles north of Ephesus. Smyrna still exists today as the town of Izmir, Turkey, with about 200,000 people.

Sometime around 107 AD, he wrote a letter to the church at Philippi—a church started by Paul in 49 or 50 AD.

In his letter he refers to "the apostles who brought us the Gospel, and the prophets who foretold the coming of the Lord (the Messiah)." At least three times he mentions Paul by name, as well as stressing the fact that Paul had preached to the Philippians and then written to them. He calls Paul's letter to the Ephesians "Scripture"—the same title used for the **Torah** of Moses—as we see in the following quotation:

> I have no doubt you are well versed in Holy Scripture…it says there, "*Do not be angry to the point of sin; do not let the sun go down on your indignation*" [quoted from Ephesians 4:26]. The happy man is he who keeps this in mind…**May the God and Father of our Lord Jesus Christ, and the eternal High Priest Jesus Christ himself, the Son of God,** help you to grow in faith and truth.[4]
>
> In him (Jesus the Messiah), endurance went so far as to face even **death for our sins**…Though you never saw him for yourselves, yet you believed in him…well knowing that it is *by grace you are saved, not of your own doing* [quoted from Ephesians 2:8].[5]

The sections in boldfaced type show that he firmly believed in the **Doctrinal Gospel**, and in this short letter of seven pages, he quotes from the Gospel according to Matthew, Acts, Romans, I Corinthians, Galatians, II Thessalonians, I Timothy, I Peter, and I John, as well as Ephesians, for a total of 10 of the 27 New Testament books.

These ten books, originating in places as far apart as Palestine, Turkey, Greece, and Rome, were well-known to Polycarp only 10 or 15 years after the death of John the Apostle, again demonstrating the early and wide dissemination of the New Testament scriptures.

Pliny the Younger—112 AD

The last person from whom we shall quote is another Roman historian. Pliny the Younger was Governor of Bithynia (northern Turkey) in 112 AD, and wrote letters to the Emperor Trajan asking for advice. **He complained that hardly anyone was sacrificing to the Roman gods (idols), and the temples had fallen into disrepair because of the Christians.** He began to kill the Christians

---

3. Haer., iii 3,4.
4. *Early Christian Writings*, Polycarp, op.cit., p 149, section 12.
5. Ibid., p 144, section 1.

if they would not sacrifice to the statues of the Emperor. He attempted to make them "curse Christ," because he was told that it was impossible to make a genuine Christian do this.

In the same letter, he says of the people being tried:

> They affirmed, however, that the whole of their guilt, or their error, was that they were in the habit of meeting on a certain fixed day before it was light, when **they sang** in alternate verse **a hymn to Christ as to a God**, and bound themselves to a solemn oath, not to any wicked deeds, but never to commit any fraud, theft, adultery, never to falsify their word, not to deny a trust when they should be called upon to deliver it up.[6]

Again, from the boldfaced words in the testimony of this pagan worshiper of idols, it is clear that the Christians were declaring their belief in the **Doctrinal Gospel**, and even dying for it.

EARLY COPIES OF
SOME OF THE GOSPEL-NEW TESTAMENT BOOKS

Papyrus Fragment of John's Gospel from 135 AD

The earliest papyrus copy of any New Testament book is a fragment of the Gospel of John at the John Rylands Library in Manchester, England, with the number p52. As you can see from Photograph 4, it is very small and contains a few words from John 18:31-33 on one side and a few more words from verses 37-38 on the other.

However, it is very important because of the date of writing and the place where it was found. Dr. Bruce M. Metzger, Professor of New Testament Language and Literature at Princeton Theological Seminary, discusses this in his book *The Text of the New Testament*. He writes:

> On the basis of the style of the script, C. H. Roberts (who discovered it) dated the fragment in the first half of the second century. Though not all scholars are convinced that it can be dated within so narrow a range, such eminent palaeographers as Sir Frederic G. Kenyon, W. Schubar, Sir Harold I. Bell, Adolf Deissmann, Ulrich Wilcken, and W. H. P. Hatch have expressed themselves as being in agreement with Roberts' judgment.
>
> Although the extent of the verses preserved is so slight, in one respect this tiny scrap of papyrus (p52) possesses quite as much evidential value as would the complete codex (book)...(For it) proves the existence and use of the Fourth Gospel (of John) during the first half of the second century in a provincial town along the Nile, far removed from its traditional place of composition (Ephesus in Ancient Turkey).[7]

---

6. Pliny the Younger, Epistles X, 96.
7. Metzger, op. cit., p 39.

Photograph 4 —

Papyrus p52 of John 18:31-33 from before 150 AD.
By permission of the John Rylands University Library, Manchester.

If we use the date of 135 AD as the time when this copy was made, we see that Christians were using the Gospel according to John in **Egypt, along the Nile River,** within 40 to 45 years of the date of its composition. This is strong evidence that by 135 AD there must have already been hundreds of copies of this Gospel in the hands of hundreds of thousands of Christians.

Therefore, if someone did wish to change either the **Written Gospel** or the **Doctrinal Gospel**, how would he go about altering the words in all these copies, and the knowledge of the words in all those minds and hearts?

Papyrus Manuscripts of 200 AD

The last two papyrus manuscripts which we want to discuss are dated around 200 AD. The first one, numbered p75, is now in the Bodmer Library of World Literature at Cologny, a suburb of Geneva, Switzerland. It originally contained Luke and John on 144 pages, of which 102 pages, or about 70%, remain. It is the oldest known copy of the Gospel according to Luke, and one of the earliest copies of the Gospel according to John.

Of great importance to any study of Christian doctrine is the fact that the middle of the codex with the last three chapters of Luke and the first 13 chapters of John are intact. The first chapter of John includes the preexistence of the divine "Word" which became flesh. The last three chapters of Luke include Jesus' death on the cross and three of his resurrection appearances. Photograph 5 of Luke 24:31-50 includes these three appearances: the first to two disciples on the road to Emmaus—the second to Peter—and the third to all the disciples except Thomas. Photograph 7 in Chapter I of Section Six shows a picture of John 14:16 from this same papyrus.

We have already seen a picture of the second manuscript, designated p46, in Photograph 1 in Part A of this chapter. It comprises eighty-six leaves, or 75%, of a papyrus codex originally made up of 114 leaves. Presently in the Chester Beatty Museum in Dublin, Ireland, it contains ten epistles of Paul in the following order: Romans, Hebrews, I and II Corinthians, Ephesians, Galatians, Philippians, Colossians, and I and II Thessalonians. As might be expected in an ancient book, part of the beginning and end are missing. **However, I Corinthians, which was written in 55 AD, quoted by Clement in 96 AD, and by Polycarp in 107 AD, is almost completely preserved.**

I make a point of the fact that 70% of the two Gospels and 75% of Paul's letters are still present, because that represents a very important sample. If the 70 or 75% which we have of these old texts is in agreement with the complete texts from 150 years later (see below), then I think that it is valid to assume that the other 25 to 30%, which is no longer present, also agreed originally. Furthermore, when considered together they represent almost 40% of the entire Gospel-New Testament.

Dr. Bucaille dismisses these papyrus manuscripts with one sentence. He writes:

> **The older documents, the papyri of the third century, one possibly dating from the second (see p52 above), only transmit fragments to us.**[8]

Surely, Dr. Bucaille, who is a medical doctor, would not say after a leg amputation that the remaining 75% of the man was only a fragment!

Anyway, in my opinion, 70 percent of the Gospel according to Luke and John is more than a "fragment." It proves conclusively that the **Written Gospel** and the **Doctrinal Gospel** were the same in 200 AD as they are now.

---

8. Bucaille, BQ&S, p 78.

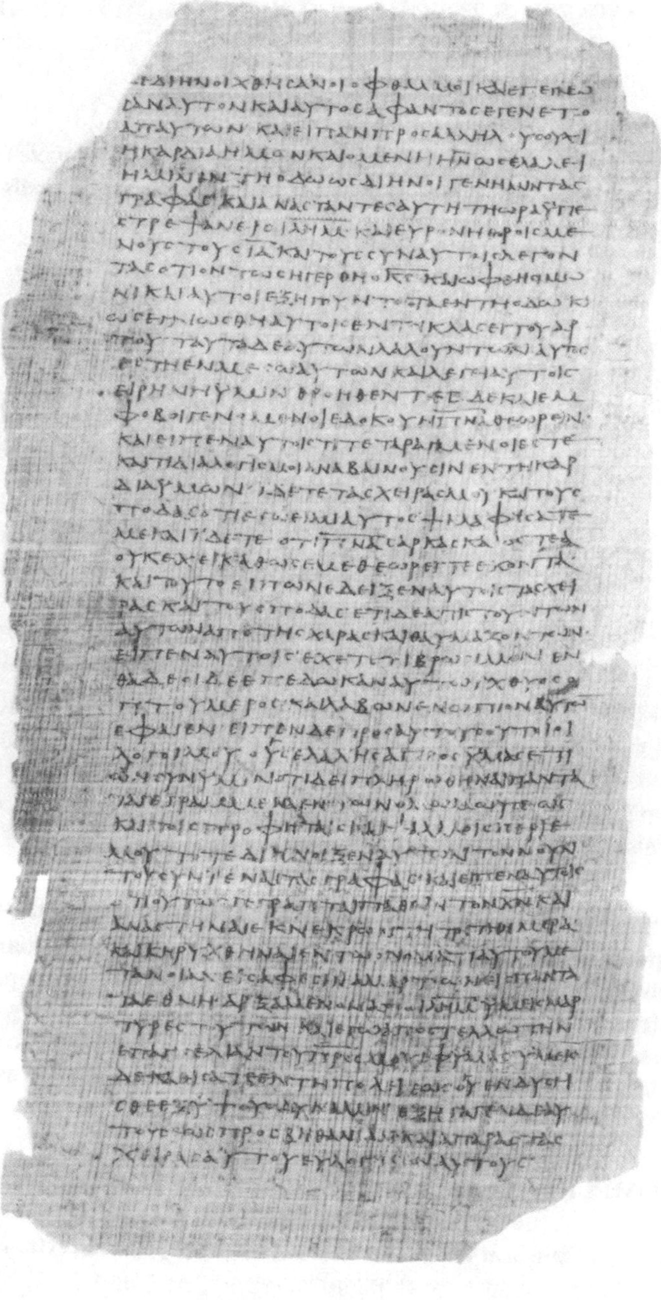

Photograph 5 —

Luke 24:31-50 as preserved in Papyrus p75 from 200 AD
including three post-resurrection appearances of Jesus.
By permission of the Bodmer Library, Geneva.

OTHER WITNESSES TO THE SECOND CENTURY TEXT OF OUR PRESENT GOSPELS

Translations

Between 150 and 180 AD, translations of the New Testament were made into old Latin and Syriac, also called Aramaic. We do not have the originals of these. We have copies from the 4th and 5th centuries.

Diagram 4

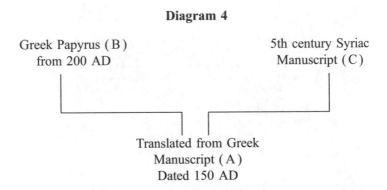

Greek Papyrus (B)
from 200 AD

5th century Syriac
Manuscript (C)

Translated from Greek
Manuscript (A)
Dated 150 AD

At first it might seem that such late copies are of little value. However, if one looks at Diagram 4 and thinks about it for a moment, it becomes clear that where a 5th century Syriac manuscript (C) agrees with a Greek papyrus (B) from 200 AD, they are two witnesses giving a clear testimony as to what the Greek text (A) said at the time of translation in 150 AD.

Quotations from the Gospel-New Testament by Early Christian Writers

To give just one example of the testimony of the early Christian writers, I will mention Tertullian. He lived from 160-220 AD and was a presbyter of the Church in Carthage in North Africa. He quotes from the New Testament more than 7,000 times, of which 3,800 are from the four Gospel accounts; and his quotations show that the text which he used is essentially the same as that which we have today.

COMPLETE COPIES OF THE GOSPEL-NEW TESTAMENT FROM 350 AD

Finally, although it is outside of the 2nd century, I shall refer again to the Codex Vaticanus which we saw in Photograph 3 in Part C of this chapter, and the Codex Sinaiticus. They both date from about 350 AD, only a little after the beginning of monasticism when the Qur'an testifies in the Sura of the Iron (Al-Ḥadīd) 57:27 that there were true Christians in the world. Photograph 6 shows a picture of the first chapter of the Gospel according to John. These codices are used to translate those parts of our present Gospel-New Testament which are

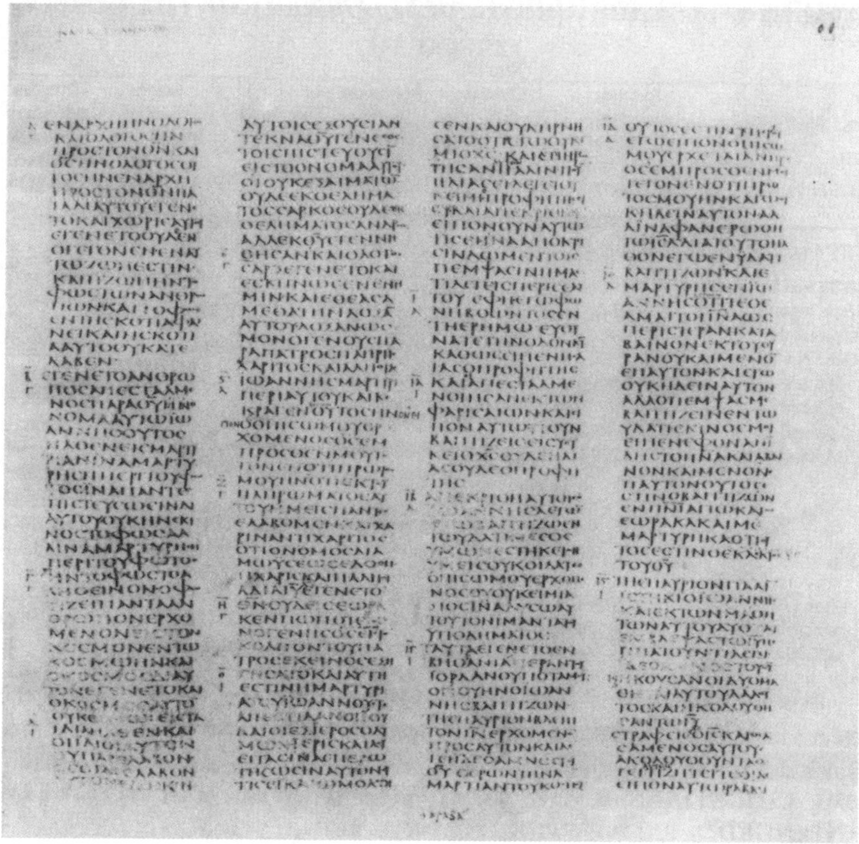

Photograph 6 —

Codex Sinaiticus from 350 AD.

Includes John 1:14, "The 'LOGOS' (Word) became flesh and dwelt among us."

By permission of the British Library.

missing from the earlier papyrus manuscripts mentioned above. Obviously they contain the **Doctrinal Gospel**.

DIAGRAM OF THE HISTORICAL DEVELOPMENT OF THE GOSPEL

In summary, we can say that by the year 200 AD, the Gospel of Jesus the Messiah which we have today was known over the whole Roman Empire. In order to clearly set forth this historical development we shall show it in the form of a diagram, just as we did with the Qur'an.

Diagram 5—THE HISTORICAL DEVELOPMENT OF THE GOSPEL

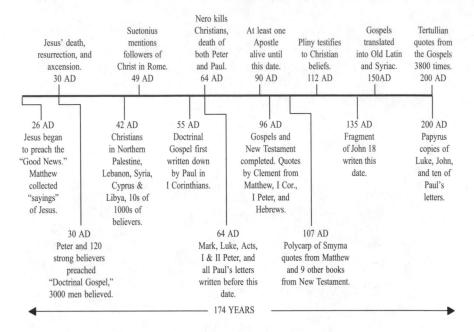

As we look at this chart, I would like the reader to reconsider the accusation that Christians have changed the Gospel. With all the above information before our eyes, we will again ask ourselves the question, **HOW DO CHRISTIANS KNOW THAT THE GOSPEL HAS NOT BEEN CHANGED?**

But this time we will answer with some other questions. **"When could it have been changed?"**

Would the disciples of Jesus have changed it while they were alive until 90 or 95 AD? No Christian believer can accept this. No Muslim would accept it about Abu Bakr and Omar. And even if the last page of the Gospel according to Mark did get lost, the TOMB IS EMPTY! and the post-resurrection appearances of Jesus to his disciples are well described in the other three Gospel accounts.

Was the Gospel changed between 90 and 150 AD? There were now tens of thousands and perhaps hundreds of thousands of believers spread over the whole Roman world. Hundreds, even thousands of these believers had heard the Gospel message from Jesus' own disciples. Could it really have been altered in any fundamental point during this period? That would be impossible.

Was it changed between 150 and 200 AD? There are translations, quotations, and important papyrus copies from this period, all testifying to essentially the same text and containing the same **Doctrinal Gospel**. Therefore, in view of all these witnesses, **WE CHRISTIANS BELIEVE that the Gospel-New Testament is the same now as it always was.**

F. SUMMING UP OF THE DEVELOPMENT OF THE QUR'AN AND THE GOSPEL

The reader will see that I have not attempted a comparable section on the Qur'an, a section covering the years between Othman's copy in 27 AH and the oldest Qur'an of 150 AH. I think that it could be done, but I am leaving that to my readers for their own personal investigation.

However, I do think that it will be helpful at this point if we compare the development of the Qur'an and the Gospel on the same time scale. The year when Muhammad and Jesus began to preach will be called "zero." In this way any similarities or differences will be easy to see.

Diagram 6

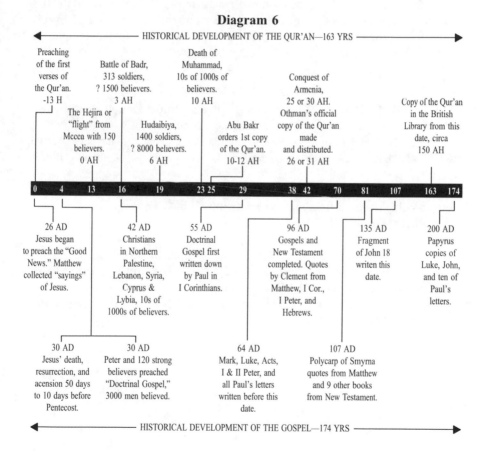

Careful examination of Diagram 6 reveals some differences. For example, the number of Christians increased at a faster rate in the beginning—3000 believers on the first day of preaching.

What strikes one, though, are the similarities. If we compare the Hejira with

Jesus' ascension to heaven, we find that there were 150 strong believers with Muhammad when he went to Medina; and Jesus left 120 strong believers when he ascended.

When we look at the situation after 10 more years we find that there were tens of thousands of Muslims when Muhammad died and his helpers became responsible. Similarly, after Jesus' disciples had preached for ten years there were tens of thousands of Christians.

The spread of the Qur'an was almost completely oral until Othman sent around the official copies 42 years after Muhammad preached the first verses. The spread of Christianity was almost completely oral until 30 to 50 years after Jesus began preaching, by which time all of the New Testament had been written except some of John's writings.

Finally, the date of the oldest known complete Qur'an, approximately 163 years after Muhammad began preaching, is essentially the same as the 174 years between the time that Jesus started preaching and our oldest papyrus copies of the Gospel accounts and other New Testament books.

IN CONCLUSION:

As you **BELIEVE** that Zaid and Othman gathered the Qur'an carefully, we **BELIEVE** that Luke and John preserved the Gospel carefully.

As you **BELIEVE** that those who copied the Qur'an did it carefully, we **BELIEVE** that the scribes who copied the Gospel-New Testament did it carefully.

As you **BELIEVE** that those leading Muslims of the first century of the Hejira would not spend their money and their lives for something that they knew to be a lie, we also **BELIEVE** that Jesus' disciples—the Apostles—would not die, as Peter and Paul did, for something that they knew was a lie.

As you **BELIEVE** that the evidence is so great in favor of the reliable transmission of the Qur'an that **you ARE SURE that you can use it with complete confidence, we BELIEVE** that the above evidence is so great in favor of the reliable transmission of the Gospel that **we ARE SURE that we can use it with complete confidence.**

FINAL CONCLUSION

NEITHER THE PRESENT QUR'AN, NOR THE PRESENT GOSPEL ACCOUNTS, HAVE SUFFERED ANY IMPORTANT CHANGE. THEY ARE ESSENTIALLY AS THEY WERE WRITTEN.

SCIENCE AND REVELATION

CHAPTER I

THE QUR'AN AND THE BIBLE: FORETELLING MODERN SCIENCE

Having now established that for matters of faith, and for our continued discussion, the texts of the Qur'an and of the Bible are both essentially as they were written, we shall take up the question of their relation to modern science. But first we must look again at the question of basic assumptions.

SMALL "BASIC ASSUMPTIONS" USED FOR RECONCILIATION

In Chapters I and II of Section One we considered major basic assumptions. The following story illustrates that we all make many smaller assumptions to bring facts into conformity with one another.

While taking a taxi from the airport in Tunisia, I got into a discussion with the taxi driver. As we talked he asked me what I thought about the Qur'an. I answered, "Well, it says that the Jews didn't kill Jesus; that they didn't crucify him, and that he didn't die. The Bible says that he did! And not only did he die, but he died for our sins, yours and mine. Now if the Qur'an means that he died but he didn't stay dead, I can go along with that and we wouldn't have any problem."

He answered, "But that would be using logic (**making a basic assumption**) to explain it in a different way" (which is true), and he went on to say, as Muslims always do, "No, Jesus didn't die!" (from Nisā' 4:157).

Then I said, "What about the verse (in the Sura of the Family of 'Imran 3:55) where God is speaking and says, **'Oh Jesus, (inna)**[1] I will cause you to die and raise you to Myself?' Doesn't that say that Jesus died before he rose again"?

The taxi driver answered, "Aaah, but statements following 'inna' don't have to be considered as being in chronological order."

I answered, "But you are using logic" (**making a basic assumption**), and we both laughed because he knew and I knew that we had both done the same thing.[2]

I mention this story because when Dr. Bucaille discusses the Bible he won't allow the commentator to make any type of "explanation" or "basic assumption" to reconcile two texts which at first might seem to contradict each other. On the other hand, when dealing with the Qur'an he is quite willing to do what every person does and make **"basic assumptions"** in his explanations.

---

1. "Inna" (merged here with the following pronoun to "innī") is an Arabic word either not translated or represented by "truly," but which intensifies the following words.

2. For those unfamiliar with the Qur'an, there are other Quranic verses which speak of Jesus' death—such as the Sura of the Table (Al-Mā'ida) 5:117 in which Jesus speaks to God and says, "When you caused me to die, you were their overseer" (note the past tense). To reconcile these verses with the verse saying "Jesus didn't die," Muslims wish to change the chronological order and say that Jesus was raised into heaven but will come back again, turn everyone to Islam, and then die.

This will be seen very clearly as we consider the following points. Dr. Bucaille claims (A) that the Qur'an shows extraordinary foreknowledge of modern science which can be accounted for only by a divine origin. He claims that (B) the Qur'an, unlike the Bible, has no scientific errors. Finally (C) he criticizes the Bible because he does not feel that it makes enough appeal to nature to show God's glory and power. We shall now examine these claims to see whether they are valid.

Dr. Bucaille, however, is not the only writer who discusses the relation between the Qur'an and science. Several other Muslim scientists have also taken up the pen, so we shall examine some of their ideas—especially some of those proposed by Dr. Bèchir Torki. Dr. Torki, a Tunisian with a Ph. D. in nuclear science, is the founder-editor of the magazine *Science et Foi* (Science and Faith) and the author of the book *L'Islam Religion de la Science.*[3]

FORETELLING MODERN SCIENCE

These apologists make great efforts to find indications of modern scientific knowledge in the Qur'an and then claim this as a miraculous proof of a divine origin. This is not wrong, but on further examination the results are not as spectacular as some would suggest; and as we shall see at the end of this chapter, there is a very definite theological problem with some of these claims.

1. Water Cycle

Dr. Bucaille[4] and Dr. Torki[5] both discuss this and claim that the Qur'an has foreknowledge of the water cycle by which water (1) **evaporates** from the seas and the earth; (2) **becomes clouds**; which (3) **give rain**; which (4a) **causes the land to bring forth**, and (4b) **replenishes the water table,** which reveals itself by gushing springs and full wells.

Dr. Bucaille declares that until the late sixteenth century "man held totally inaccurate views on the water cycle," and considers that several statements in the Qur'an which reflect a knowledge of the water cycle could not therefore have come from any human source.

He quotes Suras 50:9-11, 35:9, 30:48, 7:57, 25:48-49, and 45:5, as verses which include steps (2), (3), and (4a). As an example, we will look at the Late Meccan Sura of the Heights (Al-A'rāf) 7:57:

> (God) is the One Who sends forth the winds like heralds of His Mercy. When they have carried (2) the heavy-laden clouds, We drive them to a dead land. Then We cause (3) water to descend and thereby (4a) bring forth fruits of every kind. Thus We will Bring forth the dead. Maybe you will remember.

To demonstrate step (4b) he brings verses from Suras 23:18-19, 15:22, and the Late Meccan Sura of The Crowds (Al-Zumar) 39:21 which reads,

---

3. l'UGTT, Tunis, 1979.
4. Bucaille, BQ&S, p 173-178.
5. Torki, op. cit., p 151-152.

Have you not seen that God sent water down from the sky and led it through (**4b**) sources into the ground? Then He caused sown fields of different colors to grow."

These verses are accurate, of course, but the question is do they show special foreknowledge and thereby prove divine revelation? The answer must surely be "no." Every man or woman, even those living in a city, could describe steps (**2**), (**3**), and (**4a**). And every person in contact with farmers during a drought will hear them say that their wells and springs have dried up, thus showing common knowledge of step (**4b**) that rain is the source and origin of underground water.

But what of step (**1**)—**evaporation as the source of rain clouds**? This would be much more difficult to understand by observation and **it is not mentioned** in any of the Quranic verses cited.

Dr. Torki has recognized this lack and has proposed the Early Meccan Sura of the News (Al-Naba') 78:12-16, as a remedy. We read,

> And We have built above you seven strong (heavens) and made a dazzling lamp, and have sent down from the clouds water in abundance that with it We may bring forth grain and plants and gardens of luxurious growth."

Here he wishes to make the **basic assumption** that reference to the sun, "a dazzling lamp," followed by rain demonstrates the missing step (**1**). This is not absolutely impossible, but it seems very unlikely. The sun and rain are the 8th and 9th items in a whole list of blessings from God, a list which includes such completely unrelated things as mountains and sleep and marriage. There is no reason that either a 7th century Arab or a 20th century person should here understand a cause and effect relationship between the sun and the rain.

On the other hand, when we turn to the **Torah-Old Testament** we find three references which clearly include the difficult step (**1**).

In the book of the Prophet Amos 5:8, written 1300 years before the Hejira, we read,

> He who made the Pleiades and Orion, who turns blackness into dawn and darkens day into night, who (**1**)**calls for the waters of the sea** and (**3**)pours them out over the face of the land—the LORD is His name.

In the book of the Prophet Isaiah 55: 9-11, also 1300 years before the Hejira, it says:

> As the heavens are higher than the earth, so are My ways higher than your ways and My thoughts than your thoughts.
> As the (**3**) rain and snow come down from heaven, and do not (**1**) **return to it** without watering the earth and (**4a**) making it bud and flourish, so that it yields seed for the sower and bread for the eater, so is My word that goes out from My mouth:
> It will not return to Me empty, but will accomplish what I desire and achieve the purpose for which I sent it.

Thirdly, from the book of Job (Aiyūb) 36:26-28, a Prophet who lived on the northern borders of Arabia, we find this very detailed description of the water cycle. Written at least 1000 years before the Hejira, it says,

> How great is God—beyond our understanding! The number of His years is past finding out.
> He **(1) draws up the drops of water**, which distill from the mist as **(3)**rain; the **(2)**clouds pour down their moisture and abundant showers fall on mankind.

These verses have mentioned all the steps except **(4b)**, and in the book of the Prophet Hosea 13:15, almost 1400 years before the Hejira, we find these words showing knowledge of this step also:

> …An east wind from the LORD will come, blowing in from the desert; his spring will fail and his well will dry up…

No rain in the dry east wind, with the result that the well and spring dry up, is clearly the reverse of rain replenishing the water table. Thus the **Torah-Old Testament** describes all four steps including the difficult step **(1)**.

2. Currents in the Sea

Dr. Bèchir Torki[6] quotes the Sura of the Light (Al-Nūr) 24:39,40, from 5-6 AH, which reads,

> As for those who disbelieve, their deeds are as a mirage in a desert. The thirsty man mistakes it for water; until when he comes to it, he finds nothing…
> Or as darkness in a fathomless sea. There covers him **a wave, above which is a wave**, above which is a cloud. Layer upon layer of darkness. If he holds out his hand he can barely see it. And for whomever God has not appointed light, for him there is no light.

In his discussion of these verses, he quotes a director of one of the space projects which photographed the oceans as saying, "The waves and the currents in the depths of the ocean are more important and larger than the superficial waves." Dr. Torki proposes that when the Qur'an speaks of **"waves above waves,"** this shows foreknowledge of modern marine science, which has demonstrated that there are many ocean currents such as the Gulf Stream and the Japanese Current.

This is not impossible, although the same word is used both times for wave rather than having different words for "wave" and "current." It seems to me, however, that such a reference is really poetic prose describing the unbeliever's dark position in reference to God. But if Dr. Torki is right and this is foreknowledge of modern science, then it must be pointed out that this same information was foretold in the **Torah-Old Testament** in Jonah, and in the **Zabūr** of David.

After Jonah (Yūnus), who prophesied in 750 BC, was swallowed by the fish,

---

6. Torki, op. cit., p 159.

Jonah 2:1,3-6 says:

> From inside the fish Jonah prayed to the LORD his God.
> He said,...You hurled me into the deep,
> into the very heart of the seas,
> and the **currents** swirled about me;
> all Your **waves** and **breakers** swept over me.
> I said, "I have been banished from Your sight;
> yet I will look again toward Your holy temple."
> The engulfing waters threatened me,
> the deep surrounded me;
> seaweed was wrapped around my head.
> To the roots of the mountains I sank down;
> the earth beneath barred me in forever.
> But You brought my life up from the pit
> O LORD my God.

The Hebrew word used here for "currents" is "*nahar*," and it can also mean "river" as in Arabic. "Waves" and "breakers" are two different words—almost synonymous except that by its root "breakers" probably stands for the great, large waves of storms.

Even earlier, in 1000 BC or 1600 years before the Hejira, the Prophet David wrote the **Zabūr** by the inspiration of the Holy Spirit. In one of his great psalms of praise, Psalm 8:4,6,8, we read,

> What is man that You are mindful of him,
> the son of man that You care for him?...
> You made him ruler over the works of Your hands,
> You put everything under his feet:...
> the birds of the air, and the fish of the sea,
> all that swim **the paths of the seas**.

"**Paths of the seas**" may only be poetic repetition of the preceding line, but it is, along with the passage from Jonah, a correct description of the ocean currents as we know them in the 20th century.

3. A Barrier Between Salt and Fresh Water

In the Early Meccan Sura of The Most Gracious (Al-Rahmān) 55:19-21, a "barrier" is mentioned between two types of water. It reads,

> He (God) has let free the two bodies of flowing water meeting together. Between them is a **barrier** which they do not transgress. Then which of the favors of your Lord will you deny.

The word used here for "barrier," "barzakh," means—interval, gap, break, bar, obstruction, or isthmus.

The same information is given in a fuller form in another Early Meccan Sura, The Criterion (Al-Furqān) 25:53, which reads,

> It is He Who has let free the two bodies of flowing water—one palatable and sweet, and the other salty and bitter. And He made between them a **barrier** and **a partition that it is forbidden to pass**.

165

The phrase "a partition that it is forbidden to pass" represents two words from the same root. This is done in Arabic to stress or accent whatever is being discussed. The word "hijr" means "forbidden," "interdicted," "prohibited," all very strong words, and the second word which is the past participle of the verb has the same meanings. Therefore very literally one might translate this as "He (God) made between them a bar and a forbidden forbidding."

Dr. Bucaille discusses this briefly,[7] but Dr. Torki devotes two and a half pages to it[8] with a long discussion of osmotic pressure and how it is proved with U-tubes and semi-permeable membranes in the laboratory. He then concludes by saying,

> Muhammad had neither laboratory nor research equipment to discover all these mysteries and understand this barrier clearly cited in the Qur'an. This proves another time that this book was not written by the hand of man, but is the work of the One God.

However, the question must again be asked, Are we not faced with an observable phenomenon? Is it not presented as a known fact showing the favor of the Lord? Do not all the fishermen who fish at the outlets of rivers which empty into salt water know this fact?

While trading for Khadija, Muhammad took trips as far as Aleppo, north of Damascus in Syria. Is it not probable that at some time during these trips Muhammad went down to the coast in Syria or Lebanon; or talked to a seaman who knew that the waters were still unmixed far out in the Mediterranean?

In his latest book, Dr. Bucaille himself praises primitive people for their skill in observing and classifying. He writes,

> The naturalists tell how they have been impressed by the accuracy with which certain primitive tribes, having received no outside education in the subject, succeed nevertheless in distinguishing the animal species which surround them, and arriving at a classification almost worthy of an expert.[9]

Surely it is correct to assume that if they can observe the animals with such skill, then they can also observe the other natural phenomena which surround them, such as sweet water far out at sea.

Frankly, to read these verses as expressing modern scientific knowledge can raise more problems than it solves, because such an interpretation will also demand 20th century scientific accuracy of measurement. When God makes "a barrier and a partition that it is forbidden to pass," it sounds like a 100% prohibition. Shall we understand and translate this verse as "These waters shall never mix!"?

In fact there is no "bar," no semi-permeable membrane in the sea forbidding the mixing of the two, and the forces are actually in favor of mixing.

---

7. Bucaille, BQ&S, p 179-180.
8. Torki, op. cit., p 160-162.
9. Bucaille, *L'Homme*, p 23. (translation mine)

166

A scientist friend commenting on this said,

> It is simply that the salt and fresh water are physically separated (the effluent from the river displacing the sea water), but there is no barrier. Thermodynamically or energetically—the mixing is a spontaneous, immediate process, **highly favored by entropy considerations**. The only "barrier" is kinetic, in that it takes a little time to mix that much "stuff" together.

Dr. Bucaille recognizes this, so he has added a qualifying fact, another tiny "basic assumption." He writes, "The mixing of their waters (the rivers) with the salt water usually does not take place **until far out at sea**."

The Theological Problem

There is, however, a further problem with this effort to show foreknowledge of the fine points of modern science. Most of these Quranic descriptions are called signs. If the Qur'an calls them signs, then those listening were surely expected to understand something when they first heard it from Muhammad. Otherwise it would not be a sign.

God is all powerful and can do anything except sin. Therefore, He can obviously will to reveal a fact which is completely unknown and which could not be known at the moment of revelation, but it could not be a sign.

An example of this is found in Job 26:7 which says,

> He (God) stretches out the north over empty space.
> **He suspends the earth over nothing**.

As far as we can understand at present, Job could only know this by revelation from God.

A second example is found in Deuteronomy 23:12-14 where God gives orders for sanitation.

> You shall have a place outside the camp and you shall go out to it; and you shall have a stick with your weapons, and when you sit down outside, you shall dig a hole with it, and turn back and cover up your excrement. Because the LORD your God walks in the midst of your camp, to save you and to give up your enemies before you, therefore your camp must be holy...

As every reader will realize, this command is completely correct according to 20th century medical knowledge and public health recommendations. (And one could ask why it was not repeated in the Qur'an, which some Muslims claim has repeated everything of value from the previous books.) It prevents flies from spreading disease. But this is not explained. The reason given is that the camp should be holy in God's eyes. But God, the Eternal One, does not call any of these examples signs in the **Torah-Old Testament**. Whether those who heard these words understood the scientific information was not important.

SIGNS

Jesus said that his miracles of healing, which he called works, were signs so that people would believe. In John we read,

> "If I don't do the works (miracles) of my Father, don't believe me. **But if I do**, even though you do not believe me, **believe the works, that you may know and understand** that the Father is in me and I in the Father" (John 10:37-38).
> **"If I had not done among them the works (miracles) that no one else did, they would not be guilty of sin**. But now they have seen (the works) and yet have hated both me and my Father" (John 15:24).

Muhammad claimed that the desert coming to life after the rain was a sign so that people would believe in the resurrection and judgment. In the Sura of Iron (Al-Ḥadīd) 57:17, from 8 AH, we read,

> Know that God quickens the earth after its death. **We have made clear our signs for you, that perhaps you may understand.**

And in the Late Meccan Sura of the Cattle (Al-An'ām) 6:67, it says,

> We detail our **signs for people who know.**

In Job 28:23, 25-28, the "weight of the wind" is mentioned as an indication of the wisdom of God. It reads,

> God understands the way to it (wisdom), and He knows its place.
> **When He gave to the wind its weight**, and meted out the waters by measure; when He made a decree for the rain, and a way for the lightning of the thunder. Then He saw it and declared it; and He established it, and searched it out, and He said to man,
> "Behold, the fear of the Lord, that is wisdom; and to depart from evil is understanding."

One could enter into a long discussion here about how barometers work to measure the weight of the air, and how other instruments measure wind speed, but Job mentions this as an indication of the wisdom of God. Therefore what shall we understand? Does it show foreknowledge of 20th century science? Probably not. It probably represents an observation which Job, or anyone else, could have made by feeling the breeze in his face and having seen the sail of a ship filled and pushed by the wind.

In each of these cases, whether it be Jesus' miracles, or the desert coming to life, or the weight of the wind, the sign could be recognized and had meaning for the listeners.

The problem comes when something which is referred to as a sign was incorrectly understood until now in the 20th century.

That a prophet would use some obscure phenomenon of nature, misunderstood or unknown by his audience, to illustrate or reinforce his message is unthinkable. How could it have any effect on the minds and hearts of his hearers? **God gives the prophet simple, natural illustrations which everyone understands.**

If the currents under the sea were not understood by the people of Mecca and Medina, how could the Quranic reference to "wave above wave" have any meaning for them? They either understood it as poetry showing how deeply in trouble the sinner is without God, or they didn't understand it! Then it was not a sign.

It could be possible, in theory, for a verse to have two meanings: one obvious meaning understood by everyone when the prophet spoke, and another more complicated meaning for another time. Perhaps this is what Dr. Bucaille and Dr. Torki had in mind when they wrote about "wave above wave" or the two kinds of water. However, in the next chapter we shall look at some Quranic verses which seem to have conveyed a **wrong** meaning from the moment they were given 1400 years ago, and that creates a very difficult theological problem.

CHAPTER II

NO SCIENTIFIC PROBLEMS (ERRORS?!) IN THE QUR'AN.

A. THE EARTH, THE HEAVENS AND THE 6 OR 8 DAYS OF CREATION

1. MOUNTAINS

On pages 180-182, Dr. Bucaille has a section on "The Earth's Relief" in which he discusses the Quranic verses about mountains. The Qur'an has more than a dozen verses stating that God placed firm and immovable mountains on the earth, and in some of these verses the mountains are listed as either a blessing for believers or a warning for the unbelievers. One example of this is found in the Sura Luqman 31:10-11 where the mountains are listed as one of five warnings:

He has created the heavens without supports that you can see, and has cast (alqā ألقَى) **onto the earth firm mountains** (rawāsiya) **lest it should shake with you** (tamīda bikum تَمِيدَ بِكمْ**).

In the Prophets (Al-Anibiyā') 21:31, as one of seven warnings we read:

And We have set on the earth firm mountains (rawāsiya رَوَاسِى), lest it should shake with them (tamīda bihim**).

Finally in the Bee (Al-Naḥl) 16:15, among many "signs for the wise" we read:

And He has cast onto the earth firm mountains (rawāsiya) **lest it should shake with you** (tamīda bikum**).

The phrase "tamīda bi" from māda, yamīdu, is only used in the above three Quranic verses which are marked.** Hans Wehr's "Dictionary of Modern Written Arabic" gives the meaning of the verbal phrase "māda bi" as: **to shake something violently. "Māda bi"** is the very form used in these verses.

We see then that the believers and unbelievers are told that Allah has done this great thing. He has thrown down and placed the mountains so that the earth will not shake violently with them. Therefore, we must ask ourselves what the followers of Muhammad were supposed to understand.

In the next two verses another picture is given.

The News (Al-Naba') 78:6-7, Early Meccan.

Have We not made the earth an expanse, and the mountains as stakes. (al-jibāla autādan الجِبَالَ أَوْتَاداً) ("as those used to anchor a tent in the ground.") (Bucaille, p 191)

170

The Overwhelming (Al-Ghāshiya) 88:17,19, Early Meccan.

Do they (the unbelievers) not look...at the mountains, (al-jibal), how they have been pitched (like a tent)? (Translation Bucaille, p 191)

Here men are told that the mountains are placed as tent pegs. Tent pegs keep the tent stable so again the idea is put forward that the pegs, the mountains, will keep the earth from shaking.

A third picture is present in the word (rawāsiya) used for mountains. Wehr translates this word as unshakable mountains. The Munjid says (al-jibāl thawābat al-ruwāsikh الجِبَال الثَّوَابَت الرُّوَاسِخ) firmly established, fixed mountains. The word comes from the root (arsā آرسَا), the same root used for the Arabic word for anchor. To throw out or cast the anchor is (alqā almirsah آلقَى المِرْسَاة). So instead of "cast the anchor to keep the ship from moving," we have "cast the mountains to keep the earth from shaking."

From these pictures it is clear that Muhammad's followers understood that the Mountains were thrown down:

(a) like tent pegs to keep a tent in place.
(b) like an anchor to hold a ship in place.
(c) to stop the earth from moving, i.e., limit earthquakes.

But, in fact, this is false. Earthquakes are common events associated with the forming of mountains.

Since these verses present a definite problem, after quoting several of the above verses about mountains Dr. Bucaille says,

> Modern geologists describe the folds in the Earth as giving foundations to the mountains, and their dimensions go roughly one mile to roughly ten miles. The stability of the Earth's crust results from the phenomenon of these folds.

But is this true? Commenting on Dr. Bucaille's statement, Professor of Geology Dr. David A. Young says,

> While it is true that many mountain ranges are composed of folded rocks (and the folds may be of large scale) it is not true that the folds render the crust stable. **The very existence of the folds is evidence of instability in the crust.** [1]

In other words, mountains don't keep the earth from shaking. Their formation caused and still causes the surface of the earth to shake.

PLATE TECTONICS

Geological theories at the present time propose that the hardened crust of the earth is made up of sections or plates which slowly move in relation to each other (about as fast as the growth of a fingernail). Sometimes the plates separate, and most geologists believe that this explains the separation of North and South America from Europe and Africa.

---

1. Professor of Geology, Calvin College, Grand Rapids, Michigan, personal communication.

At other places on the earth the plates collide, and then they buckle, wrinkle and slid over each other. An example of this method of mountain formation is found in the Middle East where the migration of Arabia toward Iran has resulted in the Zagros range. The Atlas mountains in Morocco and the Alps are other examples of fold mountains caused by plate shifts. In many parts of the world, as one travels along the roads one sees a hillside where the sandstone layers, which were horizontal when they were deposited in the sea many eons ago, are now sticking up in the air at angles of 30 degrees or 50 degrees or even 90 degrees. Diagram 7 shows this type of formation.

Diagram 7

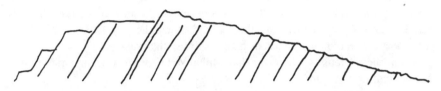

Ibn Sīnā' (Avicenna), writing in the *Kitāb al-Shifā', The Book of the Remedy*, about 412 AH/1021 AD, observed these layers. He says nothing about the tilting but discusses the layers in the following words:

> It is possible that each time the land was exposed by the ebbing of the sea a layer was left, since we see **that some mountains appear to have been piled up layer by layer**, and it is therefore likely that the clay from which they are formed was itself at one time arranged in layers. One layer was formed first, then, at a different period, a further layer was formed and piled [upon the first, and so on]...[2]

Sometimes the plates get caught on each other and stop sliding. During this period great forces are built up. When the forces of friction are overcome, the piece of plate that was stuck lurches forward, causing the shock wave of a "thrust quake." In a recent earthquake it was calculated that the Cocos plate in Mexico suddenly jumped forward three meters.

During other quakes whole sections of plate are pushed upward or downward. In 1923 there was an earthquake at Sagami Bay, Japan which laid half of Tokyo in ruins. In a chapter entitled "Mass Mortality in the Sea," Brongersma-Sanders describes the geological changes in these words:

> No other known earthquake has caused such remarkable distortions of the seabed. In the central portion of Sagami Bay "the area of distortion is of vast extent, and the seabed has subsided as much as 460 feet (140 meters) at the northwest end, 590 feet (180 meters) near the center, and 656 and 690 feet (200 and 210 meters) at

---

2. *A Source Book in Medieval Science*, Edward Grant, Harvard University Press, 1974, p. 620

the southeast end. In the northeast portion, the greatest uplift measured is 820 feet (250 meters) and in the southwest portion 328 feet (100 meters)." (quoted in turn from Davidson, 1931, p 94)[3]

Ibn Sīnā, though he thought that earthquakes were caused by winds inside the earth, accurately described the above-mentioned effect, saying,

> The formation of heights is brought about by an essential cause...when, as in many violent earthquakes, the wind which produces the earthquake raises a part of the ground and a height is formed.[4]

VOLCANOES

Another type of mountain is that formed by volcanoes. Lava and ash from inside the earth are thrown out and piled up until a high mountain is formed, even from the bottom of the sea. The Hawaiian group rises from an ocean depth of more than 1.5 km (1 mile) to the crater of Mauna Kea which is 4.2 km (2.6 miles) in the air.

On occasion the volcanoes explode, as happened in the south Pacific at Krakatoa in 1883, when the whole island was blown away, killing 36,000 people. At other times volcanoes are responsible for such severe earthquakes that surrounding towns are completely destroyed. The town of Catania, near Mt. Etna in Sicily, has been destroyed eight times during recorded history. This 3000 meter peak is still active, and in 1983 more than 200 quakes were recorded when it had a prolonged eruption and the lava almost destroyed several villages.

Diagram 8 shows both of these processes. On the left the Indo-Australia plate is moving toward the right and forcing down the Pacific plate coming from the right. In the center there are two places where liquid magma is flowing up and forming volcanoes. All this activity results in the large earthquake zone shown in the right center of the diagram.

Diagram 8

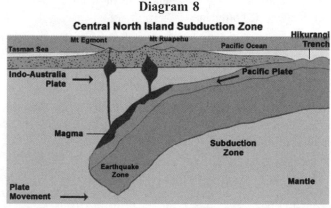

Permission granted by Heurisko Ltd, Christchurch, New Zealand

---

3. *Treatise on Marine Ecology and Paleoecology*, Vol 1, Geological Society of America, Memoir 67, 1957, p 976.
4. (Avicenna) Grant, op. cit., p 619.

We can conclude from this information that mountains were formed originally with movement and shaking of the earth's crust; and that now, in the present, many earthquakes are caused by their continued formation. When the plates buckle over each other there are earthquakes. When the volcanoes erupt associated earthquakes may occur.

Throwing the mountains down onto the earth may be poetry, but to say that mountains keep the earth from shaking is a "severe difficulty" which is out of step with modern science. It may be that Muslim writers and theologians and scientists will be able to make some basic assumptions concerning mountain formation and the shaking of the earth which will satisfy them in relation to this problem, but it is a problem.

2. SEVEN HEAVENS

The Qur'an speaks in several verses of the "seven heavens." Dr. Torki speaks of these verses and quotes them as follows:

Noah (Nūḥ) 71:15-16, Early Meccan.
> Do you not see how God has created the seven heavens one above the other, and made the moon a light in their midst, and made the sun as a lamp?

The Dominion (Al-Mulk) 67:3, Middle Meccan.
> He Who created the seven heavens, one above the other...

The Believers (Al-Mū'minūn) 23:17,86, Late Meccan.
> And We have made above you seven tracts (or roads or paths), and we are never unmindful of the creation.
> Say, "Who is Lord of the seven heavens, and Lord of the tremendous throne?"

Ḥā Mim Al-Sajda 41:12, Late Meccan.
> And He completed them seven heavens in two days and inspired in each heaven its command...

The Children of Israel (Banī Isrā'īl) 17:44, -1 before the Hejira.
> The seven heavens and the earth and all beings therein declare His glory.

The Heifer (Al-Baqara) 2:29, 2 AH.
> He it is Who created for you all that is in the earth, Then turned He to the heaven, and fashioned it as seven heavens. And He is the knower of all things.

One might easily pass over these verses as essentially poetic, but Dr.Torki attempts to show that they agree with modern astronomical knowledge.[5]

Starting with the earth's atmosphere which averages about 40 kilometers in thickness as the first heaven, he then multiplies this by 10,000 for the dimension of the second, or lunar heaven. Multiplying this by 10,000 gives the third, or solar

---

5. Ibid., p 111-114.

174

heaven; and continuing to multiply by 10,000 each time, he proposes "the heaven of the nearest stars," "the galactic heaven" (since it is about the size of our galaxy), "the heaven of the nearest galaxies," and finally "the cosmic heaven."

This scheme gives seven divisions, of course, but on analysis it is not convincing. Calling the earth's atmosphere the first heaven, and everything else the second, might have some validity; but everything else is arbitrary. Outside the earth's atmosphere, space is continuous and qualitatively similar, as Torki himself says.

It is a **basic assumption** to separate what is continuous space into a lunar and a solar heaven.

It is a **basic assumption** to separate the sun, which is a star, from the near stars, or from the galaxy which contains it.

It is a **basic assumption** to call our galaxy one heaven, and other galaxies another heaven.

Even multiplying by 10,000 seems to be a completely arbitrary **basic assumption** since no scientific reason is given, and it has no relation to any of the spiritual numbers which Dr. Torki has mentioned elsewhere, such as "7" or "19."

Making these **basic assumptions** is not wrong. The whole reason for writing this chapter is to show that **we all do it**. But they are not scientifically convincing.

Even more important from the Muslim standpoint, Dr. Torki's hypothesis does not agree with the following verses from the Qur'an,

The Ranks (Al-Ṣāffāt) 37:6, Early Meccan.

> We have indeed adorned the **lower heaven with the beauty of the stars** (kawākib اَلْكَوَاكِب).

Ḥā Mim Al-Sajda 41:12, Late Meccan.

> And He completed them seven heavens in two days and inspired in each heaven its command; and **We adorned the lower heaven with lamps** (maṣābīḥ اَلْمَصَابِيح), and rendered it guarded...

The Dominion (Al-Mulk) 67:3,5, Middle Meccan.

> He Who created the seven heavens, one above the other...
> And We have adorned the lowest heaven with lamps (maṣābīḥ اَلْمَصَابِيح)...

On page 118, Dr. Torki says that these "lamps," which the Qur'an places in the **lowest of the seven heavens**, are the stars.[6]

The **Bible** speaks of the heavens in almost 700 different verses, but it mentions more than one heaven only one time. In the Gospel-New Testament Paul writes as follows of a man who was raised up to the third heaven:

> I know **a man in Christ** who fourteen years ago **was caught up to the third heaven**. Whether it was in the body or out of the

---

6. Ibid., p 118. Yet, this is in contradiction to his own hypothetical division by which he has placed the stars in the **outer five heavens**.

body I do not know—God knows. And I know that this man…was caught up to Paradise. He heard inexpressible things, things that man is not permitted to tell (II Corinthians 12:2-4).

This clearly refers to spiritual heavens and has nothing to do with the material creation. But even if Paradise hadn't been mentioned, that would surely have to be the meaning. For otherwise what could it mean to say that this Christian was caught up to some place out in the galaxy?

3. SHOOTING STARS—METEORS AND METEORITES

We considered this a little bit in Chapter II of Section One, but now we shall look at all the verses which the Qur'an gives on the subject.

The Ranks (Al-Ṣāffāt) 37:6-10, Early Meccan.

> We have indeed adorned the lower heaven with the beauty of the stars and for guard against **every defiant devil**, so they cannot hear **the highest assembly** but be cast away from every side—repulsed for theirs is a perpetual torment—except he who snatches something by stealth, and a piercing flame (shihābun thāqibun شِهَابٌ ثَاقِبٌ) pursues him.

The Spirits (Al-Jinn, can be good or evil) 72:8-9, Late Meccan.

> A Jinn is speaking and says, "And we pried into heaven and we found it full of strong guards and **meteors** (shuhubān شُهُبًا), and we used to sit near it, perched for hearing; but **he who listens now will find a flaming fire** (shihāb الشِّهَاب) **in wait for him."**

The Dominion (Al-Mulk) 67:5, Middle Meccan.

> **And We have adorned the lowest heaven with lamps** (maṣābīḥ الْمَصَابِيح), **and We have made them missiles** (or stonings—rujūman رُجُومًا) **for the devils** and for them we have prepared the punishment of fire.

The Rocky Tract (Al-Ḥijr) 15:16-18, Late Meccan.

> It is We Who have set out the zodiac in the heaven and adorned it for the beholders, and **We have guarded it from every cursed devil (stoned satan), except he who steals a hearing and a clear flaming fire** (shihāb الشِّهَاب) **pursues him.**

The Night-visitant (Al-Ṭāriq) 86:2-3, Early Meccan.

> And what will explain to thee what the Night-visitant is?—(it is) **the piercing star** (al-najm al-thāqib النَّجْم الشَّقِيب).

There is not enough information in the context of this last verse to know about what it speaks with certainty, but since it has the adjective "piercing," it has been included for completeness.

Scientifically, what are popularly called "shooting stars" include two main classes of astronomical objects—meteors and meteorites.

a. Meteors, which are by far the more common, are rarely larger than a pin head. When they enter the atmosphere at speeds of about 18.6 miles or 30 km/ second, they become white hot from the friction and are burned up. The smallest ones, less than 1/20 of a millimeter in diameter, deaccelerate without burning up and float to earth as micro-meteorites. These have been recovered and some include iron-nickel compounds with up to 60% nickel.

In addition to sporadic meteors, there are also meteor showers during which many meteors may be observed at the same moment. It is quite widely accepted, though not proved, that meteor showers represent the debris of old comets. When the earth passes though this debris **the resulting meteors follow parallel paths**, even though visually they appear to be spreading out from a common point just over the horizon. According to Robert Hutchison, Curator of Meteorites of The British Museum, these are made up of water as ice, frozen ammonia, methane and carbon dioxide.[7]

In their notes, or by their translations, Yusuf Ali, Pickthall, and Hamidullah have all indicated that the Arabic words used in the above verses refer to meteors.

b. Meteorites are solid lumps of matter which can survive passage through the earth's atmosphere and reach the ground. While passing through the atmosphere the outer layer melts and streams away so that they are seen as a spectacularly bright fireball of light called a bolide. Perhaps this is what the Qur'an is referring to as the "night-visitant—the piercing star" in Sura 86 quoted above.

There are three principal types of meteorites: 1) the irons made up of nickel-iron; 2) the stones composed of silicates; and 3) the stony-irons made up of a mixture. Examination of light reflected from meteorite samples shows it to be very similar to the light reflected from asteroids, as seen by the telescope. This, plus the calculation of the orbits of three meteorites which have been photographed in fall, confirms the current theory that most meteorites come from the asteroid belt.

The difficulty here is obviously not with the science and composition of meteors and meteorites. The difficulty is how to understand what the Qur'an can be talking about. The word "rajīm," usually translated as "cursed" in modern translations, comes from the verb meaning "to stone," and Hamidullah translates 67:5 which is quoted above with the words,

> and We have designed them (the lamps) as a means of stoning
> the devils. (translation from French mine)

What shall we understand when it says that God throws meteors, whether made of carbon dioxide or iron-nickel, **at non-material devils who steal a hearing at the heavenly council?** And what are we to understand when the meteors come in showers and are traveling in parallel paths? Are we to understand that the devils all lined up in rows at the same moment? These are not easy questions.

---

7. *The Search For Our Beginnings*, Hutchison, Oxford U. Press, 1983.

4. CONTRADICTIONS IN TIME

a. The Quranic Days of Creation.

In Chapter II of Section One, we talked about the meaning of the word "smoke" in relation to the days of creation. In this section we want to look a little more at the number of days and their order. There are seven references which speak of God creating the heavens and the earth in six days—7:54, 10:3, 11:7 25:59, 32:4, 50:38, and 57:4. Of these it will be sufficient to quote the Late Meccan Sura of Jonah (Yūnus) 10:3, which includes all the information given by the others.

> Indeed, your Lord is God Who created the heavens and the earth in **six days**, then He mounted on the throne directing all things. There is no intercessor except after His permission. That is God your Lord, so worship Him.

That all sounds very straightforward, but in the Late Meccan Sura of Ḥā-Mim Al-Sajda 41:9-12, it reads,

> Say, "Do you deny Him Who created the earth in **two days**? And do you join equals to Him? He is the Lord of the worlds, and He placed therein firm hills rising above it, and blessed it and measured therein its nourishment in **four days**, according to (the need) of those who ask (for food)."
>
> **Then** He turned equally to the heaven when it was smoke, and said unto it and unto the earth, "Come together willingly or unwillingly."
>
> They both said, "We come obediently."
>
> And He completed them seven heavens in **two days** and inspired in each heaven its command, and We adorned the lower heaven with lamps and rendered it guarded. That is the decree of the Mighty, the Knower.

It doesn't take a genius in mathematics to read this and see that it seems to say that God made the earth in two days, and the nourishment according to the needs of each one in four days, which makes a total of six. **And after** the mountains were formed and nourishment—presumably plants and animals—**THEN** God made the seven heavens in two days for a total of eight days.

So now we have a contradiction!?

The Qur'an says seven times that God did it in six days, while here it says eight days, so what does one do? According to the rule suggested by Aristotle which was quoted at the end of Section Three, Chapter I, we should give the benefit of the doubt to the author, and not take it to ourselves.

Therefore, it seems logical to make the **basic assumption** that in Muhammad's understanding some of these days were concurrent and going along together, thus allowing a total of only six days. That still leaves the problem of the earth being formed, cooled, and growing nourishment, before the heavens are formed—a sequence which is also found in the Sura of the Heifer

178

(Al-Baqara) 2:29 which says,

> He it is Who created for you all that is in the earth. Then He
> turned to the heaven, and fashioned it as seven heavens."

These Quranic statements do not agree at all with modern theories of the
beginning of the universe, but I shall allow others to attempt a solution to that.

b. The Biblical Days of Jonah.

Perhaps the reader is asking, "Why so much time on such a minor matter?" It
is because Dr. Bucaille uses a whole page[8] to point out a similar time problem in
the Gospel-New Testament. He writes:

> The **most notable improbability** is perhaps to be found in
> Matthew. It is **the most difficult to rationalize** of all that…Jesus
> said. He (Matthew) relates in chapter 12:38-40 the episode
> concerning Jonah's sign:
>
> Jesus was among the scribes and Pharisees who addressed him
> in the following terms:
>
> "Teacher, we wish to see a sign from you."
>
> But he answered them, "An evil and adulterous generation seeks
> for a sign; but no sign shall be given to it except the sign of the
> prophet Jonah. for as Jonah was **three days and three nights** in the
> belly of the whale, so will the Son of Man be **three days and three
> nights** in the heart of the earth."
>
> Jesus therefore proclaims that he will stay in the earth three days
> and three nights.

Bucaille then goes on to show that by the account of the very same author,
Matthew, Jesus was crucified on Friday, stayed in the grave Friday night,
Saturday, Saturday night, and rose again early Sunday morning. **This gives a
part of three days, but only two nights.**

Jesus made the prophecy that he would die and be in the heart of the earth
three days and three nights sometime in the late winter or early spring of 29
AD just before the Jewish Passover.

About six months later he spoke again of his death in this very detailed
prophecy. The account reads,

> From that time on Jesus began to explain to his disciple that he
> must go to Jerusalem and suffer many things at the hands of the
> elders, chief priests and teachers of the law, and that he must be
> killed and **on the third day be raised to life** (Matthew 16:21).

A week or ten days later, he repeated the same prophecy (Mt. 17:22-23) and
finally about ten days before the Passover in 30 AD, using his title "the Son of
Man," Jesus again told his disciples,

> "We are going up to Jerusalem, and the Son of Man will be
> betrayed to the chief priests and the teachers of the law. They will

---

8. Bucaille, BQ&S, p 62.

179

condemn him to death and will turn him over to the Gentiles to be mocked and flogged and crucified. **On the third day he will be raised to life"** (Matthew 20:18-19).

Now for Dr. Bucaille there is no way that the phrase "on the third day" can equal "three days and three nights." Therefore this is a big contradiction!?! Never mind the fact that **Jesus prophesied his own death and resurrection**. The important thing is that Jesus' calculations were wrong!

But are we so sure that the author of Matthew is wrong? Do we not have to give the benefit of the doubt to the author and ask what Matthew and Jesus and other 1st century Jews would understood by the term **"three days and three nights,"** as compared with "on the third day"?

According to A.T. Robertson,[9] "The well-known custom of the Jews was to count a part of a day as a whole day of 24 hours…So then the part of Friday would count as one day, Saturday another, and the part of Sunday the third day."

The same custom is still true in North Africa. If I ask a patient, who felt a pain on Saturday night and comes to see me Monday morning, how long he has been ill, he will always answer **"three days"**; even though it is less than 48 hours. This is exactly parallel to Jesus' words in his Gospel.

Secondly, if Dr. Bucaille would read the Gospel of Matthew carefully, he would find a third phrase which provides the answer. In Matthew 27:62-64 we read,

> The next day (Saturday), the one after Preparation Day, the chief priests and Pharisees went to Pilate. "Sir," they said, "we remember that while he was still alive that deceiver said, 'After three days I will rise again.' So give the order for the tomb to be made secure **until the third day**…"

Jesus is quoted as saying, "**After three days** I will rise again." This sounds like saying, "**After three periods of 24 hours**" or "**three days and three nights**."

But the author of Matthew uses it as equal to making the tomb secure "until **the third day**."

Therefore linguistically all three of these phrases seem to be used as equal to each other and it is time to give the author "the benefit of the doubt" as Aristotle suggested.

Finally, there is a spiritual truth or argument which is convincing for many Christians.

At the beginning of Jesus' ministry near the end of 26 AD or early in 27 AD, he attended a wedding at Cana. Mary, his mother, asked Jesus to help the host who had run out of wine. He did it in a miraculous way, but also answered and said, "My hour has not yet come" (John 2:4).

More than three years later, on Thursday evening just before he was arrested, he said to his disciples, "Enough! **The hour is come**. Look, the Son of Man is betrayed into the hands of sinners" (Mark 14:41).

---

9. *A Harmony of the Gospels for Students of the Life of Christ*, Harper and Row, New York, 1922, p 290.

What hour? Christians understand "the hour" to speak of his suffering and death for our sins. This suffering started on Thursday night when Jesus was arrested, just after he said, "The hour IS COME," and it continued through the beatings, and the torture and death of the cross until his resurrection.

From the time that he said, "My hour is come" on Thursday night, until he rose from the dead with mighty power on Sunday morning, is "three nights and three days."

Whether the reader accepts this last argument or not, the point should be clear. If **"basic assumptions"** can be made for the Qur'an so that "eight days" can equal "six days," then certainly linguistic usage and spiritual **"basic assumptions"** must be allowed for the Gospel-New Testament so that "three days and three nights" can equal "after three days," and "on the third day."

B. ANATOMY, EMBRYOLOGY AND GENETICS

---

5. THE PLACE OF SEMEN PRODUCTION

One of my Muslim friends mentioned the statement in the Sura of the Women (Al-Nisā') 4:23, 5-6 AH, where it reads,

> Prohibited to you (for marriage) are...wives of **your sons from your loins** (ṣulb الصُّلْب) (as opposed to adopted sons).

He claimed that this was foreknowledge of modern medical science by which we know that the male testicles descend from the region of the kidneys during fetal development.

Logically one cannot say that this is absolutely impossible, but as a doctor it is difficult to see why God would refer to such an obscure fact in a verse which is not even discussing anatomy as a witness to God's creative power.

Surely this is a figure of speech. Speaking of "your sons from your loins" is a euphemistic way of referring to the seat of reproductive power. After the root meaning of "hard" or "solid," Wehr,[1] Kasimirski[2] and Abdel-Nour[3] all give "backbone" and "loins" as their second meaning and then, (ibn ṣulbihi إِبْن صُلْبِهِ) "his own son," as a metaphorical example.

There is even a second Arabic word which is used in this same way for the source of children. In the Late Meccan Sura of The Heights (Al-A'rāf) 7:172, it says,

> And when your Lord took from the children of Adam from their loins (ẓuhūr الظُّهُور) their descendants...

This is the usual Arabic word for "back," and again we see it being used for procreative strength or the seat of vigor. In fact, according to the specialists in language, this was a common usage among the ancient cultures of the Middle East.

Secondly, a great obstacle to the idea that this shows a Quranic "miracle of foreknowledge" is that the same idea can be found in the **Torah**. The Hebrew word "châlâts" is used exactly like the Arabic "ṣulb."

When Isaiah says, **"Put sackcloth on your loins** (châlâts)" (32:11); or Jeremiah writes, "Every man with **his hands on his loins**" (30:6), it has to mean "back" or "waist."

When God is talking to Jacob and says,

> **"And kings shall come out of your loins** (châlâts)." **Torah**, Genesis 35:11.

or when God says to David in 1000 BC,

---

1. Wehr, op. cit.
2. *Dictionnaire Arabe-Français*, A De Biberstein Kasimirski, Maisonneuve, Paris, 1960.
3. *Dictionnaire Abdel-Nour al-Mufaṣṣal*, Dar el-Ilm lil-Malayin, Beirut, 1983.

"You shall not build the house (the Temple); but **your son that shall come forth out of your loins,** he shall build the house unto my Name." (I Kings 8:19),

"châlâts" is being used figuratively as "the seat of vigor and reproduction.

In the **Gospel-New Testament** the Greek word "osphus" has much the same meaning. As recorded in Acts, when Peter was preaching he referred to the same promise given to King David, saying,

...one from the **fruit of his loins** (osphus) would sit on his throne." Acts 2:30.

The third and biggest problem, though, is that, unlike the Bible, the Qur'an uses the word "ṣulb" for loins in a verse which won't allow a euphemistic interpretation. In the Early Meccan Sura of the Night-visitant (Al-Ṭāriq) 86:5-7, it reads,

Now let man think from what he is created! He is created from a gushing fluid that issues from between the loins (ṣulb الصُّلب) and ribs (tarā'ib التَّرَ ائِب)."

Here we find that humans are made from a "gushing fluid that issues from the adult father during the "now" of the reproductive act, from a specific physical place "between the loins and the ribs." (Other translations have "backbone" instead of loins.)

Since the verse is speaking of the moment of adult reproduction it can't be talking about the time of embryonic development. Moreover, since "ṣulb" is being used in conjunction with "gushing fluid," which can only be physical— and "tarā'ib" is another physical word, for chest or thorax or ribs—it can't be euphemistic. **Therefore, we are left with the very real problem that the semen is coming from the back or kidney area and not the testicles.**

Dr. Bucaille, as a physician, recognizes this problem only too well, so he wiggles and squirms (as he accuses the Christian commentators of doing) and finally after quoting the verse as we have seen it translated above says, "This would seem more to be an interpretation than a translation. **It is hardly comprehensible.**"[4] This is the second time he has called the Qur'an **obscure or hardly comprehensible** when there was a problem.

Therefore, let us look at the translations which I have been consulting. Those made by Muslims are:

Abdullah Yusuf Ali, Egyptian, 1946 with a preface from 1938:

He is created from a drop emitted—proceeding from between the backbone and the ribs.

Muhammad Marmaduke Pickthall, English, 1977 (translation probably 1940):

He is created from a gushing fluid that issued from between the loins and ribs.

---

4. Bucaille, BQ&S, p 208.

183

Muhammad Zafrulla Khan, Pakistani, 1971:

> He is created from a fluid poured forth, which issues forth from between the loins and the breastbones.[5]

Muhammad Hamidullah, French, 1981 (10th Edition, completely revised):

> Il a été créé d'une giclée d'eau sortie d'entre lombes et côtes.
>
> He was created from a spurt of water coming out between the loins and ribs.

Made by a non-Muslim:

D. Masson, French 1967:

> Il a été créé d'une goutte d'eau répandue sortie d'entre les lombes et les côtes.
>
> He was created from a drop of spread-out water coming out between the loins and the ribs.

That these five translations are exactly equal is perfectly obvious to every reader even if he does not know French or the original Arabic.

Dr. Bucaille's Translation

What would Dr. Bucaille like to suggest? He writes, "Two verses in the Qur'an deal with sexual relations themselves…When translations and explanatory commentaries are consulted however, one is struck by the divergences between them. I have pondered for a long time on the translation of such verses (In plain English that means there is "an improbability or a contradiction, prudishly called a 'difficulty' "[6]), and am indebted to Doctor A. K. Giraud, Former Professor at the Faculty of Medicine, Beirut, for the following:

> '(Man was fashioned from a liquid poured out. It issued (as a result) of the conjunction of the sexual area of the man and the sexual area of the woman.'

"The sexual area of the man is indicated in the text of the Qur'an by the word *ṣulb* (singular). The sexual areas of the woman are designated in the Qur'an by the word *tarā'ib* (plural).

"This is the translation which appears to be most satisfactory."[7]

When compared, however, with the five translations quoted above, it is clear that Dr. Bucaille's suggestion is not a translation, nor even a paraphrase. It is an "explanation" and "interpretation" which rests on the following **basic assumptions**:

a. **That the word "ṣulb" can stand for the male sexual area.** However no examples of such a usage from the 1st century of Islam have been given.

b. **That the phrase "(as a result) of the conjunction" can be found in the**

---

5. *The Qur'an*, Curzon Press, 1981, (1st Ed. 1971). Mr. Khan has been foreign minister of Pakistan in 1947 and president of the International Court of Justice at the Hague.

6. Dr. Bucaille's comment about the Christians, BQ&S, p ix.

7. Ibid., p 208.

two Arabic words "min bain" which literally mean "from between."

c. That the word "tarā'ib" can mean "the sexual areas of the woman."

This last word occurs exactly one time in the Qur'an and you cannot establish a meaning with one usage. The dictionaries of Wehr, Abdel-Nour, and Kasimirski mention (a) the chest, (b) the upper part of the chest between the breasts and the clavicles, and (c) the ribs, and Abdel-Nour includes (d) the euphemistic extension to the breasts. It can also include the neck up to the chin and speak poetically of the area for a woman's necklace.

No dictionary includes the female genital area, and Dr. Bucaille has given no examples from literature to support his idea. He seems to be fulfilling his own complaint against others. He is trying "to camouflage (his problems) with dialectical acrobatics" -@-@-@.[8]

6. 'ALAQA (CLOT?!) AND OTHER STAGES IN THE FORMATION OF THE FETUS

It has been said that the idea of the embryo developing through stages is a modern one; that the Qur'an is anticipating (i.e., prophesying) modern embryology by describing different stages in the develpment of the embryo. In a pamphlet entitled *Highlights of Human Embryology in the Koran and the Hadith* by Keith L. Moore, M.D.,[9] Dr. Moore claims that outside the Qur'an, "The realization that the embryo develops in stages in the uterus was not discussed or illustrated until the 15th century AD."[10] In addition the claim is made that the stages described in the Qur'an match our modern knowledge.

We will weigh these claims by considering the meaning of the Arabic words used by the Qur'an and secondly by examining the historical situation leading up to and surrounding the Qur'an.

Let us start by looking at the main verses using the word **'alaqa** (عَلَقَة).

'ALAQA

The Arabic word **'alaqa** (عَلَقَة) in the singular, or **'alaq** (عَلَق) as the collective plural, is used to indicate a stage in the development of the fetus six times in five different Quranic verses.

In the Sura of the Resurrection (Al-Qiyāma) 75:37-39, we read,

> Was he (man) not a drop of sperm ejaculated? Then he became a leech-like clot (**'alaqa**) and God shaped and formed and made of him a pair, the male and the female.

In the Sura of The Believer (Al-Mū'min) 40:67, it says,

> He it is Who created you from dust, then from a sperm-drop, then from a leech-like clot (**'alaqa**), then brings you forth as a child,...that perhaps you may understand.

---

8. Another of Dr. Bucaille's acid criticisms of Christians who attempt to explain or reconcile a problem. Ibid., p 19.
9. Former Professor of Anatomy, Faculty of Medicine, University of Toronto, Toronto, Ontario, Canada.
10. Arabization and Medical Education, p 51, reprinted 1995 by Islamic Information & Da'wah Centre International, 957 Dovercourt Road, Toronto, M6H 2X6.

In the Sura of The Pilgrimage (Al-Ḥajj) 22:5, it says,

O mankind! if you have doubt about the resurrection (consider) that We have created you from dust, then from a drop of seed, then from a clot (**'alaqa**), then from a little lump of flesh, shapely and shapeless...

And finally the fullest treatment is in the Sura of The Believers (Mū'minūn) 23:12-14, which reads:

Verily We created man from a product of wet earth, then placed him as a drop of seed in a safe lodging, then We fashioned the drop a clot (**'alaqa**), and of the clot (**'alaqa**). We fashioned a lump, and of the lump We fashioned bones, and We clothed the bones (with) meat. Then We produced it as another creation.

These stages can be summarized as follows:

QURANIC STAGES OF PRENATAL DEVELOPMENT

STAGE 1. nutfa—sperm

STAGE 2. 'alaqa—clot

STAGE 3. mudagha—piece or lump of flesh

STAGE 4. 'adaam—bones

STAGE 5. dressing the bones with muscles

Over the last 100 plus years this word **'alaqa** (عَلَقَة) has been translated as follows:

— French, un grumeau de sang (a small lump of blood)—Kasimirski, 1948[11] (last Ed. during life of author was 1887)

— a leech-like clot—Yusuf Ali, (translation of 1938) 1946[12]

— a clot—Pickthall, (translation of 1940) 1977[13]

— a clot—Maulana Muhammad Ali, 1951[14]

— a clot—Muhammad Zafrulla Khan, 1971[15]

— French, de caillot de sang (clot of blood)—Hamidullah, 1981[16]

— a clot of blood—N. J. Dawood, 1980[17]

    Approved by the Supreme Sunni and Shii Councils
    of the Republic of Lebanon

— Indonesian, segumpal darah (lump of or clot of blood) —

    Indonesian Department of Religious Affairs, 1984

— Farsi, khoon basteh (a clot of blood)—Mehdi Elahi Ghomshehi

— Chinese, xue kuai (blood clot)

11. Biberstein Kasimirski, *Le Koran*, Bibliotheque Charpentier, Paris, 1948.

12. Abdullah Yusuf Ali, *The Holy Qur'an*, American International Printing Co., Washington, 1946.

13. Muhammad Marmaduke Pickthall, *The Glorious Qur'an*, Muslim World League, New York, 1977.

14. *The Holy Qur'an*, Ahmadiyyah Anjuman Ishaat Islam, Lahore, 1951.

15. *The Qur'an*, Curzon Press, 1981.

16. Muhammad Hamidullah, *Le Coran*, Le Club Français du livre, 1981.

17. N. J. Dawood, checked and revised by Mahmud Y. Zayid, *The Quran*, Dar Al-Choura, P.O. Box 11-4251, Beirut, 1980.

— Malay, darah beku (blood clot)

As every reader who has studied human reproduction will realize, **there is no stage as a clot during the formation of a fetus, so this is a very major scientific problem.**

In the dictionaries of Wehr and Abdel-Nour the only meanings given for **'alaqa** (عَلَقَة) in this feminine singular form are "clot" and "leech," and in North Africa both of these meanings are still used. Many patients have come to me to have a leech removed from their throats, and many women, believing that the fetus goes through a stage as a clot, have come to me in the dispensary asking for medicine because their periods haven't come. When I would answer that I couldn't do that because I believed that the fetus was a person, they would say, "But it's still blood."

Lastly, we must consider the first verses which came to Muhammad in Mecca. These are found in the 96th Sura called **'Alaq (Clots?)**—from this very word which we are studying. In 96:1-2, we read,

> Proclaim! in the name of your Lord Who created–created man
> from **'alaq** (عَلَق).

Here the word is in the collective plural. This word form can have other meanings because **'alaq** (عَلَق) is also the derived verbal noun of the verb **'aliqa** (عَلِقَ) which means "to hang, be suspended, dangle, to stick, cling, cleave, adhere, and to be attached." The verbal noun usually corresponds to the gerund in English as in the sentence "Swimming is fun." Therefore we could expect it to mean hanging, clinging, adhering, etc. In addition the verbal noun can have other meanings established by usage.

But the twelve translators listed above have all considered this the collective plural of **alaqa** rather than a verbal noun and used "clot" or "congealed blood" in this verse too, and Fazlur Rahman also uses "congealed blood" for this verse in his well-known book *Islam*, first published in 1966.[18]

Maulana Muhammad Ali explains why in Note 2770 on this verse. He says,

> **'Alaq** signifies a clot of blood as well as attachment and love. The former significance is the one generally adopted, because of the mention of **'alaqa** in the process of the creation of man in other places in the Holy Qur'an, and it indicates the insignificance of man's origin.[19]

In other words, the meaning of the singular form is controlling the plural even though there is great attraction to understand and use a different word which would avoid the scientific difficulty.

In spite of the number and qualifications of these translators who use the word "clot" to translate **'alaqa**, the French Doctor Maurice Bucaille has sharp words for them. He writes:

> What is more likely to mislead the inquiring reader is, once again, the problem of vocabulary...

---

18. *Islam*, 2nd Ed., U. of Chicago Press, Chicago, 1979, p 13.
19. Muhammad Ali, Op. cit.

The majority of translations describe, for example, man's formation from a "blood clot" or an "adhesion." A statement of this kind is totally unacceptable to scientists specializing in this field... This shows how great the importance of an association between linguistic and scientific knowledge is when it comes to grasping the meaning of Quranic statements on reproduction.[20]

Put in other words, Nobody has translated the Qur'an correctly until Dr. Bucaille came along.

How does Dr. Bucaille think that it should be translated? He proposes that instead of "clot," the word **'alaqa** should be translated as "something which clings" which would refer to the fetus being attached to the uterus through the placenta.[21]

We will use the good Doctor's translation for **'alaqa** and try it.

Then from the sperm-drop We created (or fashioned) the thing which clings, and from the thing which clings We created (or fashioned) chewed flesh, and from the chewed flesh We created (or fashioned) bones, and We clothed the bones with meat.

Now that we are getting very 20th century in our demands, where is the ovum? "The thing which clings" is not formed from a sperm-drop. It is formed by the fusion of the nucleus of the sperm and the nucleus of the ovum. Of course, leaving something out is not exactly an error, but we will see later that for Muhammad and the Muslims hearing him, the clot (**'alaqa**) was the female contribution.

Secondly, "the thing which clings" doesn't stop its clinging to become "chewed meat." It keeps on being "the thing which clings"—which is attached by the placenta—for 8 1/2 months until birth.

Even among scientists, though, there is disagreement about the translation of this word. Dr. Bechir Torki takes up the problem and translates Sura 96 as,

Read in the name of your Lord Who has created, Who has created man from **links (*d'attaches*)**. Read, for your Lord is most generous. It is He Who has taught by the pen.

The French word which I have translated as "links" can also mean bonds, ties, or attachments. Those meanings sound very similar to that given by Dr. Bucaille, but Torki actually proposes quite a different sense. He writes,

He (God) "created man from links (or bonds)"... (in) which is attached or suspended all the genes of the cells...The first word "read" (in the Sura) concerns the information which is contained in the first cell from which the structure of man is made. The second word "read" concerns the great Qur'an which God has taught to man by the pen.

This is a very ingenious idea, although I personally find it difficult to believe

20. *The Bible, the Qur'an and Science*, American Trust Publications, Indianapolis, 1979, p 200.
21. Bucaille, ibid., p 204.

that God's first words to Muhammad would be **"Read the gene code."** What would the people of Mecca understand? In addition, what will Dr. Torki do with the other verses where the singular form 'alaqa is used? What will it mean even with our modern education to say, "from a drop of sperm we created **"a gene code"**; and from **"a gene code"** we created a small lump of meat? The "gene code" is **in** the sperm, not created **from** it.

A few translators have used other words to translate **'alaqa**. In his translation of 1957, Regis Blache're has for 23:14,

> We have made the ejaculation **an adhesion**, We have made the adhesion a flabby mass. We have made of the flabby mass skeleton, and we have clothed the skeleton with flesh.[22]

(But it should be noted that for 75:38 he has **"a congealed drop."**)

And Muhammad Asad in his translation of 1964, published in 1980, proposes,

> And then We created out of the drop of sperm **a germ-cell** and then We created out of the germ-cell an embryonic lump and then we created within the embryonic lump bones and then we clothed the bones with flesh.[23]

Muhammad Asad has a note with 96:2 suggesting that the germ-cell **'alaqa** is the fertilized ovum.

However, I think that it is clear to the reader that:

(a) The sperm does not become an adhesion or a fertilized ovum without an unfertilized female ovum.

(b) To say that **'alaqa** means "germ-cell" means fertilized ovum is a **basic assumption.**

(c) If it is an adhesion it stays stuck during the whole pregnancy and does not become something else.

(d) To translate **"mudagha** (lump of flesh)" with the 20th century adjective "embryonic" added to lump, and to say that the bones are created "within" the embryonic lump rather than "from" the embryonic lump are both **basic assumptions**.

Lastly, in this section we must consider Dr. Keith Moore's suggestion as to the meaning of **'alaqa**. Dr. Moore, retired Professor of Anatomy and author of a text book on embryology, proposes, "Another verse in the Koran refers to the **leech-like appearance** and the chewed like stages of human development."[24] From this definition Dr. Moore has gone ahead to propose that a 23-day embryo, 3 mm long. or 1/8th of an inch, resembles a leech. This is Carnegie stage 10 from the inside front cover of Dr. Moore's own book and shown here in Diagram 9.[25]

---

22. *Le Coran, Librairie Orientale et Américaine*, Paris, 1957. (translation mine)
23. *The Message of the Qur'an*, Dar Al-Andalus Ltd., Gibraltar, 1980.
24. Moore, *Arabization*, op. cit., p 56
25. *The Developing Human*, Moore, 4th ed., 1988.

Diagram 9, STAGES 7 through 17

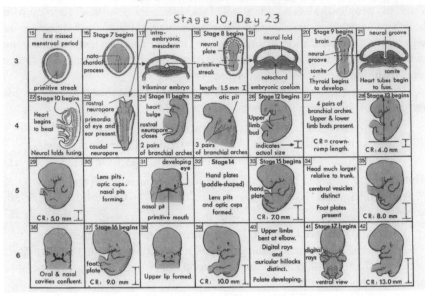

Permission granted from W. B. Saunders

Figure 5-9

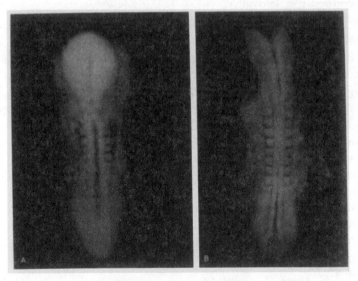

Figure 5-9 shows an x-ray enlargement of day 22 and day 23. This x-ray of the back of day 22 shows the neural groove of the backbone is still wide open.[26]

Permission granted from W. B. Saunders

26. Moore, Dev. Human, p 75.

Diagram 10

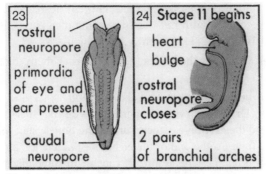

Diagram 10[27] of day 23, similar to the x-ray view, shows the rostral and caudal neuropores still widely open and the cut edges of the yolk sac.

Permission granted from W. B. Saunders

Figure 4-10

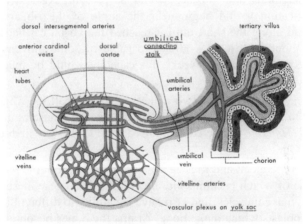

Figure 4-10[28] shows the embryo with a large ventral yoke sac and an umbilical connecting stalk. A leech has none of these characteristics.

Permission granted from W. B. Saunders

In conclusion, we can say that this 23-day, 3 millimeter (1/8th inch) embryo with its rostral and caudal neuropores still widely open, with a large ventral yoke sac and an umbilical connecting stalk, does not look like a leech at all. Furthermore, no dictionary gives "leech-like appearance" as a meaning for 'alaqa and no one has suggested that the Qur'an says that man was made from a drop of sperm which became a leech. Dr. Moore does not know Arabic and said straight out to me in a personal conversation that **if the true meaning of 'alaqa is "clot," then there is no such stage in the development of an embryo.**

27. Moore, op. cit., inside front cover.
28. Moore, op. cit. p 61.

'ADAAM—BONES BEFORE MUSCLE

Thirdly, these quranic verses say that the "lump of flesh" becomes bones and then the bones are covered with muscles. The same idea is repeated in the Sura of the Heifer (Al-Baqara) 2:259, from 2 AH, which says,

> ...Look further at the bones, how We bring them together and clothe them with flesh...

They give the impression that first the skeleton is formed, and then it is clothed with flesh. Dr. Bucaille knows perfectly well that this is not true.

The **muscles** and the **cartilage, precursors of the bones,** start forming from the somite at the same time. At the end of the eighth week there are only a few centers of ossification started but the fetus is already capable of some muscular movement.

In a personal letter dated 8/1/87 from Dr. T.W. Sadler, Ph.D., Associate Professor in the Department of Anatomy at the University of North Carolina, Chapel Hill, N.C. 27514, and author of *Langman's Medical Embryology*, Dr. Sadler states,

> At the 8th week post fertilization, the ribs would be cartilaginous and muscles would be present. Also at this time ossification would begin near the angle of the rib and would spread along the shaft until it reached the costal cartilage by the 4th month. Muscles would be capable of some movement at 8 weeks, but by 10-12 weeks this capacity would be much better developed.

It is always better to have two witnesses, so we shall see what Dr. Keith L. Moore has to say about the development of bones and muscles in his book *The Developing Human*. Extracted from Chapters 15-17 we find the following information:

> The skeletal and muscle system develops from the *mesoderm*, some of which becomes *mesenchymal* cells. These mesenchymal cells make muscles, and also have the ability to differentiate...into osteoblasts which make bone. At first the bones become cartilage models so that by the end of **the sixth week** the whole limb skeleton is formed out of cartilage but without any bony calciumas shown in **Figure 15-13**.[29]

While the bone models are forming, myoblasts develop a large muscle mass in each limb bud, separating into extensor and flexor components. **In other words, the limb musculature develops simultaneously in situ from the mesenchyme surrounding the developing bones.** So Dr. Moore agrees completely with Dr. Sadler.

Furthermore, during a personal conversation with Dr. Moore I showed him Dr. Sadler's statement and he agreed that it was absolutely valid.

Conclusion: on bone development Dr. Sadler and Dr. Moore agree. There is no time when calcified bones have been formed and then the

---

29. Keith L. Moore, *The Developing Human*, 4th ed., 1988, p 346.

muscles are placed around them. The muscles are there several weeks before there are calcified bones, rather than being added around previously formed bones as the Qur'an states. **The Qur'an is in complete error here.**

Figure 15-13

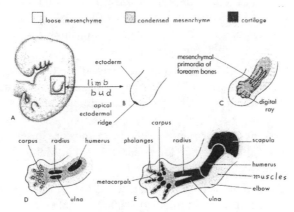

Permission granted from W. B. Saunders

THE PROBLEM

The great problem with these new definitions for words like **'alaqa** and **mudagha** is that no confirming examples of such a usage have been provided from the Arabic used in the centuries surrounding the Hejira.

Dr. Bucaille wishes to say that all of these older translators are wrong; that to correctly translate the Qur'an one must have a very good scientific education. How good? These translators would have all had modern high school biology telling about the sperm and the ovum.

Does Dr. Bucaille not understand? These translators are scientists in their field of words, and they have not found any valid linguistic facts which will allow them to change the meaning of the words in these verses. They have been honest translators, not ignorant of science.

Bucaille says that their translations are "hardly comprehensible." I am sorry but I must disagree. **Their translations are very comprehensible and correct. They just reflect the scientific problems which are present in the original Arabic.**

The only way to establish the meaning of a word is by usage. The only way to establish whether the singular form "**'alaqa**" can mean a 3mm embryo or "the thing that clings" is to bring sentences demonstrating this usage from the literature of the Arabs of Mecca and Medina close to the time of Muhammad—especially from the language of the Quraish—for the Qur'an was written in "Clear Arabic" ('arabiiyun mubinun), the Colloquial Arabic of the Quraish tribe.[30]

---

30. See Section One, Chapter 1, "Some Basic Assumptions about Words," William F. Campbell M.D., *The Qur'an and the Bible in the Light of History and Science*, Middle East Resources, P.O. Box 96, Upper Darby, PA, 1986, p 3-12.

This will not be an easy task because much work has already been done on that "clear Arabic" of the Quraish. The early Muslims understood intuitively the need to know exactly what the Quranic words mean, and for this reason they made comprehensive studies of their language and poetry.

The great historian Ibn Khaldun could say,

> Know therefore that the Qur'an descended in the language of
> the Arabs and in accordance with their style of eloquence, and all
> of them understood it and knew its various meanings in its several
> parts and in their relation to each other.[31]

His statement that "all" of the Arabs understood the Qur'an is no doubt an enthusiastic exaggeration which any one might make, but it is surely closer to the truth than Dr. Bucaille's statements that nobody has understood the Qur'an until now.

Hamza Boubakeur, former rector of the main mosque in Paris, brought up this subject at the "Colloque sur le Dieu unique" held at Montpellier on May 6, 1985. He posed the rhetorical question to the audience,

> Has the comprehension of the text (of the Qur'an) known at
> the time of Muhammad remained stable?

and his answer was,

> Ancient poetry attests to the semantic stability.

We can only conclude that if the verses which bring spiritual comfort and hope to Muslims have remained stable, then the scientific statements imbedded in those verses must also be accepted as stable unless new evidence can be brought forward.

This is especially important since some of the verses say that this information is a **sign**. The Sura of the Believer (Al-Mū'min) 40:76 says,

> He it is Who created you from dust, then from a sperm-drop,
> then from a **clot ('alaqa)...that perhaps you may understand.**

and in the Sura of the Pilgrimage (Al-Ḥajj) 22:5 we read,

> O mankind! If you have doubt about the resurrection
> (**consider**) that We have created you from dust, etc., etc...

Therefore the question must be asked, If it was a clear **sign** to the men and women of Mecca and Medina, what then did they understand from this word **'alaqa** which would lead them to faith in the resurrection?

THE ANSWER

We are going to examine the historical situation leading up to the time of Muhammad to see what Muhammad and his people believed about embryology. The trail will start with the Greek and Indian medical men.

---

31. Ibn Khaldun, Vol. II, p 391.

HIPPOCRATES

We will start with Hippocrates. According to the best evidence, he was born on the Greek island of Cos in 460 BC. His stages are as follows with the references in the text.

Semen

Sperm is a product which comes from the whole body of each parent, weak sperm coming from the weak parts, and strong sperm from the strong parts. Section 8, p 321

Coagulation of Mother's blood

The seed (embryo), then, is contained in a membrane. Moreover, it grows because of its **mother's blood, which descends to the womb**. For once a woman conceives, she ceases to menstruate...Section 14, p 326

Flesh

At this stage, with the descent and coagulation of the mother's blood, flesh begins to be formed, with the umbilicus. Section 14, p 326

Bones

As the flesh grows it is formed into distinct members by breath...The bones grow hard...moreover they send out branches like a tree... Section 17, p 328

This information is clearly summarized in the following chart.

STAGES OF PRENATAL DEVELOPMENT ACCORDING TO HIPPOCRATES

STAGE 1. sperm

STAGE 2. mother's blood descends around the membrane

STAGE 3. flesh, fed through umbilicus

STAGE 4. bones

Clearly this shows that 1000 years before the Qur'an, the development of the embryo was divided into stages.

ARISTOTLE

Next we will look at Aristotle. In his book *On the Generation of Animals*,[32] sometime about 350 BC, Aristotle gives his stages of embryology. (The section numbers are in the text.)

Semen and menstrual blood

In this section, 728a, Aristotle speaks of the male semen as being in a pure state... "It follows that what the female would contribute to the semen of the male would be material for the semen to work upon." In other words the semen clots the menstrual blood.

Then he continues, "Nature forms from the purest material the **flesh**...and from the residues thereof **bones**, sinews, hair, and also nails..." and lastly "**Round about the bones**, and attached to them by thin fibrous bands, **grow the**

---

32. Aristotle, O*n the Generation of Animals*, Translated by Arthur Platt, Vol. 9 of Great Books of the Western World, Encyclopedia Britannica, Inc., 1952.

fleshy parts…" (section 654b).

Clearly the Qur'an follows this exactly, sperm clotting the menstrual blood which forms meat. Then the bones are formed and lastly "round about the bones…grow the fleshy parts" as we see in the following chart.

STAGES OF PRENATAL DEVELOPMENT ACCORDING TO ARISTOTLE

STAGE 1. sperm

STAGE 2. catamenia—menstrual blood

STAGE 3. flesh

STAGE 4. bones

STAGE 5. around the bones grow the fleshy parts

NEXT WE SHALL CONSIDER INDIAN MEDICINE

The opinion of Charaka (123 AD) and Susruta is that both the male and female contributed seed. The "secretion" of the male is called the *sukra* (semen)…

The "secretion" of the woman is called *artava* or *sonita* (blood) and it is "derived from food by way of blood…"[33]

Here we see that in the medicine of India, they too had the idea that the child was formed from the male semen and the female menstrual blood.

NOW WE SHALL LOOK AT GALEN

Galen was born in 131 AD in Pergamum (modern Bergama in Turkey).

Our knowledge of his book, *De Semine*, depends on two Greek manuscripts of the 15th and 16th century and two Arabic copies from the 12th and 13th century of the same translation made in about 840 AD, i.e., 700 years after Galen lived. Galen's work was considered so important that copies were still being made in 1500 AD. Secondly, although the Arabic copies reflect a translation made 700 years after Galen's life, no one doubts their essential accuracy.

I mention this because in comparison we Christians have 75% of the Greek Gospel-New Testament in papyrus copies from only 150 years after Christ ascended into heaven, and we have two complete Greek copies from 350 AD. Therefore, there is no reason to doubt the essential accuracy of the Gospel-New Testament either. It has not been changed.

Galen—On Semen

Galen says, "The substance from which the fetus is formed is not merely menstrual blood, as Aristotle maintained, **but menstrual blood plus the two semens**." (p 50).

The Qur'an agrees with Galen here when it says in Sura 76:2, "We created man from a drop of mingled sperm."

33. Dr. P. Kutumbiah, M.D., F.R.C.P., *Ancient Indian Medicine*, Orient Longmans, Madras, 1969, p 2-4.

Embryological Development

Concerning Embryological development, Galen also taught that the embryo developed in stages. He wrote, "the first is that in which...the form of the semen prevails. At this time Hippocrates too, the all marvelous,...still calls it semen (*geniture*)."

The next stage is "when it has been **filled with blood**, and heart, brain and liver are (still) unarticulated and *unshaped*...this is the period...that Hippocrates (called) *foetus*."

(The Quranic Sura 22:5 reflects this saying, "...Then out of a morsel of flesh, partly formed and partly unformed...")

> And now the third period of gestation has come...Thus it
> (nature) caused **flesh** to grow on and around all the **bones**.

We saw above that the Qur'an agrees with this in Sura 23:14 where it says, "And we clothed the bones (with) meat."

> The fourth and final period (*puer* or child—verse 9) is at the
> stage when all the parts in the limbs have been differentiated.[34]

GALEN'S STAGES OF PRENATAL DEVELOPMENT

STAGE 1. The two semens

STAGE 1b. plus menstrual blood

STAGE 2. unshaped flesh

STAGE 3. bones

STAGE 3b. flesh grows on and around the bones

Thus we see that Galen also has stages. He divides them differently, but the sequence is the same.

THE 26 BOOKS OF GALEN AS THE BASIS OF MEDICAL STUDIES

Galen was so important in medicine that just about the time of the Hejira, four leading medical men in Alexandria, Egypt, decided to form a medical school using 16 books of Galen as the basis of the studies. This continued up to and including the 13th century.[35]

ARABIA AROUND 600 AD, BETWEEN GALEN AND AVICENNA

We must now ask ourselves what the political, economic and medical climate was in Arabia at the time of Muhammad.

From the Hadramaut in Yemen, the caravans of the spice trade passed north through Mecca and Medina and then reached into all of Europe.

In North Arabia in about 500 AD the Ghassanids took over and by 528 AD

---

34. Galen, op.cit., I 9, verses 1-9, p 92-95.

35. *The Role of the Nestorians and Muslims in the History of Medicine*, Allen O. Whipple, 1967, Princeton Univ. Press, p 16.

the Ghassan controlled the Syrian desert to the outskirts of Yathrib (Medina). Syriac (a form of Aramaic, related to Arabic) was their official language.

As early as 463 AD, the Jews translated the Torah and Old Testament from Hebrew into Syriac. (The British Museum has a copy.) This made it available to the Ghassan who were Christians and to the Jewish tribes in Arabia for their members who didn't know Hebrew.

During this time, Sergius al-ras Ayni (died in Constantinople in 536 AD), one of the earliest and greatest translators from Greek into Syriac (Aramaic), translated various works on medicine, **including 26 books of Galen's works** into Syriac. This made them available in the Kingdom of Khosru I and to the Ghassan Tribe whose influence extended to the outskirts of Medina.

Khosru I (Arabic Kisra), King of Persia from 531-579, was known as Khosru the Great. His troops conquered areas as far away as Yemen. He also loved learning and started several schools.

> The school of Jundi-Shapur became, during Khosru I's long reign of 48 years, the greatest intellectual center of the time. Within its walls Greek, Jewish, Nestorian, Persian and Hindu thought and experience were freely exchanged.

Teaching was done largely in Syriac from Syriac translations of Greek texts.[36] This meant that Aristotle, Hippocrates, and Galen were readily available when the medical school at Jundi-Shapur was operating during his reign.

The next step was that the conquering Arabs compelled the Nestorians to translate their Syriac texts of Greek medicine into Arabic. The translation from Syriac to Arabic was easy as the two languages had the same grammar.

Concerning the local medical situation during Muhammad's life, we know there were physicians living in Arabia during this period.

Harith ben Kalada was the best-educated physician trained in the healing art.

> He was born about the middle of the sixth century, at Ta'if, in the tribe of Banu Thaqif. He traveled through Yemen and then Persia where he received his education in the medical sciences at the great medical school of Jundi-Shapur and thus was intimately acquainted with the medical teachings of Aristotle, Hippocrates and Galen.
>
> Having completed his studies he practiced as a physician in Persia and during this time he was called to the court of King Khosru, with whom he had a long conversation. He came back to Arabia about the beginning of Islam and settled down at Ta'if. While there Abu'l-Khayr, a King of Yemen, came to see him, in connection with a certain disease from which he was suffering and, on being cured, rewarded him with much money and a slave girl.
>
> Though Harith ben Kalada did not write any book on medicine, his views on many medical problems are preserved in his

---

36. The Role of the Nestorians and Muslims in the History of Medicine, Allen O. Whipple, 1967, Princeton Univ. Press, p 16.

conversation with Khosru. About the eye he says that it is constituted of fat which is the white part, of water which is the black part, and of wind which constituted the eyesight.

All this...goes to show the acquaintance of Harith with the Greek doctors.[37] He died in the reign of 'Umar the 2nd Caliph.

Summarizing the situation in a few words in his book *Histoire de la Médecine Arabe*, Dr. Lucien LeClerc writes,

> Harith ben Kalada studied medicine at Jandi-Shapur and Muhammad owed to Harith a part of his medical knowledge. Thus, with the one as well as the other, we easily recognize the traces of Greek (medicine).[38]

Sometimes Muhammad treated the sick, but in the difficult cases he would send the patients to Harith.[39]

Another educated person around Muhammad was Nadr ben Harith—not related to the doctor. He was a Qurayshite and cousin of Muhammad and had also visited the court of Khosru. He had learned Persian and music which he introduced among the Quraish at Mecca.

However, he was not sympathetic to Muhammad, mocking some of the stories in the Qur'an. "Muhammad never forgave him for this, and when he was taken prisoner at the Battle of Badr, he caused him to be put to death."[40]

In summary, we see that

(1) Arabs living in Mecca and Medina in 600 AD had political and economic relations with people from Ethiopia, Yemen, Persia, and Byzantium of present-day Turkey.

(2) A cousin of Muhammad knew Persian well enough to do his musical studies in it.

(3) The Ghassan tribe, which ruled the Syrian desert over to the gates of Medina, used Syriac—one of the main languages used to teach medicine at Jundi-Shapur—as their official language.

(4) An ill king of Yemen came to Ta'if to consult the physician Harith ben Kalada who had been trained at Jundi-Shapur—the best medical school in that world—and to whom Muhammad sometimes sent patients.

(5) During Muhammad's lifetime a new medical school was established in Alexandria using the 26 books of Galen as their texts.

This all shows that there was ample opportunity for Muhammad and the people around him to have heard of the embryological theories of Aristotle, Hippocrates and Galen when they went to seek treatment from Harith ben Kalada and other local doctors.

Thus when the Qur'an says in the Late Meccan Sura of the Believer (Al-Mu'min) 40:67,

---

37. Dr. Muhammad Zubayr Siddiqi, *Studies in Arabic and Persian Medical Literature*, Calcutta University, 1959, p 6-7.
38. LeClerc, op.cit., p 123.
39. Le Clerc, op.cit., p 33.
40. Edward G. Brown, M.B., F.R.C.P., *Arabian Medicine*, Cambridge, 1921, p 11.

He it is Who created you from dust, then from a sperm-drop, then from a leech-like clot (**'alaqa**)...**THAT PERHAPS YOU MAY UNDERSTAND.**

And when the Sura of the Pilgrimage (Al-Ḥajj) 22:5 starts out,

> O mankind! if you have doubt about the resurrection (**consider**) that We have created you from dust, then from a drop of seed, then from a clot (**'alaqa**), etc...

it is correct for us to ask again, What were they to understand?

What were they to consider?

When we look at the Quranic stages again the answer is very clear.

QURANIC STAGES OF PRENATAL DEVELOPMENT

STAGE 1. nutfa — sperm

STAGE 2. 'alaqa — clot

STAGE 3. mudagha — piece or lump of flesh

STAGE 4. 'adam — bones

STAGE 5. dressing the bones with muscles

They were understanding and considering that which was common knowledge— the embryological stages as taught by the Greek physicians.

I do not mean that Muhammad's listeners all knew the names of the Greek physicians, but they knew the embryological stages of the Greek physicians.

(1) They believed that the male sperm

(2) mixed with the female semen and menstrual blood to cause it to clot and this became the baby.

(3) They believed there was a time when the fetal lump was "formed and unformed."

(4) They believed the lump became bones

(5) which were then covered with muscles.

Allah in the Qur'an was using that common knowledge as a sign encouraging the listeners and readers to turn to Him. The trouble is that this common knowledge was and is **not true.**

ARAB PHYSICIANS AFTER MUHAMMAD

We must now look at one hadith and two well-known physicians from the period after Muhammad. Obviously they had no effect on the Qur'an, but they demonstrate that faith in the embryological ideas of Aristotle, Hippocrates and Galen continued among the Arabs right up to the 1600's.

The **hadith** is found in the *Forty Hadiths* of An-Nawawi and reads as follows,

> This hadith is reported according to Abi 'Abd-ar-rahman 'Abdallah ben Mas'ud—may God be pleased with him—who said: "The Apostle of God—may God bless him and grant him

salvation—spoke to us and he is truthful and worthy of belief:

"The creation of any one of you is accomplished in various stages in the abdomen of your mother; **40 days a drop of sperm;** then he will be a clot (**'alaqa**) for the same period, then chewed meat (mudagha) for the same period; then the angel will be sent to him and he will blow into him the spirit (soul) and he will order four words (about the future) by writing: his monetary fortune, and his length of life, and his actions, and whether he is to be damned or happy in the hereafter.

"And I swear by God Whom there is no other God except Him: it could be that one of you will do acts as the people of heaven until there remains only one arm's-length between him and it (heaven), and the writing (of his future) will overtake him and he will do the acts of the people of the fire and he will enter it. And it could be that one of you will do acts of the people of the fire until there remains only one arm's-length between him and it, and the writing (of his future) will overtake him and he will do the acts of the people of heaven and he will enter it." (translation mine)

Transmitted by Bukhari and Muslim[41]

We have here a hadith which is reported to be from the mouth of Muhammad; attested to by the best authorities—Bukhari and Muslim; included in a special collection of hadiths by a specialist in hadiths; but which has gross scientific errors. It follows the stages of the Qur'an exactly, but here Muhammad has added other information. The drop of sperm remains a drop of sperm 40 days, then an "'alaqa" 40 days for a total of 80 days, then "chewed meat" for 40 days for a total of 120 days as shown in the following summary. Modern gynecological studies have shown that sperm remain alive less than a week inside the female genital tract, and that at 70 days organ differentiation and maturation are well advanced, except for the brain.

HADITH'S STAGES OF PRENATAL DEVELOPMENT

STAGE 1. sperm—for 40 days

STAGE 2. 'alaqa—clot for 40 days

STAGE 3. mudagha—flesh for 40 days

This makes a total of 120 days or 3 months and there are still no bones.

In truth all organs are formed, bones are beginning to calcify, and muscles are moving at 2 months.

This **hadith** says that it doesn't even become "an unformed lump" until 80 days, a clear error. Dr. Bucaille also mentions this hadith and concludes,

> This description of embryonic evolution does not agree with modern data.[42]

---

41. An-Nawawi, op. cit., p 28-29.
42. Bucaille, BQ&S, p 245.

However, it clearly shows something of what men believed only 200 years away from Muhammad, and it raises severe theological problems in relation to all the Hadith.

THE THEOLOGICAL PROBLEM

Do the scientific errors in this hadith make the theological statements of Muhammad wrong too?

If the scientific error proves that this well-attested hadith is wrong, how do we know anything about the validity of the other well-attested hadiths which don't happen to have a scientific error to betray that they are wrong?

An even more crucial question is, How do we know that this hadith is not an accurate transmission? How do we know that this does not represent Muhammad's words and understanding of the scientific facts???

Furthermore, if the correct translation of **alaqa** is "leech-like substance" as modern Muslims like Shabir Ally claim, there is no place where these post-Quranic doctors said so. In fact, it is just the opposite. The ideas of these Greek physicians were being used to explain the Qur'an and the Qur'an was quoted to enlighten the meaning of the Greek physicians.

Avicenna (Ibn Sīnā') 980-1037 AD wrote,

> 679. The human being takes its origin from two things—(1) **the male sperm**, which plays the part of "factor"; (2) **the female sperm [first part of the menstrual blood]**, which provides the matter...These give the **coagulum** ("He created man from a clot"—Q. 96,2) a certain hardiness or firmness.[43]

Thus we see that Ibn Sīnā' gave the female semen exactly the same role that Aristotle had assigned to the menstrual blood...It is difficult to overstate the importance of Ibn Sīnā' as a scientific and philosophical authority for the pre-modern Europeans.[44]

Ibn Qayyim Al-jawziyya (1291-1351)

Ibn Qayyim took full advantage of the agreement between Quranic revelation and Greek medicine.

Here Ibn Qayyim is writing a medical account which includes:

> *Hippocrates (italics)*,
>
> **the Qur'an (bold)**,
>
> Hadith (underlined),
>
> (commentaries (double underlined),
>
> and his own thoughts in (plain) in one and the same paragraph.
>
> Hippocrates said in the third chapter of Kitab al-ajinna:
> "...*The semen is contained in a membrane, and it grows because*

---

43. Gruner, op.cit., p 359.
44. Musallam, Basim F., *Sex and Society in Islam*, Birth control before the 19th century. Cambridge University Press, 1983, p 47-48.

of the blood of its mother which descends to the womb"[45]...Some membranes are formed at the beginning, others after the second month, and others in the third month..." That is why God says, "He creates you in the wombs of your mothers, by one formation after another in three darknesses" (Qur'an 39:6). Since each of these membranes has its own darkness, when God mentioned the stages of creation and transformation from one state to another, He also mentioned the darknesses of the membranes. Most commentators explain: "it is the darkness of the belly, and the darkness of the womb, and the darkness of the placenta..."

In a second example we read,

Hippocrates said, *"The mouth opens up spontaneously, and the nose and ears are formed from the flesh. The ears are opened, and the eyes, which are filled with a clear liquid."* The Prophet used to say, "I worship Him Who made my face and formed it, and opened my hearing and eyesight" etc.[46]

He could do this because, as we have seen, the educated people of Muhammad's time were familiar with Greek medicine.

However, what is important for us sitting here today to realize is that there is no place where the Qur'an corrected Greek medicine. There is no place where Ibn Qayyim was shouting "Hey you guys. You've got this all wrong. The correct meaning of 'alaqa is 'that which clings' or 'leech-like substance.'" On the contrary, Ibn Qayyim was demonstrating the agreement between the Qur'an and Greek medicine—their agreement in error.

A final witness is the commentary of Imam Naasir-addiin Baidawi who died in 1282 AD. He quotes Sura 22:5 (see next page) and then gives his understanding. He explains 'alaqa as "a piece of solid blood" and mudagha as "a piece of meat, originally as much as can be chewed."

Stages of Development—a Modern Idea?!?

As I mentioned at the beginning of this study, it has been said that the idea of the embryo developing through stages is a modern one, and that the Qur'an is prophesying modern embryology by depicting differing stages. Yet, we have seen that Aristotle, Hippocrates, the Indians and Galen have all discussed stages of embryological development during the 1000 years before the Qur'an.

And after the coming of the Qur'an, the account of the different stages as described by the Qur'an, was carried on in the teachings of the Hadiths, Avicenna and Ibn Qayyim, and is essentially the same as that taught by Galen and those preceding him.

Concerning the bone stage, it is clear, as Dr. Moore demonstrates so capably

---

45. This is exactly what we quoted from Hippocrates at the beginning of this section: "The seed (embryo), then, is contained in a membrane. Moreover, it grows because of its **mother's blood**, which descends to the womb. **For once a woman conceives, she ceases to menstruate**..." Section 14, p 326.
46. Ibn Qayyim, Tuhfat, p 248-52.

203

بِسْمِ اللَّهِ الرَّحْمَٰنِ الرَّحِيمِ

يَـٰٓأَيُّهَا ٱلنَّاسُ ٱتَّقُوا۟ رَبَّكُمْ ۚ إِنَّ زَلْزَلَةَ ٱلسَّاعَةِ شَىْءٌ عَظِيمٌ ۝ يَوْمَ تَرَوْنَهَا تَذْهَلُ كُلُّ مُرْضِعَةٍ عَمَّآ أَرْضَعَتْ وَتَضَعُ كُلُّ ذَاتِ حَمْلٍ حَمْلَهَا وَتَرَى ٱلنَّاسَ سُكَـٰرَىٰ وَمَا هُم بِسُكَـٰرَىٰ وَلَـٰكِنَّ عَذَابَ ٱللَّهِ شَدِيدٌ ۝ وَمِنَ ٱلنَّاسِ مَن يُجَـٰدِلُ فِى ٱللَّهِ بِغَيْرِ عِلْمٍ وَيَتَّبِعُ كُلَّ شَيْطَـٰنٍ مَّرِيدٍ ۝ كُتِبَ عَلَيْهِ أَنَّهُۥ مَن تَوَلَّاهُ فَأَنَّهُۥ يُضِلُّهُۥ وَيَهْدِيهِ إِلَىٰ عَذَابِ ٱلسَّعِيرِ ۝ يَـٰٓأَيُّهَا ٱلنَّاسُ إِن كُنتُمْ فِى رَيْبٍ مِّنَ ٱلْبَعْثِ فَإِنَّا خَلَقْنَـٰكُم مِّن تُرَابٍ ثُمَّ مِن نُّطْفَةٍ ثُمَّ مِنْ عَلَقَةٍ ثُمَّ مِن مُّضْغَةٍ مُّخَلَّقَةٍ وَغَيْرِ مُخَلَّقَةٍ لِّنُبَيِّنَ لَكُمْ ۚ وَنُقِرُّ فِى ٱلْأَرْحَامِ مَا نَشَآءُ إِلَىٰٓ أَجَلٍ مُّسَمًّى ثُمَّ نُخْرِجُكُمْ طِفْلًا ثُمَّ لِتَبْلُغُوٓا۟ أَشُدَّكُمْ ۖ وَمِنكُم مَّن يُتَوَفَّىٰ وَمِنكُم مَّن يُرَدُّ إِلَىٰٓ أَرْذَلِ ٱلْعُمُرِ لِكَيْلَا يَعْلَمَ مِنۢ بَعْدِ عِلْمٍ شَيْـًٔا ۚ وَتَرَى ٱلْأَرْضَ هَامِدَةً فَإِذَآ أَنزَلْنَا عَلَيْهَا ٱلْمَآءَ ٱهْتَزَّتْ وَرَبَتْ وَأَنۢبَتَتْ مِن كُلِّ زَوْجٍ بَهِيجٍ ۝

in his textbook, that muscles start forming from the somites at the same time as the cartilage models of the bones. There is no bone stage at which the limbs of the developing fetus are just bones around which muscles will later be placed.

It is equally clear, that **'alaqa** in the Qur'an means **clot** and that the Quraish who heard Muhammad speaking understood him to be referring to the menstrual blood as the female contribution to the developing baby.

Therefore we can conclude that during all these years, the Quranic verses on embryology saying that "man is created from a drop of sperm which becomes a clot" were in perfect accord with the "science" of the 1st century of the Hejira, of the time of the Qur'an.

But when compared with the modern science of our 20th century,

> **Hippocrates is in error,**
>
> **Aristotle is in error,**
>
> **Galen is in error,**
>
> **The Qur'an is in error.**

They are all in serious error.

7. THE LENGTH OF GESTATION

The verses which give information and a command concerning the duration of nursing are as follows:

Luqman 31:14, Late Meccan.

> And We have enjoined upon man concerning his parents—his mother bearing him in weakness upon weakness, and his **weaning in two years**—Give thanks to Me and to your parents...

The Heifer (Al-Baqara) 2:233, 2 AH.

> Mothers shall suckle their children for **two whole years**; for those who wish to complete the suckling...

The Winding Sand Tracts (Al-Aḥqāf) 46:15, Late Meccan.

> "And We have commended unto man kindness toward parents. His mother carried him in pain and gave him birth in pain, **and the carrying of him and the weaning of him is thirty months**...

Obviously there is no problem with this command to nurse for 24 months if possible. After many years of pushing bottle-feeding, doctors are returning to the idea that breast-feeding of babies is much to be preferred even in developed countries; and in underdeveloped areas, so that the baby will have a clean source of protein for as long as possible, breast-feeding is a matter of life and death.

The third verse, however, gives 30 months as the total for gestation and nursing. Thirty months minus 24 months, leaves **only 6 months for the period of gestation**, but normal gestation lasts 9 months. Yusuf Ali understood that there was a problem so he has a note speaking of this six months as "the *minimum* period of human gestation after which the child is known to be viable.

205

This is in accordance with the latest ascertained scientific facts."[47] (Italics his)

The reader might have been happy with that **basic assumption** when Yusuf Ali wrote it (although it is no longer accurate[48]), but even for 1938 it wasn't all that straightforward. The verse goes on,

> ...At length when he reaches the age of full strength and attains
> forty years, he says, "O my Lord, grant me that I may be grateful
> for Thy favor...truly I have repented and truly do I bow in Islam."

Such a statement speaking about 40 years seems to be for every normal man, not for some special circumstance. If the command for nursing is 24 months, a normal period of time; and man reaching 40 years of age is a normal condition; then we would expect the first part of the phrase concerning gestation to be speaking about a usual period of gestation (nine months) and not an unusual period of six months, which is really an illness.

8. INHERITANCE AND ACQUIRED CHARACTERISTICS

a. Genetics and Milk-mothers

In the past many cultures believed that what the mother saw or did could also affect the child. 100 years ago in the United States culture, people believed that if a woman saw a rabbit while she was pregnant her child might be born with a split upper lip just like a rabbit or hare. This split upper lip was called a hare-lip because of this mistaken idea, and the word still remains in usage today—even in medical books.

The Qur'an seems to have one of these same ancient ideas. In the Sura of the Women (Al-Nisā') 4:23, from 5-6 AH, there is a long list of women who are prohibited for a man to take in marriage, including the following:

> ...daughters of your (foster) mothers who breast-fed you,
> your (foster) sisters from breast-feeding...the wives of your sons
> from your loins... (as opposed to wives of adopted sons, which
> were made legal by Sura 33:37)

It is perfectly clear according to what Dr. Bucaille would call "sure" modern scientific knowledge that inheritance is controlled by the genes we receive from our biological mother and father. There is no other way. No hereditary characteristics are passed through the milk of a wet-nurse. There is no relationship of any kind between a boy who was breast-fed by a wet-nurse and the biological daughter of the wet-nurse, so there is no scientific reason to prohibit these marriages.

We might say that it was just a matter of honor to the wet-nurse, but this does not seem to be the case. Rather it seems based on the belief that breast-feeding makes you a relative. Bukhari comments on verse 4:23 mentioned above and quotes Muhammad as saying to Aisha, **"Nursing produces (the same) interdiction which childbirth produces."**[49] That is, no marriage with milk-

---

47. Yusuf Ali, op. cit., p 1370, Note 4790.
48. Now babies of 5 1/2 months weighing 600 grams are sometimes saved alive. I observed this personally in 1989.
49. Bukhari, Chapter 67, on marriage, no. 21.

sisters, but the same freedom to visit them unveiled as that allowed to blood-brothers. God is free to command that which He wishes, but it certainly does not mirror modern genetic understanding.

b. Genetics and Spotted Goats in the Torah-Old Testament

In the **Torah**, Genesis 30:32-31:13, we find the following story showing that Jacob, the grandson of Abraham, also held the unscientific belief that he could influence the color of the lambs and kids by changing what the mother goats saw.

His father-in-law, Laban, wanted Jacob to watch over his flocks and told Jacob to name his wages. Jacob suggested that Laban should take out the spotted goats and sheep. Then Jacob would guard the solid colored ones, and his wages would be the spotted lambs and kids. Laban agreed and removed the speckled and spotted goats and the dark sheep, leaving Jacob to take care of the plain-colored goats and sheep.

But Jacob had ideas about how to influence which lambs were born. The story continues:

> Jacob…took fresh-cut branches from poplar, almond and plane trees and made white stripes on them by peeling the bark and exposing the white inner wood of the branches. Then he placed the peeled branches in all the watering troughs, so that they would be directly in front of the flocks when they came to drink.

Jacob believed that putting white stripped wood where the goats mated would have an effect on the offspring, but we know by modern genetic experiments that there is no such thing as inheriting acquired characteristics. (That is, you cannot inherit a harelip and cleft palate because your mother saw a rabbit with a split upper lip.) Jacob is wrong!

However the God of Abraham and Isaac does not allow Jacob to continue in this false belief which steals credit from the Creator. He reveals the true cause to Jacob in a dream which Jacob repeated to his wives as follows:

> In breeding season I once had a dream in which I looked up and saw that the male goats mating with the flock were streaked, speckled or spotted. The angel of God said to me in the dream, "Jacob."
> I answered, "Here I am."
> And he said, "Look up and see that **all the male goats mating with the flock are streaked, speckled or spotted**, for I have seen all that Laban has been doing to you. I am the God of Bethel, where you anointed a pillar and where you made a vow to Me. Now leave this land at once and go back to your native land."

To understand how God worked this miracle one needs to know that just as blue eyes are recessive in humans, so spotting is recessive in goats. This means that under normal conditions of complete mixing, 25% of the goats would be homozygous (have two similar genes) for the dominant solid color; 25% would be homozygous for recessive spotting and be spotted; while 50% would be heterozygous with one gene for solid color and one gene for spotting. This 50% would also be solid colored because the gene for solid color is dominant and controls the color, leaving the gene for spotting hidden. Ordinary mating which happens by chance with a normal (25%-50%-25%) mix of rams and ewes, continues to result in 25% spotted kids.

When Laban removed the spotted 25%, this left a herd made up of 33% pure solid goats and 67% mixed or heterozygous goats. This would have worked against Jacob, resulting in only 16.75% of spotted goats. But then God stepped in and caused all the mating to be done by spotted (homozygous-recessive) rams.

The first-year result would be that 50% of kids born to the 67% heterozygous females would be spotted, resulting in 33% of the total number of kids being spotted and belonging to Jacob.

An additional long-term result would be that all of the solid-colored kids would be heterozygous with a recessive gene from the spotted rams which had fathered them. This would increase the percentage of heterozygous ewes to 75% the following year, and eventually almost half of the kids would be spotted, resulting in a doubling of Jacob's wages.

Thus the Biblical account from 1700 BC, while acknowledging Jacob's wrong ideas, is consistent with modern genetic understanding.

9. OTHER PROBLEMS

a. Milk. In the Late Meccan Sura of the Bee (Al-Naḥl) 16:66, it says that

> We pour out to you from what is within their (the cattle's) abdomen (buṭūn بُطُوب), between excretions and blood, milk– pure and agreeable to the drinkers.

What can it possibly mean that milk comes from between the excrement and the blood? The mammary glands which produce the milk are part of and under the skin. The excretions (feces) are spatially inside the intestines inside the abdomen, but physiologically the feces is actually outside of the body. There are no blood vessels into the feces which could connect to the mammary gland.

b. Honey. Or the problem of verse 69 in the same sura which reads,

> A multicolored drink (honey) in which there is healing for men, comes out of (the bee's) abdomen (buṭūn بُطُون).

What does it mean that honey comes out of the bee's abdomen, and what disease does honey heal?

c. Communities Like You. In the Late Meccan Sura of the Cattle (Al-An'am) 6:38, we read,

> There is not an animal on the earth, nor a being that flies on two wings, but (forms) communities like you.

What does "communities like you" mean? Dr. Bucaille mentions the bees.[50] Everyone will certainly agree that the bees are a community, but what about the

---

50. Bucaille, BQ&S, p 192.

spider where in some species the female eats the male after mating has taken place? Is that a community like mine? Like yours?

What about the lions? When the new strong lion drives out the old leader of the pride, he kills the cubs from the previous male. Now that I am more than 70 years old, is that what awaits my children?

Before leaving this subject let's re-examine even the bees. There is one queen. All the workers are eunuch female slaves. What about the male drones? When one mates with the queen all the rest are driven out of the hive to die. Is that a community like ours? I think not.

d. The Sun. Let us consider the Early Meccan Sura of the Criterion (Al-Furqan) 25:45-46, which says,

> Hast thou not turned thy vision to thy Lord? How He prolongs
> the shadow! If He willed He could make it stationary! Then do
> We (God) make the sun its guide.

Does the sun move so that it guides the shadows? They taught us in school that as the earth rotates toward the east, the shadows prolong toward the east and the sun, which does not move in relation to the earth, appears to set in the west. In 20th century science we know that the sun does not move to guide the shadow. The Qur'an is wrong.

Our second verse about the sun comes from Sura of the Cave (Al-Kahf) 18:86 which reads,

> Until when (Zul-qarnain) reached the setting of the sun, he
> found it set in a spring of murky water.

First of all, as we discussed above, the sun doesn't set. The earth rotates to bring the night. However, even modern scientists use the word sunset in their daily language. But if the sun set in a spring of murky water, it would vaporize the whole earth. This is a major problem.

Dr. Bucaille's discussion of these verses is not at all convincing!

10. MUSLIMS ABOVE THE ARCTIC CIRCLE AND PRAYING ASTRONAUTS

These last two problems have to do with information which is omitted from the Qur'an. That may sound like a rather proud statement, but I think the meaning will become clear as we continue.

a. The Qur'an claims to be a guide and a light for the entire world, and yet no person living above the arctic circle can be a Muslim!

"That's not true," you will say. "Anyone can be a Muslim. All he has to do is believe and say the shahada—the statement of faith."

"Wrong," I say. "He has got to keep the fast of Ramadan, and during the arctic summer he will starve to death because there is no sunset to mark the end of the fast. While waiting several weeks for a sunset he will have to fast and fast and fast until he's dead."

"Well then," you answer, "let him fast according to the hours of the Muslims in Stockholm or Mecca."

Yes, that is a possibility, but many Muslims won't agree that this type of "original thinking" is valid. Every year there is a big uncertainty in Morocco as to whether the new moon to end the fast of Ramadan will be seen on the 29th day of the lunar month or the 30th. In addition to the question of whether one must fast an extra day or not, people can't make a plane reservation because they don't know when their holidays start, etc.

Seeing this inconvenience year after year, I said to one friend, "But this is the 20th century and we can calculate the time of the new moon. Why don't they calculate it and be done with all this uncertainty?"

He replied, "Because the Qur'an says, 'When one of you witnesses (personally) the new moon…,' " and he pointed to his eye to emphasize that a human must see it.[51]

Tunisia does go by astronomical calculations, and if some of the Laplanders become Muslims, some type of decision will have to be made about when and how they will fast.

b. A second example of this type of problem is the space voyage of a Saudi Arabian astronaut. At an altitude of 200 km (125 miles), the orbital velocity of the space craft is 29,000 km (18,000 miles) per hour and the period of orbit around the earth is 90 minutes. So now 20th century questions must be asked. Of the 18 daily voyages around the earth, each with a sunrise and sunset, which entrance into the earth's shadow should be used for the "sunset" prayers? And how can the astronaut pray toward Mecca when, except for the rare course straight toward that town, the angle of direction would continually change even during the few minutes necessary for four rak'as of prayer?

The Saudi Arabian religious leaders decided that the astronaut should attach his feet to the space ship and pray three times during the day. This is a perfectly logical decision, but there is no place that prophesies this in the Qur'an.

I mention all this because Bucaille has a long two-page explanation proposing that the word used for "if" in the Sura of the Most Gracious (Al-Rahman) 55:33 is prophetic because it allows for "the possibility" of the conquest of space.[52] But this is of no importance compared with the unanswered questions of how the astronauts should pray toward Mecca in their rotating spaceship, or how the Laplanders above the Arctic Circle should calculate their fast of Ramadan. If we were given future answers in Muhammad's time to theological questions like these then one could speak about prophetic foreknowledge. In the Bible we actually find such detailed prophecies and we shall look at some of them in later chapters.

---

51. The Heifer (Al-Baqara) 2:185, 2 AH.
52. BQ&S, p 167-169.

C. FABLES, ALLEGORIES AND HISTORY

11. FABLE—A PARABLE TEACHING A MORAL? OR AN IMAGINARY MYTH?

A discussion of "fables" may seem out of place in a chapter on science, but it is placed in this section because "accurate history" as recorded in either the **Bible** or the **Qur'an** relates to the word "science" in its broadest sense.

Dr. Bucaille asserts that the Bible, especially the Torah-Old Testament, is not valid history but really fables and the product of men's imagination. On page 4 under the title *ORIGINS OF THE BIBLE* he writes:

> Before it became a collection of books, it was a folk tradition that relied entirely upon human memory, originally the only means of passing on ideas…
>
> E. Jacobs notes that these words (laws and records) were either passed down from family to family or channeled through the sanctuaries in the form of an account of the history of God's chosen people.
>
> **History quickly turned into fable**, as in the Fable of Jotham (Judges 9:7-21) where "the trees went forth to anoint a king over them; and they asked in turn the olive tree, the fig tree, the vine and the bramble," which allows E. Jacobs to note, "Animated by the need to tell a good story, the narration was not perturbed by subjects or times whose history was not well known…"[1]

To say that the Book of Judges came not by revelation but "by the need to tell a good story" is a very strong statement. For Christians who believe that it is revelation, the Book of Judges, where the above mentioned "fable" is found, describes real events which took place in the 12th century BC following the Exodus from Egypt and the conquest of Canaan.

According to E. Jacobs, this was a time when **there was no writing and "history quickly turned to fable."** However, the reader may remember that when we studied this question in Chapter I of Section Three, we found that writing had been known in the area from at least 2300 BC, and that **in the 13th century BC, 100 years before the Book of Judges, there were five different scripts in use in Canaan**. Clearly the specialist E. Jacobs is wrong on this point.

Now let us look at this so-called "fable," including all the necessary context so that every reader can make his own judgment.

According to Judges chapter 6, God ordered a man named Gideon, son of Joash, to tear down the altar which his father had built to a false god called Baal. Then he was to build an altar to the Eternal One, Yahweh Elohim.

Gideon did this and the next day the men of the town said to Gideon's father,

---

1. Bucaille, BQ&S, p 4.

"Bring out your son. He must die, because he has broken down Baal's altar and cut down the Asherah pole beside it."

But the father replied, "Are you going to plead Baal's cause?...If Baal really is a god, he can defend himself when someone breaks down his altar."

So that day they called Gideon "Jerub-Baal," saying, "Let Baal contend with him." Judges 6:30b-32a.

Chapters 7 and 8 tell how God used Gideon and only three hundred men to put such fear into a Midianite army of more than 100,000 men that these Midianites rushed out in the middle of the night and killed each other.

After this great victory Gideon went back to his home in Ophrah and lived there forty years. He had seventy sons from his wives and one son, Abimelech, by a concubine, who lived in the neighboring town of Shechem.

After Gideon's death, chapter 9 tells us that Abimelech said to the people of Shechem,

"Which is better for you? To have all seventy of Jerub-Baal's sons rule over you, or just one man? Remember, I am your flesh and blood" (Judges 9:2).

When the people of Shechem heard this they decided to follow Abimelech. With this support on his side,

He went to his father's home in Ophrah and on one stone murdered his seventy brothers, the sons of Jerub-Baal (Gideon); but Jotham, the youngest son of Jerub-Baal, escaped by hiding. Then all the citizens of Shechem and Beth Millo gathered...to crown Abimelech king. Judges 9:5-6.

AND NOW JOTHAM GIVES HIS FABLE

When Jotham was told about this, he climbed up on the top of Mount Gerizim and shouted to them, "Listen to me, citizens of Shechem, so that God may listen to you.

"One day the trees went out to anoint a king for themselves. They said to the olive tree, 'Be our king.'

"But the olive tree answered, 'Should I give up my oil, by which both gods and men are honored, to go waving over the trees?'

"Next the trees said to the fig tree, 'Come and be our king.'

"But the fig tree replied, 'Should I give up my fruit, so good and sweet, to hold sway over the trees?'

"Then the trees said to the vine, 'Come and be our king.'

"But the vine answered, 'Should I give up my wine, which cheers both gods and men, to go waving over the trees?'

"Finally all the trees said to the thornbush, 'Come and be our king.'

"The thornbush said to the trees, 'If you really want to anoint me king over you, come and take refuge in my shade; but if not, then let fire come out of the thornbush and consume the cedars of Lebanon!'

"Now if you have acted honorably and in good faith when you made Abimelech king, and if you have been fair to Jerub-Baal and his family, and if you have treated him as he deserves—and to think that my father fought for you, risked his life to rescue you from the hand of Midian…If then if you have acted honorably…may Abimelech be your joy, and may you be his, too! But if you have not, let fire come out from Abimelech and consume you, citizens of Shechem and Beth Millo, and let fire come out from you, citizens of Shechem and Beth Millo, and consume Abimelech!"

Then Jotham fled, escaping to Beer, and he lived there because he was afraid of his brother Abimelech. Judges 9:7-21.

Chapter 9 then goes on to tell how three years later Abimelech killed the men of Shechem, "destroyed the city, and scattered salt over it." A few days later, Abimelech himself was killed when a woman threw a millstone down from a wall and mortally wounded him. Judges 9:45-57.

Now is this a fable in the sense of "history turned to fable"?

The dictionary Larousse defines a fable as:

a. apologue, allegorical narrative, usually in verse, which hides a moral under the cover of fiction;

b. a false account, imaginary.[2]

Clearly this parable given by Jotham has a moral teaching, so **it IS** a fable if we are using the first definition. But **it IS NOT** "history turned to fable." The fable is in the middle of the history, but distinct from the history.

However, when Dr. Bucaille uses the word, quoting E. Jacobs and comparing the Torah-Old Testament with the Song of Roland, he is using the second meaning for the word "fable." He is claiming that these accounts have practically no historical value. He can only do this because in Europe so few readers have a Bible at hand with which to check up on him. But with the story in front of us, it is clear that Jotham, the remaining son, made a parable promising that those who destroyed his brothers would destroy each other. To call this a "fable" as myth is gross error.

The truth of the historical part of the account has even been confirmed by archaeology. Dr. Siegfried H. Horn, Professor of Archaeology at Andrews University, Berrien Springs, Michigan wrote in 1968,

I want to inject a personal note about the discoveries at Shechem, for I participated in its excavation. Our 1960 work at Shechem revealed that the city and its great temple of Baal were destroyed in the **twelfth century B.C.** That is exactly the time indicated in the Bible for the destruction of Shechem by Abimelech, the…son of the judge Gideon.

---

2. I have translated the French definitions because these are the French meanings for Bucaille.

The archaeological evidence—broken pieces of pottery—sets the date at **about 1150 B.C.** The agreement between the two dates, one obtained from Biblical evidence and the other from archaeological data, could hardly have been closer.[3]

HISTORICAL ACCOUNTS IN THE QUR'AN? FABLES? SOLOMON AND THE QUEEN OF SABA' (SHEBA)

From the Middle Meccan Sura of the Ant (Al-Naml) 27:15-44, we read,

And We verily gave knowledge unto David and Solomon, and they said: "Praise be to God, Who has preferred us above many of His believing slaves!"

And Solomon was David's heir, and he said, "O mankind! Lo, we have been taught the language of birds, and have been given some of all things. This is indeed evident favor."

And there were gathered together unto Solomon his armies of the jinns and humans and birds, and they were set in battle order; until when they reached the valley of the ants, an ant said, "O ants! Enter your homes lest Solomon and his armies crush you, without noticing."

Solomon smiled at the ant and said, "O Lord! May I do that which is right and well pleasing to You, so that You introduce me among Your servants the righteous."

And he took muster of the birds and said, "Why is it that I see not the Hoopoe? Is he among the absent? Truly I will punish him with a severe penalty, or execute him, unless he brings me a clear excuse."

But he was not long in coming, and said, "I have found out that which you have not found out and I have come to you from Saba' with certain news.

"I found a woman ruling over them, surrounded with every kind of possession, and having a magnificent throne. I found her and her people worshiping the sun apart from God. Satan has made their deeds pleasant unto them and has turned them aside from the right way, and they are not rightly directed, so that they do not worship God Who brings forth the hidden in the heavens and the earth, and knows what you hide and what you proclaim. God, there is no god but He! Lord of the magnificent throne!"

And (Solomon) said, "We shall see whether you are telling the truth or are from among the liars. Go with this my letter, and having delivered it to them turn aside, and see what answer they return."

(The queen) said, "O nobles! An honorable letter has been

3. Recent Illumination of the Old Testament, *Christianity Today*, June 21, 1968, p 15.

delivered to me. It is from Solomon. It is in the name of the Most Merciful God. (He says), "Be not arrogant against me, but come to me in submission." She said, "O nobles! Advise me in my affair. No affair have I decided except in your presence."

They said, "We are lords of might and lords of great prowess, but it is for you to command, so consider what you will command."

She said, "Kings, when they enter a country ruin it and make the noblest of its people the abased, and thus they will do. But I am going to send a present and we will see with what my messengers return."

So when (the envoy) came to Solomon, he said, "Will you give me wealth? Verily that which God has given me is better than that which He has given you. No, it is you who rejoice in your gift.

"Go back to them and be sure we shall come to them with such hosts as they will never be able to meet. We shall expel them from there in disgrace, and they will feel humbled."

He said (to his own leaders), "O nobles, which of you will bring me her throne, before they come submissive to me."

An 'Ifrit (devil or giant) of the Jinns said, "I will bring it to you before you rise from your place, for I am strong and trustworthy."

One who had knowledge of the book said, "I will bring it to you before the twinkling of your eye."

And when (Solomon) saw it placed before him he said, "This is a favor of my Lord, that He may try me whether I am grateful or ungrateful..." And he said, "Alter her throne, that we may see whether she will receive guidance or is from those who will not receive guidance."

So when she arrived she was asked, "Is this your throne?"

She said, "It was just like this."

And (Solomon said), "We were given knowledge before her, and we surrendered. But that which she worshiped besides had turned her aside, for she was of an unbelieving people."

It was said to her, "Enter the palace." And when she saw it, she imagined that it was a great surface of water, and she uncovered her legs.

(Solomon) said, "Verily it is a palace paved with glass."

She said, "My Lord (God), I have wronged myself. I submit (in Islam) to the Lord of the Worlds."

What shall we say of this account filled with talking birds, talking ants, giants of the jinns, and the throne brought in the "twinkling of an eye"?

Hamidullah has a note with these verses defining the word 'ifrit as, "a type of evil devil which one encounters in many **fabulous** stories." (Unlike the noun, the French adjective "fabuleux" which I translated as "fabulous" has only one meaning: **make-believe, imaginary, mythical, extraordinary.**)

What does the Bible actually say about Solomon and animals and birds? Three sentences which read,

> He (Solomon) described plant life, from the cedar of Lebanon to the hyssop that grows out of walls. **He also taught about animals and birds, reptiles and fish.** Men of all nations came to listen to Solomon's wisdom. I Kings 4:33-34a.

Yet Dr. Bucaille can write in *L'Homme, D'Ou Vient-il?*,

> In addition, I have not found in the text of the Qur'an any allusion to the myths and superstitions from the period of its communication to men, like those one finds in the Bible by the pen of authors speaking the language of their epoch.[4]

The Muslim reader may wish to place this account in class "a," i.e., a fable containing a moral teaching, but it does not seem to be presented as such in the Qur'an. It is true that there is some moral teaching, but the conversations and facts, both in the story and in the Quranic accounts before and after the story, seem to be presented as true history.

The account of Moses at the "burning bush," which comes just before the account of Solomon and the Queen of Saba', is presented in this sura and elsewhere in the Qur'an as true history.

The accounts of Salih going to the Thamud, and Lot speaking to his people—stories which immediately follow the account of Solomon and the Queen—are each presented as true history, both here and in other suras.

In addition, verses 59-66 give many appeals to nature as proof of God's greatness—including the "barrier" between two types of water which Dr. Bucaille and Dr. Torki are so keen to present as Quranic foreknowledge of modern science.

In the account of Jotham which we read above, there is a clear change between the historical material telling of the death of his 70 brothers and Jotham's parable of the trees. He knew and his listeners knew that he was saying a parable with a moral meaning, but this story of Solomon is found in the middle of historical material without any indication of change.

Furthermore, since Dr. Bucaille has been so careful to search for sources for Biblical stories, it must be asked why he has not taken the same care in relation to the Qur'an. He would find much useful material in books such as *The Sources of Islam* by W. St. Clair-Tisdall, who shows that this story was repeated among the Jews and is recorded in the Targum of the book of Esther. The account in the Targum includes the fact that the queen's legs had hair like a man. This fact, not found in the Qur'an, is however included in the Muslim traditions in the Araish al Majalis.[5]

---

4. Bucaille, *L'Homme*, p 161.
5. Op. cit., See text, T. & T. Clark, 38 George St. Edinburgh, reprinted Birmingham Bible Instit. Press, Birmingham. p 24-29.

SOLOMON'S DEATH

Another passage which needs to be considered here is the account of Solomon's death as found in the Early Meccan Sura of Saba' (Sabā') 34:12-14, which reads,

> And unto Solomon...We caused the fount of copper to gush forth for him, and there were of the jinns that worked in front of him (bain yadaihi بَيْنَ يَدَيْهِ), by the leave of his Lord, and if any one of them turned aside from Our command, We made him taste of the penalty of the blazing fire.
>
> They worked for him as he desired...then when We decreed death upon (Solomon), nothing showed them his death except a little creeping creature of the earth, which gnawed away his staff. And when he fell the jinns saw clearly how, if they had known the unseen, they would not have continued in the humiliating penalty (of work).

Here we have the great King Solomon, leaning on his staff and watching over the jinns, like any overseer that one sees managing a few workers repairing a road. He dies propped up on his staff. Not one of his servants who prepare his food, not one of his generals who come to him for orders, not one of his nobles, and not even the hoopoe bird notices or pays the least bit of attention, until a worm slowly eats away at his staff and he finally falls to the floor!?!?

What words would Dr. Bucaille use for this story if it were in the Bible? He would talk about **"l'invraisemblance"**—the unlikelihood—of the passage. He would call it a **"phantasmagoria."**[6] For any reader who does not have a dictionary close at hand, that means "a shifting series of illusions or deceptive appearances, as in a dream or as created by the imagination."[7]

Again we must ask, "What does the Bible really say about this?"

In I Kings 5:15-16 we read,

> Solomon had seventy thousand carriers and eighty thousand stonecutters in the hills, as well as thirty-three hundred foremen who supervised the project and directed the workmen.

The biggest problem, though, is the picture it gives of God. Does God Almighty, Creator of the Heavens and Earth and all that is in them, keep the jinns working by fooling them?

It is the same type of question that comes to mind about Jesus' crucifixion. Why should the great and mighty God who is called "The Truth" make it "seem as though" Jesus was crucified, if he wasn't?

In the Sura of the Family of 'Imran (āli 'Imrān) 3:52-53, from 2 or 3 AH, it says that Jesus' disciples **believed in him**.

Then it goes on in verse 54 to say,

---

6. BQ&S, French edition, p 239.
7. *The American College Dictionary*, Random House, New York, 1951.

And they (the Jews who didn't believe in Jesus) schemed (makarū مَكَرُوا), and Allah schemed (makara مَكَرَ) and Allah is the best of schemers (khair al-mākirīn خَيْرُ الْمَاكِرِينَ).

This word "schemer" (mākir الْمَاكِر) is a very strong word which Wehr and Abdel-Nour define as "sly, cunning, wily."[8] The Arabic-Arabic Munjid defines it with "khuda'a" (الْخُدَعَة) which means exactly the same thing.

According to the Gospel the leaders of the Jews did scheme to seize Jesus privately so that there wouldn't be a rebellion, but why should God allow them to think that they succeeded and then call Himself the Best of Schemers by taking up Jesus secretly? This leaves Jesus' closest followers also deceived—the very followers whom the Qur'an itself agrees believed in him. Is it really possible that the great God of Truth did this?

MATTHEW'S "INCREDIBLE" DESCRIPTIONS

In his chapter *The Four Gospels, Sources and History* Dr. Bucaille writes as follows on page 61:[9]

> He (Matthew) inserts into his book descriptions which are quite literally **incredible.**

Let us look then, at one of these passages which have been called "incredible." From the Gospel of Matthew 27:50-53 we read,

> And when Jesus (from his place on the cross) had cried out again in a loud voice, he gave up his spirit.
> At that moment the curtain of the temple was torn in two from top to bottom. The earth shook and the rocks split. The tombs broke open and the bodies of many holy people who had died were raised to life. They came out of the tombs, and after Jesus' resurrection they went into the holy city and appeared to many people.

What are Dr. Bucaille's complaints about this? First of all, it "has no corresponding passage in the other Gospels," i.e., it is only found one time. This is also true, of course, for the Quranic account saying that Jesus didn't die. It is found in only one sura.

Secondly, he says, "It is difficult to see how the bodies of the saints in question could have been raised from the dead *at the time of Jesus's death* (on Friday) and only emerge from their tombs *after his resurrection* (on Sunday)."

What shall we say? I say that though the passage gives that impression, we must give the author the benefit of the doubt. I am sure that he did not intend us to understand that those raised from the dead sat in their cold tombs, shivering from Friday until Sunday morning.

I am sure that he intended the reader to understand that the tombs were split open on Friday, and that the bodies were raised from the dead on Sunday

---

8. Wehr, op. cit., p 917.
9. Bucaille, BQ&S, p 61-62.

morning at the same time that Christ was raised from the dead—as part of his great victory over death.

In any case, compared to the account of Solomon with his talking birds and 'ifrits of the jinns; or the story about his dead body propped up on a stick; this **Biblical** account is a pearl of 20th century precision, and it was unworthy of Dr. Bucaille to even mention it.

The truth is that although the revelation in the Torah-Old Testament and Gospel-New Testament is in terms of the cultures of the people who wrote and received it, divine inspiration by the Holy Spirit prevented the Old Testament prophets and the disciples of Jesus from including the grotesque mythological ideas and the polytheism of the Babylonians, the Greeks, and the Romans.

CONCLUSION

We have seen all through this long chapter how Dr. Bucaille and others have used **basic assumptions** to reconcile differences in the Qur'an. Dr. Bucaille must allow the same freedom to those of us who love the Torah-Old Testament and the Gospel-New Testament.

When Christians propose that the genealogy in the Gospel according to Matthew is that of Joseph and the genealogy in the Gospel according to Luke is that of Mary, every person is free to say that the evidence is not convincing. But it is not valid for Dr. Bucaille to accuse Christians of being stubbornly blind and using devious means when they make such a **basic assumption** to reconcile the problem. **He has made many basic assumptions throughout his book.**

Moreover, to imply that Christians have not even been willing to admit that there is a problem is just not historically true. Eusebius, a Christian Bishop who lived in Palestine and wrote a history of the early church less than 200 years after Jesus ascended into heaven, noted the problem and suggested the solution mentioned above.

And when Dr. Bucaille makes a great point of the fact that he learned Arabic in order to read the Qur'an in the original, he must have read in the Sura of the Spider (Al-'Ankabūt) 29:14 where it says,

> We sent Noah to his people, and he tarried among them **a thousand years less fifty**...

On what basis, then, does he write,

> One knows that these (Biblical) genealogies attribute to Abraham and to his 19 ancestors until Adam lives of **unbelievable** length, which reach 969 years for Methuselah...[10]

Surely, if "969 years" is **unbelievable** for the Bible, "950 years" is **unbelievable** for the Qur'an. If "950 years" is **believable** for the Qur'an then "969 years" is **believable** for the Bible. We must weigh both books in the same balance.

---

10. Bucaille, L'Homme, p 153.

As the English proverb says,

What is good for the goose is good for the gander.

That still leaves the problem of the genealogy going back to Adam, a problem to which no totally satisfactory solution has been proposed. In his *Révélation des Origines* Henri Blocher spends three pages discussing four possible answers to this problem and then concludes, "They all have their inconveniences, so the problem remains before us."[11]

But in view of all the archaeological confirmation to the history of the Torah and the Gospel, and the many miracles which Jesus did, and the fulfilled prophecies—which abundantly confirm the truth of the Gospel—it is prudent and possible to wait and see what future studies and discoveries will produce. In 1947 no one thought that in 1948 we would find fragments of Leviticus from the Torah of Moses—fragments which were copied more than 200 years before Jesus the Messiah walked the earth—fragments which are the same as the Torah which we have in our hand today, **showing very clearly that the Torah has never been changed.**

---

11. Op. cit. in the text, p 228-230.

METHODS OF
PROOF IN REVELATION

CHAPTER I

GOD'S CREATIVE POWER AS PROOF
and
HOW TO TEST A
REVELATION ACCORDING TO THE QUR'AN

It was difficult for someone like myself who loves the Torah, the Zabūr (Psalms), and the Gospel, to understand how Dr. Bucaille could claim that the Bible does not emphasize the power of God in His creative acts. Heaven or the heavens are mentioned 75 times just in the Zabūr of David.

Many of these are poetic references about God in His heaven, comparing His qualities to the creation, as in Psalm 36:5-6,

> Your love, O LORD, reaches to the heavens, Your faithfulness to the skies. Your righteousness is like the mighty mountains, Your justice like the great deep.

Other passages appeal for God's help on the basis of His creative power as in Psalm 121:1-2,

> I lift up my eyes to the hills—where does my help come from? My help comes from the LORD, the Maker of heaven and earth.

Or they contrast the power of God with powerless idols as in Psalm 96:4-5,

> For great is the LORD and most worthy of praise; He is to be feared above all gods. **For all the gods of the nations are idols, but the LORD made the heavens**.

But 13 of these passages refer to God's creation of the heavens in a more scientific sense. David writes in Psalm 8:1,3-4,

> O LORD, our LORD, how majestic is Your name in all the earth! You have set Your glory above the heavens...When I consider Your heavens, the work of Your fingers, the moon and the stars, which You have set in place, what is man that You are mindful of him, the son of man that You care for him?

And in Psalm 19:1-4 the Holy Spirit guided him to write,

> The heavens declare the glory of God; the skies proclaim the work of His hands. Day after day they pour forth speech; night after night they display knowledge. There is no speech or language where their voice is not heard. Their voice goes out into all the earth, their words to the ends of the world.

David is saying here that the glory of the heavens is like a language which speaks to every man so that he knows that there is a great creator intellect. "There is no speech or language (no man or group of men) where their voice (the voice or vision of the creative acts of God) is not heard."

It is on the basis of these verses that the Holy Spirit led Paul to write in the Gospel-New Testament:

> For since the creation of the world God's invisible qualities— His eternal power and **divine nature**—have been clearly seen, **being understood from what has been made**, so that men are without excuse.
>
> For although they knew God, they neither glorified Him as God nor gave thanks to Him, but…they became fools and exchanged the glory of the immortal God for images…They exchanged the truth of God for a lie, **and worshiped and served created things (idols)** rather than the Creator—who is forever praised. Amen. (Romans 1:20-23a, 25).

Because we have seen the wonders of His great creation—the stars always in their courses, and the desert coming alive and blooming after the rain—we know there is a Creator God out there to whom we are accountable. Added to this in our day are the microchemical wonders, e.g., the wonder of the Krebs cycle—the enzyme system by which sugar is broken down and becomes energy in the living cell—and the wonder of the genetic code which Dr. Bucaille has described so effectively in *L'Homme D'Ou Vient-il?*[1] These things all demonstrate His creative presence, and because of these material wonders before our eyes **we have no excuse for not believing in this great Creator God!**

That still leaves a problem, however. Many "gods" are worshiped among men, and many men have claimed to be their prophets. How can we know which of these "gods" named among men is this **Creator God**?

WHICH GOD IS "THE REAL TRUE GOD"?

Is it Kali in India who orders her followers to steal and to kill?

Is it Shang Ti of the Chinese whom only the rulers could worship directly?

Is it Allah of the Qur'an who says that Jesus was not crucified?

Is it Yahweh Elohim, the Eternal One, of the Torah-Old Testament (called Theos in the Gospel-New Testament), who says that Jesus will die (Isaiah 53) and did die for our sins?

Recently I came across the book *L'Islam et la Science* by Dr. Ahmed Aroua, a medical colleague from Algeria, in which he describes the problem in very precise terms. Summarizing the relationship between science and religion, he says,

> Therefore, it will be demanded of science, not only to explain the phenomena and to act on them, but also to give answer to the why and to the ultimate development of things.
>
> The so-called objective sciences not being qualified to respond to this type of metaphysical question, and philosophy being only a

---

1. Op. cit.

speculation by adventurous extrapolation from the natural sciences, **certitude can only come from the transcendental source which dominates the reality and the destiny of the universe, and which is revealed to man by the phenomenon of prophecy.**[2]

Or, to say it in the terms we have been using, scientific observation of the universe demonstrates that there is a Creator God, but to know this God, He must reveal Himself in prophecy.

Dr. Aroua has accepted Islam as that prophecy. However, in his book he does not give us the reasons or proofs which led to his choice. He does not say how he decided which prophet to follow?

So the question remains. Which God? Which prophet is true? Every man must decide. But how?

In the Torah-Old Testament, First Kings chapter 18, the prophet Elijah gave a unique type of challenge to the prophets of the idol "Baal." He ordered them to put a bull on one altar, and he would put a bull on another altar in the name of Yahweh Elohim, but with no fire under either sacrifice. Then each side was to pray. The God who would answer by fire from heaven would show himself to be the true God.

After the priests of Baal tried for several hours, Elijah prepared his sacrifice and even wet it with water. Then he prayed and Yahweh Elohim answered with fire—fire which consumed the sacrifice and even the water. Seeing this, all the people cried out,

"Yahweh (The Eternal One), He is God! Yahweh, He is God!"

That was a great demonstration for those people, but what shall we do in our day? How shall we decide who is the One True God?

A SURA (CHAPTER) LIKE UNTO THE QUR'AN

In the Qur'an Muhammad is instructed to give another type of challenge. There are four places where Muhammad says to his opponents that if they are so sure that the Qur'an was his creation then they should produce something equal to it or better. In the Late Meccan Sura of the Children of Israel (Banī Isrā'īl) 17:88, he challenged his hearers to produce a whole book. In the Late Meccan Sura of Hūd 11:13, the requirement was reduced to ten suras. Finally in the late Meccan Sura of Jonah (Yūnus)10:38 and the Sura of the Heifer (Al-Baqara) 2:23, from 2 AH, it was reduced to one sura. The challenge in Sura 10:38 reads,

Or do they say, "He forged it"?
Say, "Bring then a sura like unto it, and call (to your aid) anyone you can, **besides God**, if it be that you speak the truth."

However, as we consider this challenge a question must be asked—a question to which there may not be a clear answer! When Muhammad threw down this challenge to the people of Mecca to bring even one other sura like the Qur'an, was he speaking about its poetic beauty? Or was he speaking of its religious truth?

---

2. *L'Islam et la Science*, 2nd Edition, Entreprise nationale du Livre, Algiers, 1984, p 8. (translation mine)

Muslims praise the Qur'an for the beauty of its language, and indeed there are many beautiful passages such as the description of God as light in the Sura of Light (Al-Nūr) 24:35-36, from 5-6 AH.[3] But was the challenge on the basis of the beauty of its language?

There does not seem to be any verse in the Qur'an which answers this question. My own feeling is that a challenge on the basis of poetic beauty would be of limited value. It is the religious content which counts. Just because Shakespeare wrote the best English prose, that does not make him a prophet of God.

When I have posed this question to Muslim friends they have always answered, though often reluctantly, that Muhammad was speaking of the religious truth. On the other hand, it must be admitted that Muslim theologians maintain that the miracle of the Qur'an is to be found, well and truly, in its literary perfection.

When I first read the Qur'an I thought that those whom Muhammad challenged included "the People of the Book,"[4] and I used to imagine which chapters from the Bible I would present for the contest. Since then I have changed my mind.

We saw above in Chapter I of Section Two that Muhammad believed in the Torah, the Zabūr, and the Gospel present **"WITH HIM"** in Mecca—books already completed. In the Middle Meccan Sura of the Prophets (Al-Anbiyā') 21:105 he quoted the words of David, "My servants, the righteous, shall inherit the earth" from Psalm 37:29. Also he claimed that the inspiration given to him was like the inspiration given to the prophets before him (Sura 4:163).

If the inspiration granted the previous prophets was the same as that granted to Muhammad, then their books would be just as true as the book granted to Muhammad. Therefore, I now believe that his challenge was to the idol worshipers of Mecca and did not include the "People of the Book."

However, in case I am wrong I would like to present the following two suras, i.e., chapters, from the Bible in answer to these challenges. Later I shall present another passage from the words of Jesus.

The first is a Psalm of David which is beautiful and poetic but in a different way. Hebrew poetry is not based on rhyming verses. The effect is achieved by repeating the same idea in different words. We might judge that it is not as pleasing without the beauty of rhyme, but it has one great advantage. **It does not suffer poetic loss in translation, because the double way of saying the same truth can be faithfully repeated in any language.**

---

3. These verses can be seen in Photograph 2, page 125.
4. Quranic term referring to Jews and Christians.

Here is Psalm 103 from the Zabūr of David.

1 Praise the LORD, O my soul;
             all my inmost being, praise His holy name.
2 Praise the LORD, O my soul,
             and forget not all His benefits.
3 IIc forgives all my sins,
             and heals all my diseases;
4 He redeems my life from the pit
             and crowns me with love and compassion.
5 He satisfies my desires with good things,
             so that my youth is renewed like the eagle's.
6 The LORD works righteousness
             and justice for all the oppressed.
7 He made known His ways to Moses,
             His deeds to the people of Israel:
8 The LORD is compassionate and gracious,
             slow to anger, abounding in love.
9 He will not always accuse,
             nor will He harbor His anger forever;
10 He does not treat us as our sins deserve
             or repay us according to our iniquities.
11 For as high as the heavens are above the earth,
             so great is His love for those who fear Him;
12 As far as the east is from thc west,
             so far has He removed our transgressions from us.
13 As a father has compassion on His children,
             so the LORD has compassion on those who fear Him;
14 For He knows how we are formed,
             He remembers that we are dust.
15 As for man, his days are like grass,
             he flourishes like a flower of the field;
16 The wind blows over it and it is gone,
             and its place remembers it no more.
17 But from everlasting to evcrlasting the LORD's love is with those who fear Him,
             and His righteousness with their children's childrcn
18 With those who keep His covenant
             and remember to obey His precepts.
19 The LORD has established His throne in heaven,
             and His kingdom rules over all.
20 Praise the LORD, you His angels,
             you mighty ones who do His bidding, who obey His word.
21 Praise the LORD, all His heavenly hosts,
             you His servants who do His will.
22 Praise the LORD, all His works everywhere in His dominion.
             Praise the LORD, O my soul.[5]

---

5. "LORD" in capitals stands for the Hebrew word "Yahweh (Jehovah)" which means "The I AM" or "The Eternal One." The French translation, L'Eternel, is excellent and absolutely correct. There is another Hebrew word, "adonai," which, like the English word "lord," can be used for God or men. By convention, this is written in the English Bible using small letters as "Lord."

Any judgment as to whether the poetry of this psalm from the Zabūr of David is as beautiful as one of the suras of the Qur'an must remain a subjective matter. But when judged by the religious truths which it contains, it is equal to many suras.

David praises the LORD who is King of all, who forgives sins, whose love is as great as the heavens are high above the earth, whose compassion for us is like the compassion of a father for his children, and who is from everlasting to everlasting. For the believer there is great comfort in all these truths.

My second passage is from The Torah-Old Testament. It appeals to the wonders of the creation. It contains modern scientific knowledge. It speaks against idols, and Yahweh Elohim, the Eternal One, affirms that there is no other god except Himself.

Isaiah, the prophet, writes in chapter 40:

1 Comfort, comfort My people, says your God.
  2 Speak tenderly to Jerusalem,
    and proclaim to her that her hard service has been completed,
    that her sin has been paid for,
    that she has received from the LORD's hand double for all her sins.

3 A voice of one calling:
  "In the desert prepare the way of the LORD;
    make straight in the wilderness a highway for our God.
4 Every valley shall be raised up, every mountain and hill made low,
    the rough ground shall become level, the rugged places a plain,
5 and the glory of the LORD will be revealed,
    and all mankind together will see it.
      For the mouth of the LORD has spoken."

6 A voice says, "Cry out."
    And I said, "What shall I cry?"
  "(Cry that) all men are like grass,
    and all their glory is like the flowers of the field.
      7 The grass withers and the flowers fall,
          because the breath of the LORD blows on them.
  Surely the people are grass.
      8 The grass withers and the flowers fall,
          but the word of our God stands forever."

9 You who bring good tidings to Zion, go up on a high mountain.
    You who bring good tidings to Jerusalem,
              lift up your voice with a shout.
        Lift it up, do not be afraid;
        Say to the towns of Judah, "Here is your God!"

10 See, the Sovereign LORD comes with power, and His arm rules for Him.
    See, His reward is with Him, and His recompense accompanies Him.

11 He tends His flock like a shepherd:
    He gathers the lambs in His arms and carries them close to His heart;
    He gently leads those that have young.

12 Who has measured the waters in the hollow of his hand,
> or with the breadth of his hand marked off the heavens?
Who has held the dust of the earth in a basket,
> or weighed the mountains on the scales and the hills in a balance?
13 Who has understood the Spirit of the LORD,
> or instructed Him as His counselor?
14 Whom did the LORD consult to enlighten Him,
> and who taught Him the right way?
Who was it that taught Him knowledge,
> or showed Him the path of understanding?

15 Surely the nations are like a drop in a bucket;
> they are regarded as dust on the scales;
> > He weighs the islands as though they were fine dust.
16 Lebanon is not sufficient for altar fires,
> nor its animals enough for burnt offerings.
17 Before Him all the nations are as nothing;
> they are regarded by Him as worthless and less than nothing.

18 To whom, then, will you compare God?
What image will you compare Him to?

19 As for an idol, a craftsman casts it,
> and a goldsmith overlays it with gold
> > and fashions silver chains for it.
20 A man too poor to present such an offering selects wood that will not rot.
> He looks for a skilled craftsman to set up an idol that will not topple.

21 Do you not know?
> Have you not heard?
Has it not been told you from the beginning?
> Have you not understood since the earth was founded?

22 **He sits enthroned above the circle of the earth**,
> and its people are like grasshoppers.
He stretches out the heavens like a canopy,
> and spreads them out like a tent to live in.
23 He brings princes to naught
> and reduces the rulers of this world to nothing.
24 No sooner are they planted,
> no sooner are they sown,
> > no sooner do they take root in the ground,
than He blows on them and they wither,
> and a whirlwind sweeps them away like chaff.

25 **"To whom will you compare Me?**
> > **Or who is My equal?" says the Holy One.**

26 Lift your eyes and look to the heavens: **Who created all these?**
> > **He who brings out the starry host one by one,**
> > > **and calls them each by name.**
Because of His great power and mighty strength,
> > not one of them is missing.

27 Why do you say, O Jacob,
   and complain, O Israel,
"My way is hidden from the LORD;
   my cause is disregarded by my God"?

28 Do you not know?
   Have you not heard?
The LORD is the everlasting God,
   the Creator of the ends of the earth.
He will not grow tired or weary,
   and His understanding no one can fathom.
29 He gives strength to the weary
   and increases the power of the weak.
30 Even youths grow tired and weary,
   and young men stumble and fall;
31 but those who hope in the LORD will renew their strength.
   They will soar on wings like eagles;
      they will run and not grow weary,
      they will walk and not be faint.

In this passage as in the Psalm of David, there are many beautiful thoughts to encourage the believer. Verse 6 says that Isaiah was told, "Cry" or "Cry out": the same command which was repeated in the first words of the Qur'an in the Sura of the Clot (Al-'alaq) 96:1-2. And the message of the succeeding three verses, that man is like grass which will pass away, is similar to verses 6-8 of the same sura saying that,

> man transgresses all bounds...verily to thy Lord is the return
> (of all).

Isaiah points out the futility of idols made by man from gold and wood, just as the Qur'an does many years later.

God is clearly the Creator of all things. The Holy One Himself asks, "To whom will you compare Me? Or who is My equal? Lift your eyes and look to the heavens. Who created all these?" And Isaiah answers, "**The LORD is the everlasting God, the Creator of the ends of the earth.**"

Lastly, we see that this prophet who wrote in about 750 BC mentions in verse 22 that **God "sits enthroned above the circle of the earth"—a statement which can certainly include our modern knowledge that the earth is round**.

CONCLUSION

Though the verses and chapters given in this section show clearly that the Torah-Old Testament appeals many times to the creation as a proof (or sign) that there is a great **Creator God**, in the final analysis I agree with Dr. Bucaille's evaluation.

This argument does not receive the same emphasis in the Bible that it does in the Qur'an, but there is a valid and important reason. It is because Yahweh Elohim, the Eternal One of the Torah-Old Testament, proposes quite a different method for knowing whether a prophet speaks from God or not, and we shall examine this method in the next chapter.

CHAPTER II

HOW TO TEST A REVELATION ACCORDING TO THE TORAH

In the Torah-Old Testament, at Deuteronomy 18:17-20 God gives the first test. He tells us through Moses how to recognize a true prophet with these words:[1]

> The LORD said to me "What they say is good. I will raise up for them a prophet like you from among their brothers; I will put My words in his mouth, and he will tell them everything I command him. **If anyone does not listen to My words that the prophet speaks in My name, I Myself will call him to account**. But a prophet who presumes to speak in My name anything I have not commanded him to say, or a prophet who speaks in the name of other gods, must be put to death."

The command and the punishment for disobeying the command are stated very clearly. Yahweh, the Eternal One, says, "If anyone doesn't listen to My words that the prophet speaks in My name, I Myself will call him to account." Then He goes on (verses 21-22) to mention the very problem which has been on our minds,

> You may say to yourselves, **"HOW CAN WE KNOW WHEN A MESSAGE HAS NOT BEEN SPOKEN BY THE LORD?"**

How can we know a false prophet from a true? How can we know whether a man speaks for God or not? And the LORD then gives His answer. He says,

> **"IF WHAT A PROPHET PROCLAIMS IN THE NAME OF THE LORD DOES NOT TAKE PLACE OR COME TRUE, THAT IS A MESSAGE THE LORD HAS NOT SPOKEN**. That prophet has spoken presumptuously. Do not be afraid of him."

In other words,

YOU KNOW A TRUE PROPHET WHEN HIS PROPHECY COMES TRUE.

A very clear example is found in I Kings 17 and 18. Elijah prophesied to King Ahab that it was not going to rain with these words,

> As the LORD, the God of Israel whom I serve, lives, there will be neither dew nor rain in the next few years except at my word.

Then everyone waited to see what would happen. When it didn't rain for a few months, people just thought that it was a bit unusual. But when it didn't rain for three and a half years until Elijah told the King "Go down before the rain stops you," and a strong rain came—then everyone knew that Elijah was a true prophet of God who must be feared.

---

1. See page 12 for a discussion of this same passage and the claim that it is a prophecy about Muhammad.

The second test is to evaluate the teaching of the person claiming to be a prophet and consider whether his doctrine contradicts previous revelation. In the Torah, Yahweh, the Eternal One, guides Moses to say,

> If a prophet, or one who foretells by dreams, appears among you and announces to you a miraculous sign or wonder, and if the sign or wonder of which he has spoken takes place, and he says, "Let us follow other gods"—gods you have not known—"and let us worship them," **you must not listen to the words of that prophet or dreamer...**
>
> **It is the LORD your God (Yahweh Elohim) you must follow, and Him you must revere.** Keep His commands and obey Him; serve Him and hold fast to Him (Deuteronomy 13:1-4).

Miraculous signs are not enough by themselves. If the person's words contradict previous teaching, he is not to be believed and accepted. These two points are shown quite well in the next example where two men are both claiming to be prophets of Yahweh Elohim but are giving contradictory and opposing messages.

THE TRUE AND THE FALSE PROPHET

This striking example is to be found in the life of Jeremiah. While living in Jerusalem he had to prophesy that because the people had forsaken God, the Eternal One, and worshiped false and powerless idols, God was going to destroy the city using Nebuchadnezzar, King of Babylon.

God ordered him to wear a yoke like the yoke of an ox on his neck and then to speak to Zedekiah, King of Jerusalem, with these words:

> "Bow your neck under the yoke of the king of Babylon; serve him and his people, and you will live. Why will you and your people die by the sword, famine and plague with which the LORD has threatened any nation that will not serve the king of Babylon?" (Jeremiah 27:2,12-13).

But there were also prophets prophesying who said exactly the opposite. The prophet Jeremiah describes the situation in chapter 28 of his prophecy as follows:

> In the **fifth month** of that same year...the prophet Hananiah son of Azzur, who was from Gibeon, said to me in the house of the LORD in the presence of the priests and all the people: "This is what the LORD Almighty, the God of Israel, says, 'I will break the yoke of the king of Babylon. Within two years I will bring back to this place all the articles of the LORD's house that Nebuchadnezzar king of Babylon removed from here and took to Babylon...For I will break the yoke of the king of Babylon.'"
>
> The prophet Jeremiah replied, "...From early times the prophets who preceded you and me have prophesied war, disaster and plague

against many countries and great kingdoms. But the prophet who prophesies peace will be recognized as one truly sent by the Lord only if his prediction comes true."

(**Here Jeremiah applies the two tests**. He reminds the listeners that his words are in accordance with previous prophecy and that they will know the true prophet when the prophecies are fulfilled.)

Then the prophet Hananiah took the yoke off the neck of the prophet Jeremiah and broke it (Jeremiah 28:1-4,8-10).

Now let us imagine that we are living in Jerusalem at that time. Jeremiah tells us that God is set on destroying the city, and that we will die by famine, by plague, or by the sword unless we surrender to Nebuchadnezzar, the king of Babylon. He will take us to Babylon as slaves, but we will stay alive, and after 70 years God will bring our children back again (Jeremiah 29:10). These words are treason in the eyes of the king of Israel, of course; but who wants to die being against God?

On the other hand, Hananiah says that God is going to deliver Israel. If that is true, it's better to stay here as a free man. Who wants to be a slave? In addition, if we desert to the enemy and then the king of Israel captures us back, he will probably put us to death because we deserted.

It's a matter of life and death, of freedom and slavery. How shall we decide? In the end we will know which prophet is right by which king wins the battle, but by then, if Jeremiah is right, it will be too late to act.

So the LORD, the Eternal One, sends more information. Chapter 28 continues:

> Shortly after the prophet Hananiah had broken the yoke off the neck of the prophet Jeremiah, the word of the LORD came to Jeremiah: "Go and tell Hananiah, 'This is what the LORD says: You have broken a wooden yoke, but in its place you will get a yoke of iron...I will put an iron yoke on the necks of all these nations to make them serve Nebuchadnezzar king of Babylon...'"
>
> Then the prophet Jeremiah said to Hananiah the prophet, "Listen, Hananiah! The LORD has not sent you, yet you have persuaded this nation to trust in lies. Therefore, this is what the LORD says: 'I am about to remove you from the face of the earth. **This very year you are going to die**, because you have preached rebellion against the LORD.'"
>
> In the **seventh month** of that same year, **Hananiah the prophet died** (Jeremiah 28:12-17).

Those living in Jerusalem did not have to wait very long before they had their answer. Hananiah made his false prophecy in the **fifth month**. Shortly afterward Jeremiah told him, "You will die for your false prophecy," and he died in the **seventh month**. Jeremiah's word was confirmed by God, and those who were looking for leading from God knew that they must surrender and go to Babylon.

Five years later Jerusalem fell, again confirming Jeremiah's words. We read in Jeremiah 39:6-7 that,

> ...the king of Babylon slaughtered the sons of Zedekiah before his eyes and also killed all the nobles of Judah. Then he put out Zedekiah's eyes and bound him with bronze shackles to take him to Babylon.

OTHER FULFILLED PROPHECIES IN THE
TORAH-OLD TESTAMENT

There are many other such fulfilled prophecies in the Torah-Old Testament. For some of them the length of waiting between the prophecy and the fulfillment was short. In Elijah's case it was three and a half years, in Jeremiah's a few weeks. Thus the people living at the time could see the fulfillment and believe in the prophet. Other prophecies were not fulfilled until centuries later, and some have still not been fulfilled. Here are several examples.

A. In Section Two, Chapter II we quoted Daniel's prophecy that Babylon would fall to the Medes and the Persians; that next the Greeks would take over (which happened 270 yrs later), that the Messiah would come and "be cut off, but not for himself"; and that Jerusalem and the Temple would be destroyed a second time, as happened in 70 AD. (Daniel 8:20-21 and 9:25-26)

B. Isaiah, to whom the word of the Lord came around 750 BC, prophesied that the Persian general who would conquer Babylon according to Daniel's prophecy would be called Cyrus. In addition, Isaiah prophesies that Cyrus will order the Jews to return to their homeland and rebuild their temple. The prophecy reads:

This is what the LORD says...

> **"I am the LORD,** who has made all things,
> Who alone stretched out the heavens,
> Who spread out the earth by Myself,
> **Who foils the signs of false prophets**,
> and makes fools of diviners...
> **Who carries out the words of His servants**
> **and fulfills the predictions of His messengers**,
> Who says of Jerusalem, 'It shall be inhabited...'

> Who says of **Cyrus**, 'He is My shepherd
> and will accomplish all that I please;
> **he will say of Jerusalem, "Let it be rebuilt,"**
> **and of the temple, "Let its foundations be laid." '**
>   Isaiah 44:24-25a,26a,28.

The fulfillment is recorded in the book of Ezra. Writing sometime before 400 BC, more than 300 years after the prophecy, Ezra records:

> In the first year of **Cyrus king of Persia**…the LORD moved the heart of Cyrus…to make a proclamation throughout his realm and to put in writing:
>
> This is what Cyrus king of Persia says:
>
> "The LORD, the God of heaven, has given me all the kingdoms of the earth and **He has appointed me to build a temple for Him at Jerusalem in Judah**…"
>
> Moreover, King Cyrus brought out the articles belonging to the temple of the LORD, which Nebuchadnezzar had carried away from Jerusalem and had placed in the temple of his god…(and sent them back) (Ezra 1:1-2,7).

This prophecy is really very remarkable. Cyrus, who was the king of Persia (Iran), came in 539 BC and defeated Babylon (Iraq) where the Jews were prisoners. His policy was to return all peoples to their homelands **with orders to rebuild their temples**. Each people was then to ask its "god" to intercede with the great "gods" which Cyrus worshiped, called Bel and Nebo.

This policy is explained in a text called the Cyrus Cylinder (now in the British Museum). It reads,

> May all the gods whom I have resettled in their sacred cities ask daily Bel and Nebo for a long life for me and may they recommend me (to them).

In summary, to fulfill Isaiah's prophecy, God raised up a king in Persia to defeat the Babylonians—a king whose unusual and tolerant religious policy was to return captured people to their homelands so that they could pray for him. One of these captured people happened to be the Jews of Israel—a small, unimportant people of no consequence—except that God used them to send the Messiah, the Saviour of the world.

This prophecy and its fulfillment are so remarkable that those men who constructed the "documentary hypothesis" discussed in Chapter I of Section Three concluded that since miraculous prophecies are impossible, the prophecy of Isaiah had to have been written after 500 BC—after Cyrus had become King and fulfilled the prophecy.

C. Ezekiel prophesied around 590 BC that Nebuchadnezzar would take Tyre (in present-day Lebanon) and that the town **"shall be a place to spread nets"** and **"shall be built no more"** (Ezekiel 26). In 586 BC Nebuchadnezzar laid siege to Tyre, and thirteen years later, in 573 BC, he took it. Thus the first part was fulfilled in Ezekiel's day when people who heard him give it were still alive.

However the second part is true until this day. For, although there is a modern Tyre, **the original site has never been rebuilt**, and **the fisherman wash and spread their nets there.**

D. Micah, prophesying in 750 BC about the town of Samaria, foretells its destruction hundreds of years later, saying, "I will make Samaria as a **heap of rubble**, a place for **planting vineyards**." (Micah 1:6)

The town continued as an important center until the time of Jesus and afterward, but it was eventually destroyed. The foundation stones were rolled into the valley, and **today the site is covered with vineyards**.

E. In the Torah-Leviticus 26:31-33a, written by the hand of Moses more than 1200 years before the Messiah, God tells the 12 tribes of Israel that if they do not follow Him with their whole heart then He will send the following punishments:

> I will turn your cities into ruins and lay waste your sanctuaries, and I will take no delight in the pleasing aroma of your offerings. I will lay waste the land...I will scatter you among the nations and will draw out My sword and pursue you.

As everyone knows, there were two main occasions when the Jewish people were exiled. The first was the exile to Babylon in the time of Jeremiah, and the second occurred after they rejected the "Messiah" in 30 AD. Forty years later, in 70 AD, the Roman General Titus destroyed Jerusalem. Most of the Jews were scattered among the nations and until the present time they have no temple in which to offer their sacrifices.

Now, having looked at these examples of fulfilled prophecy, we must ask ourselves whether there is some principle which we are to learn from this. The answer is **"YES."**

THERE MUST ALWAYS BE TWO (OR MORE) WITNESSES

When God said through Moses that no prophet should be accepted until his prophecy comes true, He was saying that there must be two witnesses. When Elijah said that it wouldn't rain, Elijah was the first witness. By withholding the rain for three and a half years until Elijah prayed for it, God Himself became the second witness as He fulfilled Elijah's words.

When Jeremiah prophesied that Hananiah the false prophet would die, he was the first witness. When God caused Hananiah to die a few weeks later, He showed Himself as the second witness confirming Jeremiah's words. In the Torah we find that God established this basic principle even for human law. Deuteronomy 17:6 says,

> On the testimony of **two or three witnesses** a man shall be put to death; but no one shall be put to death on the testimony of only one witness.

and in Deuteronomy 19:15 the same principle is stated to apply to all types of crime,

> One witness is not enough to convict a man accused of any crime or offense he may have committed. A matter must be established by the testimony of **two or three witnesses**.

This need for two witnesses is also found in the Qur'an. In the Sura of the Heifer (Al-Baqara) 2:282, from 2 AH, it says,

If the party liable is mentally deficient, or weak, or unable himself to dictate, let his guardian dictate faithfully. **And get two witnesses out of your own men, and if there are not two men, then a man and two women.**

The same requirement is given for making a last will and testament. The Sura of the Table (Al-Mā'ida) 5:109, from 10 AH, reads,

O ye who believe! When death approaches any of you, **(take) witnesses among yourselves when making bequests—two just men.**

The Sura of the Light (Al-Nūr) 24:4, from 5-6 AH, requires four witnesses in order to sustain an accusation of marital infidelity. It reads,

And those who launch a charge against chaste women, and produce not **four witnesses**, flog them with eighty stripes; and reject their evidence ever after: for such men are wicked transgressors.

Obviously, if two or four witnesses are necessary in human matters, **how much more important it is to have two or more witnesses establishing a word as "the Word of God" come by revelation!**

If a man walks into a city in Iran or Egypt and says that he is the "Mehdi," how will anyone decide whether it is true?

If anyone walks into New York or Jerusalem and says that he is the "Messiah" returned, how will we know whether to accept him or not?

The first test, of course, is that his doctrine or teaching must not contradict previous revelation. As we saw at the beginning of this chapter, miraculous signs are not enough by themselves. The teachings of a man who claims to be Christ returned to earth cannot contradict the teaching he gave when he came the first time.

Secondly, we would want a confirming sign—a miracle or the fulfillment of previous prophecy—to confirm that the person speaking to us spoke from God.

From this we understand that when Muhammad spoke to the people of Mecca saying that he was a prophet and the Meccans and the Jews demanded that Muhammad should show them some confirming miracle, it was not just because of hard-hearted unbelief. That may have been true of many of them, but as the Qur'an itself admits, some of the Jews were honorable and feared God. The Jews and others in Mecca were saying, "One witness is not enough. We need a confirming witness from God." They were doing exactly what God has commanded men to do, because Yahweh, the Eternal One, has ruled for our sake that **there must be two or more witnesses.**

JESUS AND MUHAMMAD, TWO PROPHETS FOR A LOST WORLD?

CHAPTER I

MUHAMMAD'S PROPHETHOOD

In the last chapter we saw that God requires two witnesses for human legal matters; and He expects to provide at least two witnesses in divine, heavenly matters. We saw that if a man stands up in Jerusalem or Mecca or anywhere else, and claims that his words have been given by the Great Creator, we have been instructed to ask ourselves and him the question, "How do we know that you speak from the Great Creator God—the God of heaven and earth? What or who is your second witness?"

Perhaps some readers will be unhappy or uneasy that this question should be asked. It throws doubt on the person speaking the prophecy. It implies that the person asking it is thinking, "I don't believe you."

That may be true, but imagine how it makes Christians feel to be told, as I have been told hundreds of times, "You changed the Gospel." Does that not mean, "I don't believe you"?

No matter how we may feel, however, the question must be posed to both Christians and Muslims, "What are the proofs? What are the confirming witnesses that the words of the Gospel which Jesus spoke came from God? What are the confirming witnesses that the words of the Qur'an which Muhammad spoke came from God?"

When Muhammad walked into Mecca, or now walks into the mind of one who reads the Qur'an, and says that God spoke to him and told him about the day of judgment, how will the person hearing or reading know? **Muhammad is only one witness—the first witness.**

A SECOND WITNESS

When I have asked whether anyone other than Muhammad heard the Angel Gabriel, every person, except one, has answered that he was the only one. That man brought a hadith which is found in Nawawi's collection of 40 Hadith.

This hadith, which was transmitted by Muslim, tells of a man coming and asking Muhammad questions with the tone of voice used by a teacher, and approving of Muhammad's answers. When he left, Muhammad told Omar and the others present that the man was Gabriel. Perhaps so, but again we are left with Muhammad as the sole witness. It was not Gabriel who identified himself; it was Muhammad who made the claim.

It is a single witness in another sense, too. With all the doubt there is concerning the **hadith**, to base our belief on one **hadith** transmitted by one specialist is not very satisfactory.

On the other hand, it is characteristic of most prophets that only the prophet heard the voice of God or His angel. We have no record in the Torah-Old Testament of anyone else hearing God speak to Isaiah or Jeremiah; just as there

241

is no record in the Qur'an that anyone else heard God speak to Hud or Salih. Two important exceptions to this were Moses and Jesus.

From Mt. Sinai God spoke to Moses and all the Children of Israel. They were so terrified that they asked God not to repeat it, and it was on the basis of this request by the people that God said that He would send "a prophet like (Moses) from among their brothers" (Torah-Deuteronomy 18).[1]

During the life of Jesus there were three times that God spoke openly **as a second witness**. The first time was when Jesus was baptized by John the Baptist (Yaḥyā Ibn Zakarīyā):

> When all the people were being baptized, Jesus was baptized too. And as he was praying, heaven was opened and the Holy Spirit descended on him in bodily form like a dove. **And a voice came from heaven. "You are My beloved Son, with you I am well pleased"** (Luke 3:21-22).

Obviously, John and those being baptized at the same time heard this voice.

The second time occurred in the presence of his three disciples—Peter, James and John. He took them up on a high mountain where he was transfigured. His clothes became dazzling. Moses and Elijah, who had each been dead for more than 900 years, appeared to Jesus. The account reads,

> Then a cloud appeared and enveloped them, and **a voice came from the cloud, "This is My beloved Son. Listen to him!"**
> Suddenly, when they looked around, they no longer saw anyone with them except Jesus" (Mark 9:7-8).

The third occasion is recorded by John and happened with a whole crowd of people present.

> (Jesus said), "Father, glorify Your name!"
> **Then a voice came from heaven, "I have glorified it and will glorify it again."**
> The crowd that was there and heard it said it had thundered; others said an angel had spoken to him.
> Jesus said, **"This voice was for your benefit, not mine..."**
> John 12:28-30.

However, most prophets are not confirmed by a voice from heaven. Therefore God must provide some other type of second witness. In the past God has usually used three types.

A. The prophet is given miracles to confirm his words.

B. Prophecies made by former prophets are fulfilled by the new prophet.

C. The new messenger prophesies concerning future events and the fulfillment of his words by God confirms his message.

We will now examine each one of these possibilities.

---

1. Discussed in detail on page 12.

A. MIRACLES AS A SECOND WITNESS

Both the Torah and the Qur'an tell how God confirmed the apostleship of Moses with many miracles. The Torah-Old Testament refers to miracles given to a number of other prophets including Elijah and Elisha, and the Gospel and the Qur'an both tell of the miracles given to confirm the ministry of Jesus. Therefore it was natural that the people of Mecca would ask Muhammad to show them a miracle in order to have a second witness.

According to the Qur'an, Muhammad was instructed to answer that he was sent only as a **warner**. After naming the heavens, the sun and moon, the earth with mountains standing firm, rivers, fruit, gardens, palm trees as signs, we read in the Late Meccan Sura of the Thunder (Al-Ra'd) 13:4b,7:

> ...Behold, verily in these things there are signs for those who understand...
>
> And the unbelievers say, "Why is not a sign sent down to him from his Lord?"
>
> **But thou are truly a warner**, and to every people a guide.

In verse 27 the demand is repeated,

> The unbelievers say, "Why is not a sign sent down to him from his Lord?"

And the answer in verse 31 is that they wouldn't believe even if there was power in the Qur'an by which "the dead were made to speak."

That there are many hard-hearted unbelievers, for which that conclusion is true, cannot be doubted for one minute. After Jesus had fed 5000 people by multiplying five loaves and two fish and then claimed on the basis of this miracle that he, himself was the true bread come down from heaven, they said, "**What miraculous sign then will you give that we may see it and believe you? What will you do?**" (John 6:30)

But there are always two groups. Though many are hard-hearted and choose to remain in unbelief no matter what God does, there are always some who want to know God's will. They are waiting for the **second witness** by which they can know the right path to follow.

In answer to this need, the Qur'an mentions signs. The problem is that the Quranic signs quoted above are all signs of nature which prove only one thing. They prove that there is a powerful Creator God. **They do not prove that the speaker recounting them is a prophet.**

Dr. Bucaille has written two books recounting the marvels of God's creation. In the second book, he has even described marvels that are not mentioned in the Qur'an. **But does that make him a prophet?** Of course not, and he would be the first to deny that he is a prophet.

Are there any miracles which Muslims suggest as a possible second witness? Some mention the Mi'rāj or night journey. This is found in the Sura of the Children of Israel (Banī Isrā'īl) 17:1, from one year before the Hejira.

> Glory to (God) who took His servant for a journey by night

from the Sacred Mosque to the Farthest Mosque, whose precincts
We blessed, in order that We might show him some of Our signs...

The majority of commentators believe this to be a physical transportation, though a few, including Hamidullah, consider it a vision. All consider that the "Farthest Mosque" refers to Jerusalem, except for Hamidullah who thinks that it refers to heaven. Pickthall mentions a "heavenly steed," Yusuf Ali speaks of Muhammad ascending from Jerusalem to the sublime throne in the highest heaven, while Hamidullah adds that Muhammad was there given the five official prayer times; but these beliefs all come from the Hadith literature. The above verse says nothing about these ideas, and we are again left with one witness. It is something which only Muhammad experienced and reported.

This demand of the unbelievers in Mecca is mentioned again in the Middle Meccan Sura of the Spider (Al-'Ankabūt) 29:50 where they are quoted as saying,

Why are signs not sent down to him from his Lord?

And now another answer is given in verses 50b-51:

Say: "The signs are with God only, and **I am but a clear warner. Is it not enough for them that We have sent down to you the book** which is rehearsed to them?"

Now we have followed the reasoning down to the final step. Miracles or signs are in the power and will of God. Muhammad is told to say that he is only a "clear warner." From that we understand that God has **not** chosen to give Muhammad any miracle, and then the question is asked "**Is the Qur'an not more than sufficient?**" as the second witness.

But this is using the question as the answer. We have been told to accept the words of a prophet, in this case the Qur'an, only when there has been a second witness. Now the Qur'an wants to turn it around and say that the words of the prophet are the second witness. This is not possible. The prophet and his words are not separate. They are one, and together they represent the first witness.

Supposing that I declare to you, "The moon is made of butter."

You are going to answer in these days, "That isn't what the astronauts found. Prove it to me."

As a proof I take a piece of paper and write, "The moon is made of butter." Then I turn to you and say, "There, that piece of paper says so! Look at it."

When demonstrated in this way, it is perfectly clear that my spoken words and my written words are exactly the same words. They represent only one witness, and you will say, "No! Bring another proof outside of yourself." You will not accept my written copy as a second witness of my oral word.

Sura 29 then goes on in verse 52 to appeal to God as Muhammad's witness by saying,

Say: "Sufficient is God as a witness between me and you. He knows whatever is in the heavens and the earth..."

and the argument is turned back to appealing to "the heavens and the earth"—to the creation, which is a proof that there is a Creator God, but not a proof of Muhammad's prophethood. Therefore, we still have no answer to the question we are instructed by God in the Torah to ask of any prophet, **"Where is your confirming sign—your second witness that you are speaking for this Creator God?"**

B. PROPHECIES IN THE FORMER SCRIPTURES ABOUT MUHAMMAD

On page 65 we examined the following hadith in connection with its testimony to the validity of the Bible. Now we must re-examine it as a prophecy about Muhammad. It reads,

> 'Ata b. Yasar told that he met 'Abdallah b. 'Amr b. al-'As and asked him to inform him of the description of God's messenger given in the Torah. He agreed, swearing by God that he was certainly described in the Torah by part of the description of him given in the Qur'an (Al-Ahzāb 33:45) when it says, "O prophet, We have sent you as a witness, a bearer of good tidings, and a warner, and a guard for the common people."
>
> (Then continuing from the Torah-Old Testament) "You are My servant and My messenger; I have called you the one who trusts, not harsh or rough, nor loud-voiced in the streets. He will not repulse evil with evil, but will pardon and forgive, and God will not take him till He uses him to straighten the crooked creed so that people may say there is no god but God, and He opens thereby blind eyes, deaf ears and hardened hearts."
>
> Bukhari transmitted it, and Darimi also gives something to the same effect on the authority of "Ata" who gave as his authority Ibn Salam.

The passage quoted above from the Torah-Old Testament can be found now, today, in the prophecy of Isaiah written about 750 BC. It reads,

Here is My servant, whom I uphold,
> My chosen one in whom I delight;
I will put My Spirit on him
> and he will bring justice to the nations.
He will not shout or cry out,
> or raise his voice in the streets.
A bruised reed he will not break,
> and a smoldering wick he will not snuff out...
I, the LORD, have called you in righteousness...
> I will keep you and will make you to be a covenant for the
> > people...
to open eyes that are blind,
> to free captives from prison,
> and to release from the dungeon those who are in darkness.
> > > Isaiah 42:1-3,6a,7.

Here is a hadith, then, that one can be **sure** is authentic because it has **two witnesses**. We have the transmission by the Muslim community, and we have the original quotation in the Book of Isaiah. This is exactly the type of confirmation which is found in dozens of prophecies in relation to Jesus the Messiah.

This same passage, in fact, is one of those quoted in the Gospel as applying to Jesus. In Matthew 12:15-18 we read,

> Jesus...withdrew from there, and many followed him and **he healed them all**...This was to fulfill what was spoken by the prophet Isaiah,
>
> "Behold, My servant whom I have chosen, My beloved with whom My soul is well pleased:
>
> I will put My Spirit upon him, and he shall proclaim justice to the Gentiles."

And the passage goes on in verse 22 to say that **Jesus healed a blind and mute demon-possessed man**, following which all the people said, **"Can this be the Son of David?"—the Messiah?**

Whether Isaiah wrote his words about Muhammad or about Jesus each reader will have to decide, but because of the two witnesses we can be 99% sure that the conversation recorded in the above hadith really took place.

Why just 99%? Because there is the slight possibility that someone invented it to support a doctrine. But even if that were true, **it shows that someone in the Muslim community was quoting Isaiah as the true Word of God.**

The "Paraclete" as a prophecy of Muhammad (Ahmad)?

On pages 102-106 of his book comparing the Bible and the Qur'an, Dr. Bucaille has a lengthy treatment of the Biblical verses in John, chapters 14-16, which mention that a "Paraclete" will come. Except for his discussion of Genesis chapter 1 and the genealogies, he deals with no other verses of the Bible in such detail.

In these four pages, after claiming to have quoted all the relevant verses, Dr. Bucaille makes six attacks or criticisms against the validity of this Biblical passage. For example, he maintains that some material was suppressed from the Gospel, that other words were added, that Greek words are wrongly used, and that most translations are in complete error.

These are very serious attacks, and Dr. Bucaille pursues them with a fine-tuned literary skill which gives the impression that there is great scholarly support for his ideas. Therefore, we are going to consider each one of these six criticisms, plus a seventh false claim.

Christians believe that this word "paraclete" (*paracletos* in Greek) refers to the Holy Spirit of God, and that this Holy Spirit comes to live in each Christian in order to help him fight sin.[2]

---

2. According to the Gospel, the Holy Spirit is the guiding Spirit of God and not the angel Gabriel.

Muslims have proposed that it is a prophecy of Muhammad. A Muslim believes that there is such a prophecy because of the following words found in the Sura of the Battle Array (Al-Ṣaff) 61:6, from 3 AH.

> And remember, Jesus, the son of Mary, said: "Oh Children of Israel! I am the Apostle of God to you...giving glad tidings of an apostle to come after me, whose name shall be AHMAD." But when he came to them with clear signs, they said, "This is clearly sorcery!"

In Arabic the names aHMaD (more praiseworthy) and muHaMmaD (praised) have the same root letters[3] and related meanings. Therefore Muslims believe that this is a slightly veiled prophecy by Jesus saying that Muhammad will come.

Since a quick reading of the Gospel does not reveal such a prophecy in any obvious form, a more detailed search has continued over the years; and many Muslims now claim that Jesus' promise of the Counselor or Paraclete in John 14 is that very prophecy. Professor Katkat claims this in an article on the subject in *Manār Al-Islām*,[4] and Yusuf Ali expresses the same idea in the following note on Sura 61:6:

> "Ahmad," or "Muhammad," the Praised one, is almost a translation of the Greek word *periclytos*. In the present Gospel of John, 14:16, 15:26, and 16:7, the word "Comforter" in the English version is for the Greek word "*Paracletos*." Our doctors contend that Paracletos is a corrupt reading for Periclytos, and that in the original saying of Jesus there was a prophecy of our holy Prophet Ahmad by name.[5]

The first thing to be understood is that in Greek, unlike Arabic, the vowels are written into the text. Thus to change from periclytos to paracletos would require the alteration of three written letters.

Secondly, there is absolutely no textual evidence for such a reading. Not one copy of the Gospel of John, from the oldest Greek copy of 200 AD until now, shows *periclytos* in place of *paracletos*. Photograph 7 of Papyrus p75 from 200 AD shows John 14:9-26a. The last word on the page clearly shows "PARACLETOS" (Παρακλητος) from verse 26. Verse 16 has been partly destroyed, but in the middle of the line marked by the two arrows one can still see "PARACL—N" for paracleton. ("ON" signifies a direct object.) In the first case the whole word is visible and in the second, two of the three letters under discussion can be clearly seen.

---

3. You would find them both under **H M D** in the Arabic dictionary.
4. Katkat, op. cit., p 59; see also page 11 earlier in this book.
5. Yusuf Ali, op. cit., p 1540.

Photograph 7 —

John 14:9-26a from Papyrus p75 from 200 AD,
showing the word "PARACLETOS" in verse 16
and in verse 26, where it is the last word on the page.
By permission of the Bodmer Library, Geneva.

Thirdly, although *periclytos*, which means famous or renowned, was used by Homer when he wrote the Iliad and the Odyssey in the classical Greek of the 10th century BC, there is not one instance where this word, or any of the other members of its word group, is used in the Koine Greek of the **New Testament** or the Septuagint translation of the **Old Testament**.

Thus there is neither textual or linguistic support for *"periclytos."*

a. Dr. Bucaille's preliminary remarks

By placing his comments about the Paraclete, or Holy Spirit, at the end of his chapter on *Contradictions and Improbabilities*, Dr. Bucaille pushes the reader to assume that there is a contradiction or improbability even before reading the information.

Next, claiming that only one author mentions this Paraclete who is to come, he asks how a matter of such "fundamental importance" could be mentioned in only one of the four Gospel accounts?

This then leads to two suggestive and critical questions.

1. "Was it originally in the other accounts and then suppressed?"

Suppression? Who said anything about suppression? Then without having provided even one fact of confirming evidence to prove that something was suppressed, he asks,

2. "Why was it suppressed?"

Thus, without any facts at all, he has created a contradiction and implied that Christians suppressed part of the Gospel.

He then concludes,

"No answer is possible. So the mystery remains."

Now we have a mystery—a mystery made entirely out of worthless words. Notice I did not say powerless words. These are very strong words, but they are worthless because they are not supported by any facts. It is about words like this that Jesus spoke when he warned,

> Men will have to give account in the day of judgment for every careless (idle) word they have spoken (Matthew 12:36).

The first thing to be said is that Dr. Bucaille is wrong when he claims that this matter of such "fundamental importance" is reported by only one Gospel writer. Though he does not use the name **Paraclete**, Luke tells of Jesus' promise of the Holy Spirit and the fulfillment of the promise in Acts chapters 1 and 2.

Secondly, behind Dr. Bucaille's questions there seems to be the assumption that IT IS IMPOSSIBLE FOR THE ALL-POWERFUL GOD TO DIRECT ONLY ONE WRITER TO REPORT AN EVENT.

If this assumption is valid it also holds for the Qur'an. The entire Qur'an came through one human author—Muhammad. In addition, many events, such as the young men who slept over 300 years in a cave,[6] are mentioned only once

---

6. The Meccan Sura of the Cave (Al-Kahf) 18:9-26.

in the Quranic text. Even the words placed in Jesus' mouth that "Ahmad" will come are found only once. Are we therefore to assume a contradiction and mystery?!? How many readers will accept that logic?

And if his negative assumption is valid, are we allowed to infer the opposite: that something mentioned by two, three, or four of the Gospel writers **IS TRUE**? If so, then it must be noted that Jesus' death for our sins and the empty tomb following his resurrection are mentioned by **all four Gospel writers, plus Paul**.[7] This is very strong evidence.

b. The verses concerning the "Paraclete" as quoted by Dr. Bucaille

Before going further we need to look at the verses which mention the "paraclete." On page 106 Dr. Bucaille quotes them as follows:

> John 14:15-16. "If you love me (Jesus), you will obey what I command, and I will ask the Father and he will give you another **Paraclete**."

> John 14:26. "But **the Paraclete, the Holy Spirit**, whom the Father will send in my name, will teach you all things and will remind you of everything I have said to you."

> John 15:26. "He will testify about me."

> John 16:7-8, 13-14. "It is for your good that I am going away. Unless I go away, **the Paraclete** will not come to you; but if I go, I will send him to you. When he comes, he will convict the world of guilt in regard to sin and righteousness and judgment...

> But when he, **the Spirit of Truth**, comes, he will guide you into all truth. He will not *speak* on his own; he will *speak* only what he *hears*, and he will tell you what is yet to come. He will bring glory to me... (Boldface and italics mine)

After the above quotations, Dr. Bucaille has a special note:

> **It is to be noted that the passages from Chapters 14 to 17 of the Gospel according to John which are not cited here,** *do not modify in any way (ne modifient aucunement) the general sense of these verses.* <sic>

c. Improbabilities??

Is his problem, then, with *Improbabilities*? Yes, it is, and on the basis of the verses given above he makes the following criticisms.

3. It is "curious" and "inconceivable" that one can attribute to the Holy Spirit the powers of "*speaking and saying what he hears*" because in Greek these words are invalid for a spirit.

4. Since it is invalid to use these words for a spirit, it could be that the text was tampered with and the words "Holy Spirit" were added to John 14:26 at a later time.

5. Why were they added later? The words could have been added "deliberately, in

---

7. Even in Mark the tomb is empty before the missing ending.

order to modify the original sense of a passage which, by announcing the coming of a prophet after Jesus, was in contradiction with the teaching of the early Christian churches, which desired that Jesus would be the last of the prophets."[8] In other words, the Christians wanted to suppress a prophecy by Christ that any other prophet would come after him.

6. The translation of the word "paraclete" is totally inaccurate.

We shall now evaluate the validity of each of these criticisms, starting with the fourth.

4. The reliability of the text

Dr. Bucaille starts his discussion of this point by saying, "Every serious study of a text starts with the search for variant readings." In other words, he is looking for any evidence that the words "Holy Spirit" were added to the text at a late date. We considered this question of variants for both the Qur'an and the Bible in Chapter IIIC of Section Three and concluded that in almost all cases they could be shown to be scribal errors by comparing the various copies with each other.

So what is the result of Bucaille's investigation? Are there any variant readings for John 14:26? Only one! In a 4th or 5th century translation into the Syriac Language. It omits the adjective "Holy" but retains the noun "Spirit." The verse in question then reads, "But the **Paraclete, the Spirit**, whom the Father will send in my name..."

What weight of importance shall we give this one variant in a translation? John wrote his Gospel account in Greek, and when we examine the Greek Papyri from 200 to 400 AD, they all read "Holy Spirit." The Codex Sinaiticus and the Codex Vaticanus from 350 AD do not show the variant. The Codex Alexandrius from 450 AD also reads "Holy Spirit."

This is exactly similar to finding a variant in the Persian translation of the Qur'an made by a committee in 345 AH, of which there are still copies available today.[9] What weight would you give to such a variant in a Persian translation?

Is it valid to make a doctrinal decision on the basis of this type of single reading in either the Qur'an or the **Bible**?

Surely this is no more than a scribal error and the answer is **NO!**

Dr. Bucaille also admits the possibility of a scribal error when he asks, "Did the scribe merely miss out a word?" However, he wants to think that the omission was intentional, so he asks,

> ...or, knowing full well that the text he was to copy claimed to make the Holy Spirit hear and speak, did he perhaps lack the audacity to write something that seemed absurd to him?[10]

But the Bible and Qur'an are both full of verses saying that God speaks and hears, so why is it absurd to say this of God's Spirit?

---

8. Bucaille, BQ&S, French Edition, p 109. (translation mine)
9. Hamidullah, *Le Coran*, Op. cit., p xxxvi.
10. Bucaille, BQ&S, p 104-105.

251

3. Can one use "akouo" (hear) and "laleo" (speak) for a spiritual being?

Dr. Bucaille claims that the Greek words *akouo* (hear) and *laleo* (speak), printed in boldfaced type in John 16:13-14 above, have a material character and could not be used for the Holy Spirit. He says, "The two Greek verbs *akouo* and *laleo* define concrete actions which can only be applied to a being with hearing and speech organs. It is consequently impossible to apply them to the Holy Spirit." From this he reasons that these passages could only be speaking about another man or prophet coming.

When we consult a Classical Greek Dictionary we see that Dr. Bucaille is correct for early **Classical Greek usage**. In the *Dictionary of New Testament Theology*, Vol. 2, p 172, edited by Colin Brown, it says:

> *Akouo* (from Homer in the 10th century BC on) means to hear and refers primarily to the perception of sounds by the sense of hearing.

That agrees 100% with Bucaille, but then the dictionary goes on to say,

> Hearing, however, covers not only sense perception but also the apprehension and acceptance by the mind of the content of what is heard. **This led to differences of linguistic usage** which are discussed below in connection with Heb. *shâma* and **which also occur in secular Greek**.

But! and it is a big but. We are not speaking of 950 BC. We are dealing with the Koine dialect of Greek used by the man in the street and in the business world of the 1st century AD.

We saw on pages 4 and 5 that the meaning of a word is determined by its usage in the context of sentences and paragraphs at the time of writing. Therefore, we will examine the **Gospel-New Testament** as a source of Christian Greek usage. We will examine the Septuagint—the Greek translation of the Torah-Old Testament made by the Jews from Hebrew around 200 BC—as a source of Jewish usage. And for Islamic usage we shall also examine the Quranic words for speaking and hearing as applied to God.

a. Other New Testament verses where *akouo* (or its compounds) and *laleo* are used.

Are there other verses in the **Gospel-New Testament** where *akouo* is used with God as the one who is listening? Yes there are. *Akouo* or its compounds are found in John 9:31, John 11:41-42, II Corinthians 6:2, Luke 1:13, and Acts 10:31. Here are three of these verses printed out in full with the corresponding English word in boldfaced italics.

akouo

1. John 9:31. "We know that God does not *listen* to sinners. He *listens* to the godly man who does His will."
2. John 11:41-42. "...Then Jesus looked up and said, 'Father (God), I thank You that You have *heard* me. I knew that You always *hear* me.'"

252

eisakouo

3. Luke 1:13. "But the angel said to him: 'Do not be afraid, Zechariah; your prayer has been *heard*. Your wife Elizabeth will bear you a son, and you are to give him the name John.' "

It is clear from these examples that *akouo* can be used for a spiritual being, including God Himself. Moreover, the first two examples being from the Gospel of John demonstrate usage by the very same author who wrote the passages about the Paraclete.

Laleo is used with God in John 9:29, Acts 7:6, Hebrews 1:1 and 5:5, Mark 13:11, and Acts 28:25. Here are three examples.

1. John 9:29. "We know that God *spoke* to Moses..."

2. Hebrews 1:1. "In the past God *spoke* to our forefathers through the prophets in many different ways."

3. Acts 28:25. "The Holy Spirit *spoke* the truth to your forefathers when He said through Isaiah the prophet..."

Thus a simple examination of the **New Testament** shows that *akouo* and *laleo* were used with God as the subject by five of the **Gospel-New Testament** writers including John.

b. God speaking and hearing in the Septuagint

The Septuagint is a Greek translation of the Hebrew Torah-Old Testament. It was made by Jewish scholars for Jewish believers about 200 BC, and was still in current use in the 1st century AD by both the Jewish and Christian communities.

When we examine it, we find that *akouo* and *laleo* are used many times with God as the subject. There are dozens of verses but we shall give only three, it being understood that *akouo* represents the Hebrew word *shâma* and *laleo* the Hebrew *dabar*.

1. Exodus 6:2-3. "God also *said* to Moses, 'I am the LORD. I appeared to Abraham, to Isaac and to Jacob as God Almighty...' "

2. Psalm 115:4-6. "But their idols are silver and gold, made by the hands of men. They have mouths, but cannot *speak*...they have ears but cannot *hear*."

3. Psalm 94:7,9. "They say, 'The LORD does not see. The God of Jacob pays no heed...' Does He who implanted the ear not *hear*? Does He who formed the eye not see?"

From these verses it is very clear that the idols are blamed and laughed at because **they do not *akouo* and *laleo*,** but **the LORD, Yahweh (Jehovah), the Eternal One hears**—*akouo* and **speaks**—*laleo*.

Dr. Bucaille has claimed that these words should be used only for a human because they require a material organ of hearing and speech. What more beautiful answer can be given than Psalm 94:9 quoted above:

"Does He who implanted the ear not hear (*akouo*)?"

c. God speaking and hearing in the Qur'an

When we examine the Qur'an we find that even though Muslims are very careful to stress that Allah is completely transcendent, the actions of speaking and hearing are often attributed to Him. Here are four examples.

1. The Believer (Al-Mū'min) 40:60, Late Meccan. "And your Lord **says**: 'Call on Me; I *will answer* you.'"

2. The Heifer (Al-Baqara) 2:30. "Behold, the Lord *said* to the angels..." Note: Here a spiritual being, God, is speaking to other spiritual beings—angels.

3. Ṭā-Hā 20:46, Middle Meccan. "He (God) **said**, 'Fear not: for I am with you. I *hear* and see everything.'"

4. The Heifer (Al-Baqara) 3:38. "There did Zakarīya pray to his Lord, saying: 'O my Lord! Grant to me from You a pure child. For You are *The Hearer* of prayer!'"

The fifth verse gives the same account of Zakarīya asking for Yaḥyā (John the Baptist) as that found in the Gospel of Luke where the compound verb *eisakouo* is used to describe God hearing. Here are the two verses placed side by side.

5. Āli 'Imrān 3:38. "There did Zakariya pray to his Lord, saying: 'O my Lord! Grant to me from You a pure child. For You are **The Hearer of prayer!'"**	Luke 1:13, 58 AD. "But the angel said to him: 'Do not be afraid, Zechariah; your prayer has been **heard**. Your wife Elizabeth will bear you a son, and you are to give him the name John.'"

Therefore, it seems correct to assume that *The Hearer* (سَمِيع) in Sura 3:38 would be translated using the Greek verb *eisakouo* found in Luke's original account of the story written 600 years earlier.

Recently I had an opportunity to confirm this assumption by examining a Greek translation of the Qur'an.[11] When I opened it to the verse quoted above, Sura 3:38 (verse 33 in this Greek edition) it read:

> O my Lord! Grant to me from You a pure child. For you are
> *eisakouo (The hearer)* of prayer.

However I hope that the reader is getting wise enough by now to realize that although it is a strong indication that our reasoning is correct, it does not offer conclusive proof concerning the use of *akouo* in the Gospel of John or in the Qur'an. Why? Because the translation was made in 1928. Therefore it can not be an example of either 1st century Christian usage or of 7th century Muslim usage.

In summary:

1. Since *akouo* and *laleo* are used in other verses in the **Gospel-New Testament** for God **hearing** and **speaking**,

---

11. *TO KORANION*, translated into Greek by G. I. Pentakh, printed in Greece, 1928.

2. and since the Jewish translators of the Septuagint used *akouo* and *laleo* with God as the subject,

3. and since a **modern Greek translation of the Qur'an uses** *eisakouo* **for God hearing,**

4. and since the very same events are described in both the Bible and the Qur'an, with the Greek Qur'an using *eisakouo* for *samī'un*;

it is abundantly clear that these Greek words are used for spiritual beings and Dr. Bucaille's argument has no foundation in fact.

5. Did the Christian church teach that Jesus is the last of the prophets?

The answer to this question is a straight "NO!"

The **New Testament** says that **there WILL BE prophets after Jesus.** God revealed through Paul in the letter to the Ephesians,

> It was he (the ascended Christ) who gave some to be **apostles**, some to be **prophets**... (Ephesians 4:11).

And when we examine the New Testament we find men mentioned **who received their revelations long after Jesus ascended**.

Thirty-five years after seeing the risen Christ, the **Apostle Peter** received two revelations **for all people** and **prophesied** concerning the last days.[12]

By revelation the Apostle John wrote his Gospel account **to all people** 50 or 60 years after knowing Jesus alive here on earth. In addition, the last book in the Bible, also by John, is a warning to us and a **prophecy** of what will happen in the days of Jesus' return and the last judgment.[13]

Agabus prophesied that there would be a famine (Acts 11:28), and "**Judas and Silas**, also being **prophets**, exhorted the people" (Acts 15:32). These men all came after Jesus.

And in Revelation 11:3-6, we are told about two prophets who are yet to come in the future:

> And I will give power to my **two witnesses**, and they will **prophesy** for 1,260 days...it will not rain during the time they are **prophesying** (like Elijah); and they have power to turn the waters into blood (like Moses).

Clearly the early Christians believed there were apostles and prophets who came after Jesus ascended, and at least two more are still to come.

On what basis, therefore, would the early Christians wish to suppress a prophecy about Muhammad's coming?

They would not know what he was going to say nor what his doctrine would be.

In conclusion, we see that Dr. Bucaille's theory that the church wished to suppress a prophecy about Muhammad is an empty accusation without substance.

---

12. I Peter, II Peter.
13. Gospel according to John, and Revelation.

6. Mistranslation of the word "paraclete"

A 6th accusation made by Dr. Bucaille is that the word "Paraclete" has been incorrectly translated. In a footnote on page 106, we read,

> Many translations of the Gospels and commentaries, especially the older ones, translate the word (paraclete) by comforter, which is **totally inaccurate**.[14]

A wrong translation is always a possibility, but this accusation is not against one translator, but many. In fact it is not limited to one language either. "Paraclete" was translated by mu'azzī (مُعَزِّيْ) in Arabic, by comforter in English, as well as consolateur in French. Could it really be that everyone is wrong except Dr. Bucaille?

When it is realized that elsewhere he has said about the Qur'an that,

> There are still many translations and commentaries (of the Qur'an) in circulation today that can give a completely false idea of the Quranic revelation…to the scientist who reads them.
>
> …We shall see the reasons why distinguished Arabists who lack a scientific background have made such blunders.[15]

one can only stand in awe and amazement before this man who is able to judge that the quasi-totality of translators and commentators of both the Bible and the Qur'an are in error.

Then how has Dr. Bucaille translated "paraclete"? He has not! He has used a translation where the Greek word "paraclete" is left untranslated!?!

That avoids the problem, of course, but has it helped you? Probably not. Most people do not know what this Greek word means.

A paraclete is someone who can be called on for help. Therefore the meaning depends on what kind of help you need, whether defense by an "advocate—a lawyer," or comfort by a "comforter" in time of sadness. A small dictionary defines it as (1) intercessor, (2) advocate, (3) consoler or comforter and (4) exhorter. There is no single English or French or Arabic word which includes all these meanings. So we are back to context!

To be translated correctly it has to be **in a context**. Most of the older translators chose "comforter" because one of the words in the context is orphan (John 14:18). An orphan is alone without father and mother and needs comforting. The *New International Version* translates paraclete as "counselor." This is a real improvement as it includes two of the four meanings—exhorting and comforting.

In 1 John 2:1 it says, "If we sin we have a 'Paraclete' with the Father, Jesus Christ the righteous." Here the context makes clear that we do not need a comforter, we need an intercessor or an advocate, so the translators have used "advocate" in English, "avocat" in French, and "intercessor" (shafi' الشَّفِيع) in Arabic.

---

14. Bucaille, BQ&S, p 106.
15. Ibid., p 200.

256

Though "paraclete" is used only 5 times in the New Testament, the related noun "paraklesis" which can mean comfort, consolation, exhortation, and entreaty, is used on 29 occasions and was translated **comfort** 20 times.

The verb "parakaleo" which means to beseech, call for, comfort, desire, exhort, and entreat is used 107 times and was translated 24 times by **to comfort**.

As one example of the use of these words we will look at II Corinthians 1:3-4.

> Praise be to the God and Father of our Lord Jesus Christ, the Father of compassion and the God of all **comfort (paraklesis)**, who **comforts (parakaleo)** us in all our troubles, so that we can **comfort (parakaleo)** those in any trouble with the **comfort (paraklesis)** with which we ourselves are **comforted (parakaleo)** of God.

In these two verses the two words are used 5 times and each time the context demands "comfort" or "comforter." Clearly Dr Bucaille's claim that "comforter" is **"totally inaccurate"** as a translation for "Paraclete" is found to be empty.

7. Has Dr. Bucaille quoted all the verses and given the whole context concerning the word "paraclete" as he claims?

Near the beginning of this chapter the verses on the Paraclete from the Gospel of John were given just as Dr. Bucaille quoted them. We also saw his special note which declares,

> **It is to be noted that the passages from chapters 14 to 17 of the Gospel according to John which are not cited here,** *do not modify in any way (ne modifient aucunement) the general sense of these verses. <sic><sic>*[16]

Many people do not have a **Gospel-New Testament** in their homes or easily available, so we will now reprint the verses which Dr. Bucaille quoted in the left column. On the right the passages are repeated but they include eight other verses which also speak about the "Paraclete." Let the reader, himself, judge whether they modify or limit the interpretation of the passage or not.

John 14:15-16. [15] "If you love me (Jesus), you will obey what I command, [16] and I will ask the Father and he will give you another **Paraclete.**"

John 14:15-18. [15] "If you love me (Jesus), you will obey what I command, [16] and I will ask the Father and he will give you another **Paraclete to be with you forever**—[17] **the Spirit of Truth. The world cannot accept him, because it neither sees him nor knows him. But you know him, for he lives with you and will be in you.** [18] I will not leave you as **orphans**; I will come to you."

---

16. Bucaille, BQ&S, French Edition, p 107. (translation mine)

John 14:26. "But **the Paraclete the Holy Spirit**, whom the Father will send in my name, will teach you all things and will remind you of everything I have said to you."

John 15:26.
"He will testify about me"

(Note: Even the word "Paraclete" was omitted by Dr. Bucaille.)

John 16:7-8. [7] "It is for your good that I am going away. Unless I go away, **the Paraclete** will not come to you; but if I go, I will send him to you. [8] When he comes, he will convict the world of guilt in regard to sin and righteousness and judgment…"

John 16:13-14. [13] "But when he, **the Spirit of Truth,** comes, he will guide you into all truth. He will not *speak* on his own, he will *speak* only what he *hears*, and he will tell you what is yet to come. [14] He will bring glory to me…"

John 14:26. "But **the Paraclete, the Holy Spirit**, whom the Father will send in my name, **will teach you all things and will remind you of everything I have said to you.**"

John 15:26-27. [26] "When **the Paraclete** comes, whom I will send you from the Father, **the Spirit of Truth** who goes out from the Father, he will testify about me; [27] **but you also must testify, for you have been with me from the beginning.**"

John 16:7-12. [7] "It is for your good that I am going away. Unless I go away, **the Paraclete** will not come to you; but if I go, I will send him to you. [8] **When he comes, he will convict the world of guilt in regard to sin and righteousness and judgment:** [9] **in regard to sin, because men do not believe in me;** [10] **in regard to righteousness, because I am going to the Father where you can see me no longer;** [11] and in regard to judgment, because the prince of this world (Satan) now stands condemned. [12] I have much more to say to you, more than you can now bear."

John 16:13-15. [13] "**But when he, the Spirit of Truth, comes, he will guide you into all truth**. He will not *speak* on his own; he will *speak* only what he *hears*, and he will tell you what is yet to come. [14] He will bring glory to me by taking from what is mine and making it known to you. [15] All that belongs to the Father is mine. That is why I said the Spirit will take from what is mine and make it known to you."

Dr. Bucaille said that he had quoted all the important verses. "The rest," he claimed, "do not modify in any way the general sense" of the passage.

Yet it is perfectly clear to every reader that many of these **eight** omitted verses do "modify the general sense" of the seven verses which he quoted.

Dr. Bucaille makes a great point of the fact that one manuscript copied 300 years after the original does not include the adjective "holy" and implies that the entire phrase "holy spirit" is a late addition. On page 80 he refers to this problem, saying,

> We shall see...how a single word in a passage from John concerning the Paraclete radically alters its meaning and completely changes its sense when viewed from a theological point of view.[17]

But when we read the above omitted verses we find that this is just not true. The whole doctrine does not rest on John 14:26. The Paraclete is called spirit—the Spirit of Truth—in three other verses: in omitted verses 14:17 and 15:26, as well as 16:13, which Dr. Bucaille does include. This makes a total of four times that the Paraclete is called a "Spirit."

Dr. Bucaille quotes John 14:16 as,

> "I will ask the Father and he will give you another Paraclete."

but he has stopped in the middle of the verse. The whole verse reads,

> "I will ask the Father and he will give you another Paraclete **to be with you forever.**"

Omitted verse 14:17 says that the world **"neither sees him (the Paraclete) nor knows him."**

In the same verse Jesus says to his disciples, **"he (the Paraclete) lives with you and shall be in you."**

He is saying that the Paraclete **"lives with"** Peter, James, John, Matthew, and the others, **"and will be in"** Peter, James, John, Matthew, and the others **"forever."**

In omitted verse 15:27, Jesus tells the disciple-apostles that, **they "must testify"** along with the **"Paraclete"** who **"will testify about me."**

In omitted verse 16:9 Jesus says, "He (the Paraclete) will convict the world of...sin, **because men do not believe in me."**

In addition, to have a complete study, Dr. Bucaille should have included the other verses in the Gospel of John which speak about the Holy Spirit, such as the following,

John 1:33 says that Jesus will baptize with the Holy Spirit.

John 7:39 speaks of the Holy Spirit "which those who believed in him (Jesus) were later to receive."

He also should have given the information recorded by Luke that Jesus told his disciples,

> Do not leave Jerusalem, but wait for the gift my Father promised...For John baptized with water, but in a few days you will be baptized with the Holy Spirit (Acts 1:4-5).

Together, these verses show that the Paraclete, the Holy Spirit, the Spirit of Truth, can be in all of the 11 disciples at once. They were to wait in Jerusalem

---

17. Bucaille, BQ&S, p 80.

and receive this Holy Spirit while they were still alive. This Paraclete would do a convicting work in the hearts of all men and women who would hear the disciples preach—whether Thomas preaching in India or Peter in Rome.

The Paraclete can only be a spiritual being.

The only being that can be in the 11 disciples at the same time, the only being that can be in all the Christians alive at the same time, is a spiritual being. It cannot be true of the man Moses who came before the promise. It cannot be true of Peter who heard the promise. And it cannot be true of Muhammad.

Was Muhammad with Peter and the others in Jerusalem? Was he around to teach Peter and the others all things? Can we say of Muhammad that the men of this world could "not see him," or that he was "with them forever" as it says of the Paraclete?

The answer is obviously NO.

This takes nothing away from Muhammad and his great success as a warner, but it shows clearly that Dr. Bucaille has purposely omitted the context and deformed the quotations in order to support his idea.

He made six accusations as to why this Biblical passage is not true, plus a false statement claiming that he had quoted all relevant verses. We have examined each one and found that his accusations are empty. **One can only conclude that he has not been serious and scholarly in his investigation, and that the verses about the Paraclete cannot be a prophecy about Muhammad.**

C. PROPHECIES BY MUHAMMAD

We saw above that God confirmed the prophethood of Elijah and Jeremiah by fulfilling their prophesies about future events, and in the case of Elijah by sending fire from heaven in answer to his prayer. We must now see whether Muhammad made any prophecies about future events, the fulfillment of which would be a sign of his prophethood.

1. Some commentators have suggested that verse 45 of the Early Meccan Sura of the Moon (Al-Qamar) 54, is a prophecy of the victory at the battle of Badr. It reads,

> Soon will their multitude be put to flight, and they will show their backs.

However, when we add the context found in verses 43 to 48, we find that the subject is the day of judgment.

> Are your unbelievers better than they (the Egyptians who were destroyed)? Or do you have an immunity in the sacred books?
> Or do they say, "We are a host victorious"?
> **Soon will their multitude be put to flight, and they will show their backs.**
> Nay, the hour (of doom) is their appointed promise, and that

hour will be most grievous and most bitter. Truly those in sin are in error and madness.

On the day they will be dragged through the fire on their faces (they will hear) "Taste the touch of hell."

Neither Yusuf Ali nor Hamidullah claim it as a prophecy, although it is possible, of course, for a verse to have two meanings.

2. In the Sura of the Spoils of War (Al-Anfāl) 8:43, from 2 AH, another dream is mentioned. The verse reads,

Remember in your dream (Muhammad), God showed them to you as few. If He had shown them to you as many, you (Muslims) would surely have been discouraged and would have disputed in your decision. But God saved, for He is a Knower of the secrets of the hearts.

This verse, which came after the battle of Badr, refers to a dream which Muhammad had before the battle, but it leaves more problems than it solves. It does not claim that the dream showed a victory, and it depicts God as showing the 300 Muslim fighters that there will only be a few enemy soldiers instead of 1000. **Thus, it shows God using deception to achieve His aims in His own community of believers**.

For me personally, this is a real difficulty. Is this the way the God of heaven and earth, Mighty and All-powerful, named the Truth and the Holy One, acts and carries on His affairs?

We see this same type of action in other places. In Sura 19:26 God tells Mary to say that she is fasting when in fact she is eating water and dates. (Yusuf Ali is usually very good, but in his comment on this problem he suggests that it means fasting from words?! @-@) In Sura 34:12-14 God keeps the jinns working by fooling them that Solomon is still alive. In Sura 4:157 Jesus didn't die, he wasn't crucified, it just looks like it.

Does this not make the reader uneasy in his spirit? How do you convince yourself that these actions which the Qur'an attributes to Allah are not lying actions?

3. In the Sura of the Victory (Al-Fath) 48:27, from 6 AH, we read about another vision.

Truly did God fulfill the vision for His Apostle. You shall enter the Sacred Mosque, **if God wills (In sha' Allah)**, with minds secure, heads shaved, hair cut short, and without fear. For He knew what you did not know…

Muhammad told his men that he had a vision of making the pilgrimage before they set out toward Mecca to do it. The Meccans stopped them at Hudaibiya and wouldn't let them do the pilgrimage, but a treaty was made which would allow the Muslims to do the pilgrimage in the future. According to the **hadith**, some of the Muslims were very upset because the dream was not fulfilled, at which point this verse was given, promising that it would be fulfilled in the future.

Each reader must assign his own value to this verse, since we do not have the details of the original dream. But the biggest problem is this phrase **"if God wills"** in the middle of a prophetic word from the mouth of God.

If God has "fulfilled the vision of the Apostle" and said, "You shall enter," how can He dictate to His Apostle the words "If God wills." He is God and He knows what He wills. That is the whole point of calling something a prophecy of the future: **IT WILL COME TO PASS!**

4. Finally, there is one case where a prophecy was clearly fulfilled. This is found in the Middle Meccan Sura of the Roman Empire (Al-Rūm) 30:1-4 which reads,

> The Romans have been defeated in a land close by; but they,
> after their defeat, will be victorious within a few years. With God
> is the command, in the former case and in the latter—and in that
> day believers will rejoice.[18]

This verse was given, according to the commentators, in 615 or 616 AD when the Persians were threatening to take Constantinople. Eight years later in 624 AD, the tide had turned and the Romans were entering Persia. The historical experience that a losing nation turns the battle around and defeats its opponent is certainly not rare. Therefore, this prophecy could have been fulfilled by chance perhaps 1 in 4 or 1 in 5 times, but that it was fulfilled is plain for all to see.

There are other miraculous accounts in the Hadith material and oral stories which are told throughout the Muslim world, but we have examined all of those which have any basis in our understanding of the Quranic words and phrases. We must now consider a recent attempt to demonstrate a miracle by a mathematical study of the words and letters of the Qur'an.

5. A Numeric Miracle of the Number 19?

This modern attempt to find a second witness is found in the monograph by Rashad Khalifa, Ph.D., entitled *Computer-manifested Miracles in the Holy Qur'an*. In his introduction he admits very openly to this need for **two witnesses** with the following words:

> Throughout the times, the Almighty God has sent a succession
> of messengers who guided the humankind and delivered the
> scripture. **These messengers were invariably supported by
> divine miracles which proved to the believers that they were
> indeed sent by God**. Thus, Moses (peace be upon him) went to
> Pharaoh supported by such miracles as turning his staff into a
> serpent. Jesus…was supported by such miracles as reviving the
> dead and healing the hopelessly blind.[19]

---

18. If "the believers" mentioned here refers to or includes the Christians of Constantinople, then it represents a Qur'anic statement that true Christians were alive during the life of Muhammad—"believers" who would not have changed their Scriptures.

19. Monograph Page 1. Recently enlarged and published as *The Computer Speaks God's Message to the World*, Renaissance Productions International, Tucson.

Dr. Khalifa goes on to point out that these miracles were limited by time and place in the sense that only those present could see them. He believes that he has found a different type of confirming miracle for the Qur'an. It is a miracle revealing itself today by numerology which can be demonstrated only now in our time by the computer. He writes,

> The key to Muhammad's perpetual miracle is found in the very first verse of the Qur'an, "IN THE NAME OF GOD, MOST GRACIOUS, MOST MERCIFUL = BiSM ALLaH, AL-RaHMaN, AL-RaHIM (بسم الله الرحمن الرحيم)..."
>
> When we count the (capital) letters that make up the first Quranic verse, we find them 19.[20] This is of course a physical fact. And, it was discovered that each word in this verse is mentioned throughout the Qur'an a number of times which is consistently a multiple of 19. The first word "ISM (اسم)" is found...19 times; the second word, "ALLaH (الله)" is mentioned 2,698 times, a multiple of 19 (19 x 142); the third word, "AL-RaHMaN (الرحمن)" is found in the Qur'an 57 times, (19 x 3); and the last word, "AL-RaHIM (الرحيم)" is mentioned in the whole Qur'an 114 times, 6 multiples of 19.[21]

Dr. Khalifa then claims, "This computerized study of God's final message deals with strictly physical facts: no guesswork, human interpretation, or conjecture is involved"; in other words, **no basic assumptions along the way.** He has many other numerical examples in his work, but we shall take time to look at only this one in detail.

In spite of Dr. Khalifa's claim that no human conjecture is involved, there is a **basic assumption** in the very first statement claiming that this phrase from the Qur'an has 19 letters. When we rewrite the English transcription of the Arabic, eliminating the vowels which aren't written, but only understood, the phrase looks like this: "BSM ALLH ALRHMN ALRHIM," which counts out to 19 letters. However, there is a little mark in Arabic grammar called a "shadda" which means that the letter underneath the mark is doubled. "ALLaH" or "ALLH" has a "shadda" on the second "L," and could (should?) be written "ALLLH"—which would then make 20 letters.

In his presentation Dr. Khalifa has not explained how he made his decision to exclude the doubling of the letter; nor, for that matter, how he decided to omit the unwritten vowels.

The next problem concerns the word "BiSM." This is a word which is really two words contracted together—the preposition "Bi" (بـ) which in this case is translated as "in"; and the word "ISM" (اسم) or "name."

When we look up the word "ISM" in the Arabic Concordance which Dr.

---

20. In the Arabic language many vowels are not written (see page 124). To try and make the discussion understandable for those who don't know Arabic, I have chosen to write the written letters in capitals, and the understood vowels in small letters. It is further complicated by the fact that when the noun "ISM" stands alone the "I" is a written letter. When it is contracted with the preceding preposition "Bi," the written "I" disappears and it becomes "BiSM."

21. Ibid., p 3.

Khalifa has recommended, called *Index to the Words of the Glorious Qur'an*, by Abdul-Baqi,[22] what a surprise to find the following information:

"BiSM," the word which is written in the first verse of the Qur'an, and which we are supposed to be studying, **occurs only three times:** in Suras 1:1, 11:41, and 27:30.

"ISM," the unconnected noun, **does occur "nineteen times."**

But, there is also a third listing: "ISMuHu (اسمه)" meaning "his name," and written as one word in Arabic, **occurs five times.**[23]

Clearly 3 + 19 + 5 = 27 and does not divide by 19.

We have, then, further **basic assumptions** in front of us for which Dr. Khalifa has given no reason. On what basis did he ignore the three times where the word BiSM is mentioned, the very word about which he is writing? On what basis did he count only the separated form "ISM" standing by itself, and eliminate the noun connected to its following pronoun as in "ISMuHu"?

Is there a reason to be found in the meaning of the words? Perhaps Dr. Khalifa decided to count only those verses which speak of God, for example. But when we look at the following two verses we find that this is not the case. The Sura of the Table (Al-Mā'ida) 5:5 reads,

> …but pronounce God's name (ISM ALLaH) over it…

and the Sura of the Heifer (Al-Baqara) 2:114 reads,

> And who is more unjust than he who forbids in places for the worship of God, that His name (ISMuHu) should be pronounced?

In the English translation, as in the Arabic, there is no difference between these words except that "God's name" is used as a direct object and "His name" as the subject. The maker of the concordance arbitrarily listed them separately on the basis of their written expression.

Furthermore, on what basis should the 12 occurrences of the plural of the noun be excluded?—especially in the following usage from the Sura of the Heights (Al-A'rāf) 7:180 which reads,

> The most beautiful names belong to God…

The only apparent reason is that if all the usages—singular and plural—had been counted, the total would be 39 and not divisible by 19.

Examination of the way ALLAH is used again reveals a contraction. When the preposition "Li (ل)" meaning "to" is used in the phrase "to God," it is contracted with the following noun and they are written together as "LiLaH," or "LiLLah" (لله) with the "shadda." (See Sura 2:22 as an example.) Grammatically, this corresponds exactly to "BiSM" as discussed above. However, this time the contracted form "LiLaH" has been included in the 2698 usages which is a multiple of 19, a procedure which seems absolutely logical.

---

22. Published by Dar Ihiaa Al-Turath Al-'Araby, Beyrouth, Lebanon, 1945, p 361-362.
23. This is the normal way of writing the possessive pronoun in Arabic. It is as though we were to write "hisname" and "yourname" as one word in English.

The contradiction is that "BiSM" and "LiLaH" have not been treated the same. If "LiLaH" is to be included so that the total will divide by 19, then "BiSM" must be included and in that case the total won't divide by 19.

In the case of AL-RaḤMaN there are no complications. It occurs only 57 times or (19 x 3) as the author has stated.

Finally we come to the word AL-RaḤIM. Dr. Khalifa says that it occurs (6 x 19) or 114 times, but according to Abdul-Baqi's concordance it occurs only 34 times in the exact form with the definite article. It occurs another 81 times without the definite article for a total of **115 times, plus one time in the plural which would make 116**. Obviously neither 115 or 116 are divisible by 19.

Dr. Khalifa's findings are quoted with approval by many people. Dr. Be'chir Torki devoted more than four pages to a summary of this study.[24] Yet the following four basic assumptions have been made without any explanation.

Dr. Khalifa has made a decision to ignore both the doubling of the "L" in "ALLaH" and the unwritten vowels.

He has decided to omit "BiSM" from his study of "ISM" although "LiLaH" is included in the count of the word "ALLaH."

He has decided to omit "ISMuHu" from his count even though grammatically it is exactly equal to "ISM."

He has decided to omit the plural usage of "ISM" and "AL-RaḤIM."

In addition, his count for "AL-RaḤIM" seems to be in error.

If his findings are to be a second witness, an attesting miracle to the Qur'an, then Dr. Khalifa's reasoning must be clear to all. Perhaps in the future, he will show how he arrived at these decisions, but until that is done Dr. Khalifa has not proved his case.

CONCLUSION

We have examined all the evidence which we could find in the Qur'an concerning miracles and prophecy. Now each reader will have to make his own evaluation and decide whether **the second witness** is there and satisfactory.

In the next chapter we shall examine some of the Torah-Old Testament prophecies concerning Jesus the Messiah, and see whether God has provided a second witness for his ministry by fulfilling them.

---

24. Torki, op.cit., p 92-96.

CHAPTER II

PROPHETHOOD AND MESSIAHSHIP OF JESUS

We must now ask ourselves the same questions about Jesus of Nazareth, the son of Mary. How could the people of 1st century Palestine know whether he was a prophet? Did God provide a second witness? Did He cause Jesus to fulfill prophecies from previous scriptures? Or did He give miracles? Or after Jesus made prophecies did God cause them to be accomplished?

Fulfilled Prophecies from Previous Scriptures

Since many people have looked with approval on the mathematical study of the Qur'an attempted by Dr. Khalifa, we are going to make a mathematical analysis of some of the prophecies which were made in the Torah-Old Testament concerning "the Messiah."

First we will examine several prophecies and their fulfillment. Then we will make an estimate as to the possibility that "chance" alone could account for the fulfillment of all of the prophecies by one person.

As an example of this type of mathematics we shall assume that you own 10 shirts, each of a different color—colors which are known to me; and I say to some of our mutual friends, "Tomorrow he will wear a red shirt."

When you arrive the next day at the cafè where we always meet, behold you are wearing a red shirt, so I say to everyone, "Look! I'm a prophet!"

But you can say, "Ah, but it was just chance. You had one chance in 10 of being right just by luck."

Now supposing that you also have five hats, each of a different style, and three pairs of shoes: a white pair, a black pair, and a pair of sandals. Now I have one chance in ten of getting your shirt correct, one chance in five for your hat, and one chance in three for your shoes. In order to calculate my chances of getting all three correct just by luck, we must multiply $1/10 \times 1/5 \times 1/3$. This equals $1/150$ or one chance in one hundred and fifty.

Now that we have some idea of how the mathematics work we shall look at ten of the following 12 prophecies and their fulfillment. We shall omit the first one from our calculations—the virgin birth—because it is too unique; and we shall omit the last one—the resurrection of Jesus from the dead—because that is what we are trying to give evidence for.

We shall assign a probability to each of the other prophecies and then calculate the possibilities that the prophets could have written them by chance alone; or put the other way, that Jesus of Nazareth, the son of Mary, could have fulfilled all of these prophecies by chance alone. Because if chance could not account for the fulfillments, then they are signs and proofs to us that the **Gospel WITH US TODAY is true**; and that the Eternal One, Yahweh Elohim, sent Jesus to save us from our sins.

THE PROPHECIES AND THEIR FULFILLMENTS

1. The Prophecy. A virgin shall bear a son so special that he is called "Immanuel" which means "God with us."

> Therefore the Lord himself will give you a sign: **Behold, a virgin shall conceive, and bear a son, and shall call his name Immanuel.** Isaiah 7:14, from 750 BC.

2. The Prophecy. The Messiah must be of the posterity of David.

> "The days are coming," declares the LORD, "when **I will raise up to David a righteous Branch**, a King who will reign wisely and do what is just and right in the land. In his days Judah will be saved and Israel will live in safety.
>
> "This is the name by which **he will be called: The LORD Our Righteousness.**" Jeremiah 23:5-6 from 600 BC.

The Fulfillment of both 1 and 2.

> In the sixth month the angel Gabriel was sent from God to a city of Galilee named Nazareth, to **a virgin** betrothed to a man whose name was **Joseph of the house of David**; and the virgin's name was Mary...
>
> The angel said to her, "Do not be afraid Mary...Behold, you will conceive in your womb and bear a son, and you shall call his name Jesus. He will be great, and will be called the Son of the Most High; **and the Lord God will give to him the throne of his father David**...and **of his kingdom there will be no end.**"
>
> And Mary said to the angel, "How can this be, since I have no husband?"
>
> And the angel said to her, **"The Holy Spirit will come upon you**, and the power of the Most High will overshadow you; therefore the child to be born will be called holy, the Son of God..."
>
> And Mary said, "Behold I am the handmaid of the Lord; let it be to me according to your word." Luke 1:26-27,30-35,38.

We must now ask: One in how many Jewish people belonged to the family of David?

Originally David's family was one of hundreds of families in the tribe of Judah. But of course when his family became the royal family, the king's sons and daughters would have been married into all the other eleven tribes for political reasons, and everyone would remember their kinship with the royal family. Therefore we shall assume that 1 in 200 or 2×10^2 were related to the family of David.

3. The Prophecy. An everlasting ruler is to be born in Bethlehem.

> But you, O **Bethlehem Ephrathah**, who are little to be among the clans of Judah, from you shall come forth for me one who is to be ruler in Israel, whose origin is from of old, from ancient days. Micah 5:2, also from around 750 BC.

The Fulfillment.

Though Joseph and Mary lived in Nazareth in the north, because of an order from Caesar Augustus for a census, Joseph had to take Mary to Bethlehem, his native town.

> In those days a decree went out from Caesar Augustus that all the world should be enrolled...And all went to be enrolled, each to his own city.
>
> And Joseph also went up from Galilee, from the city of Nazareth, to Judea, **to the city of David, which is called Bethlehem, because he was of the house and lineage of David...And while they were there...she gave birth to her first-born son...** Luke 2:1,3-4,6-7.

This prophecy predicts that the Christ is to be born in Bethlehem, so our question is: One man in how many, the world over, has been born in Bethlehem?

The best answer that has been determined assumes that from the time of the prophet Micah until now, the average population on the earth has been two billion people and the average population of Bethlehem has been about 7000. Therefore $2,000,000,000/7000 =$ one man out of every 280,000 men or one man in 2.8×10^5 has been born in Bethlehem.

4. The Prophecy. A messenger will prepare the way for the Messiah.

> "Behold, **I send my messenger to prepare the way before me**, and the Lord whom you seek will suddenly come to his temple; the messenger of the covenant in whom you delight, behold, he is coming," says the LORD of hosts. Malachi 3:1, from about 400 BC.
>
> **A voice cries: "In the wilderness prepare the way of the LORD**, make straight in the desert a highway for our God." Isaiah 40:3.

The Fulfillment.

> And this is the testimony of John (Yaḥyā Ibn Zakarīyā), when the Jews sent priests and Levites from Jerusalem to ask him, "Who are you?"
>
> He confessed..., "I am not the Christ."
>
> They said to him then, "Who are you?"
>
> **He said, "I am the voice of one crying, 'In the wilderness, make straight the way of the Lord,' as the prophet Isaiah said."**
>
> The next day he saw Jesus coming toward him, and said, "Behold the Lamb of God who takes away the sin of world! **This is he of whom I said, 'After me comes a man who ranks before me**, for he was before me.'" John 1:19-20,22-23,29-30.

And to this the Qur'an agrees in the Sura of the Family of 'Imran (Āli 'Imrān) 3:39,45, from 2-3 AH, when it says that Yahya is to come,

"witnessing the truth of a Word from God" (مُصَدِّقًا بِكَلِمَةٍ) (مِنْ أَللَّه) whose **"name will be Christ Jesus, the son of Mary."**

Thus the Qur'an also records both the prophecy that Yaḥyā (John the Baptist) would come to prepare the way for Jesus *and* the fulfillment.

Our question here is: Of the men who have been born in Bethlehem, one man in how many has had a forerunner to prepare the way? But since there appears to be no material difference between the people of Bethlehem and those born any other place in the world, the question can just as well be general: One man in how many, the world over, has had a forerunner to prepare his way?

For example, the Bahai say that a man called the Bab foretold the coming of Bahaullah. It seems very conservative to propose that one man in 1000 was a leader who had a forerunner, so we shall use one man in 1×10^3.

5. The Prophecy. The Messiah will do many signs and miracles.

> Say to those with fearful hearts, "Be strong, do not fear; your God will come, he will come with vengeance; with divine retribution, he will come to save you."
>
> Then will **the eyes of the blind be opened** and **the ears of the deaf be unstopped**. Then will **the lame leap like a deer**, and **the tongue of the dumb shout for joy**... Isaiah 35:4-6a, from 750 BC.

The Fulfillment.

The Gospel states (as does the Qur'an) that Jesus did many miracles. The Biblical record speaks of only four prophets who did a large number of miracles—Moses, Elijah, Elisha, and Jesus. Of these, Jesus did many more than all the others put together and is the only one who did all four types of miracles mentioned in the prophecy. In Appendix A you will find a list of **the 37 miracles which are described in detail** in the four Gospel records. In addition, he sometimes healed "all who came to him." When all the information is considered, it is clear that Jesus did more than 1000 miracles.

Therefore, one could say Jesus was the one man in all men who fulfilled the prophecy. However, since many Muslims believe that there were 124,000 prophets, we will use that number and say that Jesus was the one man in 124,000 or 1.24×10^5.

6. The Prophecy. In spite of these signs, his brothers were against him.

> ...**I have become a stranger to my brethren, an alien to my mother's sons**. Psalm 69:8, from 1000 BC.

The Fulfillment.

> So his brothers said to him, "Leave here and go to Judea...If you do these things, show yourself to the world." **For even his brothers did not believe in him.** John 7:3a, 4b-5.

Our question here might be posed as: One ruler in how many would find his family against him?

This cuts two ways, of course. Many kings in the past placed their own brothers and relatives in positions of power. The other side is that many kings were overthrown by their own relatives. Therefore, we shall use the figure 1 in five or 2×10^1.

7. The Prophecy. The Messiah king will come riding on a donkey.

> "Rejoice greatly, O daughter of Zion; shout, O daughter of Jerusalem: behold, **your King comes unto you**: he is just, and **having salvation**; lowly, **and riding upon an ass**—a colt the foal of an ass" Zechariah 9:9, from around 520 BC.

The Fulfillment.

> The next day the great crowd that had come for the Feast heard that Jesus was on his way to Jerusalem. They took palm branches and went out to meet him shouting,
> "Hosanna!
> "Blessed is he who comes in the name of the Lord!
> **"Blessed is the King of Israel!"**
> **Jesus found a young donkey and sat upon it**...
> John 12:12-14.
>
> Note: Obviously Jesus chose to ride on the ass, but the crowd fulfilled the prophecy when they praised him and spoke of him as a king.

Our question here can be worded: One man in how many, entering Jerusalem as a ruler, has entered riding on a donkey?

We know from the Bible that up to the time of his death King David rode only a mule (I Kings 1:33), but after that kings seem to have ridden on horses or in chariots. Today it is probable that a ruler would come in a Mercedes. We will use the estimate of one man in 100 or 1×10^2.

8. The Prophecy. Kings and rulers shall plot against the Messiah.

> Why do the nations conspire, and the peoples plot in vain? The **kings** of the earth set themselves, and the **rulers** take counsel together, **against the LORD and his anointed (Messiah)**...
> Psalm 2:1-2.

The Fulfillment.

> Kings. "And when (Pilate) learned that he (Jesus) belonged to (King) Herod's jurisdiction, he sent him over to Herod...And **Herod with his soldiers treated him with contempt and mocked him**, then...he sent him back to **Pilate (Caesar's governor)**." Luke 23:7a,11.
>
> Rulers. "So **the chief priests and the Pharisees** gathered the council, and said, 'What are we going to do? For this man performs many signs.'...So from that day on they **took counsel how to put him to death.**"
> John 11:47,53.

In this case we might state our question as: One man in how many after raising someone from the dead, is sentenced to death? That is too restrictive a question (only three are mentioned in the Bible), so we shall rephrase the question as: One man in how many, after doing only good, has had the whole government against him?

This could happen quite often, since what is good to one man may seem bad to another. Therefore, we will use the estimate of one in five or 2×10^1.

9. The Prophecy. The Messiah will be crucified.

> ...a band of evil men has encircled me, **they have pierced my hands and my feet**... Psalm 22:16, written by David 1000 BC.

The Fulfillment.

> When they came to the place called the Skull, **there they crucified him**, along with the criminals—one on his right, the other on his left. Luke 23:33.

The Jews are still looking for the coming of their Messiah. He might have come at any time up to the present, or even in the future. So our question is: One man in how many, from the time of David on, has been crucified?

Many methods of execution have been used over the years—the sword, the guillotine, hanging, the electric chair, etc; but the Jews used stoning. **Crucifixion was not used by them**, which makes this prophecy written by David all the more specific. Therefore, I am sure that it is a very conservative estimate if we say that over the centuries one man in 10,000 or 1×10^4 was executed by crucifixion.

10. The Prophecy. They will divide his garments and cast lots for his robe.

> **They divide my garments among them and cast lots for my clothing.** Psalm 22:18.

The Fulfillment.

> When the soldiers crucified Jesus, **they took his clothes, dividing them into four shares**, one for each of them, with the undergarment remaining. This garment was seamless, woven in one piece from top to bottom.
>
> "Let's not tear it," they said to one another. "Let's decide by lot who will get it." John 19:23-24.

For the soldiers to divide the garments of those who were crucified was probably standard procedure, but that the crucified person would have a seamless garment and they would cast lots for it was probably fairly unusual. We will use 1 in 100 or 1×10^2.

11. The Prophecy. Though he was innocent, he would be counted with the wicked transgressors; and he would be with the rich in his death.

> He was assigned **a grave with the wicked**, and **with the rich in his death** though he had done no violence, nor was any deceit in his mouth...**He was numbered with the transgressors**. Isaiah 53:9,12b.

The Fulfillment.

> **They crucified two robbers with him**. Mark 15:27.
>
> And when Jesus had cried out again in a loud voice, **he gave up his spirit**. Matthew 27:50.
>
> As evening approached, **there came a rich man from**

Arimathea, named Joseph...a disciple of Jesus. Going to Pilate, he asked for Jesus' body...Joseph took the body, wrapped it in a clean linen cloth, **and placed it in his own new tomb**...
Matthew 27:57-60.

There are two parts to this prophecy. The first question is: One man in how many of those executed is innocent?

I hope that the truth is a much smaller number, but we shall use an estimate of 1 man in 10.

The second question is: One man in how many who are executed are from a rich family or would be "with the rich in their death"?

Since the rich have less reason to steal or instigate rebellions, and they have friends to intercede and money to pay lawyers, we shall use the figure of one man in 100. Multiplying 1 in 10 by 1 in 100 gives one man in a 1000 or 1×10^3.

12. The Prophecy. After dying he will rise from the dead.

For he was cut off from the land of the living...and though the LORD makes his life a guilt offering, **he will see his offspring and prolong his days**..." Isaiah 53:8b,10.

The Fulfillment. (The Sunday after he was killed by crucifixion)

...**Jesus himself stood among them and said to them, "Peace be with you."**
...**"**Look at my hands and my feet. It is I myself! **Touch me and see; a ghost does not have flesh and bones, as you see I have**..."
...They gave him a piece of broiled fish, and he took it and ate it in their presence." Luke 24:36,39,42-43.

(As I said above, we will not assign a value to this prophecy of Jesus' resurrection from the dead, since this is what we wish to prove.)

THE CALCULATIONS

If the above estimates are considered fair the question may now be asked: One man in how many men, the world over, will fulfill all ten prophecies?

This question can be answered by multiplying all of our estimates together, or **one** in 2×10^2; x 2.8×10^5; x 10^3; x 1.24×10^5; x 2×10^1; x 10^2; x 2×10^1; x 10^4; x 10^2; x 10^3. This gives one chance in 2.78×10^{28}, where 28 means that we have 28 ciphers following the 2.78. Let us simplify and reduce the number by calling it 1×10^{28}. Written out, this number is 1 chance in 10,000,000,000,000,000,000,000,000,000.

This is the answer to the question: One man in how many men would have fulfilled these ten prophecies by chance alone? But we are really concerned with the answer to the question: What is the chance that any man might have lived from the day of these prophecies down to the present time and have fulfilled all of the ten prophecies by luck?

We can answer this question by dividing our 10^{28} by the total number of people who have lived since the time of these prophecies. The best information available indicates the number to be about 88 billion or 8.8×10^{10} which we will simplify to 1×10^{11}. By dividing these two numbers we find that the chance that any man might have lived down to the present time and fulfilled all ten prophecies by luck is 1 in 10^{17}.

Let us try and visualize this chance. Suppose that we take 10^{17} French 5 franc pieces and lay them over France, Belgium, Holland, Luxembourg, Denmark and Switzerland, a total of 702,000 square kilometers (271,000 square miles). They will cover this whole area to a depth of one meter. Now mark one of these 5 franc pieces with a radioactive mark and stir all the coins over the whole area. Then choose a man and tell him to go in any direction that he wishes, but he must pick up **one** 5 franc piece and say that it is the **right** one.

Where is that coin?

Just imagine the problem! Where will he start looking? It might be near Marseille in southern France. It might be on some northern peninsula of Denmark. It may be on the top of Mont Blanc. What chance would he have of getting the right one? Just the same chance that the prophets would have had of writing these ten prophecies and having them all come true in any one man by luck, if they wrote them in their own wisdom.

CONCLUSION

This means that the fulfillment of these ten prophecies alone proves that God inspired the writing of them to a precision which lacks only one chance in 1×10^{17} of being absolute. Furthermore, these are not all the prophecies. We did not include Jesus' birth from a virgin. The chance would be one person in all the 88 billion people that ever lived, for that one prophecy. In addition, there are many other prophecies which we did not have time to look at. Appendix B shows that at Jesus' crucifixion alone 16 prophecies were fulfilled. We considered only four of them in our list of ten.

If we were to assign probabilities to Jesus' birth from a virgin, and to each one of the prophecies from the Torah-Old Testament which we saw in Chapter II of Section Five; and then add them to our present number; we would have such a large number that you could fill the whole universe with electrons and have only one chance to choose the marked electron.[1]

That is the measure of the reliability of the Torah-Old Testament and the Gospel-New Testament. **The great Creator God, Yahweh Elohim, guided the prophets and told them what to write by the Holy Spirit. Then He fulfilled their words, so that we could know that Jesus' death and resurrection for our sins is true.**

Distributed among the many false problems which Dr. Bucaille has created in his criticism of the Bible are a few real problems to which we do not have good answers. But because of the many fulfilled prophecies and the miracles

---

1. This study is adapted from Chapter 3 of *Science Speaks* by Peter W. Stoner, Moody Press, Chicago, 3rd Edition, 1969.

which Jesus did to prove that his words were from God, we Christians are quite willing to wait and see what the future brings. Every new archaeological discovery, every new discovery of an ancient copy of the Scripture, confirms the truth of **the Gospel which is WITH US**, and shows that the criticisms mounted against it were wrong.

Likewise, it is on the basis of the many miracles which Jesus did and the prophecies which he fulfilled that we accept claims which are difficult for us to understand—such as his claim that he is "in the Father (God) and the Father is in him"; and his claim that the Father loves him because he "lays down his life for his sheep."

The first Christians did not make up and fabricate these doctrines. The first Christians were serious Jews who believed in the oneness of God. They had great difficulty accepting Jesus' statement that he could forgive sins, and that he had the right to call God "his Father." It was only because of **the second witness, the attestation of God Himself** in the miracles and the fulfilled prophecies, and finally in Jesus' resurrection from the dead, that these Jews were able to accept and believe Jesus' claims.

CHAPTER III

PROPHETHOOD AND MESSIAHSHIP OF JESUS
CONTINUED

In the last chapter we began to consider how the people of 1st century Palestine could know whether Jesus the son of Mary was a prophet and the Messiah, and we found that there was one difference between the coming of Jesus and the coming of other prophets. The Jewish nation already believed that God was going to send a special anointed one—"a Messiah." We examined prophecies from the Torah-Old Testament stating that this "Messiah" would be from the descendants of King David; that he would be born in Bethlehem; that he would have mighty miraculous powers; and that he would be called righteous and holy in an exceptional way.

Further information was revealed to the Prophet Isaiah who described this special child from the house and family of David with these words:

> For to us **a child is born**...And **he will be called Wonderful Counselor, Mighty God, Everlasting Father, Prince of Peace.** Of the increase of his government and of peace there will be no end. **He will reign on David's throne**...establishing and upholding it with justice and righteousness from that time on and **forever.** Isaiah 9:6-7.

And, as we saw in the last chapter, they believed the description written by Jeremiah in 600 BC that this special "Messiah" would rule with justice was so correct that it would be like a divine righteousness. He prophesied:

> "The days are coming," declares the LORD, "when **I will raise up to David a righteous Branch**, a King who will reign wisely and do what is just and right in the land. In his days Judah will be saved and Israel will live in safety."
>
> "This is the name by which **he will be called: The LORD Our Righteousness**" (Jeremiah 23:5-6).

Now let us imagine that you the readers, and myself, along with a neighbor Elias, are serious believing Jews living in first century Palestine under Roman occupation. We are fed up with these idolatrous Romans who carry images around and worship more than one God. We long for the Messiah to come, hoping and expecting that with his great and miraculous power he will deliver us from these uncircumcised pagans.

But we have a problem. When a man comes along and claims to be the Messiah, how can we know whether his claim is true? How can we know that he really is the Messiah promised by God?

Over the last 100 years several men have come claiming to be the "Messiah." They all tried to restore the kingdom to Israel by their own force, and they all failed and were killed along with their followers.[1] Therefore, we want to be very

---

1. According to the Bible (Acts 5:34-38), and according to secular historians such as Josephus, many men had come claiming to be the "Messiah" in the years before Jesus was born.

sure that someone who claims to be the promised "Messiah" really is "THE MESSIAH" before we risk our necks following him. The following story shows how our friend Elias solved this problem.

JESUS' TEACHING AND HIS MIRACLES AS A SECOND WITNESS

The Beginning of His Ministry

My name is Elias (Elijah) and my wife and I live in the city of Nain. Nain is eight or nine kilometers from Nazareth, and three or four years ago we began to hear stories that a rabbi was doing miracles over in Capernaum. Our neighbor, a poor widow woman with one son, has a cousin who lives over there and this is what she told us.

My cousin, named Obadiah, lives in Capernaum, and one Saturday at the synagogue service there was a visiting rabbi from Nazareth who was very different. First of all they <were amazed at his teaching, because he taught them as one who had authority,>[2] as though he knew God personally. Secondly, just as he finished speaking, <a man in their synagogue who was possessed by an evil spirit cried out,

"What do you want with us, Jesus of Nazareth? Have you come to destroy us? I know who you are—the Holy One of God!">

Everybody turned around to see what was going on and all of a sudden this rabbi, called Jesus, stood up and said sternly,

<"Be quiet! Come out of him!"

The evil spirit shook the man violently and came out of him with a shriek.>

My cousin says that the synagogue was like a madhouse. There were more than 200 people present and everyone was talking at once. Some were crying and embracing the man who was healed. A few were upset because the evil spirit called this rabbi "the Holy One of God," but most of them were just amazed, saying, <"What is this? A new teaching—and with authority! He even gives orders to evil spirits and they obey him."> (Mark 1:22-27).

My cousin, Obadiah, says there's even more. He has a good friend who's a fisherman. The man's name is Simon Peter. Simon and his brother Andrew had been fishing all night and they didn't get even one fish. Then this same rabbi, Jesus, came along with a crowd of about 100 people and asked to sit in Simon's boat while he spoke. <When he finished speaking he said to Simon,

Put out into deep water, and let down the nets for a catch.>

Well, according to Obadiah, Simon got sort of upset. He's one of the best fishermen on the Sea of Galilee and hadn't caught anything. For this rabbi to start telling *him* when to go fishing was too much. But he didn't want to offend a religious teacher, so he said,

<Because you say so, I will let down the nets.

---

2. All the words included between the marks <> are quoted exactly from the text of the New Testament.

When they had done so, they caught such a large number of fish that their nets began to break.> They had to call their partners in the other boat, and they filled both boats so full of fish that they almost sank. (Luke 5:3-6).

With all those fish, my cousin decided to help Simon Peter and Andrew carry their fish home. When they got there they found <Simon's mother-in-law was in bed with a fever.> Peter had invited the rabbi home for a meal, therefore <they told Jesus about her. So he went to her, took her hand, and helped her up. The fever left her> just like that, <and she began to wait on them> (Mark 1:30-31). That made two miracles that my cousin had seen in one day, in addition to the one in the synagogue, but you haven't heard anything yet!

<That evening after sunset the people brought to Jesus all the sick and demon-possessed. The whole town gathered at the door, and Jesus healed many who had various diseases. He also drove out many demons, but he would not let the demons speak because they knew who he was.> (Mark 1:32-34).

I've never been to Capernaum, but Obadiah says that it's about the same size as Nain—about 4000 people. He says that there must have been about 500 people around that door. Nearly every family in town had brought a sick person, and he figures that Jesus healed 50 people that night. He says that the people in Capernaum are saying, <"**Nothing like this has ever been seen in Israel**"> (Matthew 9:33).

Death and Then Life

Well, our neighbor lady is nice enough, but she talks quite a bit; so my wife and I, we took this with a grain of salt. But we kept hearing stories like this from all over the region of Galilee, and then we had the shock of our lives. The neighbor-lady's son died. He had been coughing for years, but this one night it got very bad, and in spite of all the medicines and herbs she gave him, that was the end. She was grief-stricken, of course, and since it was her only son it was worse.

We felt really sorry for her, but there wasn't anything we could do except go to the funeral. So after they read over the body we started out toward the cemetery. She was just a poor woman and there weren't very many of us—about fifty maybe—so, even though I'm not as strong as I used to be, I was taking a turn carrying the coffin.

When we came out of the city gate there was a large crowd coming down the road. Usually people get out of the way when a funeral comes, and they started to move over—but this time a lane opened up in the center of the crowd and a man came right toward us. I didn't pay much attention until he reached up <and touched the coffin.> Then, with the way he looked at us, we just stopped and <stood still (and) he said,

Young man, I say to you, get up!>

Well! you won't believe it, but <the dead man sat up and began to talk!> We just gasped and people started whispering "It's Jesus of Nazareth." We put the young man down and took off the graveclothes; <and Jesus gave him back to his mother.> (Luke 7:14-15).

After that first silence, people started shouting and praising God. You've never seen anything like it! I was jumping and shouting and waving my arms. I congratulated the mother three times and the son five. And I wanted to say something to Jesus or slap him on the back for thanks, but I didn't dare. How can you slap a rabbi on the back?

Then all of a sudden he said something to his disciples and they turned off on a side road and were gone.

A Few Months Later

Sometime later my wife and I decided that we were really going to look into this situation. We had two reasons. The first was that her mother was all stiff with arthritis. It was so painful that she could only walk a few steps; so we figured that we might as well see whether the healing power of this Jesus wouldn't work for her too.

But for me, the real reason was that I wanted to hear what he had to say with my own ears. Some people said that he was going to be king. Others said that he talked about a "kingdom of God" but then said that it was inside of you. After all, if he was really "THE MESSIAH," then I wanted to know.

Therefore when the weather turned good and warm, I got my brother to milk my two cows and my goats, and we hired a cart to carry my mother-in-law and started out. The first night we stayed with the neighbor-lady's cousin, Obadiah, in Capernaum. He's the one that knows Simon Peter and Andrew, two of Jesus' disciples.

It took us another day to get to a place northeast of the Sea of Galilee called Bethsaida. It was hard on the mother-in-law and we had to stop pretty often so she could rest. But without those Roman roads it would have been even harder. I hate their guts, but I have to admit that they build good roads.

The rabbi was way out in the country on the other side of the Jordan river, but lots of people were traveling in the same direction, so we knew we weren't lost. About mid-morning of the third day we arrived and there were crowds of people. We sat on the side of a hill while Jesus spoke.

*** His Message (My Third Sura) ***[3]

The first thing which I heard was when he talked about fasting and said,

> <"When you fast, do not look somber as the hypocrites do, for they disfigure their faces to show men they are fasting. I tell you the truth, they have received their reward in full. But when you fast, put oil on your head and wash your face, so that it will not be obvious to men that you are fasting, but only to your Father, who is unseen; and your Father, who sees what is done in secret, will reward you"> (Matthew 6:16-18).

---

3. All these readings are from Matthew chapters five through seven, called "The Sermon on the Mountain," which I propose as my third reading for a sura like in the Qur'an, which I promised previously.

Then he spoke about what should be the most important thing, saying,

> <"Do not store up for yourselves treasures on earth, where moth and rust destroy, and where thieves break in and steal. But store up for yourselves treasures in heaven, where moth and rust do not destroy, and where thieves do not break in and steal. For where your treasure is, there your heart will be also...
>
> "No one can serve two masters. Either he will hate the one and love the other, or he will be devoted to the one and despise the other. You cannot serve both God and money"> (Matthew 6:19-24).

Then he stopped and walked around through the crowd for fifteen or twenty minutes healing people who were ill and ordering the demons to come out, and some of those demons recognized him and called him strange things. One of them even called him <"the Son of the Most High God."> (Mark 5:7).

When he started speaking again he said,

> <"Do not judge, or you too will be judged. For in the same way you judge others, you will be judged, and with the measure you use, it will be measured to you.
>
> "Why do you look at the speck of sawdust in your brother's eye and pay no attention to the plank in your own eye? How can you say to your brother, 'Let me take the speck out of your eye,' when all the time there is a plank in your own eye? You hypocrite, first take the plank out of your own eye, and then you will see clearly to remove the speck from your brother's eye."> (Matthew 7:1-5).

Jesus did this over and over again through the whole day,[4] and about three o'clock in the afternoon he came in our direction. He had that same stern but compassionate look in his eyes that I saw when he wakened the neighbor boy from the dead. He passed from one ill person to another until he came to my mother-in-law. Then he reached down and took her hand and said,

> "Come, my mother, stand up!"[5]

She stood up immediately, straight as an 18-year old. For about a minute she just stood there moving her legs and arms and fingers and praising the Lord. Then jumping and shouting, she went running after him to thank him. When she got there he turned to her and said as he did to almost all of the people, <"Your faith has healed you."> (Mark 5:34).

But sometimes he would say to someone,

> <"See, you are well again. Stop sinning or something worse may happen to you"> (John 5:14).

just as though he knew about the person's past and that the illness was a result of sin.

---

4. I believe that Jesus gave the same teachings over and over in each village where he spoke. Therefore I have felt free to include here teachings and healings which are recorded for other times and places in the Gospel; on the basis of Luke, who in his account of the feeding of the 5000 wrote, "But the crowds...followed him. He welcomed them and spoke to them about the kingdom of God, and healed those who needed healing" (Luke 9:11).
5. This miracle is exactly similar to the one recorded in Luke 13:11-13.

He said many things that day. I've already told you some of them, and here are some others. He talked about prayer and said,

> <Ask and it will be given to you; seek and you will find; knock and the door will be opened to you. For everyone who asks receives; he who seeks finds; and to him who knocks, the door will be opened.
>
> Which of you, if his son asks for bread, will give him a stone? Or if he asks for a fish, will give him a snake?
>
> If you, then, though you are evil, know how to give good gifts to your children, how much more will your Father in heaven give good gifts to those who ask him!>

He told us that if something wasn't covered in the law then the rule is,

> <In everything, do to others what you would have them do to you, for this sums up the Law and the Prophets.>

He warned us that it takes a real effort to follow in the way of God. He called it entering the narrow gate.

> <Enter through the narrow gate. For wide is the gate and broad is the road that leads to destruction, and many enter through it. But small is the gate and narrow the road that leads to life, and only a few find it.>

He warned us about false prophets, saying,

> <Watch out for false prophets. They come to you in sheep's clothing, but inwardly they are ferocious wolves. By their fruit you will recognize them. Do people pick grapes from thorn bushes, or figs from thistles?
>
> Likewise every good tree bears good fruit, but a bad tree bears bad fruit. A good tree cannot bear bad fruit, and a bad tree cannot bear good fruit. Every tree that does not bear good fruit is cut down and thrown into the fire. Thus by their fruit you will recognize them.>

Next he spoke some hard words. He said,

> <Not everyone who says to me, "Lord, Lord," will enter the kingdom of heaven, but only he who does the will of my Father who is in heaven. Many will say to me on that day, "Lord, Lord, did we not prophesy in your name, and in your name drive out demons and perform many miracles?" Then I will tell them plainly, "I never knew you. Away from me, you evildoers!">

Finally he ended this group of sayings with a parable about two men. One built his house on the sand and the other on a rock foundation. When a storm came the house on the sand was soon washed away, but the house built on the rock stood firm. When Jesus finished the story he said,

<"Therefore everyone who hears these words of mine and puts them into practice is like (the) wise man who built his house on the rock...

"But everyone who hears these words of mine and does not put them into practice is like (the) foolish man who built his house on sand."> (Matthew 7:7-26).

All day he taught with great authority—not like the usual religious teachers who just quote what was said by Rabbi this and Rabbi that.

The Sacred Restaurant

Finally, late in the afternoon people began to get a bit restless, with the children crying and running around. Our food was all gone and we were starting to talk about going back home when Jesus turned to one of his disciples called Philip and said,

<"Where shall we buy bread for these people to eat?..."
Philip answered him, "Eight months' wages would not buy enough bread for each one to have a bite."
Another of his disciples, Andrew,...spoke up, "Here is a boy with five small barley loaves and two small fish..."
Jesus said, "Have the people sit down."> (John 6:5-9).

There was plenty of grass in that place, and they had us sit <down in groups of hundreds and fifties> (Mark 6:40); and you know, I counted them and there were at least 100 groups of 50. That makes 5000 people!

<Jesus then took the loaves, gave thanks, and distributed to those who were seated as much as they wanted. He did the same with the fish> until we were full.

I've never experienced anything like it before! I was part of a miracle! I ate a whole loaf of bread and six fish myself, and there were only two fish and five loaves of bread to start with! It was absolutely incredible!!

When we finished <they gathered (the leftover pieces) and filled twelve baskets.> Every one of his twelve closest disciples was carrying a full basket of extra bread.

<After the people saw the miraculous sign that Jesus did, they began to say, "Surely this is **the Prophet** who is to come into the world,">[6] and they started to talk about crowning him king right there on the spot, but he refused!! (John 6:11,13-15).

Then Jesus preached to us with really strange words. He said,

<"I am the bread of life. He who comes to me will never go hungry, and he who believes in me will never be thirsty...For I have come down from heaven not to do my will, but to do the will of Him who sent me.

---

6. They are referring to God's promise that He would send a prophet like Moses. See page 12 for a full quotation and discussion of this prophecy.

"For my Father's will is that everyone who looks to the Son and believes in him shall have eternal life, and I will raise him up at the last day"> (John 6:35,38,40).

We had to leave after that in order to get back. But now that the mother-in-law was well we could go home as fast as the cart would go, and it only took us a day and a half. What an experience!

The Questions

There are still some questions about all this, though. They really are big questions and I don't know what to do with them. Jesus calls God his Father! What can he mean?

Of course, David said in Psalm 68 that God is "a Father to the fatherless, a defender of widows"; and God calls Abraham "my friend" (Isaiah 41:8). Maybe it's a relationship like that.

The trouble is that Jesus doesn't talk in that distant kind of way. He keeps referring to God as his Father—and not only that, but he said to us that day, "How much more will **your Father in heaven** give good gifts to those who ask him." And he told us to pray saying, "Our Father in heaven." I have to admit that it would be comforting to think that God was interested in us like a "father"; but what if it's blasphemy?

Then he said, "I came down from heaven." Does he mean to say that he was in heaven with God before? Who can believe that? And he said, "Many will say to me on that day, 'Lord, Lord; then I will say, 'I never knew you.'" That sounds like he is claiming that he will have some sort of power at the day of final judgment.

Another problem concerns the information I heard from the neighbor-lady's cousin when we stayed overnight in Capernaum. He said that one day Jesus was in a house speaking to a whole crowd of people. Some were religious leaders who had come all the way from Jerusalem. All of a sudden there was a lot of noise as four men started taking the tiles off the roof. They had this friend who was paralyzed—and no one would back away and let them in so they made a hole in the roof and let their friend down right in front of Jesus.

People were getting sort of used to seeing miracles by this time, and they thought that Jesus would just heal him and start preaching again—but it didn't happen like that at all. For <…When Jesus saw their faith, he said to the paralytic, **"Son, your sins are forgiven."**>

Obadiah, the neighbor-lady's cousin, said that you could have heard a pin drop. He can read and he knows the Torah real well, so he and the other scribes sitting there were <thinking to themselves, Why does this fellow talk like that? He's blaspheming! Who can forgive sins but God alone?>

Then Jesus looked at them just as though he knew what they were thinking and said to them,

<"Which is easier? To say to the paralytic, 'Your sins are forgiven'? Or to say, 'Get up. Take your mat and walk'"?>

The neighbor-lady's cousin said, "I started to answer him and say that it was easier to heal the man—when suddenly I realized that he might turn around to me and tell me to heal him myself if it's so easy. So I was very quiet."

When no one answered him, Jesus said to them,

> <"But that you may know that the Son of Man has authority on earth to forgive sins"
>
> —he said to the paralytic—
>
> "I tell you, get up, take your mat and go home."

He got up, took his mat and walked out in full view of them all.> (Mark 2:5-12).

Now what can you say about a thing like that? He claimed to have power to forgive sins!! In case you are wondering who the "Son of Man" is, Obadiah says that that's another name which he calls himself. It doesn't change the problem at all. How can he forgive sins?

It was just as though he was saying to them, "If I am lying, then God won't give me the power to heal this man. But if he gets up when I tell him to get up—a thing which you *can* see—then you know that I have power on earth to forgive sins—a thing which you *can't* see."

So now you can see our problem. My wife and I have talked about it many times. Jesus says that he came down from heaven, that he's going to have power at the day of judgment, and that he can forgive sins. The demons call him "the Holy One of God" and "the Son of the Most High God."

We could say that it is all lies and blasphemy, but what about the neighbor-lady's son? He's just as alive as you and I, and without even one cough! And my mother-in-law has been doing a full day's work ever since we came back! And what about me?

I ate those fish! I saw those fish which that boy brought over to Jesus with my own eyes! There were only two to start with and I ate six myself!

I would say that he *has* to be **"The Promised Messiah,"** yet he refused with great insistence when they wanted to make him king! *It just won't fit in my head.*

CHAPTER IV

A MESSIAH TO SUFFER

In the last section we left our friends with a very disturbing question in their minds—a question which seemed to defy understanding. If Jesus was "the Messiah," why did he refuse when they wanted to make him king? We, ourselves, looked at three prophecies from three different prophets stating that the Messiah would be a king from the tribe of David, so we too might ask the question—why did he refuse?

The answer is to be found in other prophecies which describe "the Messiah" as a righteous servant who will suffer and die. The first of these prophecies was written around 600 BC and is found in Daniel 9:21-26.

> While I was still in prayer, (the angel) Gabriel...came to me in swift flight...
>
> He instructed me and said to me, "Daniel, I have now come to give you insight and understanding...
>
> "Seventy 'sevens' (of prophetic years) are decreed for your people and your holy city to finish transgression, **to put an end to sin, to atone for wickedness, to bring in everlasting righteousness**...
>
> "Know therefore and understand this: From the issuing of the decree to restore and rebuild Jerusalem until **the Anointed One (Messiah), the ruler, comes**, there will be seven 'sevens,' and sixty-two 'sevens'...After the sixty-two 'sevens,' **the Anointed One will be cut off, and will have nothing.**"

This phrase "will have nothing" has also been translated as "but not for himself" or "and will have no one." Regardless of which translation is the best, they all convey the meaning that this Anointed One will not realize his kingdom at that time, but that these things will happen in order to **put an end to sin, to atone for wickedness, (and) to bring in everlasting righteousness.**

The second prophecy, written by Isaiah some 750 years before Christ came, can be seen on the following page in Photograph 8. This very manuscript from the caves of Qumran was copied 150 years before Jesus started preaching, and remained buried in the caves until 1948. There is no question of anyone changing this portion of God's word during those years, so we can be sure that it represents part of the Torah-Old Testament which the Qur'an testifies was in Jesus' presence and **"BETWEEN HIS HANDS."** The prophecy reads,

> Who has believed our message
>   and to whom has the arm of the LORD been revealed?
> He was despised and rejected by men,
>   a man of sorrows, and familiar with suffering...
>
> But he was pierced for our transgressions,
>   he was crushed for our iniquities;

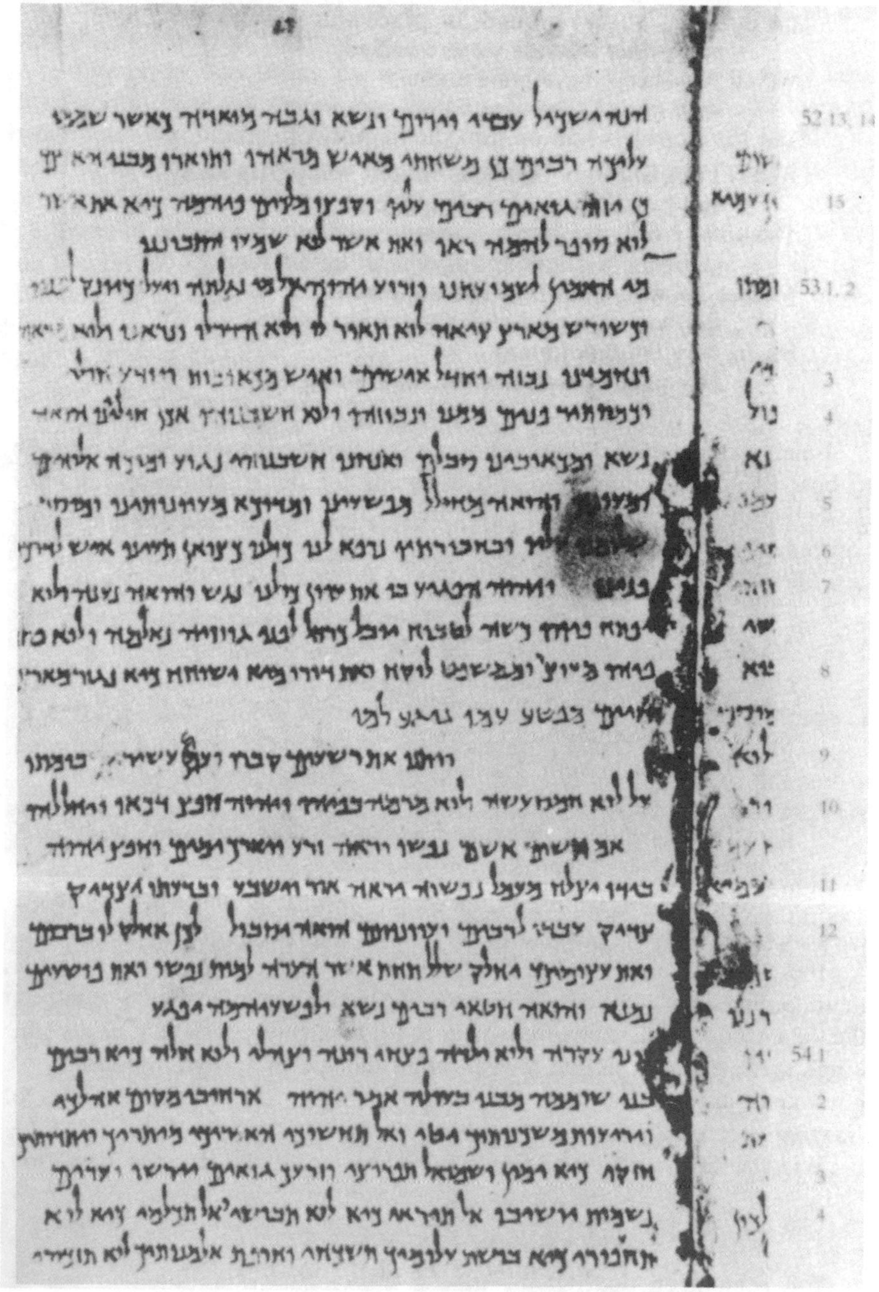

Photograph 8 —

Isaiah 53 as found in the "Dead Sea Scroll" (IQIs[a]), dated *ca.* 125-100 B.C.
By permission of the Israel Museum, Jerusalem.

the punishment that brought us peace was upon him,
    and by his wounds we are healed.
We all, like sheep, have gone astray,
    each of us has turned to his own way;
and the LORD has laid on him the iniquity of us all.

By his knowledge **my righteous servant will justify many**,
    and he will bear their iniquities.
Therefore I will give him a portion among the great,
    and he will divide the spoils with the strong,
because he poured out his life unto death,
    and was numbered with the transgressors.
For he bore the sin of many,
    and made intercession for the transgressors.
                                        Isaiah 53:1,3a,5-6,11b-12.

Isaiah prophesies that there is going to be a "righteous servant" who will die to bear the sins of many and will intercede for the transgressors. Stanley Rosenthal, a Jewish writer who became a Christian, mentions this seeming contradiction between the idea of a mighty king and a suffering servant and describes the attempt of Jewish scholars to resolve it with these words:

> It is no wonder that many of the ancient rabbis wrote in the Jewish Talmud of two Messiahs who would appear on the stage of history. Studying intensely as they did, it was obvious to them that not only would there be a Messiah whom they called Mashiah ben David (Messiah, son of David) who would reign and rule as David did, but that there also would be a Messiah whom they called Mashiah ben Joseph (Messiah, son of Joseph) for he would suffer as Joseph suffered.[1]

How can this be reconciled? A first century Jew had no answer and there was no answer until Jesus explained it.

By revelation Jesus showed his disciples that he, the Son of Man, was with them the first time "to be cut off" in order "to bear the sin of many." Secondly, in the future he would return from heaven with mighty power to establish his kingdom on earth. What the Jewish rabbis thought of as "two Messiahs," we now understand to be two appearances of the "one Messiah—Jesus of Nazareth."

With that further understanding in mind let us return to Elias, our friend from Nain.

DISCUSSIONS IN JERUSALEM

You remember that rabbi I was telling you about—Jesus of Nazareth—well things are not getting any clearer. The other day a man from Jerusalem to whom I sell my goats was here. He was raised in Nain and knows everyone well, so every year just before the feast of the Passover he comes up here to

---

1. *One God or Three?* by Stanley Rosenthal, CLC Publications, Fort Washington, Pa., 1978, p 63.

Nain and buys the best healthy one-year-old rams he can find for the Passover sacrifice.

Anyway, he was telling me about some things which really make your head spin. One day during the feast of Tabernacles several months ago, when Jesus was talking to a crowd of people in the Temple, he <said, "If you hold to my teaching, you are really my disciples. Then you will know the truth and the truth will set you free."> (John 8:31-32).

Some of our Jewish theologians got pretty upset at this and said, "What do you mean? We've <never been slaves of anyone. How can you say that we shall be set free?"

Jesus answered, "I tell you the truth, everyone who sins is a slave of sin."> Then he went on and said, <"If the Son sets you free, you will be free indeed."> (John 8:33-34,36).

Later on, according to the sheep-trader, he told them, <**I tell you the truth, if a man keeps my word, he will never see death**."">

At this the theologians got really excited and exclaimed, <"Now we know that you are demon-possessed! Abraham died and so did the prophets, yet you say that if a man keeps your word, he will never taste death. Are you greater than our father Abraham? He died, and so did the prophets. Who do you think you are?"

Jesus replied, "…Your father Abraham rejoiced at the thought of seeing my day; he saw it and was glad." [Abraham lived about 1800 years before Jesus.]

"You are not yet fifty years old," the (theologians) said to him, "and you have seen Abraham!"">

And now get this answer. Without a moment's hesitation, as though it was the most normal and obvious thing in the world, he said, <"I tell you the truth. **Before Abraham was born, I AM!**"">

He called himself "**I AM!**" But "**I AM**" is a name of God! No human can have that name!

The sheep-trader says that a lot of them started looking around for stones <to stone him> to death for blasphemy.[2] But they were sort of slow as though they couldn't make up their minds, and Jesus went over behind a pillar and <slipped away from the Temple grounds.> (John 8:51-53,56-59).[3]

It certainly would be blasphemy if anyone else said it! But what about those miracles?

The sheep-trader says that the very next day Jesus healed a man who had been born blind. He'd never seen a thing in his whole life. He didn't know red from blue, or even black from white for that matter.

When Jesus came by he told his disciples, <"While I am in the world I am the light of the world."

Having said this, he spit on the ground, made some mud with the saliva, and put it on the man's eyes. (Then) he told him, "Go. Wash in the Pool of Siloam.">

---

2. Stoning as the punishment for blasphemy is found in the Torah at Deuteronomy 13:6-10.
3. These verses can be seen in Photograph 3 of the Codex Vaticanus from 350 AD, on page 132.

A couple of people helped him get up and started him on his way. <He went and washed, and came home seeing.> Just like that—a man who had never seen anything in his whole life!

Later when someone asked him about this miracle, <Jesus said, "For judgment I have come into this world, so that the blind will see...">—just as though he had done the miracle as a lesson. (John 9:1,5-7,39a).

And that's the way it goes. One day he says some terrible, unbelievable thing and then the next day he does an unbelievable miracle.

The sheep-trader says that just before coming up to Nain on his buying trip, he heard Jesus speak as though he were going to die—as though it is all planned. <He said,

> I am the good shepherd. I know my sheep and my sheep know me—just as the Father knows me and I know the Father—and **I lay down my life for the sheep**...The reason my Father loves me is that **I lay down my life—only to take it up again**.> (These verses from John 10:14-15,17 can be seen on the following page in Photograph 9.)

Who can understand it? Jesus always speaks in these allegories, but it sure sounds like he is saying that he is going to die and then come back to life. But what kind of a "Messiah" is that? And why?

At this point, the sheep-trader says there was a big discussion in the Temple. <Many of them said, "He is demon-possessed and raving mad. Why listen to him?"

But others said, "These are not the sayings of a man possessed by a demon. Can a demon open the eyes of the blind?"> (John 10:20-21).

When the sheep-trader told me that, I felt pretty good. I'm just as puzzled as I was before, but according to him our greatest religious teachers are equally puzzled.

Another day the Jewish leaders said to Jesus, <"If you are the Messiah tell us plainly."

Jesus answered, "I did tell you, but you do not believe. The miracles which I do in my Father's name speak for me...Do not believe me unless I do what my Father does. But if I do it, even though you do not believe me, believe the miracles, that you may learn and understand that the Father is in me, and I in the Father.">

When he said that, <they tried to seize him again, but he escaped from their grasp.> (John 10:24-25,37-39).

The next thing the sheep-trader heard was that Jesus had healed ten lepers with one command. <As he was going into a village, ten men who had leprosy met him. They stood at a distance and called out..."Jesus, Master, have pity on us."

When he saw them, he said, "Go, show yourselves to the priests."

And as they went, they were cleansed.> (Luke 17:12-14).

Now, there it is again! How can he be "in the Father and the Father in him"? I can't blame them for wanting to stone him, but he always gives the impression

14 καὶ ὁ λυκος αρπαζει αυτα· καὶ
σκορπιζει· οτι μισθωτος εστιν
και ου μελι αυτω περι των
προβατων· εγω ειμι ο ποιμη
ο καλος και γινωσκω τα εμα
και γινωσκουσι με τα εμα

15 καθως γεινωσκει με ο πηρ
καγω γινωσκω τον πρα και
την ψυχην μου διδωμι ϋ

16 περ των προβατων και αλ
λα δε προβατα εχω α ουκ εστι
                    λ
εκ της αυης ταυτης κακεινα
δει με συναγαγειν· και της
φωνης μου ακουσουσιν· και
γενησεται μια ποιμνη εις

17 ποιμην δια τουτο με ο πηρ αγα
πα· οτι εγω τιθημι την ψυ
χην μου ϊνα παλιν λαβω αυ

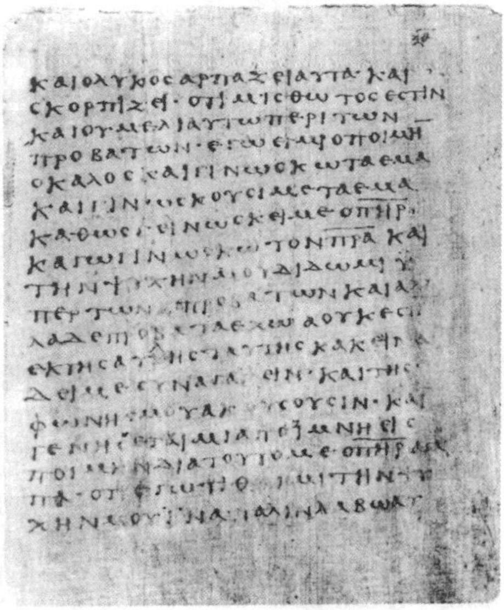

So when he (the hired hand) sees the wolf coming, he abandons the sheep and runs away. [[Then the wolf attacks the flock and scatters it. [13] The man runs away because he is a hired hand and cares nothing for the sheep.

[14] "I am the good shepherd; I know my sheep and my sheep know me— [15] just as the Father knows me and I know the Father— and I lay down my life for the sheep. [16] I have other sheep that are not of this sheep pen. I must bring them also. They too will listen to my voice, and there shall be one flock and one shepherd. [17] The reason my Father loves me is that I lay down my life—only to take it up again.]]

Photograph 9 —

John 10:13-17 as preserved in Papyrus p66 from 200 AD.
By permission of the Bodmer Library, Geneva.

his words are truth and that he wants them to go right into your heart. In fact it's as though he himself is the truth standing right in front of you.

The last thing the sheep-trader told me was that he has a friend who is one of Jesus' disciples—not one of the closest twelve, but one of the seventy. This friend told the sheep-trader that on the way to Jerusalem, Jesus said clearly to the twelve that he, <the Son of Man, will be betrayed to the chief priests and teachers of the law. They will condemn him to death and will hand him over to the Gentiles, who will mock him and spit on him, flog him and kill him; and three days later he will rise.> (Mark 10:33b-34).

Now why would he want to prophesy his own death? It's unbelievable. He has all that power to do those miracles. Why, one time they say he stopped the wind and waves of a storm just by speaking to it! (Mark 4:37-41).

If he has all that power how could they even touch him, let alone seize him and kill him? It's true that a long time ago I heard a rabbi speak about a suffering "Messiah," but I told him that was ridiculous. If somebody is the "Messiah" he is going to reign as king and throw out these horrid uncircumcised Romans! The rabbi didn't insist, but he did say something about a "righteous suffering servant."

You know, I think a lot about these things—especially when I'm sitting milking my goats and my mind is free. I wonder what it will be like to be under him as a king? He certainly spoke sternly to some of those people the day he fed the 5000, but when he spoke of God as Father and said that the Heavenly Father loves us, it was very reassuring. I still remember those words when he said, "If you know how to give good gifts to your children, how much more will your Father in heaven give good gifts to those who ask him!"

Oh, I have some good news. My uncle who lives near Cyrene in Libya, whom we haven't seen for 15 years, is coming for the Passover and the feast of Pentecost. I can't go to Jerusalem with him for the Passover, because it is my turn to watch the goats and do the milking for my two brothers and myself. But when Pentecost comes, if the Lord wills, I'm going to go up to Jerusalem with my uncle. Then I'm hoping to hear Jesus speak again. I think he really *is* bearing witness to the truth and *they know it*!

CHAPTER V

THE POWER OF INTERCESSION

We saw in the last chapter that at least some of the Jewish rabbis believed in a Messiah who would come to suffer and intercede. However, when we Christians say that Jesus is the Messiah who came to intercede for all who accept him as Saviour, Muslims usually reply, "No, it is Muhammad who has the power to intercede." The principal of a primary school in Tunisia told me that no Muslim will stay in hell, because Muhammad will speak on behalf of each one of them.

If the Christian goes on to claim that only Jesus has the right to intercede because he was perfect and sinless, someone almost always answers, "But all the prophets are restrained or guarded (ma'ṣūm مَعْصُوم) from sin."

And when Christians say that Jesus died for our sin, a Muslim often responds with the statement that God would not let one of His chosen prophets be killed.

Therefore, we shall turn again to the Qur'an and see whether it has anything to say concerning these claims. Starting with the last question first, we shall look at all the passages which seem to have any bearing on these three points.

DOES GOD EVER ALLOW ANY OF HIS CHOSEN PROPHETS TO BE KILLED?

There are eight Quranic verses which mention this subject, all of which seem to be addressed to the Jews. The first group of verses speak of prophets and are as follows:

The Heifer (Al-Baqara) 2:91, from 2 AH.

> When it is said to them "Believe in what God has sent down," they say, "We believe in what was sent down to us"; and they disbelieve in that which comes after it. And it is the truth confirming what is WITH THEM.
> Say, "**Why did you kill the prophets of God in times gone by, if you are believers?**"

The Family of 'Imran (Āli 'Imrān) 3:112, from 3 AH.

> ...they rejected the signs of God, and **killed the prophets unjustly**...

The Family of 'Imran (Āli 'Imrān) 3:181.

> ...We shall certainly record their word and **their killing of the prophets unjustly**...

The Women (Al-Nisā') 4:155, from 5-6 AH.

> Then because of their breaking of their covenant, and their disbelief in the clear proofs of God, and **their killing of the**

291

prophets unjustly, and their statement, "Our hearts are uncircumcised"…they believe not, except a few.

Then in the Sura of the Family of 'Imran (Āli 'Imrān) 3:21, from 3 AH, we find the accusation broadened. In addition to the prophets, the unbelievers seek to slay even ordinary men if they "command justice."

> As to those who deny the clear proofs of God and **kill the prophets,** and **kill those of men who command justice**; announce to them a painful punishment.

Finally, in a third group of verses we find that in addition to prophets, even apostles were killed.

The Heifer (Al-Baqara) 2:87, from 2 AH.

> We gave Moses the Book and **followed him up with a succession of apostles**; and we gave Jesus the son of Mary clear proofs and strengthened him with the holy spirit. Is it that whenever there comes to you an apostle with what you yourselves desire not, you are puffed up with pride? Some you called liars, **and some you killed**.

The Family of 'Imran (Āli 'Imrān) 3:183, from 3 AH.

> Say (Muhammad), "**There came to you apostles before me** with clear signs and even with what you ask for. **Why then did you kill them**, if you speak the truth?"

The Table (Al-Mā'ida) 5:70, from 10 AH.

> **We** took the covenant of the Children of Israel and **sent them apostles**. Every time an apostle came to them with what they themselves disliked—some of them they called liars, and **some they killed**.

These eight verses state clearly that **(a) righteous men who taught justice, (b) prophets of God, and (c) apostles of God were killed** at one time or another—often at the hands of the Jewish leaders.

A well-known example is the prophet Yaḥyā Ibn Zakarīyā (John the Baptist). Though his death is not mentioned in the Qur'an, it is found in the Gospel, and it is mentioned by the Jewish historian Flavius Josephus. In book XVIII, chap. 5 of *The Antiquities of the Jews* he writes,

> For Herod (King of the Jews) slew him (Yaḥyā), who was a good man and *commanded the Jews to exercise virtue*. (italics mine)

The words in italics are almost exactly the same as the Quranic verse saying that they "killed those who commanded justice."

We must conclude, therefore, that it is completely false for a Muslim to say that God could never let a prophet, or an apostle like Jesus, be killed. The Qur'an states clearly that the Sovereign, All-Powerful Lord has already done so in the past.

ALL PROPHETS ARE GUARDED (MA'ṢUM) FROM SIN

1. The first prophet according to the Muslims was Adam, and the Qur'an says that he was thrown out of the heavenly garden because he sinned. The Middle Meccan Sura of Ṭā-Hā 20:120-121 reads,

> But Satan whispered evil to him (Adam)...
> In the result they both ate of the tree...**Thus did Adam disobey** ('aṣā عَضَى)[1] **his Lord and went astray** (ghawā غَوَى),

and though Adam and Eve are not mentioned by name in the Late Meccan Sura of the Heights (Al-A'rāf) 7:189-190, it certainly seems to be the intention of these verses (and 4:1 where the same phrase is used) when we are told,

> He it is Who did create you from a single soul, and therefrom did make his mate that he might take rest in her...
> But when He gave to them a goodly child, **they ascribed unto Him partners** (shurakā' شُرَكَاء).

To "ascribe partners to God" is the unforgivable sin in Islam. It is worse than rebellion.

2. Concerning Noah, in the Late Meccan Sura of The Prophet Hud (Hūd) 11:45-47, we read,

> And Noah called upon his Lord, and said, "O my Lord! surely my son is of my family (and should be saved)..."
> He (God) said, "O Noah! he is not of thy family, for his conduct is unrighteous. **So ask not of Me that of which you have no knowledge. I give you counsel, lest you act like the ignorant!**"
> He (Noah) said, "O my Lord! I do seek refuge with You, lest I ask You for that of which I have no knowledge. **And unless You forgive me and have mercy on me, I will be of the lost.**"

What shall we say of this? Noah's request that his unbelieving son should be spared is so human, "so normal" to us, that we would hardly call it sin. But God rebukes him with strong words; and Noah recognizes that he has sinned in refusing God's will, and asks for forgiveness and mercy.

3. Abraham, the father of three religions, also has something to say. In the Middle Meccan Sura of Abraham (Ibrāhīm) 14:41, Abraham speaks:

> Our Lord! **Forgive me** and my parents and believers on the day when the account is cast.

and again in the Middle Meccan Sura of the Poets (Al-Shu'arā') 26:77,81-82, he says,

> ...Not so the Lord and Cherisher of the Worlds...
> who will cause me to die and then give me life, and who, I hope, will **forgive me my sin** (khaṭī'ati خَطِيئَتِي) on the day of judgment.

---

1. This is a very strong word meaning to defy, oppose, rebel, and revolt—the exact opposite of submission.

293

Here, Abraham not only asks forgiveness in a general way as in the first quotation, but he specifically asks forgiveness for **his own sin**.

4. When we examine Moses, this great apostle of God to whom the Lord spoke "directly," we find that he too is rebuked. In the Late Meccan Sura of the Narration (Al-Qaṣaṣ) 28:15,16 we read,

> And he (Moses) entered the City...and he found two men fighting—one of his own sect, and the other of his foes. Now the man of his own sect appealed to him against his foe, and Moses struck him with his fist and finished him off. (Then) he said, "This is of the work of Satan; for he is a clearly misleading enemy."
>
> He prayed, "**O my Lord, I have indeed wronged my soul! Forgive me**!" and He **(God) forgave him**, for He is the Forgiving One, the Most Merciful.

The interpretation of Yusuf Ali is that Moses did not intend to kill the Egyptian but only to deliver the Jewish fighter. Therefore, Moses asked God's forgiveness for killing this man.

5. The next man to be considered is the apostle David who wrote the Zabūr or Psalms. In the Early Meccan Sura of Ṣād 38:21-25 it is written,

> Has the story of the disputants reached you? Behold, they climbed over the wall of the private chamber.
>
> When they entered in front of David...they said, "Don't be afraid. We are two disputants...Decide now between us with truth...This man is my brother. He has nine and ninety ewes, and I have one ewe; and he says entrust her to me, and he is harsh to me in speech."
>
> He (David) said, "He has undoubtedly wronged you in demanding your ewe to be added to his ewes...Not so do those who believe and do good works, and they are few."
>
> And David guessed that We had tried him and **he asked forgiveness of his Lord** and he fell down prostrate and repented.
>
> So **We forgave him THIS**... (capital letters mine)

Yusuf Ali does not believe that this story refers to David's crime of committing adultery with Bathsheba and then killing her husband to hide the sin as recorded in the Torah-Old Testament.[2]

Hamidullah, though, has no doubt that it does refer to this very serious crime, and that is also my opinion for two reasons. Firstly, the parable of the 99 ewes and one ewe as found here is similar to the Biblical account, and secondly verse 26 of the Qur'an goes on to say,

> O David...judge between men with truth and don't follow **the passion** (al-hawā الْهَوَى) (of the heart), for **it will beguile you** from the path of God...

Anyway, whether it refers to his adultery or not, it clearly speaks of some

---

2. See II Samuel 11 and 12 and David's Psalm of repentance—Psalm 51.

specific sin referred to as **"THIS,"** for which David asked forgiveness and for which he was so overcome that he fell on his knees and bowed down.

6. In the Early Meccan Sura of Ṣād 38:35 Solomon too says,

> ...O my Lord! **Forgive me**...

although his sin is not very clear, unless it was loving horses more than the remembrance of God.

7. Finally we come to the Prophet Jonah. He purposely refused to obey God's command to go and warn the people of Nineveh, and took ship to run away. After which, according to the Early Meccan Sura of the Ranks (Al-Ṣāffāt) 37:142-144,

> ...the fish swallowed him, and he was **blameworthy** (mulīm مُلِيمٌ) **and had he not been one of those who glorify (God), he would have stayed in its belly till the day when they are raised.**

His words of repentance from the belly of the fish are found in the Middle Meccan Sura of the Prophets (Al-Anbiyā') 21:87 where it says that,

> ...he cried out in the darkness, saying, "There is no God save you! Glory to you! Indeed, **I have been one of the oppressing transgressors** (al-ẓālimīn الظَّالِمِينَ)."

So Jonah admits that he was an "oppressing sinner" and God calls him "blameworthy," the very same word used in Sura 51:40 where the Qur'an reports that God threw Pharaoh into the sea because he was "blameworthy."

In these verses we have seen that seven prophets, two of whom were also apostles, either called themselves sinners or were called sinners by God and told to repent. While the sins of Noah and Solomon seem such small sins of heart attitude to us as to be almost "normal," they were still told to ask for forgiveness. But of Adam, the Qur'an says that he "rebelled ('aṣā)" and "ascribed partners (shurakā') to God," and Jonah, after refusing God's command, is called "blameworthy (mulīm)."

Abraham specifically asks forgiveness for "sin (k̲h̲aṭī'a)," and the two apostles, Moses and David, must repent for murder and adultery. Moses' killing of the Egyptian was accidental, but David was completely responsible for his sinful actions.

Some Muslims have wanted to say that the prophets and apostles were held back from great sins, but we have seen that even this is not true.

A judge from the Court of Appeals in Tangier once claimed that actions which were sins for ordinary people were not sins for the prophets. Then I asked him who would be more blameworthy and receive a greater punishment in his court: one who knew the law when he broke it, or one who was ignorant of the law? He quickly answered that it was the person who knew the law who deserved the greater punishment. The lesson is obvious. **The responsibility of a prophet or an apostle is greater, not less.**

To this the Qur'an also agrees. In the Sura of the Confederates (Al-Aḥzāb) 33:7-8, from 5-6 AH, it says that God took a "sacred covenant" from the prophets and apostles: a covenant which He did not demand from other people; and on the basis of which He would judge their faithfulness. The verses read,

> And remember We took from the prophets their covenant; and from you (Muhammad) and from Noah and Abraham and Moses, and Jesus the son of Mary; and **we took from them a sacred covenant, that He (God) may ask (call to account) the faithful ones concerning their truthfulness.**

In conclusion, we can only say that it is obvious and clear that according to the Qur'an prophets and apostles also sin.

8. This brings us then to a very delicate subject—delicate because it may cause pain in the heart of the reader—but if we are to continue our search right down to the last grain of truth, we must discuss it anyway.

What does the Qur'an say about Muhammad and sin? We shall look at the verses in the order of their revelation.

One Wrapped Up (Al-Mudaththir) 74:1-5, Very Early Meccan.

> O you, the wrapped up one, arise and warn,
> and your Lord magnify,
> and **purify your garments**,
> and flee abomination.
>> (or "that which provokes God's anger"—Hamidullah)

Morning Light (Al-Ḍuḥā) 93:6-7, Early Meccan.

> Did He not find you (Muhammad) an orphan and protect?
> Did He not find you **straying** (ḍallan ضَالًّا) **and He guided?**

This is the word used in the Early Meccan Sura of the Opening (Al-Fātiḥa) 1:6-7 which every Muslim prays many times a day:

> Show us the straight path.
> The path of those whom You have favored—not (the path) of those who earn Your anger, **nor of those who go astray** (al-ḍāllin الضَّالِّين).

The Expansion (A lam nashrah) 94:1-7, which reads,

> Have We not expanded your breast (Muhammad), and **removed from you your burden** (wizrak وِزْرَك) **which crushed your back**, and exalted your fame? Along with trouble comes ease...So when you are free, toil and strive to please your Lord.

This must be compared with the Late Meccan Sura of the Cattle (Al-An'ām) 6:31 which describes the unbelievers in hell by saying,

> ...**They bear upon their backs their burdens** (auzārahum أَوْزَارَهُمْ) **and evil is that which they bear!**

The reader may also remember that on pages 5-7 we studied this word for burden and we saw that "no burdened one can bear the burden of another"—that is, "No sinner can bear the sin of another."

He Frowned ('Abasa) 80:1-11, Early Meccan.

> (The Prophet) frowned and turned away, because there came to him the blind man. But what could tell you but that perchance he might grow (in righteousness)? Or that he might receive admonition and teaching might profit him?
>
> As to one who regards himself as self-sufficient, to him you attend. Yet it is no blame to you if he does not grow (in righteousness).
>
> But as for him who came to you striving earnestly and with fear, of him you were unmindful.
>
> No. **It is indeed an admonishment**.

Here Muhammad is rebuked for showing favoritism and Hamidullah has a note at these verses saying, "Thus the revelation is not always pleasing to the prophet."

The Believer (Al-Mū'min) 40:55, Late Meccan.

> Then have patience (Muhammad) for the promise of God is true; and **ask forgiveness for your sin** (danbika ذَنْبِكَ) and celebrate the praise of the Lord in the evening and the morning.

Muhammad 47:19, from 1 AH.

> And know (O Muhammad) that there is no god but God, and ask **forgiveness for your sin** (danbika ذَنْبِكَ), and for the men and women who believe...

Since the sins of Muhammad and of the other believers are mentioned together in the same sentence, it would seem that they must be similar in character.

The Women (Al-Nisā') 4:105-107, from 5-6 AH.

> Lo! We have sent down to you the book with truth, that you may judge between mankind by that which God shows you. And don't be a pleader for the treacherous,
>
> and **ask forgiveness from God** (for your wrong intention), for God is Ever-forgiving, most Merciful,
>
> and plead not on behalf of those who deceive themselves. Lo! God does not love one who is treacherous and sinful.

The words in parentheses, added by one translator, are placed there on the basis of the explanation given by most commentators and quoted by Yusuf Ali: that this revelation came when Muhammad was tempted to judge against an innocent Jew in favor of a guilty Muslim.

The Victory (Al-Fath) 48:1-2, from 6 AH.

> Truly We have granted you a clear victory, that **God may forgive you your sin** (danbika ذَنْبِكَ) **that is past and that which is to come**, and finish His favor to you and guide you on the straight path.

Repentance (Al-Tauba) 9:43, from 9 AH.

> **God give you forgiveness** (Muhammad)! Why did you grant
> them exemption until those who told the truth were seen by you in a
> clear light and you knew the liars?

Muhammad is rebuked for not inquiring of God, or for judging too hastily in
giving some men exemption from battle.

Help (Al-Naṣr) 110:3, from 10 AH, a few week's before Muhammad's death.

> Celebrate the praises of your Lord (Muhammad) and **pray for**
> **His forgiveness**; for He is ever ready to show mercy.

We may summarize this information by saying that Muhammad did no great
sins like those which the Qur'an attributes to Adam and Jonah and David. The
acts of Muhammad which are described and rebuked in the above verses are
those into which it would be exceedingly easy for any leader to fall, and they can
be found in the lives of other prophets who have gone before. What we are to
understand by the words "your sin" (ḍanbika) is not explained, but we are
forced to the conclusion that Muhammad, like the other prophets and apostles
whom we studied above, was not sinless.

The reader may be very upset by this information—even angry; but these
verses have not been included because they bring joy. It is because of the
question of intercession.

Intercession Yes or No? Two Opinions

At the beginning of this section, I quoted the principal of a primary school
who said that because of the intercession of Muhammad, no Muslim will remain
in hell.

In support of the same opinion, a book called *Proofs of Blessing* (دَلاَئِلُ
الْخَيْرَات dalā'il al-khairāt) by Abī ʿAbdallah Muhammad Sulimān Al-jazūli, one
of the "yellow books" sold all across North Africa and even in Marseille,
describes Muhammad as,

> Intercessor of the Nation, and the Intercessor among Inter-
> cessors of the Resurrection Day.[3]

In a chapter entitled the "Two Hundred and One Names of Muhammad" he is
called,

> ...Perfect...Truth...Intercessor...the Spirit of Holiness...the
> Spirit of Truth...the Key of Heaven...Forgiving of Sins...and the
> Holder of Intercession...[4]

In other places further names are added, such as,

> "Light of Lights...Lord of the Righteous,"[5] and even names of

---

3. Edition, Al-Manār, Tunis, 1964, p 63-64.
4. Ibid., p 25-30.
5. Ibid., p 92.

298

God such as "The Gracious" (al-ra'ūf الــرَّؤُوف) and "The Compassionate" (al-raḥīm الرَّحِيم).[6]

This book is so well known that two male nurses in one of the North African dispensaries where I worked could sing long passages by heart.

Finally, consider the following story which I have heard in both Morocco and Tunisia.

On the day of resurrection,
Moses' people said to him, "O Moses! Intercede for us."
He answered, "Myself. Myself."[7]
Jesus' people said to him, "O Jesus! Intercede for us."
He answered, "Myself, Myself."
Muhammad's people said to him, "O Muhammad! Intercede for us."
He answered, "My nation, My nation."

Hearing beliefs and stories like these repeated over and over again gives the people of North Africa the idea that the intercession of Muhammad is a sure thing. Therefore, we shall again make a detailed study of the Qur'an to see if there are verses which support this belief in Muhammad's power to intercede on the day of judgment—a belief held almost universally in popular Islam!

INTERCESSION ON THE DAY OF RESURRECTION ACCORDING TO THE QUR'AN

In the Qur'an we find that the verb and nouns formed from the verb "he intercedes" (shafa'a شَفَعَ) are used 26 times in relation to God.[8] Except for one verse which I have treated separately, the references divide themselves naturally into three groups. We shall now look at each passage in detail, including as much context as is necessary to demonstrate the usage.

1. THERE WILL BE NO INTERCESSION BY IDOLS OR FALSE GODS

One Wrapped Up (Al-Mudaththir) 74:48, Very Early Meccan. (Used twice as different noun forms)

> Then will **NO INTERCESSION** of (any) **INTERCESSORS** profit them.

Yā-Sīn 36:23, Early or Middle Meccan.

> If (God) most gracious should intend some adversity for me (Muhammad), of **NO USE** whatever will be **THEIR INTERCESSION** for me, nor can they deliver me.

The Roman Empire (Al-Rūm) 30:13, Middle Meccan.

> **NO INTERCESSOR** will they have among their false gods and they will themselves reject their false gods.

---

6. Ibid., p 158.

7. It should be noted that this story contradicts the Sura of the Heights (Al-A'rāf) 7:148-156 in which Moses prays for himself and his people saying, "Forgive us and have mercy upon us." See page 294 later in this chapter.

8. Words formed from this root are also used four times in Sura 4:85 and one time in Sura 89:3, but without reference to intercession with God.

The Poets (Al-Shu'arā') 26:100-101, Middle Meccan.

Now that we have **NONE TO INTERCEDE** (for us) nor a single friend to feel (for us).

The Heights (Al-A'rāf) 7:53, Late Meccan. (Used twice—once as a verb and once as a noun)

On the day (judgment day) the event is finally fulfilled, those who disregarded it before will say, "The apostles of our Lord did indeed bring truth. Have we **NO INTERCESSOR** now **TO INTERCEDE** on our behalf?" (In the context it means "Where are our false gods to help us now?")

The Believer (Al-Mū'min) 40:18, Late Meccan.

NO intimate friend nor **INTERCESSOR** will the wrong-doers have, who could be listened to.

The Cattle (Al-An'ām) 6:94, Late Meccan.

WE SEE NOT with you **YOUR INTERCESSORS** (false gods) whom ye thought to be partners in your affairs.

Jonah (Yūnus) 10:18, Late Meccan.

They serve besides God, things that hurt them not, nor profit them and they say, "THESE (FALSE GODS) ARE OUR INTERCESSORS with God."

The Heifer (Al-Baqara) 2:48, 2 AH.

Then guard yourselves against a day when one soul shall not avail another, **NOR SHALL INTERCESSION BE ACCEPTED** from it, nor shall compensation be received from it, nor shall they be helped.

The Heifer (Al-Baqara) 2:123, 2 AH.

Then guard yourselves against a day when one soul shall not avail another, nor shall compensation be accepted from it, **NOR SHALL INTERCESSION** (of another) **PROFIT IT** nor shall they be helped.

The Heifer (Al-Baqara) 2:254, 2 AH.

Before the day comes when **NO** bargaining (will avail) nor friendship nor **INTERCESSION**.

2. GOD ALONE HAS THE POWER OF INTERCESSION

The Crowds (Al-Zumar) 39:43,44, Late Meccan.

What! Do they take for **INTERCESSORS** others BESIDES GOD? Say: "Even if they have NO POWER whatever and no intelligence?" Say: "**TO GOD BELONGS ALL INTERCESSION.**"

The Cattle (Al-An'ām) 6:70, Late Meccan.

> But proclaim (to them) this (truth): that every soul delivers itself to ruin by its own acts: it will find for itself **NO** protector or **INTERCESSOR EXCEPT GOD**: if it offered every ransom (or reparation), none will be accepted.

The Cattle (Al-An'ām) 6:51, Late Meccan.

> Give this warning to those who fear (because they know) that they will be gathered unto their Lord. **EXCEPT FOR HIM**, they will have **NO** protector, nor **INTERCESSOR**: that they may live righteously.

Adoration (Al-Sajda) 32:4, Middle Meccan.

> Ye have **NONE BESIDE HIM, TO** protect or **INTERCEDE** (for you).

3. INTERCESSION IS BY GOD'S PERMISSION ALONE

The Star (Al-Najm) 53:26, Early Meccan.

> How many-so-ever be the **ANGELS** in the heavens, their **INTERCESSION WILL AVAIL NOTHING, EXCEPT AFTER GOD HAS GIVEN LEAVE FOR WHOM HE PLEASES AND** IS ACCEPTABLE.

The City of Saba (Sabā) 34:23, Early Meccan.

> **NO INTERCESSION** can avail in His presence **EXCEPT FOR HIM FOR WHOM HE HAS GRANTED PERMISSION.**

The Prophets (Al-Anbiyā') 21:28, Middle Meccan.

> And they (angels or apostles) offer **NO INTERCESSION EXCEPT FOR THOSE WHO ARE ACCEPTABLE** and they stand in awe and reverence of His (glory). ***

*** This says clearly, along with the preceding verses, that the person who is to receive intercession must be acceptable to God.

Mary (Maryam) 19:87, Middle Meccan.

> **NONE SHALL HAVE POWER OF INTERCESSION, BUT SUCH A ONE AS HAS RECEIVED PERMISSION** (or promise) **FROM GOD** most gracious.

Ṭā-Hā 20:109, Middle Meccan.

> On that day **NO INTERCESSION SHALL AVAIL EXCEPT HE TO WHOM THE MOST MERCIFUL PERMITS IT AND WHOSE WORD IS ACCEPTABLE.**

Jonah (Yūnus) 10:3, Late Meccan.

> **NO INTERCESSOR** (can plead with Him) **EXCEPT AFTER HIS PERMISSION** (has been obtained).

The Heifer (Al-Baqara) 2:255, 2 AH.

> His are all things in the heavens and on earth. **WHO CAN INTERCEDE** in His presence **EXCEPT AS HE PERMITS?** ***

*** These four verses say clearly that no one can intercede except as God permits.

4. INTERCESSION ONLY BY HE WHO BEARS WITNESS TO THE TRUTH

Finally there is one other verse which I have treated separately because it gives another characteristic of one who can intercede. In the Late Meccan Sura of the Gold Adornments (Al-Zukhruf) 43:86, we read,

> And THOSE (FALSE GODS) whom they invoke besides God have **NO POWER OF INTERCESSION; ONLY HE WHO BEARS WITNESS TO THE TRUTH** and they know.

The question is—who is this person who bears witness to the truth?

Yusuf Ali in his note on this verse says that many commentators interpret it to mean any apostle who preached the Gospel of Unity. Others, including Yusuf Ali, would interpret it to mean Muhammad.

The verse does not say. One can only pose the question: Is it Abraham? Is it Muhammad? Is it Moses? Is it Jesus? Jesus is the only prophet who ever said of himself, "**I am...the truth**." But in the end we don't know. We are not told.

In summary, we have found words derived from "he intercedes" used 13 times in 11 verses to say that it is foolish and useless to think that dead idols will intercede at the day of judgment. We have found such derivatives used five times in four verses to say that God alone has the power of intercession. Thirdly, the question of who can intercede is discussed in eight verses where it is stated that:

a) No one can intercede—even angels—except with God's permission.

b) Only those acceptable to God can have intercession offered in their behalf.

c) Only he who bears witness to the truth can intercede.

5. OTHER VERSES ON THE SUBJECT BUT WITHOUT THE WORD INTERCESSION

The same teachings as those mentioned above, but expressed by different words and expressions, are also found in other Quranic verses.

The Cleaving Asunder (Al-Infiṭār) 82:19, Early Meccan.

> **The day when no soul shall have power (to do) anything for another**: for the command that day, will be (wholly) with God.

The News (Al-Naba') 78:37-38, Early Meccan.

> ...**None shall have power to argue with Him** the day that the Spirit and the angels will stand forth in ranks. **None shall speak except him whom the Most Gracious allows**, and he will say what is right.

The Cattle (Al-An'ām) 6:164, Late Meccan.

> ...Every soul gathers the result of its acts on none but itself. **No bearer of burdens can bear the burden of another.** Your goal in the end is towards God. He will tell you the truth of the things wherein you disputed. ***

*** As we have seen on pages 6-7, the portion in bold-face is also found four other times in Suras 17:15, 35:18, 39:7, and 53:38.

PROPHETS WHO WERE ORDERED TO PRAY FOR OTHERS

There are verses in the Qur'an where prophets are told to pray for people or ask forgiveness for them. We shall take the verses concerning each prophet in their order of revelation.

1. Verses concerning Muhammad are as follows:

Muhammad 47:19, from 1 AH.

> And know (O Muhammad) that there is no god but God, and ask **forgiveness for your sin** (danbika ذَنْبِكَ), **and for the men and women who believe**.

The Family of 'Imran (Āli 'Imrān) 3:159, from 2 AH. Muhammad is told in relation to the soldiers who were disobedient at Uhud to

> pass over (their faults), and **ask for forgiveness for them**.

The Hypocrites (Al-Munāfiqūn) 63:5, from 4-5 AH, speaks of hypocrites who pretend to believe but

> ...when it is said to them, "**Come, the Apostle of God will pray for your forgiveness**," they turn aside their heads...

The Women (Al-Nisā') 4:64, from 5-6 AH, speaking of hypocritical believers who refused to come, says,

> And if, when they had wronged themselves, they had but come unto you and asked forgiveness of God, and **the Apostle had asked forgiveness for them, they would have found God Forgiving**, Merciful.

The Light (Al-Nūr) 24:62, from 5-6 AH, speaking in relation to those who ask to be excused from a matter needing collective action, says,

> ...when they ask for your permission (to go) for some business of theirs, give permission to those of them whom you wish and **ask God to forgive them**.

The Examined Woman (Al-Mumtahina) 60:12, from 8 AH. Speaking in relation of women who wish to become Muslims, this verse says,

> O Prophet, when believing women come to you, taking oath of allegiance to you...then accept their allegiance and **ask God to forgive them**.

Repentance (Al-Tauba) 9:103, from 9 AH, speaks of the desert Arabs, saying,

> Of their goods take alms...and pray for them. Verily **your prayers are a source of security** for them.

At first glance these verses might seem to lend support to a doctrine of special intercession by Muhammad, but first of all, none of them have to do with the day of judgment, and secondly the Qur'an tells us that other prophets prayed in this way.

2. Noah prayed for his family and his people, as well as himself. His preaching is recorded in the Early Meccan Sura of Noah (Nūḥ) 71:2-4,7,10.

> He (Noah) said, "O my people! I am to you a clear warner, that you should worship God and fear Him and obey me; so that He may forgive you of your sins..."
> He said, "Lord!...**whenever I call to them that you may forgive them**, they thrust their fingers in their ears...and I have said, **ask forgiveness of your Lord**. He is a Forgiving One."

And in verse 28 of the same sura we read,

> Lord! **Forgive me, and my parents, and him who enters my house believing, and believing men and believing women...**"

3. Abraham also prayed for others as well as himself.

Abraham (Ibrāhīm) 14:41, Late Meccan.

> (Abraham said) **O our Lord! Forgive me, my parents and all believers.**

The Poets (Al-Shu'arā') 26:86, Middle Meccan, says that Abraham prayed,

> **Forgive my father. Indeed, he is of those who go astray** (al-ḍāllīn الضَّالِّين).

It was, of course, later revealed in 9:113-114, from 9 AH, that Abraham, Muhammad and the believers are not to pray, even for next of kin, after they understand and refuse.

The Sura of the Prophet Hud (Hūd) 11:74, Late Meccan, tells us that Abraham even pleaded for the people of another prophet, his nephew Lot.

> When fear had passed from Abraham...**he began to plead with us** (yujādiluna يُجَادِلُنَا) **on behalf of Lot's people**. [The Arabic word here would mean argue if used of two men; and Hamidullah translates it "dispute."]

4. Jacob, too, is stated to have asked forgiveness for the sins of his ten sons. In the Late Meccan Sura of Joseph (Yūsuf) 12:97-98, we read,

> They said, "**O our father! Ask forgiveness of our sins** (ḍunūbanā ذُنُوبَنَا) **for us**; for indeed we were sinners (khāṭi'īn خَاطِئِين)." He said, "**I shall ask forgiveness for you of my Lord** for He is the Forgiver, the Merciful."

5. In the Late Meccan Sura of the Heights (Al-A'rāf) 7:148-156 the Qur'an gives the story of the golden calf, and verse 155 records how **Moses** prayed for his people, saying,

> ...O my Lord! If it had been Your will You could have destroyed, long before, both them and me. Will You destroy us for the deeds of the foolish ones among us? This is no more than Your trial. By it You cause whom You will to stray; and You lead whom You will into the right path. You are our Protector. **So forgive us and have mercy upon us**; and You are the Best of forgivers.

THE BIBLICAL RECORD OF PROPHETS WHO PRAYED FOR OTHERS

The Bible also speaks of prophets who prayed in this way.

1. The Torah: Exodus 32:31-32 records the same prayer of **Moses** as that given above.

> ...Oh, what a great sin these people have committed! They have made themselves gods of gold. But now, **please forgive their sin—** but if not, then blot me out of the book You have written.

2. The prophet **Daniel** describes his praying with these words:

> O Lord, listen! **O Lord, forgive!** O Lord, hear and act! For Your sake, O my God, do not delay, because Your city and Your people bear Your Name. (Daniel 9:19-20).

3. The prophet **Amos** prays for his people, saying,

> ...I cried out, **"Sovereign LORD, forgive!** How can Jacob (the Nation) survive? He is so small!" (Amos 7:2).

4. Job was told to pray for those who had accused him of sin.

> After the LORD had said these things to Job, He said to Eliphaz the Temanite, "'I am angry with you and your two friends, because you have not spoken of Me what is right, as My servant Job has. So now take seven bulls and seven rams and go to My servant Job and sacrifice a burnt offering for yourselves. **My servant Job will pray for you, and I will accept his prayer and not deal with you according to your folly...**" and the LORD accepted Job's prayer (Job 42:7-9).

5. Paul prays for his brothers of the Jewish nation:

> Brothers, **my heart's desire and prayer to God for the Israelites is that they may be saved** (Romans 10:1).

And the depth of his feeling and prayer are shown in these words,

> I have great sorrow and unceasing anguish in my heart. **For I could wish that I myself were cursed and cut off from Christ for**

the sake of my brothers, those of my own race, the people of Israel. (Romans 9:2-4).

In the Bible, too, **Jeremiah** is finally told by God not to plead anymore. God says,

> So **do not pray for this people nor offer any plea or petition for them**; do not plead with Me, for I will not listen to you. Do you not see what they are doing in the towns of Judah and in the streets of Jerusalem?...**They pour out drink offerings to other gods** to provoke Me to anger. (Jeremiah 7:16-18).

Having examined these many passages, in both the Qur'an and the Bible, we find that they all speak of living prophets praying for living people with whom they are in contact. We have not found one single verse in the whole Qur'an which promises that any of these prophets, from Noah to Muhammad, will have power to intercede on the day of judgment. This leaves only the Hadith as a possible source for further information.

INTERCESSION ON THE DAY OF JUDGMENT ACCORDING TO THE HADITH

About the time that I decided that I would have to consult the hadith literature on this subject, I found a copy of An-Nawawi's *Forty Hadiths* in a bookstore. There, I thought, this should make it easy. If there are any hadiths on "intercession," this great specialist in hadith literature will surely include at least one in his special collection. But to my surprise there was not one hadith on the subject—not even a short one!

In his *Dictionary of Islam* under the heading "intercession," T.P. Hughes gives the following information concerning the Hadith on page 214.

> The statements of Muhammad, as contained in the Traditions, are as follows:
>
> "He is most fortunate in my intercession in the Day of Judgment, who shall have said from his heart, without any mixture of hypocrisy, 'There is no deity but God.' "
>
> "I will intercede for those who shall have committed great sins."
>
> "Three classes will intercede on the Day of Judgment, the Prophets, the Learned, the Martyrs." *Mishkat*, book xxxiii, ch. xii.
>
> The author of the *sharh-i-Mawaqif* says (p 588): According to the Sunnis, the intercession of Muhammad is specially for those who have committed great sins (ahlu 'l-kabair), for the purpose of removing punishment; for Muhammad has said, "My intercession is for those who have committed great sins." But the Mu'tazilas say the intercession of Muhammad is for the increase of merit, and not for the prevention of punishment; for it is said in the Qur'an, Sura ii.48: "Fear the day wherein no soul shall pay recompense for another soul. **Nor shall intercession be**

accepted for it, nor shall compensation be taken from it, nor shall they be helped." (This is one of the verses which we saw above in group 1.)

I have not made my own study of the Hadith as I did of the Qur'an, but it is clear from this summary that hadiths on the subject are scarce and contradictory; and there is so little evidence to support intercession by Muhammad at the day of judgment that the Mu'tazilas—the Muslim rationalists from the second century of the Hejira—could say categorically that intercession by Muhammad is not for the prevention of sin.

One does not have to look as far back as the Mu'tazilas, though, to find this doctrine. The founder of the Wahhabis, Muhammad ibn 'Abd al-Wahhab, wrote a book called *The Book of Unity* toward the end of the 18th century. In this book "**he attacked** the commonly held beliefs in the powers of the saints and pious men and the practices consequent upon these beliefs—worship of and at saints' tombs, **reliance upon the intercessions of the Prophet** and the saints, indeed, the whole gamut of popular religion."[9]

A very modern statement of the Islamic belief concerning "intercession" is found in *The Muslim World League Journal* of May-June 1983. In an article entitled "The Islamic Concept of God and Prophet," Shaikh Gamal al-Banna writes,

> Islam stresses the human character of the Prophet... Therefore, **any kind of mediation is not permissible or recognized in Islam**. Prophets are mere messengers of God; they cannot forgive anyone if he commits a sin or exempt him from the punishment he deserves. **They cannot also intercede with God on anybody's behalf**, for **Islam does not recognize the idea of intercession as such**.[10]

In support of Shaikh al-Banna's statement and the beliefs of the Wahhabis are the following two hadiths which go strongly against any idea of intercession by Muhammad. The first is recorded by Bukhari, in the book *Testimonies*, Chapter XXX, on "Casting Lots to Solve Problems," where it tells about Othman, one of the strongly convinced Muslims who fled from Mecca with Muhammad. Shortly afterward he became ill and died. Muhammad entered the home at that moment and heard Omm-El-Ala, a woman who had cared for Othman in his illness, say over the body, "The mercy of God be with you. I witness in your favor that God was generous toward you."

Muhammad asked her how she knew this, and when she admitted that she didn't he said,

> As for Othman, he is dead, and by God the Certain One, I wish only good for him, but by God, (even though) I am the Apostle of God, I do not know what God will do with him.

9. Rahman, *Islam*, op. cit., p 197.
10. *The Muslim World League Journal*, Vol. 10, No. 8, p 9.

The second hadith is found on page 128 of the book, *Prophet Muhammad and His Mission* (1967) by Athar Husain, where the author tells us,

> Muhammad said,
> "O People of Quraish, be prepared for the hereafter. I cannot save you from the punishment of God,
> O Bani Abd Manaf…I cannot protect you either,
> O Safia, aunt of the Prophet, I cannot be of help to you;
> O Fatima, daughter of Muhammad, even you I cannot save."
> Transmitted by Bukhari and Muslim

What can one say? If Muhammad could not intercede for a Muslim follower who was so convinced that he left his home and family to follow Muhammad, or for his own believing daughter, who is left?

In conclusion, there is nothing in the Qur'an or the hadiths to support the popular story mentioned above which ended with Muhammad saying, "My nation. My nation." Rather than interceding, the Sura of the Children of Israel (Banī Isrā'īl) 17:57, from 1 AH, says that the prophets themselves are looking for a means to get close to God. It reads,

> Those whom others call on (angels and prophets) wish a means
> to their Lord, **even those who are nearest. They hope for his
> mercy and fear his wrath.**

And rather than finding verses which say that Muhammad will pray for the believers, as one might expect, the Sura of the Confederates (Al-Ahzab) 33:56 says that God and the angels pray for Muhammad; and the believers are also commanded to pray for him and his salvation. It reads,

> **God and His angels pray for the Prophet, and you who
> believe, pray for Him and ask for his salvation.**

It is because of this command that every time a Muslim mentions Muhammad by name, he adds his prayer for Muhammad's salvation.

The 200-page "yellow book" *Proofs of Blessing*, mentioned earlier, is filled with encouragements to pray for Muhammad. Many times praying for Muhammad is linked with Muhammad's intercession for the person praying, as in the following examples:

> Whoever prays for Muhammad 100 times on Friday will have
> 80 years of sins forgiven.

> Gabriel speaking: "If anyone prays for you (Muhammad),
> seventy thousand angels will pray for him, and he whom the
> angels pray for will be of the family of paradise."

> And Muhammad himself, saying, "The more from you prayers
> for me, the more for you wives in heaven."[11]

Unfortunately people believe these ideas, repeat them, and hope that they are true even though there is no support for them in the Qur'an.

---

11. Sulīmān Al-Jazūlī, op. cit., p 15-16.

TWO OF THE FIRST MUSLIMS

Finally, to close this chapter we shall look at the attitude of two of the earliest and greatest Muslims, which shows how they were feeling as death approached. Jens Christensen, after many years of Islamic studies, wrote,

> One of the things that often surprised me in my first studies of Islam was the note of despondency and insecurity that is found in the deathbed utterances of so many of Islam's great men.
>
> Abu Bakr, for example, was a prince among men, of sterling character and a true Muslim. Yet it is said of him that he was so fearful of the future and labored so much under distress that his breath was often as of a roasted liver. According to two traditions he is supposed to have said to Aisha on the day of his death,
>
> > "Oh my daughter, this is the day of my release and of obtaining of my desert:—**if** gladness it will be lasting; **if** sorrow it will never cease."[12]
>
> **Do you see those two "ifs"?** Nothing in Islam can remove them; not even the fact that Abu Bakr was given the title 'Atīq (Free) because Muhammad is supposed to have told him: "You are free (saved) from the fire."

T. P. Hughes quotes Omar as saying, "It had gone hard with my soul, if I had not been a Muslim,"[13] but in telling of Omar's death Christensen writes:

> When Omar was lying on his deathbed, he is reported to have said,
>
> > "...I am not other than as a drowning man who sees a possibility of escape with life, and hopes for it, but fears he may die and lose it, and so plunges about with hands and feet. More desperate than the drowning man is he who at the sight of heaven and hell is buried in the vision...Had I the whole East and West, gladly would I give up all to be delivered from this awful terror that is hanging over me." And finally touching his face against the ground he cried aloud: "Alas for Omar, and alas for the mother of Omar, **if** it should not please the Lord to pardon me."

Do you see Omar's difficulty? It is the uncertainty expressed in the "if" of the last sentence. That "if" does not express any feeling of uncertainty regarding Omar's faith, Omar's belief in one God, Omar's trust and confidence in the prophet, or Omar's lack of having lived a moral life. All of these things are in order as far as a human being could do that which is right.

No. **The "if" refers to Allah; "if" it should not please the Lord to pardon him.**

---

12. This and the following quotations about Omar are found in *The Torch of Guidance to the Mystery of Redemption*, translated by Sir W. Muir, printed by the Religious Tract Society, London.
13. Hughes, op. cit., p 654.

When Yazid was burying Omar his father, he is quoted as saying: "I will not magnify him before the Almighty in whose presence he has gone to appear. **If** He forgives him it will be of His mercy; **if** He takes vengeance on him, it will be for his transgressions."

> Here again you have the two **"ifs"**
> **If Allah forgives...**
> **If Allah takes vengeance...**

This remark of Yazid's seems to me to epitomize the whole of Islam.[14] No man from Muhammad himself, right down to the least educated non-Arabic speaking Muslim who knows only a few prayers, would ever presume to know, or dare to predict what "if" will mean for him.[15]

Or to put it another way, Allah demands complete submission from each man, but He never commits Himself in any revealed way to His servants as individuals. There is no way that a man can know whether he will be saved or not.

This uncertainty is seen clearly in the Middle Meccan Sura of the Poets (Al-Shu'arā') 26:82, where Abraham speaks of

> The Lord of the Worlds...Who will cause me to die and then to live (Abraham believes this and is sure of it); and Who, **I hope** (atma'u أَطْمَعُ), will forgive me my sins on the day of judgment. (For his forgiveness he can only say, "I hope so.")

In verse 52 of the same sura, Moses and Aaron say to Pharaoh,

> **We hope** (natma'u نَطْمَعُ) that our Lord will forgive us our sins.

And in 17:57, as we saw above,

> even those (the angels and prophets) who are nearest. **They hope** (yarjūna يَرْجُونَ) **for His mercy and fear His wrath**.

Finally, three more verses from the Qur'an state very clearly that even those who have done their best are given only a **"maybe"** from Allah. In the Late Meccan Sura of the Narration (Al-Qaṣaṣ) 28:67, Allah says to His believers,

> But as for him who shall repent and believe and do right, **perhaps** ('asā an عَسَى أَنْ) **he may be** one of the successful.

---

14. *Practical Approach*, Pakistan, 1960, as correspondence course. Republished 1977, p 379.
15. Ibid., p 381.

The same idea is repeated in the Sura of the Forbidding (Al-Tahrim) 66:8, from 7 AH, where the believers are told,

O ye who believe, Repent toward Allah with a sincere repentance. **It may be** ('asa an أَنْ عَسَى) that your Lord will remit from you your evil deeds and admit you to gardens beneath which rivers flow.

In the Sura of Repentance (Al-Tauba) 9:18, from 9 AH, almost the end of the Qur'an, Allah says,

Those only shall worship in the Mosques of Allah, who believe in Allah and the last day and observe proper worship and give alms and fear none except Allah; and **it might be** ('asa an أَنْ عَسَى) **that these are of the rightly guided.**

In the end, it is a very lonely choice. If a person does not believe, then he is sure to go to hell; but even if he does believe, on the day of judgment he stands there all by himself in front of Allah. There is no intercessor or friend, and he can only **hope that maybe, perhaps, he might be** among the blessed.

CHAPTER VI

JESUS AS A RIGHTEOUS SERVANT
AND INTERCESSOR

Having examined intercession in the Qur'an, we must now do the same for the Torah-Old Testament and the Gospel-New Testament. We have already seen that a "**righteous servant**" who can intercede is foretold by the prophet Isaiah. But of course to say that Jesus came as a servant is only to say what Muslims always claim.

Whenever a Christian mentions the miracles which Jesus performed and points out that they are a proof—a second witness—that his teachings were from God, Muslims quickly respond that they were done only "with the permission of God." Then they add that Jesus was just a servant or slave (**'abd** عَبْد) of God like every other man. And finally they sometimes finish by quoting the Middle Meccan Sura of Mary (Maryam) 19:30, in which Jesus says as a baby in the cradle,

"I am indeed a servant of God ('Abd Allah). He gave me the
Book and made me a prophet."

The first thing I would like to say in response to these statements is that just because his miracles were done "by the permission of God" does not subtract from their value as a second witness. They still serve as one of the proofs that Jesus' words and actions came from God.

Secondly, it may be a surprise to the reader to know that, although Christians believe that Jesus was and is more than a servant, they agree completely with the statement that during his time here in the world he lived as an 'abd—as a servant or slave of God.

In his prophecy that a "righteous servant" would come, the Hebrew word used by Isaiah for "servant" is " **'ebed.**" This is written with the Hebrew letters 'ayin, bêth, and dāleth which correspond exactly to the Arabic letters 'ain, bā', and dāl. It means "slave" or "servant," and when one looks at the root verb, one finds that it means "to work, to serve, and to worship" just like the root verb " 'abada" in Arabic.

" 'Ebed" can be compounded with the names of God just as one does in Arabic to form 'Abdallah. With "El" it makes 'Abdiyel or "slave of God," and from "Yah" (a shortened form of YaHWeH) comes 'Obadyahweh for "Serving Yahweh." This name 'Obadyahweh, written in English as "Obadiah," is even the name of one of the prophets in the Torah-Old Testament.

Therefore, we may understand from Isaiah's Old Testament prophecy that a special **"righteous 'abd"** is going to come to do the will of God.

The equivalent Greek word in the Gospel-New Testament is "doulos." In Philippians 2:7-8, God guides Paul to say of Jesus that in

taking the very nature of a **servant (doulos)**...he humbled
himself and became obedient to death—even death on a cross.

312

In his Gospel Jesus claimed that he was obedient in repeating the words which God had given him. He said,

> For I did not speak on my own authority, but **the Father who sent me commanded me what to say and how to speak**. I know that His command leads to eternal life. So **what the Father has said to me, that is what I speak.** (John 12:49-50).

He also claimed to have fulfilled the idea of servanthood in all his actions, saying,

> **My food is to do the will of Him who sent me** and to finish His work." (John 4:34).

> By myself I can do nothing. I judge only as I hear, and my judgment is just, for **I seek not to please myself but Him who sent me**. (John 5:30).

> For **I have come down from heaven** not to do my will but **to do the will of Him who sent me**. (John 6:38).

These verses show that Jesus came down from heaven at the command of God. All that he said and did here was in obedience to the Father. **In everything he was a "righteous servant"—a "righteous 'abd."**

In addition he came to be a servant, an 'abd, to us. Paul writes by revelation in Romans 15:8,

> Jesus became a servant (doulos) of the Jews...to confirm the promises made to the patriarchs (Abraham and Isaac), so that the Gentiles (non-Jews) might glorify God for His mercy.

In other words, Jesus showed himself a servant, or 'abd of God, by being a servant to us, whether we are Jews or non-Jews. In his Gospel he said about himself,

> For even **the Son of Man did not come to be served, but to serve**, and to give his life as a ransom for many. (Mark 10:45).

None of these verses have said explicitly that Jesus was perfect or sinless. As we continue our study, however, we find other verses which do confirm that Jesus was without sin.

In John 8:28-29 Jesus says,

> ...I do nothing on my own but speak just what the Father has taught me...He has not left me alone, for **I always do what pleases Him**.

Farther on, in John 8:46, after making his listeners unhappy with him by calling them sons of the Devil, Jesus says,

> **Can any of you prove me guilty of sin?**

When Peter preached after Jesus' resurrection, he said to his listeners,

> You disowned the **Holy and Righteous one**... (Acts 3:14).

313

Luke tells us in chapter 1:35 that Gabriel used this word "holy" when he spoke to Mary about the birth of Jesus,

> The Holy Spirit shall come upon you, and the power of God shall overshadow you; so **the child born to you will be called holy**…

Although it uses a different word, the Qur'an agrees to this when it says in the Middle Meccan Sura of Mary (Maryam) 19:19 that the angel came and said to Mary,

> Indeed, I am a messenger of your Lord to give to you a (ghulāman zakīyan غُلَامًا زَكِيًّا) ⌐ **holy son**." Yusuf Ali
> ⌐ **faultless son**." Pickthall
> ⌐ **pure son**." Hamidullah

As one of my friends says, "Jesus is the only prophet who never had to ask forgiveness." (يَسُوعُ هُوَ النَّبِيُّ الْوَحِيدُ الَّذِي لَمْ يَسْتَغْفِرْ اللهَ قَطّ مِنْ أَجْلِ تَفْسِهِ)

The author of Hebrews describes Jesus as a great high priest,

> …one who has been tempted in every way, just as we are—**yet was without sin**. (Hebrews 4:15).

Further on the same author, writing always by revelation, says,

> But because Jesus lives forever, he has a permanent priesthood…Such a high priest meets our need—**one who is holy, blameless, pure, set apart from sinners**, exalted above the heavens. (Hebrews 7:24-26).

and again in Hebrews 9:14,

> How much more, then, will the blood of Christ, who through the eternal Spirit **offered himself unblemished to God**, cleanse our consciences from acts that lead to death.

Finally Peter, an eye-witness who lived with Christ several years, writes,

> …you were redeemed…with the precious blood of Christ, a lamb **without blemish or defect**. (I Peter 1:18b-19).

We conclude, therefore, that Jesus was without sin, and this now brings a whole new dimension to the equation. The Qur'an says that "no burdened one can bear the burden of another." But what about a prophet without sin? An apostle without a burden? An intercessor who is perfect? The Quranic verses which we saw in Chapter I of Section One and Chapter V of the present section say nothing about this situation. The Bible, however, does speak about it, so now we shall look at all the Biblical verses which speak of intercession.

INTERCESSION (SHAFĀ'A شَفَاعَة) FOR THE BELIEVERS BY THE SINLESS MESSIAH

In a previous chapter we saw that there were prophecies of a suffering servant. We must now look again at one of those prophecies which, along with a sister verse, speaks of intercession by an "arm of the LORD"—a "righteous servant."

The first passage tells us that since the Eternal One found no one to intercede He will do it with "His own arm." Prophesying about 750 BC Isaiah wrote,

> He (the LORD) saw that there was no one, He was appalled that there was NO ONE TO INTERCEDE; so **His own arm** worked salvation for Him, and His own righteousness sustained Him. (Isaiah 59:16).

On page 285 of this section we quoted the following passage from Isaiah in reference to a Messiah who would suffer. Now we must look at it again in reference to intercession by the "arm of the LORD." It reads,

> To whom has **the arm of the LORD** been revealed?...
> (He was) a man of sorrows,
>   and familiar with suffering...
> but he was pierced for our transgressions,
>   he was crushed for our iniquities;
> the punishment that brought us peace was upon him
>   and by his wounds we are healed...
> By his knowledge, My **righteous servant** will justify many,
>   and he will bear their iniquities...
> he poured out his life unto death,
>   and was numbered with the transgressors.
> For he bore the sin of many,
>   and **MADE INTERCESSION** for the transgressors.
>   (Isaiah 53:1,3,5,11b,12b).

These verses say that a man called "the arm of the LORD" is going to come. He will suffer and be "pierced" for our transgressions. He will receive a punishment which will bring us peace. He will have "poured out his life unto death." **And he will "make intercession for the transgressors."**

This clear prophecy, that an intercessor will come, was given some 750 years before Christ came, and Photograph 8 on page 273 shows a copy of this very passage—a copy which was itself made 100 years before Jesus lived—a copy just like that which the Qur'an testifies was in Jesus' presence and "between his hands."

Has anyone fulfilled the prophecy?

We saw above that Jesus was sinless. Since he was sinless, his death on the cross could not have been a punishment for his own sin. The Injīl says that he died to bear the punishment for our sins, and the proof is that God raised him from the dead. Men who die for their own sins stay dead until the day of judgment.

In the words of the Gospel-New Testament it says,

God made him who had no sin to be sin for us.

II Corinthians 5:21.

In Quranic terms it could be stated,

Jesus, who had no burden, bore our burden.

He then ascended into heaven and, as the following verses show, he is alive in the presence of God to intercede for us.

Hebrews 7:25-26.

> ...He (Jesus) is able to save completely those who come to God through him, because **he always lives to INTERCEDE for them**. Such a high priest meets our need—one who is holy, blameless, pure, set apart from sinners, exalted above the heavens.

Romans 8:34.

> **Christ Jesus**, who died—more than that, who was raised to life—**is at the right hand of God and IS also INTERCEDING for us**.

I John 2:1-2.

> My dear children, I write this to you so that you will not sin. But if anybody does sin, **we have an INTERCESSOR with the Father—Jesus Christ, the Righteous One**. He is the atoning sacrifice for our sins, and not only for ours, but also for the sins of the whole world.

THE HOLY SPIRIT, THE PARACLETE, AS INTERCESSOR

Finally there is another one who intercedes. God says in the Gospel-New Testament that when we don't know what to pray or how to pray, **the Holy Spirit** intercedes for us with groans, that is prayers, which words cannot express.

Romans 8:26-27.

> In the same way, the Spirit helps us in our weakness. We do not know what we ought to pray, but **the Spirit himself INTER-CEDES for us** with groans that words cannot express. And He who searches our hearts knows the mind of the Spirit, because **the Spirit INTERCEDES for the saints in accordance with God's will.**

From these verses we understand and believe that Jesus the Messiah, the Eternal Word of God (kalimat Allah كَلِمَةُ ٱللهِ), and the Eternal Holy Spirit stand with us and intercede for us with the Father today and every today while we live.

Then tomorrow, on that great and terrible day of judgment, no Christian will have to stand alone without any friend or intercessor in the awesome presence of Yahweh Elohim, the Eternal One. Because Jesus, the Righteous 'Abd, the friend of sinners, will be there on that day of resurrection to speak and intercede for every person who has accepted him as Saviour.

It is so written in the Injīl, the Gospel-New Testament, in which there is no doubt and no change.

Now, with all that we have studied from the beginning of this book until the present as a background to our thoughts, let us return for one more visit with Elias, our friend from Nain.

CHAPTER VII

EACH IN HIS OWN LANGUAGE

Well, we've been to Jerusalem and what a time it was! I'll never be the same again. You remember that my uncle was coming from Libya to be in Jerusalem for the Passover. He and my two brothers went down for the feast just as they had planned and had the Passover meal on Thursday night with some relatives; but Friday a terrible thing happened. That wonderful rabbi that I told you about was seized by our high priests and *executed by the Romans*.

When I heard the news from my brothers, I had to go out behind the cattle shed and be by myself. Men aren't allowed to cry, so I won't admit whether I did or I didn't, but I felt terrible. The whole thing was incredible—especially that they were able to catch him. As I told you before, if he could stop the storm with one word, how could they get near him?

Anyway, according to the stories going around they actually had a trial early Friday morning. At the trial they asked Jesus, <"Are you the Christ, the Son of the Blessed One?"> When he answered, <"I am"> they said he was a blasphemer and sentenced him to death, and that was it (Mark 14:61-63). They took him outside of town and crucified him with two thieves, just like he was any old criminal.

Of course, when I heard all these things, I didn't care whether I went to Jerusalem for Pentecost[1] or for any other feast ever again! I even began to think that if God let a man like that die—who was so great and did all those miracles, and helped people—then He wasn't much of a God.

Oh, I know. You will tell me that those words are blasphemy too; and you are right. But what I thought is what I thought. Nevertheless, I had promised my uncle that I would go up to Jerusalem for the feast, so I felt that I had to keep my word. I just asked him to please excuse me if sometimes I was a little sad.

We arrived a couple of days early, so by Sunday morning we had seen most of the sights and we went to the Temple fairly early, about eight-thirty in the morning. All of a sudden my uncle stopped and said, "Listen to that voice!"

I said, "Listen to what voice? There's dozens of people talking."

"Look!" he said, and pointed to a man about five steps away—"That man! Though he's dressed like a Galilean, he is praising the Eternal One, Yahweh Elohim, in the Libyan language of my village! But I am the only Jew who came this year from my whole area. How did he learn my language? And without an accent!"

There were two other fellows from Nain with us, but they laughed and said, "Don't be silly. He's just drunk."

"No. No!" my uncle said, "He's talking about Jesus of Nazareth, the rabbi you spoke of, except that he says that he was the Christ; and something about the Holy Spirit."

---

1. Pentecost is a Jewish feast held 50 days after the Passover to celebrate the beginning of the wheat harvest, and Jews who did not live in Palestine would try to come back and celebrate these two feasts.

Just then a man with a strong voice started speaking to us from the steps of the Temple. A lot of other people must have been saying that people were drunk, because the very first thing he said was, <"These men aren't drunk, as you suppose. It's only nine in the morning! No, this is what was spoken by the prophet Joel,"> and he went on to say that they were filled with the Holy Spirit just as the prophet Joel had foretold would happen (Acts 2:15-16).

Then he started speaking about the Rabbi Jesus; and after mentioning the signs and wonders which God did through him, he said, <"This man was handed over to you by God's set purpose and foreknowledge; and you, with the help of wicked men, put him to death by nailing him to the cross.">

And then he said, <"But God raised him from the dead"> (Acts 2:23-24a).

When he said that, I felt a tightness in my chest as though I couldn't breath and chills all over me. I grabbed the shoulder of my uncle so tightly that he cried out in pain.

Next the speaker (whom I later found out was Peter, one of Jesus' disciples from Capernaum) went on and quoted the 16th Psalm of David which says,

> <Therefore my heart is glad and my tongue rejoices… because
> you will not abandon me to the grave, nor will you let your Holy
> One see decay> (Psalm 16:9-10).

After that he continued saying, <"Brothers, I can tell you confidently that the patriarch David died and was buried, and his tomb is here to this day. But he was a prophet and knew that God had promised him on oath that He would place one of his descendants on his throne. Seeing what was ahead, he spoke of the resurrection of the Messiah, that he was not abandoned to the grave, nor did his body see decay"> (Acts 2:29-31).

And his next words I shall never forget. He said, <"God has raised this Jesus to life, and we are witnesses of the fact,…(and) He has made this Jesus, whom you crucified, both Lord and Messiah."> When I heard that, my chest expanded and I could finally breath again (Acts 2:32,36).

I started walking through the crowd until I was just a few steps from Peter and I said along with several other people, <"What shall we do?"

Peter replied, "Repent and be baptized, every one of you, in the name of Jesus the Messiah for the forgiveness of your sins; and you will receive the gift of the Holy Spirit…Save yourselves from this corrupt generation"> (Acts 2:37b-38,40b).

When he finished those words, everybody started talking and asking questions, and I went up to Peter and I said, "You don't know me, but I know your friend Obadiah in Capernaum, and I was present when Jesus fed the 5000 people. Now I want to know one thing. In the name of the Eternal One, the Lord God of Abraham, Isaac and Jacob, did you really see Jesus alive after he was crucified?" Peter looked me straight in the eye and said, "Yes!"

Then I said, "How many times did you see him?"

He answered, "Jesus showed himself to me by myself, and then to all of us the Sunday after Passover—the day he rose from the dead. A week later, I was present when he revealed himself to give a special message to Thomas. A few days later, when seven of us went fishing on the Lake of Galilee, he caused us to have a miraculous catch of fish; and when we landed he had prepared a breakfast for us. Then, he showed himself to more than 500 of us at one time, and the last time was a week ago Thursday when he ascended into heaven right in front of our eyes."

"Is it true then," I asked, "that he prophesied that he would give his life for his sheep to pay for their sins, and that he would rise from the dead and come back to life the third day?"

"Yes, it's true!" Peter answered.

"Okay," I said, "I believe you. I believe that Jesus died for my sins and rose again. Now, baptize me like you said."

Immediately he took me over to a pool and baptized me in Jesus' name. Maybe I was the first one. There were <about three thousand> of us baptized that day and my uncle was baptized too (Acts 2:41). He said, "When that Galilean preached to me in my own language, I knew it had to be true. There was no doubt about it."

So now my sins are all forgiven and I am free. Just like Jesus promised, "If the Son shall make you free, you shall be free indeed!"

* * *

To end, I would like to remind the reader of a Quranic verse found in the Sura of the Cattle (Al-An'ām) 6:9, from 6 AH. In Pickthall's translation it reads,

> "Had We appointed an angel (as our messenger), We assuredly had made him (as) a man (that he might speak to men)..."

That is what God did when He came in Christ, reconciling the world unto Himself. He came as a man that He might speak to men and open Paradise for all who will accept His great gift of salvation.

320

APPENDIX A

SPECIFIC MIRACLES REPORTED IN THE FOUR GOSPEL ACCOUNTS

The information for each miracle will be presented as follows:

Type of miracle   Town or place where it occurred

The Biblical text telling of the miracle

Number cured	Number of Witnesses who saw the miracle	Estimate of those who knew the person as ill and then perceived him as cured.

1. Water to wine.   Cana

    "Now six stone jars were standing there each holding between 75 and 115 liters. Jesus said to them, 'Fill the jars with water,' and they filled them to the brim...

    When the steward of the feast tasted the water now become wine...(he) called the bridegroom and said to him...'You have kept the good wine until now.'" (John 2:6-7,9,10b).

           Disciples and servants ?=20   Maybe all the guests

2. Jesus knew the past of a Samaritan woman at a public well.   Samaria

    "Jesus said to her, 'Go, call your husband, and come here.'
    "The woman answered him, 'I have no husband.'
    "Jesus said to her, 'You are right in saying, "I have no husband"; for you have had five husbands, and he whom you now have is not your husband; what you have just said is quite true.'
    "The woman said to him, 'Sir, I can see that you are a prophet.'" (John 4:16-19).

    1

3. Jesus heals the son of an official without seeing him.   Cana

    "And there was a certain royal official whose son lay sick... (he) went to (Jesus) and begged him to come and heal his son, who was close to death.
    "...Jesus replied, 'You may go. Your son will live.'
    "The man believed the word that Jesus spoke to him and departed. While he was still on the way, his servant met him with the news that his boy was living...'The fever left him yesterday at the seventh hour.'
    "Then the father realized that this was the exact time at which Jesus had said to him, 'Your son will live,' so he and all his house believed." (John 4:46b,47b,50-52b,53).

        1   Household of official ?=10   If short illness ?=30 family and friends

4. The healing at the pool of a man   Jerusalem
   who had been ill for 38 yrs.

   "One man was there who had been ill thirty-eight years.

   "...Jesus asked him, 'Do you want to get well?'

   "The sick man answered him, 'Sir, I have no one to put me into the pool...'

   "Then Jesus said to him, 'Get up! Pick up your mat and walk.'

   "At once the man was cured. He picked up his mat and walked."
   (John 5:5,6b-7a,8-9).

1	Disciples	Long illness — many would know ?=200

5. Miraculous catch of fish.   City of Capernaum

   "...Jesus was standing by the Lake of Gennesaret, with the people **crowding** around him and listening to the word of God...He got into one of the boats...and taught the people from the boat. When he finished speaking he said to Simon, 'Put out into deep water, and let down the nets for a catch.'

   "...When they had done so, they caught such a large number of fish that their nets began to break." (Luke 5:1,3-4,6).

4 fishermen	"crowd" ?=100

6. Jesus drives out an evil spirit.   Capernaum

   "Just then a man in the synagogue who was possessed by an evil spirit cried out, 'What do you want with us, Jesus of Nazareth? Have you come to destroy us? I know who you are–the Holy One of God!'

   " 'Be quiet!' said Jesus sternly. 'Come out of him!' "The evil spirit shook the man violently and came out of him with a shriek."
   (Mark 1:23-26).

1	Synagogue full ?=200	others in town ?=200

7. Peter's mother-in-law in bed with a fever.   Capernaum

   "So he (Jesus) went to her, took her hand, and helped her up. The fever left her and she began to wait on them." (Mark 1:31).

1	Some disciples and family ?=10

A. Many were healed.   Capernaum - Roman troops
                                        there. City of ? 4000

   "That evening after sunset the people brought to Jesus all the sick and demon-possessed. **The whole town gathered at the door,** and Jesus healed many who had various diseases. He also drove out many demons, but he would not let the demons speak because they knew who he was."
   (Mark 1:32-34).

1 in 10 of those who came were ill ?=50	? 500 who came with the ill people	?=4000 would know at least one ill person

322

8. Jesus heals a leper. Galilee

"A man with leprosy came to him and begged him on his knees, 'If you are willing you can make me clean.'

"Filled with compassion, Jesus reached out his hand and touched the man. 'I am willing,' he said. 'Be clean!' Immediately the leprosy left him and he was cured." (Mark 1:40-42).

1   Disciples   his family & friends ?=200

9. Jesus heals a paralytic as proof that he, Capernaum
the Son of Man, has power to forgive sins.

"Some men came bringing to him a paralytic, carried by four of them.

"...When Jesus saw their faith, he said to the paralytic, 'Son, your sins are forgiven.'

"Now some of the scribes were sitting there, questioning in their hearts, 'Why does this man speak thus? It is blasphemy! Who can forgive sins but God alone?'

"...'but that you may know that the Son of Man has authority on earth to forgive sins'—he said to the paralytic—'I say to you rise, take up your pallet and go home.' And he rose..." (Mark 2:3,5-7,10-12a).

1   House & yard full ?=150   long illness ?=200

10. Jesus heals a man's shriveled hand on the Sabbath. Capernaum

"And he (Jesus) said to the man who had the shriveled hand, 'Stand up in front of everyone.'

"Then Jesus asked them, 'Which is lawful on the Sabbath: to do good or to do evil, to save life or to kill?' But they remained silent.

"He looked around at them in anger and, deeply distressed at their stubborn hearts, said to the man, 'Stretch out your hand.'

"He stretched it out, and his hand was completely restored." (Mark 3:3-5).

1   Synagogue full ?=100   long illness ?=200

B. People were coming from as far as Tyre and Sidon to be healed.

"When they heard all he was doing, **many people came to him from Judea, Jerusalem, Idumea, and the regions across the Jordan, and around Tyre and Sidon**...For he had healed many, so that those with diseases were pushing forward to touch him. Whenever, the evil spirits saw him, they fell down before him and cried out, 'You are the Son of God.'" (Mark 3:8,10-11).

1 of 10 ill ?=200   ?=2000 came   100 people knew each
                                                       healed person ?=20,000

11. Healing of the centurion's servant   Capernaum
    without seeing him.

"Now a centurion had a slave who was dear to him, who was sick and at the point of death. When he heard of Jesus, he sent to him elders of the Jews...And Jesus went with them. When he was not far from the house, the centurion sent friends to him, saying to him, 'Lord, do not trouble yourself, for I am not worthy to have you come under my roof...But say the word, and my servant will be healed. For I myself am a man under authority, with soldiers under me. I tell this one, "Go," and he goes, and that one "Come," and he comes. I say to my servant "Do this," and he does it.'

"When Jesus heard this...he said, 'I tell you, I have not found such great faith even in Israel.' Then the men who had been sent returned to the house and found the servant healed." (Luke 7:2-3a,6-8,9b-10).

      1   Centurion's household?=10

12. Jesus raises a widow's son   Nain
    from the dead.

"As he approached the town gate a dead person was being carried out—the only son of his mother, and she was a widow...

"Then he went up and touched the coffin...He said, 'Young man, I say to you, get up!'

"The dead man sat up and began to talk, and Jesus gave him back to his mother" (Luke 7:12,14-15).

      1   Poor widow, small funeral?=50   other people?=50

13. Jesus calms the storm.   Sea of Galilee

"And a great storm of wind arose, and the waves beat into the boat...but he was in the stern, asleep on the cushion...He awoke and rebuked the wind, and said to the sea, 'Peace, be still!' and the wind ceased and there was a great calm.

"And they (the disciples) were terrified and asked each other, 'Who is this that even the wind and the waves obey him?'"
(Mark 4:37-38a,39,41).

                    His disciples

14. Healing of a demon-possessed man.   Gerasa (Jordan)

"...There met him out of the tombs a man with an unclean spirit...He had often been chained hand and foot, but he tore the chains apart and broke the irons on his feet. No one was strong enough to subdue him...When he saw Jesus from a distance, he ran and fell on his knees in front of him. He shouted at the top of his voice, 'What do you want with me, Jesus, Son of the Most High God? Swear to God that you won't torture me,' for Jesus was saying to him, 'Come out of this man, you evil spirit!'

"...the evil spirits came out and went into the pigs...(which) rushed down the steep bank into the lake and were drowned.

"(The town people) saw the man who had been possessed by the legion of demons, sitting there, dressed and in his right mind, and they were afraid." (Mark 5:2b,4,6-8,13,15).

| 1 | The disciples | whole area ?=500 |

15. Jairus' daughter raised from the dead.   Capernaum

"Then came one of the rulers of the synagogue, Jairus by name...and pleaded earnestly with him, 'My little daughter is dying...' So Jesus went with him.

"(Jesus) went in and said to them, 'Why all this commotion and wailing? The child is not dead but asleep.' But they laughed at him.

"...(He) went in where the child was. He took her hand and said to her, 'Talitha koum!' (which means, 'Little girl, get up!')

"Immediately the girl stood up and walked around (she was twelve-years-old)..." (Mark 5:22-23a,24b,39-40,41-42b).

| 1 | Disciples and parents | important person ?=400 |

16. A woman with a twelve year   Capernaum
history of bleeding healed.

"A woman was there who had had a flow of blood for twelve years...she touched his cloak...Immediately her bleeding stopped...At once Jesus realized that power had gone out of him."
(Mark 5:25,27b,29a,30a).

| 1 | ? crowd of 50 | poor woman ?=100 |

17. Two blind men are healed.   ?outside Capernaum.

"And as Jesus passed on from there, two blind men followed him crying out, 'Have mercy on us, Son of David!'

"When he had gone **indoors**, the blind men came to him, and he asked them, 'Do you believe that I am able to do this?'

"'Yes, Lord,' they replied. Then he touched their eyes...and their sight was restored." (Matthew 9:27-29a,30a).

| 2 | House full ?=20 | ?100 x 2 =200 |

18. Immediately afterward casts out a demon.   Same village.

"While they were going out, a man who was demon-possessed and could not talk was brought to Jesus, and when the demon was driven out, the man who had been dumb spoke. **The crowd** was amazed and said, 'Nothing like this has ever been seen in Israel.'" (Matthew 9:32-33).

| 1 | Crowd of ?=100 | whole village ?=500 |

19. Feeding 5000 people with five loaves   Near Bethsaida in
and 2 fish.   Jordan

"...Jesus crossed to the far shore of the Sea of Galilee...When Jesus looked up and saw a **great crowd** coming toward him, he said to Philip, 'Where shall we buy bread for these people to eat?'

"Philip answered him, 'Eight months' wages would not buy enough bread for each one to have a bite.'

"Another of his disciples...spoke up, 'Here is a boy with five small barley loaves and two small fish...'

"Jesus said, 'Have the people sit down.' There was plenty of grass in that place, and the men sat down, **about five thousand of them**. Jesus took the loaves, gave thanks, and distributed to those who were seated as much as they wanted. He did the same with the fish.

"...they gathered (the leftover pieces) and filled twelve baskets...

"After the people saw the miraculous sign that Jesus did, they began to say, 'Surely this is **the Prophet** who is to come into the world.'" (John 6:1,5,7-10,13-14).

Then Jesus preached to them and said, "I am the bread of life...For I have come down from heaven not to do my will, but to do the will of Him who sent me." (John 6:35,38).

5000 were both witnesses and
partakers of the miraculous food.

20. Jesus walks on the water.   Sea of Galilee

"When evening came, his disciples...got into a boat and set off across the lake for Capernaum...When they had rowed five or six kilometers, they saw Jesus approaching the boat, walking on the water, and they were terrified.

"But he said to them, 'It is I; don't be afraid.'

"Then they were willing to take him into the boat..." (John 6:16,19-21a).

His disciples

C. All who touched him were healed.   Region of Gennesaret

"When they had crossed over, they landed at Gennesaret... People recognized Jesus. **They ran throughout that whole region and carried the sick on mats to wherever they heard he was, and everywhere he went—into villages, towns or countryside**—they placed the sick in the marketplaces. They begged him to let them touch even the edge of his cloak, and all who touched him were healed." (Mark 7:53-56).

1 of 10 ?=400   ?=4000 from 20 villages   400 x 100 friends
                                                                ?=40,000

21. Jesus cures the daughter of a Greek woman.   In a house in Tyre

"Jesus...went to the vicinity of Tyre. He entered **a house** and did not want anyone to know it; yet he could not keep his presence secret...A woman whose little daughter was possessed by an evil spirit came...(she) was a Greek, a Syrophoenician by birth. She begged Jesus to drive the demon out of her daughter...

"Then he told her, 'For such a reply, you may go; the demon has left your daughter.' She went home and found her child lying on the bed, and the demon gone." (Mark 7:24-26,29-30).

           1   House full?=20   ?200

22. Healing of a deaf and dumb man.   Decapolis–large region of Jordan

"Then (Jesus) returned...through the region of the Decapolis, and they brought to him a man who was deaf and had an impediment in his speech...and **taking him aside** from the multitude privately, he put his fingers into his ears, and he spat and touched his tongue; and looking up to heaven, he sighed, and said to him 'Ephphata,' that is 'Be opened.'

"And his ears were opened, his tongue was released, and he spoke plainly." (Mark 7:31-32a,33-35).

           1   ?=200

D. Great Crowds east of sea of Galilee.   Decapolis

"And Jesus...passed along the Sea of Galilee, and...up on the mountain, and sat down there. And **great crowds** came to him, bringing with them the lame, the maimed, the blind, the dumb, and many others, and they put them at his feet, and he healed them...and they glorified God." (Matthew 15:29-30,31b).

1 of 10?=200   "Great crowd" ?=2000   each one x 100
                                                                ?=20,000

23. Feeding of the 4000.   Decapolis

"...again a **great crowd** had gathered...and he commanded the crowd to sit down on the ground, and he took the seven loaves, and having given thanks he broke them and gave them to his disciples to set before the people...and they had a few small fish...and they ate and were satisfied, and they took up the broken pieces left over, seven baskets full. And they were about 4000 people." (Mark 8:1a,6-7a,8-9).

"Great crowd" of 4000 witnessed and ate

24. A blind man healed.   Village of Bethsaida

"...**Some people** brought to him a blind man...(he) led him out of the village, and when he had spit on his eyes and laid his hands upon him, he asked him, 'Do you see anything?'

"And he looked up and said, 'I see men; but they look like trees walking.'

"Then again he laid his hands upon his eyes, and he looked intently and was restored, and saw everything clearly."
(Mark 8:22,23b-25).

| 1 | "some people" ?=10 | 100 |

25. Casting out of an epileptic-like
    demon.

    Region of Caesarea Philippi
    toward Damascus

"...(the other disciples) were surrounded by a **great crowd**...

"So they brought (the boy). When the spirit saw Jesus, it immediately threw the boy into a convulsion...He rebuked the evil spirit. 'You deaf and dumb spirit,' he said, 'I command you come out of him and never enter him again.'

"The spirit shrieked, convulsed him violently and came out...But Jesus took him by the hand and lifted him to his feet and he stood up."
(Mark 9:20,25b-26a,27).

| 1 | "Great crowd" ?=500-1000 | 200 |

26. Catching a special fish

    Capernaum

"...the collectors of the two-drachma tax came to Peter and asked, 'Doesn't your teacher pay the temple tax?'

"'Yes he does,' he replied.

"...Jesus said to him, '...go to the lake and throw out your line. Take the first fish you catch. Open its mouth and you will find a four-drachma coin. Take it and give it to them for my tax and yours.'" (Matthew 17:24b-25a,27).

1

27. Healing of a man born blind.

    Jerusalem

"As he went along he saw a man blind from birth.

"(He said), 'While I am in the world I am the light of the world.'
"Having said this, he spit on the ground, made some mud with the saliva, and put it on the man's eyes. 'Go,' he told him, 'wash in the pool of Siloam'...

"So the man went and washed and came home seeing.

"...Jesus said, 'For judgment I have come into this world, so that the blind will see...'" (John 9:1,5-7,39a).

| 1 | | Friends + those from whom he begged?=300 |

E. 72 disciples traveling in pairs
    also did miracles.

    Whole country

"After this the Lord appointed seventy-two others and sent them two by two ahead of him...

"The seventy-two returned with joy and said, 'Lord, even the demons submit to us in your name.'" (Luke 10:1,17).

| 36 pairs x 2 miracles = 72 | ?72 x 100 = 7200 |

28. Healing of a dumb man.   Region of Judea

"Jesus was driving out a demon that was mute. When the demon left, the man who had been dumb spoke, and the **crowd** was amazed" (Luke 11:14).

     1   "Crowd" ?=100   200

29. Crippled woman is healed.   Region of Judea

"On a Sabbath, Jesus was teaching **in one of the synagogues**, and a woman was there who had been crippled by a spirit for eighteen years. She was bent over and could not straighten up at all...Then he put his hands on her and immediately she straightened up and praised God." (Luke 13:11,13).

     1   Synagogue full ?=100   200

30. Healing of a man with dropsy   Perea in middle Jordan

"One Sabbath, when Jesus went to eat **in the house of a prominent Pharisee**...there in front of him was a man suffering from dropsy... taking hold of the man he healed him and sent him away." (Luke 14:1-2,4).

     1   Prominent household ?=20   200

31. Raising of Lazarus who had been   Bethany near Jerusalem
    dead four days.

"When Martha (Lazurus' sister) heard that Jesus was coming, she went out to meet him. 'Lord,' Martha said to Jesus, 'if you had been here, my brother would not have died...'

"Jesus said to her, 'Your brother will rise again.'

"Martha answered, 'I know he will rise again in the resurrection at the last day.'

"Jesus said to her, 'I am the resurrection and the life. He who believes in me will live, even though he dies...'"

"Jesus, once more deeply moved, came to the tomb...'Take away the stone,' he said.

"'But Lord,' said Martha...'by this time he smells, for he has been there four days.'

"...Then Jesus looked up and said, 'Father, I thank You that You have heard me. I knew that You always hear me, but I said this for the benefit of **the people standing here**, that they may believe that You sent me."

"When he had said this, Jesus called in a loud voice, 'Lazarus, come out!'

"The dead man came out, his hands and feet wrapped with strips of linen, and a cloth around his face." (John 11:20-25,38a,39,41b-44).

     1   the people standing ?=50   200

32. Jesus heals 10 lepers.   Samaria

   "As (Jesus) was going into a village, ten men who had leprosy met
him. They stood at a distance and called out... 'Jesus, Master, have pity
on us.'
   "When he saw them, he said, 'Go, show yourselves to the priests.'
And as they went, they were cleansed." (Luke 17:12-14).
              10   The disciples   10 men x ?100 = 1000

33. Two blind men are healed.   Jericho

   "As Jesus and his disciples were leaving Jericho, a **large crowd**
followed him. Two blind men were sitting by the roadside and...they
shouted, 'Lord, Son of David, have mercy on us!'
   "Jesus had compassion on them and touched their eyes. Immediately
they received their sight and followed him." (Matthew 20:29-30,34).
              2   "Large Crowd" ?=500   2 men x ?100 = 200

34. The fig tree withers as a symbol.   Jerusalem

   "The next day as they were leaving Bethany, Jesus was hungry.
Seeing in the distance a fig tree in leaf, he went to find out if it had any
fruit. When he reached it, he found nothing but leaves, because it was
not the season for figs. Then he said to the tree, 'May no one ever eat
fruit from you again.' And his disciples heard him say it.
   "...In the morning as they went along, they saw the fig tree withered
from the roots. Peter remembered and said to Jesus, 'Rabbi, look! The
fig tree you cursed has withered!'" (Mark 11:12-14,20).
                           The disciples

35. Jesus prophesies that Peter will deny   Jerusalem
   him three times.

   "Peter declared, 'Even if all fall away, I will not.'
   "'I tell you the truth,' Jesus answered, 'this very night, before the
cock crows twice, you will deny me three times.'
   "And after a little while again the bystanders said to Peter, 'Certainly
you are one of them; for you are a Galilean.'
   "But he began to invoke a curse on himself and to swear, 'I do not
know this man of whom you speak.'
   "And immediately the cock crowed a second time. And Peter
remembered...and he broke down and wept." (Mark 14:29-30,70b-72).
                           The disciples

36. Jesus heals Malchus, one of those   Jerusalem
   who came to arrest him.

   "While he was still speaking, there came a **crowd**, and the man
called Judas, one of the twelve, was leading them...

"But Jesus said to him, 'Judas, would you betray the Son of man with a kiss?'

"And one of them struck the slave of the high priest and cut off his right ear.

"But Jesus said, 'No more of this!' and he touched his ear and healed him." (Luke 22:47-48,50-51).

1   Disciples and "crowd" ?=50

37. Jesus reveals himself after his resurrection   Lake of Galilee
   from the dead by a miraculous catch of fish.

"After this Jesus revealed himself again to his disciples…in this way.

"Simon Peter said to them (the other six disciples), 'I am going fishing.' They said, 'We will go with you.'

"They went out and got into the boat; but that night they caught nothing. Just as day was breaking, Jesus stood on the beach; yet the disciples did not know that it was Jesus.

"Jesus said to them, 'Children, have you any fish?'

"They answered him, 'No.'

"He said to them, 'Cast the net on the right side of the boat, and you will find some.'

So they cast it, and now they were not able to haul it in, for the quantity of fish. The disciple whom Jesus loved said to Peter, 'It is the Lord!'

"When they finished breakfast, Jesus said to Simon Peter, 'Simon, son of John, do you love me more than these?'

"He said to him, 'Yes Lord, you know that I love you.'

"(Jesus) said to him, 'Feed my lambs (the believers).'

"…After this he said to him, 'Follow me.'" (John 21:1,3-7a,15,19b).

7 disciples

In the above accounts there are 37 miracles, 26 of which are miracles of healing describing in some detail the healing of 37 different people. There are four additional passages (A,B,C,D), plus the healings at the feeding of the five thousand, stating that Jesus healed *all* who came. By rough estimate, it is proposed that at least 1000 people were healed in these mass healings.

In addition there were surely as many as 14,500 to 15,000 people who observed these healings and other miracles, including the 5000 on one occasion and the 4000 on another who actually ate of the multiplied bread as well as witnessing the miracle. Even if we assume that half of the witnesses saw two miracles, that would still leave 11,000 witnesses to the almost 1000 miracles.

Thirdly, there were probably at least another 86,000 people who knew these ill men and women when they were demon possessed or crippled and would be able to see that a healing had taken place, even though they had not been present. If two million people lived in Palestine at that time this would mean that

331

one out of every 20 people had seen a miracle or knew someone who had been healed.

Thus the true believers at the time of Christ had an abundance of confirming signs that Jesus had indeed been sent by the great Creator God, Yahweh Elohim.

APPENDIX B

PROPHECIES OF THE DETAILS OF CHRIST'S DEATH AND THEIR FULFILLMENT

Jesus' Own Prophecy

"We are going up to Jerusalem," he said (to the twelve), "and the Son of Man will be betrayed to the chief priests and teachers of the law. **They will condemn him to death and will hand him over to the Gentiles, who will mock him and spit on him, flog him and kill him. Three days later he will rise.**"

Mark 10:33-34.

Daniel's Prophecy

"In my vision at night I looked, and there before me was **one like a son of man, coming with the clouds of heaven. He approached the Ancient of Days (God) and was led into His presence. He was given authority, glory and sovereign power; all peoples, nations and men of every language worshiped him. His dominion is an everlasting dominion that will not pass away.**"

Daniel 7:13-14a (600 BC)

Isaiah 53 (750 BC)

He was oppressed and afflicted, **yet he did not open his mouth...**

Verse 7.

By oppression and judgment, he was taken away...though he had done no violence, nor was any deceit in his mouth.

Verses 8a-9b.

The Gospel

Then the high priest stood up before them and asked Jesus, "Are you not going to answer? What is this testimony that these men are bringing against you?"

But Jesus remained silent and gave no answer.

Again the high priest asked him, **"Are you the Messiah, the Son of the Blessed One?"**

"I am," said Jesus, "and you will see the Son of Man sitting at the right hand of the Mighty One and coming on the clouds of heaven."

The high priest tore his clothes. "Why do we need any more witnesses?" he asked. "You have heard the blasphemy."

They all condemned him as worthy of death. Then some began to spit at him...and the guards took him and beat him.

Mark 14:60-65.

Psalm 2 (1000 BC)

Why do **the nations** conspire, and the peoples plot in vain? **The kings** of the earth take their stand, and **the rulers gather together against the LORD and His Anointed One (Messiah).**
Psalm 2:1-2 (1000 BC)
.

Isaiah 53 (750 BC)

He was despised and rejected by men, a man of sorrows…
Verse 3.

The Gospel

Then the whole assembly rose and led him off to Pilate. And when (Pilate) learned that he belonged to (King) Herod's jurisdiction, he sent him over to Herod…**And Herod with his soldiers treated him with contempt and mocked him, then…he sent him back to Pilate (Caesar's governor).**
Luke 23:1,7a,11.

They brought Jesus to the place called Golgotha…Then they offered him wine mixed with (bitter) myrrh, but he did not take it.

Psalm 22 (1000 BC)

They have pierced my hands and my feet. I can count all my bones. Verses 16b-17a.
They divide my garments among them and cast lots for my clothing. Verse 18.

But I am a worm and not a man, scorned by men and despised by the people. **All who see me mock me. They hurl insults, shaking their heads.** Verses 6-7.

But he was pierced for our transgressions, he was crushed for our iniquities. Verse 5.

He poured out his life unto death, and **was numbered with the transgressors.** Verse 12.

And they crucified him.

Dividing up his clothes, they cast lots to see what each would get. Mark 15:22-24

They crucified two robbers with him, one on his right and one on his left.
Those who passed by hurled insults at him, shaking their heads and saying, "So! You who are going to destroy the temple and build it in three days, come down from the cross and save yourself!"

Psalm 22 (1000 BC)

He trusts in the LORD. **Let the LORD rescue him. Let Him deliver him, since He delights in him.**
                              Verse 8.

My God, my God, why have you forsaken me? Why are you so far from saving me, so far from the words of my groaning?   Verse 1.

I am poured out like water, and all my bones are out of joint...My strength is dried up like a potsherd, **and my tongue sticks to the roof of my mouth.**
                       Verses 14a-15.

"...**And (they) gave me vinegar for my thirst**"   Psalm 69:21.

Isaiah 53 (750 BC)

Yet it was the LORD's will to crush him and cause him to suffer...   Verse 10a.

The Gospel

In the same way the chief priests and the teachers of the law mocked him among themselves. **"He saved others," they said, "but he can't save himself! Let this Christ, this King of Israel, come down now from the cross, that we may see and believe."**

Those crucified with him also heaped insults on him.

At the sixth hour (noon) darkness came over the whole land until the ninth hour (3pm). And at the ninth hour Jesus cried out in a loud voice, **"Eloi, Eloi, lama sabachthani?"–which means, "My God, my God, why have you forsaken me?"**

When some of those standing near heard this, they said, "Listen, he's calling Elijah."
                       Mark 15:27-35.

Jesus said, "I am thirsty."   John 19:28.

One man ran, filled a sponge with wine vinegar, put it on a stick, and offered it to Jesus to drink...

335

Psalm 22 (1000 BC)	Isaiah 53 (750 BC)	The Gospel
You (God) lay me in the dust of death. Verse 15b.	**For he was cut off from the land of the living;** for the transgression of my people he was stricken. For he bore the sin of many, and made intercession for the transgressors. Verses 8b and 12b.	**With a loud cry, Jesus gave up the spirit.** The curtain of the temple (the entrance to the Most Holy place = the presence of God) was torn in two from top to bottom. Mark 15:36-38.
	He was assigned a grave with the wicked, and **with the rich in his death...** Verse 9a.	**Joseph of Arimathea, a prominent member of the Council**, who was himself waiting for the kingdom of God, went boldly to Pilate and **asked for Jesus' body.** Pilate was surprised to hear that he was already dead... When he learned from the centurion that it was so, he gave the body to Joseph. **So Joseph... took down the body, wrapped it in the linen, and placed it in a tomb cut out of rock.** Then he rolled a stone against the entrance of the tomb. Mary Magdalene and Mary the mother of Jesus saw where he was laid. Mark 15:43-47.

PROPHECIES OF JESUS' RESURRECTION AND THEIR FULFILLMENT

Psalm 22 (1000 BC)

Isaiah 53 (750 BC)

The testimony of the Apostle Paul (55 AD)

And though the LORD makes his life a guilt offering,

For what I received I passed on to you... that Christ died for our sins...that he was buried, that he was raised the third day according to the Scriptures, and

I will declare Your name to my brothers; in the congregation I will praise You.

Verse 22.

he will see his offspring and prolong his days.

Verse 10.

1) that he appeared to Peter,

2) and then to the Twelve.

3) After that he appeared to more than 500 of the brothers at the same time, most of whom are still living, though some have fallen asleep.

4) Then he appeared to James,

5) then to all the apostles.

I Corinthians 15:3-7.

In addition to the above appearances, **Jesus showed himself (6) to Mary Magdalene** (John 20:10-18); **(7) to one of the other women** along with Mary (Matthew 28:8-10); **(8) to two disciples** on the road to Emmaus (Luke 24:13-32); **(9) to Thomas** one week after the resurrection (John 20:24-29); and sometime after this **(10) to seven of his disciples** who went fishing (John chapter 21).

This makes a total of ten recorded appearances of Jesus to more than 500 different people over a period of 40 days (Acts 1:3).

INDEX

E

F

I

347

M

N

Q

T

U

V

W

Transcription of Arabic into English

Arabic	International Symbol	English Adaptation	Arabic	International Symbol
ا	a		ق	q
ب	b		ك	k
ت	t		ل	l
ث	t	th	م	m
ج	j		ن	n
ح	ḥ		ه	h
خ	ḵ	kh	و	w
د	d		ي	y
ذ	ḏ		ء	'
ر	r		**Short vowels**	
ز	z		ﹷ	a
س	s		ﹻ	i
ش	š		ﹹ	u
ص	ṣ		**Long vowels**	
ض	ḍ		ـا	ā
ط	ṭ		ـي	ī
ظ	ẓ		ـو	ū
ع	'		**Diphthongs**	
غ	ḡ	gh	ـو	au or aw
ف	f		ـي	ai or ay